TRINITY COUNTY
HISTORIC SITES

This photo was taken in 1930 from Center Street and shows the Rush Creek-Minersville road leaving Weaverville. The barns on the left were owned by the New York Hotel, and were on the site of the present P. G. & E. office. The Montague house then facing Center Street was on the site now occupied by the Maddalena accounting office.

Alice Goen Jones, Editor
Richard Krieg
Elizabeth Bigelow Langworthy
Henry C. Meckel
Florence Scott Morris
Walter Robb
Herbert Woods

TRINITY COUNTY HISTORIC SITES

Published by
Trinity County Historical Society
1981

The printing of this book was funded, in part, by a grant from The James Irvine Foundation, San Francisco.

First printing 1000 copies
Copyright©1981 Trinity County Historical Society
All rights reserved

Library of Congress Catalogue Number 81-82756
ISBN #0-9607054-4-9

Published in 1981 by Trinity County Historical Society
  in Weaverville, California
Design and typography by Golden State Printers, Weaverville, California
Cartography by David Winegardner
Printed in the United States of America
  by Curtis Media Inc., Bedford, Texas

Second Printing 1982
Revised Printing 1988
Fourth Printing 1998

DEDICATED TO
THE MEMORY OF:

Emma A. Dawson
Henry Sutherland
Elaine Fetzer Moran
Helen Elizabeth Warnock
Leroy Harrison
Florence Heryford
Ivo Haven Hussey
Andrew Brenneis
Bing Wah Lee
Benjamin Franklin Adamson
Nellie Mortensen
Myrtle Skinner Luhmann
James Thomas Smallen
Zelita Todd Jones
Mildred Ryan Hurd
George Leas Anderline
Clinton Chapin
John Cox
John Davis
Laurence Vernon Jordan
Lemuel Theodore Jackson

Earl Montgomery
Edward Hans Mortensen
Lonnie J. Pool
Lloyd Snyder
Ann Sullivan
Errol Dean Senter
Edward Gideon Smith
Janet Goodyear Turner
Amy Lucille Todd Vick
Christian George Christensen
Orville Charles Ward
L. Stanford Scott
Alice Kapusta Denison
Irene Burks
William X. Garrett
Elsie May Tye
Charles Henry Crews
Margaret Brown
Emil V. Lehmann
Grace Chiolero
Dixon Douglas Jones
John E. Hinson
Marian E. Pollard
Wilbur Scott Pollard
Mary B. Rennick
J. Walter Wilson, M.D.
Sherwood McCartney
Rex Cecil McGee

TRINITY COUNTY AREAS

COFFEE CREEK

I

IV

III

WILLOW CREEK

NEW DENNY

SALYER

DEDRICK

TRINITY CENTER

II

BURNT RANCH

HELENA

BIG BAR

WEAVERVILLE

JUNCTION
CITY

LEWISTON

DOUGLAS CITY

HYAMPOM

V

HAYFORK

VI

MAD
RIVER

WILDWOOD

RUTH

ZENIA

HOAGLIN

VII

LAKE MT.

N

AREAS

I. Northeast Trinity
II. Weaverville
III. Helena-Junction City
IV. Lower Trinity-New River
V. Lewiston-Douglas City
VI. Hayfork-Hyampom-Wildwood
VII. Southern Trinity

CONTENTS

PREFACE

Trinity County is an area of unusual historic significance. Its very special character led, in 1978, to receipt by the county of a $10,000 grant through the California State Office of Historic Preservation and the National Park Service of the Department of the Interior for the purpose of making a survey of the county's cultural and historical resources. As a result of the National Historic Preservation Act of 1966, California was under pressure to complete a statewide inventory of places of historic importance as part of a long range plan to protect the state's historical resources. Federal funds available under this act were granted to the county for this purpose. It was the first attempt in the state to survey an entire rural county.

This historical resources survey was carried out under the direction of the Trinity County Historical Society with Walter Robb employed as Director and Florence Scott Morris serving as a volunteer Co-director. Through the tireless efforts of these two individuals a thorough, creative, and professional job was accomplished. A wealth of historical information was recorded. The Trinity County Historical Society has brought this and other material together in this book. The contents are from the research of the authors and do not necessarily reflect the views and opinions of the Department of Interior. It is hoped that the book will stimulate public awareness of the county's history and character and that it will serve to encourage public officials to face the challenge of preserving the historical character of the county.

The authors of this book are a committee appointed by the Board of Directors of the Trinity County Historical Society to develop the material into book form. Although the book is based upon the survey, its scope has been greatly expanded. Much additional historical information gathered by Walter Robb in the course of the survey has also been incorporated into the book. Since the state limited the survey to only those resources of architectural or historic importance that are still existent or visible and for which there is available data, many sites of historic importance were not included. An attempt has been made here to expand the survey's coverage of Trinity County's historic sites to include as many as possible of those sites which did not qualify for inclusion in the state survey. In many cases information is sketchy; in other cases sites have been omitted for lack of available information. The authors regret that the book cannot be more comprehensive. It is hoped, however, that by recording in this book those facts that we have been able to gather together we will have preserved in one place that part of Trinity County's history that still remains in the memories of a few old-timers or their descendants. We were fortunate, for example, to have as one of the co-authors, Henry C. Meckel, who is a direct descendant of one of the first pioneers to settle in the area of the North Fork of the Trinity River. Because of the extent of his personal knowledge of the history of Helena and Junction City, we have included a more comprehensive coverage of the history of these two places than was possible for much of the rest of the county.

Many individuals have contributed much helpful information, either for the book directly or for the survey from which this book began. These people have been listed as sources of information, by areas, at the end of the book.

Architectural descriptions of the structural resources comprised a major part of the material gathered for the survey. This facet of the work was contributed by Emily Robb who served as architectural consultant. Her professional expertise was of great value. Area coordinators assisted in gathering information for the survey. Those who were especially helpful were Mary Scott Hamilton (Trinity Center-Coffee Creek), Florence Scott Morris (Weaverville), Henry C. Meckel (Junction City-Helena), Marion Karch (Lewiston), Ray Patton (Hayfork), and Louise Garrett (Hyampom).

In the preparation of the book itself many people volunteered their time and talent. The authors spent countless hours bringing the material together. Rita Hanover was especially helpful in sharing historical information gathered from personal research, as was Patricia J. Hicks. Walter Miller volunteered his darkroom and talent in the reproduction of some of the old photos and Jean Breeden photographed many of the Weaverville buildings for which older photographs were lacking. Wallace Kibbee's professional expertise in preparing these photos for publication was greatly appreciated. Senta Moore and others were helpful with typing. The extra service provided by Doris Callahan, Librarian, and her Trinity County Library staff as well as service by the staff of the Trinity County Courthouse and the Trinity County Museum was of great assistance when historical information or county records needed checking. There were still others who lent assistance in many ways. The time and help of all these people is gratefully acknowledged.

Besides the work required for the preparation of the manuscript the Trinity County Historical Society was faced with the problem of funding its publication. A grant from The James Irvine Foundation of San Francisco made this possible. To augment this grant, the Board of Directors designated all funds contributed to the Trinity County Historical Society as memorials to loved ones during the period between June 1, 1979, and June 30, 1981. These memorials are listed on the memorial page of the book.

For the purpose of this book, Trinity County has been divided into seven geographical areas. Each area comprises one chapter. Maps have been included to assist the reader in locating the various historic sites. Reference material pertaining to the sites in each area from which historical information was obtained has been listed by their respective areas. The photographs are largely from the files of the Trinity County Historical Society but there are also photographs from private family collections. Without the generosity of these people our photographic record of Trinity County's historical sites would not be as complete.

It is hoped that this book will help all who read it to understand and appreciate the rich heritage that Trinity County's history embraces.

—Alice Goen Jones, Editor

NORTHEAST TRINITY

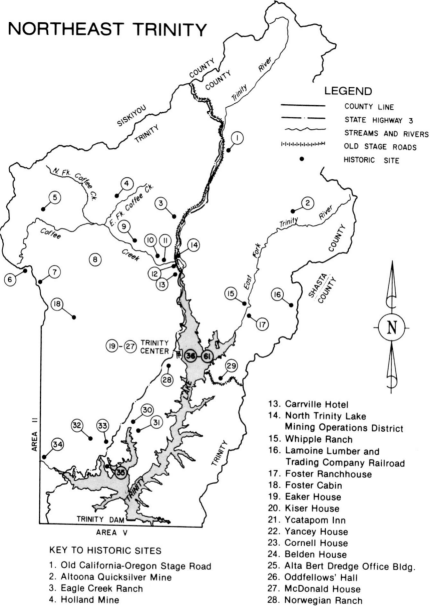

13. Carrville Hotel
14. North Trinity Lake
    Mining Operations District
15. Whipple Ranch
16. Lamoine Lumber and
    Trading Company Railroad
17. Foster Ranchhouse
18. Foster Cabin
19. Eaker House
20. Kiser House
21. Ycatapom Inn
22. Yancey House
23. Cornell House
24. Belden House
25. Alta Bert Dredge Office Bldg.
26. Oddfellows' Hall
27. McDonald House
28. Norwegian Ranch
29. Delta Road
30. Covington Mill
31. Bowerman Barn
32. Heath Ranch
33. Diener House, Mine, and Trestle
34. Trinity Alps Resort
35. Ridgeville Town Site
36-61. Sites covered by Trinity Lake
       (see detailed map on page 33)

KEY TO HISTORIC SITES

1. Old California-Oregon Stage Road
2. Altoona Quicksilver Mine
3. Eagle Creek Ranch
4. Holland Mine
5. Upper Coffee Creek Mining
   Operations District
6. Mountain Meadow Ranch
7. Dorleska Mine
8. High Country Place Names
9. Coffee Creek Ranch
10. Double Cabin
11. Old Trinity Center Jail
12. Cross House

AREA I
NORTHEAST TRINITY

Historical Overview

The broad valley along the upper reaches of the Trinity River became one of the most populous and thriving early mining centers in Trinity County. Following the discovery of gold near Douglas City in 1848 gold seekers spread throughout the Trinity mountains, and by 1853 many of them had made their way up the Trinity River and had begun mining in the Trinity Center area. Prior to this time only the Wintu Indians had inhabited the broad Trinity valley. Their territory extended downstream from the headwaters of the Trinity River to Big Bar. The heaviest concentration of these Wintus was in permanent villages on land adjacent to the river throughout this broad valley. The Trinity River Wintus traded freely with all of their neighbors, especially with the Shasta Indians to the north and with the Upper Sacramento Wintus to the east. Periodic warfare, however, did occur between the tribes. In fact the Trinity River Wintu referred to the tribe to the north as Wiayuki, a word which meant "north enemy".

The Hudson Bay Company started sending fur expeditions into California in 1825. A brigade under Michel Laframboise passed through this region in 1833 following instructions "to hunt and explore the country along the coast between Bodega Bay and McLeods River." Another party led by Tom McKay returned in 1836 to trap the headwaters of the Trinity River. It was not until the early 1850's that the white man came into the area in any number. The early miners followed the original Indian trails into the Trinity Valley and later, as travel between the Sacramento Valley and Oregon increased, these trails became established pack trails which, by 1860, had been replaced by a wagon road. This became the main transportation link between California and Oregon and contributed much to the development of this northeastern portion of the county. A small ranch and trading post started in 1851 by Moses Chadbourne grew to be the thriving settlement of Trinity Center.

Besides the stage route and the influx of miners into this part of the county, agriculture also contributed to the growth of the area. The fertile soil of the Trinity Valley and an abundance of gravity flow water for irrigation led to the establishment of many productive ranches. Notable among them was the Trinity Farm and Cattle Company which, shortly after the turn of the century, became one of the most important cattle operations in northern California.

1

Extensive mining eventually took place throughout the Valley and along most of the tributaries of the upper Trinity River, notably Coffee Creek where gold strikes around 1897 started a small gold rush which vied with the gold rush of the Klondike for attention. Mining continued off and on throughout the area until the advent of World War II drew the miners into the armed services or into defense industries. The depressed price of gold during the mid-1900's was also a major factor in bringing the mining era to an end. An increase in the price of gold during the late 1970's has reactivated an interest in mining throughout Trinity County including this northeastern area.

The course of history in this part of the county was further changed when the Trinity Valley became inundated with the waters which backed up behind the Trinity Dam in 1962 covering forever old Trinity Centre, Stringtown, and many beautiful ranches and other historic sites. Although the building of the Trinity Dam served the state of California by becoming a part of the Central Valley Project, it had a devastating effect upon the people who lived there. Anita Van Matre Shuford stated it well when she wrote, "No one who has not experienced it can know what a heartbreaking event this was to the members of the Van Matre family, young and old alike." And Ed Scott wrote upon being uprooted from the ranch he had occupied for so many years, "It was like leaving part of me behind—having lived at the ranch for over fifty years. We finally left on December 12, 1959, and now, since the clearing contractor has finished, there is not a building standing, not a fence or a tree . . . many people had spent so many happy hours at the ranch over the years. It is now a scene of total devastation!"

Site 1. Old California-Oregon Stage Road and Historic District

The old California-Oregon Stage Road follows closely the route of State Highway 3. Only scattered portions of the original road remain. These are fairly narrow sections of dirt road with vegetation crowding in upon them. The Carrville, Derrick Flat and Eagle Creek Loop Roads along Highway 3 roughly follow portions of the old stage route.

The old stage road from Shasta to Callahan and Yreka was the first main artery of commerce leading from California into Oregon. In 1856 travel through the Trinity County portion was still by saddle mule, but in 1857 construction of a road was started through Trinity County from the foot of Trinity Mountain to the foot of Scott Mountain. James E. Carr had been given the contract to push the road through at a cost of $40,000. In September, 1860, it was finished and opened to the public. Mr. Carr then began to operate it as a private toll road for the California and Oregon Stage Company. It remained an important transportation link between California and Oregon until 1888 when the railroad was completed through the Sacramento Canyon. After that time use of the road greatly diminished. It became so unprofitable and maintenance became so inadequate that the franchise was revoked and the road became part of the county road system.

There were many stage stops along the upper Trinity River portion of this route. At the top of Scott Mountain, where winter snows could be deep, oxen were kept and used to tramp down the snow in order to keep the road open in winter. A large barn for the animals was located here as well as a hotel for the travelers and team drivers. All traces of these buildings have disappeared.

About halfway down Scott Mountain towards Trinity Center was a small flat area which was used as a camping spot for teamsters or men working on the road. At the bottom of the mountain on a big flat near the mouth of Tangle Blue Creek was the American House, a stage stop for the Portland-Sacramento

This view of the Trinity River in the vicinity of old Trinity Center is gone forever. This once fertile valley lies buried under the waters of the Trinity Lake.

Stage operated by the Wilbur Dodge family. This was operated as a hotel to serve not only the travelers but the miners of the area as well. Sometime after the turn of the century Frank Trumble took over the property and homesteaded it. It has since been known as the Trumble Ranch. A small house, considerable fenceline and cattle chutes still remain at this site. The original hotel building was rebuilt at least twice over the years but is no longer standing.

About nine miles down river from the American House is the site of the New York House. This was a fashionable and popular roadhouse that burned in the early 1880's and was not rebuilt. The present Highway 3 passes over the site of the hotel, but an old stone fence that formed the south edge of the corral still stands on the east side of the highway.

Approximately five miles farther downstream near the junction of Davis Creek with the Trinity River is the old Iowa Ranch, now called Eagle Creek Ranch. It was one of the earliest agricultural land claims in the county. Because of its proximity to the New York House it was not used as a hotel, but it did serve as a freight team stopping place. It has, in more recent years, operated as a guest and cattle ranch.

The Carrville Hotel is another important historic place along this portion of the California-Oregon Stage Road in northern Trinity County. It was a productive 160 acre ranch owned by James E. Carr who operated this portion of the stage road. Mr. Carr was also a man prominent in northern California mining and business ventures and his ranch became an important stop along the route.

The last stage traveled this road in 1924. Known locally as the Old Oregon Road, the places mentioned here are significant because they played such an important role in its history.

Site 2. The Altoona Quicksilver Mines

The Altoona Mines are located in the headwaters of the East Fork of the Trinity River and are reached via the Ramshorn Creek Road from Highway 3.

Cinnabar was discovered at the site of the Altoona Mine in 1871. At first it was a placer operation, but with the formation of the Altoona Quicksilver Mining Company in 1875 underground workings began which eventually reached a depth of 600 feet.

The Altoona Mine had only two periods of real production: 1875-1880 and 1895-1901. During these two periods the mine yielded 27,200 flasks of mercury and ranked fifth in the state of California in output. Since 1901 production has been sporadic. There were several reasons for this: the most easily available source of the mineral had become exhausted; its isolated location had made transportation costly; severe winter weather conditions made year-round mining difficult; and drainage problems were encountered at the 600' depth. In 1943 World War II brought on an increase in the demand for mercury, causing a short spurt in production. There were again attempts to mine in 1955-60 and in 1964-65.

At the turn of the century, when the mine was experiencing its greatest activity, it was one of the largest operations in the county and possibly in northern California. It boasted a boarding house at the site which could accommodate 150 workers. There were also a commissary, a saloon, a one-room schoolhouse, a company doctor in residence, and a power plant that provided electricity for a lighted recreational ski run. Today, one can view in various stages of disrepair, the obvious remains of a variety of buildings including bunk and boarding houses, an office, a machine shop, storage rooms, a residence or two, and other mill related buildings as well as pipes, a trackbed, vats, furnaces and chutes. Dumps and open cuts in addition to the main adit and shaft sites are

4

Site 2. This picture of the Altoona Quicksilver Mine smelter and other mill-related buildings was taken in 1898 during the mine's greatest activity. Note the pack animals at the left of the picture — an essential element in the mine's operation.

also plainly evident. Because of the relatively recent attempts to operate this mine, there are a number of buildings that are not as old as those that predate the turn of the century; even the older buildings show evidence of later additions and maintenance.

To the north of the Altoona operation is a related mine, the Integral Mine. Here the buildings and site are not as well preserved as those at the Altoona.

Site 3. Iowa Ranch (Stoddard Ranch) (Eagle Creek Ranch)

Iowa Ranch, now known as Eagle Creek Ranch, is along Highway 3 near where Ripple Creek enters the Trinity River.

The Davis family first settled on this ranch in the 1850's. They named it the Iowa Ranch after their home state. It was one of the earliest agricultural land claims in Trinity County. The ranch was built along the route followed by the early supply trains which packed between California and Oregon. the California and Oregon Stage Road which was completed through Trinity County in 1860 followed this early supply route and thus the Iowa Ranch became a stopping place for the freight teams. But since the ranch was only five miles from the New York House, an established roadhouse on the stage road, it was not used as a hotel stopping place. The freight teams, however, stopped here for repairs and shelter. The original wagon shed still stands with its big double doors through which the teams could drive. Upstairs in the shed were sleeping quarters for the team drivers. It is a board and batten building with hand hewn beams pegged with one-inch dowels.

In 1878 the ranch was sold for $2400 to John R. Stoddard who then homesteaded it. The Stoddards ran many head of cattle, using the Stoddard Meadows in the Alps for their summer grazing. An old drift fence four miles up Eagle Creek dates from this time.

The two-story hand-hewn log cabin on the ranch, known as the Stoddard House, was probably built soon after the Stoddards acquired the property. The building has been substantially remodeled, but one original corner has been retained which shows the original two-story porch and the dovetailed 12" logs. This building was once used as a telegraph office, the second such telegraph office in Trinity County.

There is an old orchard on the property containing apple trees over 100 years old. The old fence line is still in evidence, and nearby there is a family cemetery which is now overgrown with vegetation.

The ranch was taken over by Jim and Gussie Lee about 1930. The Lees continued running it as a cattle ranch, but they also operated it as a guest ranch. It was the Lees who gave it its present name of Eagle Creek Ranch. The ranch is currently being restored by Mr. and Mrs. Karl Van Matre who have recently acquired a portion of the property.

Site 4. Holland Mine

The Holland Mine extended along more than two miles of the East Fork of Coffee Creek and is significant because, by 1926, it had operated continuously for more than fifty years. As such it had the longest continuous period of operation of any of the mines in this part of the county and at the turn of the century was considered to be one of the area's most famous mines. It was not a particularly large operation nor an outstanding producer of gold. Only 5000-6000 sq. ft. of bedrock was cleaned each season, but nuggets ranged from $200 to $600 in value.

The most striking feature of the mine was its three-mile long wooden flume, 3' high by 3' wide, supported by huge rough sawn timbers 12' high. Portions of the flume still exist although in a state of considerable deterioration. Remains of various buildings used in the mining operation as well as small pieces of machinery are also in evidence. Signs of small dams, which had been placed along the East Fork to aid in the utilization of power and water for the mining operation, may also be found. Stoddard Lake at the headwaters of the East Fork was dammed in an attempt to control flooding by the stream that, during periods of high water, could have scoured out the stream channel where the mining was occurring.

The mine is a good example of a small, privately owned mining operation that was durable. It was owned and operated by Pat Holland until his death. His wife, Kate, and her brother, J. A. Coyle, continued the operation until the mid-1920's.

Site 5. The Upper Coffee Creek Mining Operations District

The mines of the upper Coffee Creek drainage from the East Fork of Coffee Creek to Big Flat have been grouped together here as the Upper Coffee Creek Mining Operations District. In the late 1880's and early 1890's there had been a rush of miners into the entire Coffee Creek area following the discovery of a rich pocket of gold near the mouth of Coffee Creek by the Graves brothers. But various mining activities had been taking place here ever since the 1850's. The Abrams brothers who had established a trading post at Big Flat in 1851 had the first claim along the upper Coffee Creek.

An extensive series of placer, hydraulic, and dredge tailings is found throughout the general area. These tailings, along with extensive dump, pit, ditch, and shaft sites, are residues of over 100 years of mining activity. These evidences of past mining activity are to be found along much of the North Fork of Coffee Creek, on the upper benches of Deacon and Hickory Creeks, in the Union Creek drainage, along the South Fork of Coffee Creek, at Adams Lake, upon the side of Battle Mountain, and on many of the small tributaries.

At the mouth of Saloon Creek, a tributary of the North Fork of Coffee Creek, there was once a bustling community known as Saloon City. Election records show that 700 votes were cast here in one mid-1850's election. This place was a trading post and source of supplies for numerous mines in the area. Only one small lone cabin remains at the site of the once active community. It is said that 300 people also lived in the nearby Chipmunk Meadows area along what became known as Milk Ranch Creek. Billiard balls found in Chipmunk Meadows in recent times would indicate that this community, like nearby Saloon Creek, had a billiard saloon among its business enterprises. But a more important business, no doubt, was its dairy business, for cows that were kept there provided milk for the miners as far away as the Nash Mine along Coffee Creek.

The Nash Mines, both the Lower Nash and later the Upper Nash, were sizeable operations along the upper end of Coffee Creek. These operations were known as the Nash Deep Gravel Gold Mining Company. James E. Carr, Louis Maitland, Gordon Abrams, and others were active in the mine's ownership and operation. By the 1890's 649 acres covering approximately seven miles of a narrow strip of ground along Coffee Creek above its junction with Hickory Creek had been deeded by the government to the Nash Company.

The gold in this region was generally coarse; the gravels ran 14 to 16 feet deep and the nuggets ran up to $50.00 in value. By the 1890's hydraulic efforts had replaced the original placer operation. This lasted but a few years for the gravels were soon well worked over. With the turn of the century a period of inactivity began. In the 1920's the Nash Mine came under the control of a San Francisco engineer, E. L. Joseph, who eventually leased the properties out for a

Site 5. This 1907 picture of an early day miner's cabin on Coffee Creek is typical of miner's cabins throughout the Trinity mountains.

Site 6. This very small log cabin, once used as the dairy building, is the only original building remaining from the days of the Abrams Trading Post.

dredging operation. In May 1947, a dredge, generally known as the Mires and Underseath, began its slow upstream grind. With a succession of owners and partners, dredging activities continued off and on until September, 1951, when the frequent changes in personnel, high costs, breakdowns, and boulders too large to handle brought the operation to a close. It has been reported that 10,000 ounces of gold were removed from the site of the Nash Mines from 1896-1951.

There have been numerous other mines in the area which were active either during the early mining boom of the 1850's, the Coffee Creek gold rush at the turn of the century, or during the depression years of the 1930's. These include the Hardscrabble Prospect on Hardscrabble Creek (1900-1909), Steve's Gulch Placer on Steveale Creek (1897-1898), the Schlomberg on the upper North Fork of Coffee Creek (1916-1937), and the Gypsy Queen on Deacon Creek. There were also the Geneva, the Niedra, the Andy, the Prince Albert, the Mary Queen, the Lady Slipper, and the Francis Mine. Most of these latter were relatively small mines which operated during the depression years of the 1930's.

Site 6. Abrams Trading Post (Big Flat) (Mountain Meadow Ranch)

Big Flat is the location of an old trading post or stopping place on the South Fork of the Salmon near the headwaters of Coffee Creek. Although it is located just over the boundary in Siskiyou County, it is included here because it is closely related to Trinity County's early history. It was probably into the Big Flat area that the first white men came when they ventured into the higher elevations searching for gold. In 1849 a party of four men, including a man named James Abrams, followed an old Indian trail up Swift Creek, across the mountains near Preacher's Peak, and into the Big Flat area. They found no gold at that time, but Abrams returned the next year (1850) and started building a stopover place for the miners who were coming through there on their way from the Sacramento Valley to the gold diggings along the Klamath. The following year (1851) a younger brother, Francis, arrived from Illinois and joined his brother in fencing the natural meadow and building cabins, a store, a butcher shop, and a dairy. The meadows supported a herd of cattle that supplied meat for the butcher shop and milk for the miners. The brothers also packed food and materials in from Shasta and French Gulch in Shasta County and from Callahan in Siskiyou County to supply the miners.

James later returned to his home in Illinois to marry his sweetheart. He brought her back to Big Flat to live and raise their family. Descendants of James have followed him as postmaster, merchants, and packers in the area. Francis did not marry.

Only one cabin of the original buildings remains. It is a very small log cabin covered with shakes which was used as the dairy building.

Big Flat is now the location of the Mountain Meadow Ranch, a resort tnat is operated as a summer hotel for vacationers.

Site 7. Dorleska Mine

The Dorleska Mine is within the Trinity Alps Primitive Area. It is located on a high and remote ridge at the 6700' elevation at the head of the Union Creek drainage west of Bullard's Basin.

There is much evidence that this was once a substantial gold mining operation. Adit, shaft, pit, dump and tailing areas, as well as piles of scrap wood and metal are in evidence. There are the obvious remains of a mill complete with a large boiler and several support buildings that are either totally collapsed or nearly so. The one building that as late as 1979 remained somewhat upright had double walls filled with sawdust and a high and interestingly weathered roof line. All of the mine tunnels and shaft openings have caved in leaving their interiors essentially inaccessible.

The Dorleska Mine was started during the Coffee Creek gold rush of 1897-98 by R. D. Laurence who named the site after his wife Dorleska. In spite of its extremely remote location much heavy equipment had to be sledded in by mule teams. This included a steam engine, a boiler, pumps, and all of the material necessary to set up a sawmill, a five-stamp mill, a ten-stamp mill, and the necessary buildings to support a community of 15-20 people who would live there for the next several years. The route followed to sled much of this equipment in was up Swift Creek, then Parker Creek to its head, thence over the pass into the Union Creek drainage, and on to the site of the Dorleska, a distance of 16 miles.

Close to 2000' of tunnels were dug and a protective snowshed was built over the outside tracks which carried the ore from the tunnel to the stamp mill nearby. This enabled the mining operations to continue throughout the winter when snows could vary from 10' to 25' in depth. The Dorleska became a substantial mining operation. It is said that the ore shipped by mule from the Dorleska netted $1100 to $2000 per ton after expenses. At its peak, $200 per day was realized. This mine was a major producer until about 1912. After that, production dwindled and it was difficult to meet ordinary expenses of the operation. Mining continued off and on through the 1920's and 1930's and essentially ceased in 1938. $200,000 is the estimated production of this mine between 1898 and 1926. It remains today a fine example of a typical major high country underground gold mine of the turn of the century.

Site 8. High Country Place Names

Many of the lakes and meadows in the high country of the Trinity Alps have been associated with Trinity County's pioneers and particularly with its cattlemen. Until 1940 stock raising was a large industry in the county, and the high country was used as summer grazing land for the cattle. Some of the places which have been named for, or associated with, these pioneers are:

Morris Meadows on the Stuart Fork was named for James Morris, a Weaverville cattleman.

Portugese Meadows and Portugese Camp on the Stuart Fork has reference to Jesse Costa, a Portugese cattleman who had a ranch on Rush Creek.

Foster Lake in the upper Union Creek drainage and Foster Cabin at Parker Meadows on Swift Creek are named for William Foster, Trinity Center cattleman who operated the Trinity Farm and Cattle Company.

Van Matre Meadows and Van Matre Creek in the Stuart Fork drainage were named for Mart Van Matre, a Lewiston cattleman.

Siligo Meadow and Siligo Peak near Deer Lake and Deer Creek Pass were named for Louis Siligo, another Lewiston cattleman.

Stoddard Lake and Stoddard Meadows, west of the Trinity River and north of Coffee Creek were named for John Stoddard, a cattleman and miner whose ranch was along the upper Trinity River in the vicinity of Ripple Creek.

Ward Lake at the headwaters of Swift Creek was named for Whit Ward, the number one cowhand for the Trinity Farm and Cattle Company of Trinity Center.

Tapie Lake at the headwaters of the Boulder Creek drainage, tributary of Coffee Creek, was named for Raymond Tapie who owned the Coffee Creek Chalet, now the Coffee Creek Ranch.

Conway Lake, near Tapie Lake, is named for Fred Conway, pioneer cattleman from Trinity Center. He discovered Lake Eleanor and named it for his wife.

Site 7. Mining activity was carried on throughout the year at the Dorleska Mine. A protective snowshed (not visible in this 1906 picture) was built over the outside tracks making it possible to carry the ore from the mine tunnels to the stamp mill even though snow depths were substantial.

Site 7. A pile of rocks, a tree limb and some old boards mark the corner of the Dorleska mining claim.

Site 11. No prisoners have ever occupied this one-room jail, built in Trinity Center in 1918, but never put to use!

Bowerman Meadows in the headwaters of the East Fork of Stuart Fork gets its name from Jake Bowerman, Minersville cattleman.

Black Basin in the upper Deer Creek drainage, a tributary of Stuart Fork, is named for an early Trinity Center sheepman.

Scott's Cow Camp along Bear Creek in the Swift Creek drainage was used by the cattlemen from Scott's Ranch, Trinity Center.

McDonald Lake, near Stoddard Lake, was named in memory of Warren P. McDonald, son of Elmer and Louise McDonald of Trinity Center and grandson of Pete McDonald, Trinity Center pioneer. Warren was killed while working for the Trinity County Road Department shortly after World War II. His name was submitted for this honor by the Trinity County Sportsmen's Association of which he was president.

Seven-up Peak was given its name by Irvin and Stanford Scott of Scott's Ranch, Trinity Center, as they were playing a game of seven-up while tending their cattle nearby.

Stonewall Pass is a narrow pass separating Siligo and Van Matre Meadows from Red Mountain Meadows. The cattlemen, using these meadows as grazing lands, built a wall of boulders across this pass, topped it with barbed wire, and closed the opening with pole bars in order to keep their cattle from drifting from one grazing area to another. This stone wall is responsible for the name which has been given this pass.

Site 9. The Ben Pinkham boarding house, built to serve the miners coming into the Coffee Creek area, was remodeled and expanded into a 17-room hotel by 1908 and became a well known vacation spot.

Site 9. Pinkham's Hotel (Coffee Creek Chalet) (Coffee Creek Ranch)

Coffee Creek Ranch, five miles up Coffee Creek Road, was originally the 140 acre homestead of Ben Pinkham, for which he received the patent in 1908. He was a Maine Yankee who came to California during the gold rush, first settling in the Santa Clara Valley.

Upon hearing of the gold strikes in the Coffee Creek area, Pinkham came to Trinity County to mine and eventually bought out the interest of a Mr. Hensley in a mining claim. Mr. Pinkham soon decided that there was more of a future to be had in establishing a farm and supplying the miners, than in mining his claim. Pinkham grew hay and vegetables and opened a boarding house for the miners. This had expanded into a 17 room hotel by 1908. There was such an influx of miners and their families into the area that a school was established here in 1908; Coffee Creek Post Office was located here as well. Although the hotel started out to serve the miners coming into the area, it gradually became popular with vacationers from the cities. It was given the name Coffee Creek Chalet by Mr. Pinkham's stepdaughter, Viva Tapie, who, together with her husband Raymond, operated the resort for many years. In 1946 the ranch was purchased by John and Margaret Neubauer who for a brief period ran it as a boys' camp. Soon it was again being operated as a resort. It was the Neubauers who changed the name to Coffee Creek Ranch. The property was sold again in 1965 and in 1976 and continues to be operated as a resort.

The Coffee Creek Ranch occupies land on both sides of the creek. On the north side is the main resort building which is a replacement for the original hotel-boarding house that burned on Easter Sunday in 1966. Several cabins are nearby including two of the original outbuildings. These date back to World War I or slightly later. They are of board and batten construction and are still in use.

Across the creek is a large pasture, a barn of recent origin, and the old caretaker's house. This house is considered to be the oldest building on the property. It was built in 1889 on a different spot and was moved to its present location in 1935. It is a one and one-half story gable, board and batten structure.

Parts of the old packer's bridge, parts of the old corral fence, and parts of the old road to the Golden Jubilee Mine, as well as an old irrigation ditch, are in evidence.

Site 10. Double Cabin

Double Cabin is approximately three miles up Coffee Creek Road from Highway 3.

Presently uninhabited and posted, this building was originally two log cabins under one shake roof with a walkway between. In 1913 the middle part was enclosed with vertical boards to make it warmer for winter living. The wide horizontal planks on the two original cabins cover the original logs. The shake roof has been replaced with metal.

The "Double Cabin" was built in 1879 and is the oldest cabin along Coffee Creek. The builder is known only as a "Mr. Bighouse". The cabin is in fair condition but has begun to deteriorate for it has stood vacant for many years.

One story associated with this building is that two miners once lived here, had a fight, and ended up building the second cabin separated by the open breezeway — thus explaining the second cabin under one roof.

Site 11. Old Trinity Center Jail

The old Trinity County Jail is about three miles up Coffee Creek Road from Highway 3.

About the time of World War I Trinity Center was filled with men constructing the Estabrook Dredge or working in their sawmill. These men were frequent visitors to the local saloon. This gave the deputy sheriff reason to fear that someday there might be need for a jail. In 1918 he had a small, one room metal structure built complete with bars on the front door. It is a unique structure in that it is a jail in which there has never been an occupant! It sat, largely vacant, until 1959 when it was moved from its original site to its present location on the Coffee Creek Road.

Site 12. Atkins House (Laura Atkins Cross House) (Cross House)

The Cross house on Carrville Loop Road was originally one of the buildings at the Headlight Mine located one mile southeast of Carrville.

This log building was constructed about the turn of the century as a residence for the mine's superintendent. When the mine ceased operation about 1915, the sister of the mine's superintendent and her husband, Mr. and Mrs. G. H. Atkins, purchased the house and moved it across the river to its present location on the Carrville Loop Road. To make the move the building was taken apart piece by piece with each log numbered and then reassembled at the new location exactly as they were originally.

It is a one and one-half story, steep pitch, gable roofed structure with massive vertical unpeeled logs supporting a veranda across the front. The dormer windows contain multiple small panes of glass 3" x 5" in size.

Mrs. Atkins later became Mrs. Cross accounting for the name given this house.

Site 13. Currey and Noyes Ranch (Carrville Hotel)

The original Carrville Hotel, located on Carrville Loop Road about six miles north of Trinity Center, was built in 1867 and was completely destroyed by fire on April 10, 1917. It was rebuilt in 1918 and modeled after the original building. However, essential differences exist, the most important being the roof which was a rambling cross gable but now is a consolidated hip roof structure. It is a beautiful, dignified, two and one-half story former hotel with a double story veranda across the front reminiscent of a southern mansion. It was originally built of logs, but improvements were continually being made until eventually the logs were completely covered with shiplap siding.

The Carrville property consisting of 160 acres was originally settled in 1854 and was known as the Currey and Noyes Ranch. It was excellent farm land, but these gentlemen kept a hotel here. The property was acquired by James E. Carr in 1861. Carr was a prominent northern California businessman who was manager of the mule express trains of the California-Oregon Stage Road. The story goes that Carr's wife fell in love with the ranch when she saw it while accompanying her husband on an inspection tour of the stage road. This led to its purchase by the Carrs. Mr. Carr later became involved with a large number of mines including the well known Nash and Altoona properties. His son, George L. Carr, was the successful proprietor of a general store in Trinity Center.

Situated along the old stage road, the Carrville Hotel became one of the most attractive and popular hostelries and, later, resorts in California. It continued to be operated by the Carrs until the late 1940's. It was sold out of the family in 1968. Since that time several attempts have been made to revive it.

Besides the hotel, there were a blacksmith shop, a post office, a freight depot, and a general store which was first run by the Carr Mercantile Company and later by the McCormick-Saeltzer Company. There were also a saloon and a dance hall, as well as several cabins behind the main hotel building. Most of these buildings date from the 1915-1952 period when Carrville was run as a summer resort and pack station. One of its most prominent and frequent visitors was President Herbert Hoover who had spent many of his younger days as a mining engineer on the North Fork of the Trinity River.

A private cemetery is situated in the woods on the hill behind the hotel. The site of the Carr bungalow which was destroyed by fire was south of the main building.

Site 13. The stage leaves the Carrville Hotel. This is a 1913 photo of the original hotel which was destroyed by fire in 1917.

Site 14. North Trinity Lake Mining Operations District

The mines that were along both sides of the Trinity River north of Trinity Center up to and including the lower portion of Coffee Creek have been grouped together here as the North Trinity Lake Mining Operations District. Particularly noticeable in this area are massive gold dredge tailings which are the residue of three major dredge operations. The region also embraced numerous placer, hydraulic and lode mines.

The first gold mines were worked here in 1852, but the first major mining venture occurred in 1871 with the establishment of Frank Bloss and David McClary's mine in the gravel bench area between Hatchet and Swift Creeks. These benches, up to 45 feet in depth, were thoroughly covered by a relatively elaborate system of tunnels, open cuts, ditches, pipes, giants, and over 80 sluice boxes. Water for this hydraulic operation was supplied by two ditches out of Swift Creek, one eight miles long and the other three miles long. This provided sufficient water to operate the mine ten months out of the year. By 1891 the Bloss and McClary Mine was considered to be one of the most valuable gravel gold properties in the state. Part of this operation continued at the turn of the century as the Sykes Hydraulic Mine.

Various other mines contributed to the historical significance of this area as a mining district. Mining activities occurred in Hostetter Gulch, at the Graves Mine, and at the claim of A. P. Haskin on Hatchet Creek, the placers on Buckeye Creek, and at the Blythe properties near Carrville where various members of the Carr family were active in the late 1890's and early 1900's. The following are some of the other mines that have operated in the area:

The Golden Jubilee on Boulder Creek was an active quartz mine employing 60 men. Considerable wood and metal from its ten-stamp mill and cyanide plant can still be found in the area as well as several adit and dump sites and several large vats.

The Wagner Mine on Wagner Creek operated around the turn of the century. Two adits, a dump, the frame of a small cyanide plant, and a three-seater outhouse remain as evidence of this former mine.

The Strode Mine on the Trinity River just north of Coffee Creek was the site of a ten-stamp mill and a cyanide plant. Only various dumps and the roadbed of a wide-gauge, cable-operated, vertical tramway are left.

The Headlight Mine on the east side of the Trinity River, one and one-half miles southeast of Carrville, was a large 40-stamp mill and cyanide operation. It had a power plant, a sawmill, and numerous residences but now very little remains. It was most active about 1910.

The Blue Jay Mine on Morrison Gulch was famous for its rich pockets of gold. One pocket alone brought in $42,000. The gold strike here was made in 1892 by John B. Graves when his very first panning effort paid off with gold worth $400-$500.

The Copper King and Copper Queen Mines differed from the others in that gold was not the mineral being mined. All that remains as evidence of this operation is a roadbed or two, dumps, a probable shaft area, and a few scattered boards around the old building sites.

The Bonanza King and Queen group of mines were active from 1893 until 1922. A few building sites and two grave sites in the vicinity are all that are left.

During and after World War I the more level grounds of some of these early mines were worked over by large gold dredges. The first successful dredge operation was started about 1916 by the Pacific Gold Dredging Company and the Guggenheim interests at the mouth of Coffee Creek. This dredge later moved to the meadow at the Graves Ranch two miles north of Trinity Center where it continued in operation until 1925. The dredge camp established there later became known as Stringtown because of the manner in which the camp was strung out.

About the same time an ambitious project began which involved the construction and operation of what was the largest wooden gold dredge in the world, the Estabrook. It had followed the short-lived operation of the Alta Bert Dredge that had sunk not long after it had started in 1912. The Estabrook began working in 1918. It was a giant piece of machinery which, along with the mine buildings, utilized 15 million board feet of lumber in it construction, including 64' timbers from a sawmill established on Rancheria Creek. Like the Pacific Dredge, the Estabrook was electrically driven. Power was brought into the area on lines from the outside especially built for the purpose. This electricity enabled the Estabrook to move 12,000 yards of gravel per day and work six and one-half acres of ground to a depth of 50 feet in a period of one

16

month. The Estabrook continued operation through the 1920's but eventually shut down due to gravels that were too heavy for it to handle.

The last dredge in this area was designed on a scale that, it was hoped, would enable it to work in hard areas. This all steel dredge was built in 1938-39 by the Yuba manufacturing Company of San Francisco for the Carrville Gold Company of Minnesota. It was operated in the Carrville area and had some early successes. For example, one year during ten days of cleanup 1900 ounces of gold were netted. The dredge employed 32 men making it the largest operation in the area at the time. Financial problems, war interruptions, troublesome equipment breakdowns, as well as heavy gravels, finally led in 1947 to the end of this effort in large scale industrial mining.

This north lake area is a notable example of successive mining efforts in a concentrated area which, over a period of years, had a significant impact on the economy of the region. At the same time scarred land that was left behind is a weighty reminder of a greed-oriented past.

Site 14. Mill and store building at the Bonanza King Mine.

Site 14. A long span of the aerial tram carrying ore across Cedar Creek at the Bonanza King Mine.

Site 14. The Golden Jubilee Mine was an active lode mine during the early 1900's.

Site 15. The Whipple Ranch barn has had many names and many owners over the years. It is presently called The Wildcat after the nearby mountain that overlooks it.

Site 15. Whipple Ranch Barn (Wagner Ranch) (Wildcat Ranch)

The Whipple Ranch is now known as the Wildcat after the nearby peak which overlooks it. Located on the East Fork Road, it was built in 1884-5 by Louis Girard. Its next owner was Milton Shoemaker who patented the land. A succession of owners followed including George Leisz, E. A. and F. A. Bassham, Bud Wagner, W. H. Key, John C. Whipple, his son Jack Whipple, and C. Mark Groves the present owner. It is the last major ranch left along the East Fork of the Trinity River. Power for the Bonanza King, at one time, was generated at this site.

The Whipple Barn is similar in construction to the well known Bowerman Barn (see page 28). The barn is 60' x 54'; its 45' roof is its most dominant feature. The construction is log and pole. The huge supporting beams are hand hewn and held together with wooden pegs. It has not been altered except for a metal roof installed in 1954. It remains in excellent condition, having not succumbed to the threat of fire, neglect, or development.

Site 16. Lamoine Lumber and Trading Company Railroad Grade, Trestles and Camps

The remains of the Lamoine operation are in an isolated area near Slate Mountain in Townships 36N and 37N, R6W.

In 1894, Sam, Cliff and Lowell Coggins from Lamoine, Maine, formed the Lamoine Lumber and Trading Company and went into the sawmill business. In the late 1890's the company bought timberland west of Slatonis on the old Oregon Trail and changed the name of Slatonis to Lamoine in honor of their hometown. To facilitate the logging of their timberlands the company, in 1903, started building a railroad. Fifty miles of railroad grade were constructed extending from a point near Lamoine to within 12 miles of Trinity Center. There were 35 miles of narrow guage railroad track. The track was rotated and put into use along the grade wherever logging was occurring in order to bring the logs to the mill. This Lamoine logging railroad was located in the Hall's Gulch area of the Shasta-Trinity divide and is one of two railroads which have operated within Trinity County. It also extended into the Clear Creek area of Shasta County. It was a remarkable engineering accomplishment as the topography was rough and steep, and the cuts were made by pick and shovel or by using a horse with a Fresno scraper. Since the railroad was not connected to any railroad on the outside, all materials, including those for more than a dozen large donkey engines, had to be hauled in by pack animals and reassembled.

The Lamoine Company also built a large box factory and a V-type flume which extended from the railroad terminus at the sawmill down the steep Slate Creek Canyon for about five miles to the planing mill and box factory at Lamoine. The Coggins controlled the company until 1904. The operation continued under different management until a large fire in the area in 1917 eventually led to its cessation and the sale of the railroad to a Castella firm in 1927.

The area through which the railroad grade passes is forest land with heavy vegetation. There is considerable evidence of past logging in the area. The railroad grade itself is fairly discernible although it has washed out in places. In some spots the ties, though rotting, are still in place. The trestles are in various stages of deterioration. At first the trestles had been built of second grade lumber, but after an accident in which a locomotive and a number of cars went through a trestle only first quality timbers were used. The camp sites along either side of the grade contain considerable downed building lumber and artifacts from the railroad such as bars, spikes, rail sections, and wheels from the logging cars.

Site 16. The Lamoine logging railroad, operating in rough, steep country on the Trinity-Shasta Divide, was a remarkable engineering accomplishment.

Site 17. Foster Ranchhouse

The Foster Ranchhouse is located about two miles up the East Fork of the Trinity River from Trinity Lake. It is a simple two-story structure which was built in 1917 by D. O. Ferguson for the Trinity Farm and Cattle Company. It was lived in by William Foster, Sr. and his family. Mr. Foster, together with his five sons, William Jr., Milton, Melvin, Harvey and George, established and operated the Trinity Farm and Cattle Company which became one of the largest cattle operations in northern California.

The ranchhouse originally stood among a cluster of other ranch buildings along the east bank of the Trinity River near the mouth of the East Fork about three miles from Trinity Center on the road to French Gulch. It was moved from its original setting to its present location on the East Fork when the Trinity Lake formed. It was a functional building which had seven bedrooms, one bath, a large kitchen and pantry, an office and a large dining room which could seat 16 people comfortably. The hired hands slept in a bunkhouse nearby.

Site 18. Foster Cabin (Foster Cow Camp)

Foster Meadows, at the head of Parker Meadows, in the upper Swift Creek drainage, is believed to have been the location of a midway stopping place along the early supply trail between Norwegian Ranch and the trading post at Big Flat. Later it became the site of the Foster Cow Camp. The meadows were summer grazing lands for cattle belonging to the Trinity Farm and Cattle Company operated by William Foster, Sr. and his five sons. Quarters for the cowhands who stayed with the cattle during the summer months were located here.

TRINITY CENTER

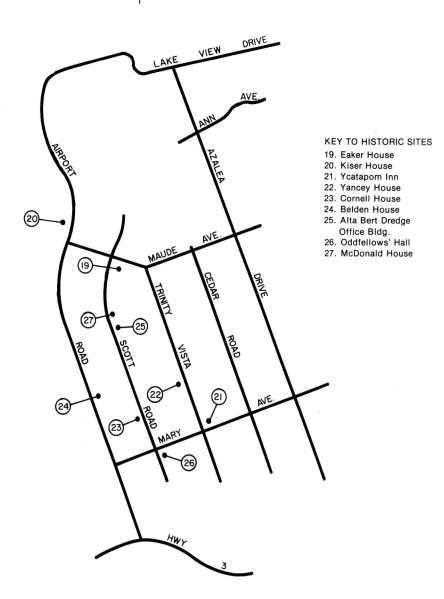

KEY TO HISTORIC SITES
19. Eaker House
20. Kiser House
21. Ycatapom Inn
22. Yancey House
23. Cornell House
24. Belden House
25. Alta Bert Dredge
    Office Bldg.
26. Oddfellows' Hall
27. McDonald House

The collapsed remains of the first Foster cabin and a nearby small barn are still in evidence. These buildings were constructed of logs and date back to 1915. The present cabin was built nearby in 1944 by Fred McHugh for Mr. Foster and for the U.S. Forest Service which put it to use as a snow survey cabin. Construction of this more recent building is of 6x6 hand hewn timbers cut on the site.

About four miles beyond Foster Cabin at the headwaters of Swift Creek is Ward Lake. It is named for Whit Ward, Mr. Foster's #1 cowhand.

Site 18. Foster Cow Camp, located at Parker Meadows, was used by Trinity Farm and Cattle Company cowhands in the summer when cattle grazed in the high mountain meadows of the Swift Creek drainage.

Site 19. Estabrook Dredge Office (Eaker House)

Estabrook Dredge Office is located at the corner of Maude and Scott Roads in Trinity Center.

This one-story, medium gable, clapboard structure with a veranda across the front was built by the Estabrook Dredge Company as an office in 1918 and was used for that purpose until 1927 when the dredge ceased operation. Since that time it has been a residence. It was moved from its original location in old Trinity Center by Elmer McDonald in 1959. The present owner is Bill Eaker.

Site 20. Estabrook Dredge Building (Kiser House)

The Estabrook Dredge Building at 16 Airport Road in Trinity Center is now a residence. This house was built by the Estabrook Dredge Company in 1918 and was used by the company as a residence until 1927. At that time the dredge ceased operation and the house was sold. Marion and Mary Rae Dickey purchased it and lived in it for over thirty years. It was originally located in old Trinity Center but moved to new Trinity Center upon construction of the Trinity Dam.

This building is a one-story high gable structure with shiplap siding. Of special note are the shutters which have a cut-out pattern of a Christmas tree in them. It is now the residence of Mrs. Margaret Kiser.

Site 21. Estabrook Home (Ycatapom Inn)

Now part of the Ycatapom Inn at 71 Mary Avenue, Trinity Center, the Estabrook Home was built in 1918 in old Trinity Center. It was a two-story house built of fir logs. Only part of one side wall and the projecting logs in part of one gable end remain of the original building. The house was moved to new Trinity Center in 1959 where it was reconstructed and attached to the Ycatapom Inn which had also been moved from old Trinity Center. The Inn portion is a low, board and batten structure.

The Estabrook house was the home of Bill Estabrook who built and operated the Estabrook Dredge. The Estabrook was the largest wooden dredge in the world. It had a wood hull and superstructure, was electrically driven and had buckets of 20 to 22 cubic feet capacity. The main line drive belt was 5' wide. The dredge had the capability of moving 400,000 tons of gravel a month while covering an area of six and one-sixth acres.

The 1500 tons of machinery for the dredge were manufactured in Michigan, hauled by rail to Delta, then trucked over the old Delta Toll Road to Trinity Center. Fifteen million board feet of lumber were needed for construction of this dredge and its buildings. The hull alone required 650,000 bd. ft. A small sawmill set up on Rancheria Creek was reportedly the first in the world equipped to cut 64' timbers. The Estabrook Dredge was fairly successful, but the heavy gravels of the upper Trinity took their toll and the dredge closed down in 1927. The Estabrook home was then sold and the woodshed and garage were turned into a saloon. In its new location at new Trinity Center the home is still a saloon as well as a restaurant.

Site 22. Larson House (Yancy House)

The Larson House on Trinity Vista Road, Trinity Center, is a one and one-half story board and batten structure with a veranda surrounding it on four sides. It was moved to its present site from old Trinity Center in 1959 at the time of the construction of the Trinity Dam. It is one of three pre-1900 buildings in Trinity Center. The house was built in the 1870-1880 era by John Larson who ran a store and blacksmith shop in Trinity Center. John Larson was originally from Copenhagen, Denmark. He had jumped his ship in San Francisco in the 1850's and headed for the gold country. He married Margaret Coyle, the daughter of an immigrant Irishman. Ownership of the house passed to their daughter, Anna Yancey, and then on to her daughter, Margaret Hall.

Site 23. Hall House (Cornell House)

Hall House, at 43 Scott Road in Trinity Center, was moved to this location to escape the waters of Trinity Lake.

The Hall House, a one and one-half story wood building with shiplap siding, was built around 1890 and originally was situated just west of the school in old Trinity Center. In 1959 it was moved to new Trinity Center and is one of the three buildings built prior to 1900 that has been moved to a site in the new town.

From 1914 until 1930 the Forest Service rented this building for use as a ranger station. In 1930 it was moved off the Ranger Station grounds and sold to Jim Basham who used it as a family residence. The present owner is Joan Cornell.

Site 21. The Ycatapom Inn was originally the home of Bill Estabrook, the builder and operator of the Estabrook Dredge. It was moved from old Trinity Center to its present location in 1959.

Site 22. This original Larson house in old Trinity Center is one of three pre - 1900 buildings that have been relocated in new Trinity Center.

Site 24. Alta Bert Dredge Building (Joe Belden House)

This building, located at 30 Airport Road, Trinity Center, was originally constructed of rough-cut 1x12 vertical planks which had been part of an old house that had been located just north of what is now the Wyntoon Resort. The old house had been torn down about 1912 and hauled to old Trinity Center where it was rebuilt for use by employees of the Alta Bert Dredge Co. About 1916 the building was purchased by the Estabrook Dredge Company for use as the home of their office manager. It remained the property of the Estabrook Company until it was closed down in 1927.

A cross gable containing two rooms was added to one side in the 1950's by Ray Glassburn who was the owner at that time. The building was moved to new Trinity Center in 1959. Several alterations have been made to this building such as the addition of composition shingle siding and dormer windows in the hip roof. Joe and Sophie Belden are the present owners.

Site 25. Alta Bert Dredge Office (McDonald Rental)

This building on Scott Road, Trinity Center, was built as a dredge office for the Alta Bert Dredge Company about 1911-1912. Later it was sold to the Estabrook Company. Elmer McDonald renovated the house in the 1930's adding a gable to the west side. A new roof and siding were added when the house was moved to new Trinity Center from old Trinity Center in 1959. Although it is now a residence, it has served as a doctor's office in the past.

Site 26. I.O.O.F. Comet Lodge #84 (Oddfellows' Hall)

Located at the corner of Scott Road and Mary Avenue, Trinity Center, the Oddfellows' Hall is the best surviving example of the buildings which once comprised old Trinity Center. It is listed in the California Inventory of Historic Resources and is present day Trinity Center's best link with its past. It does, however, have a definite "transplanted" look in its new location. It was moved to its present location at the time of the construction of Trinity Dam. Although it has not been structurally altered, the move to its new location has stripped this dignified building of some of its historic charm and character.

The building was constructed in 1905-1906 to replace an earlier building which had burned on December 25, 1903, when a Christmas tree caught fire. It was used for regular meetings by both the Oddfellows and the Rebekah Lodges until the time came when the lodges merged with those of Weaverville. A period in which the building stood vacant followed. Recently, a group of citizens formed the North Lake Improvement Association and acquired funds to purchase and recondition it. The integrity of the original building has been maintained in its renovation. It is now used as a community hall.

Site 27. McDonald House

The McDonald House at 60 Scott Road, Trinity Center, is an excellent example of a pioneer residence and is believed to have been built in the 1870's. It is a one and one-half story, rectangular building with a high pitch, gable roof, a veranda on three sides, and a lean-to porch at the rear. Originally, it was only a four room dwelling with a center hallway and was used as a lodging house. Later a kitchen and dining room were added to the back of the building and it became a family dwelling. There were various early owners, but it has belonged to the McDonald family since the 1890's when it was purchased by Pete McDonald from George Carr. About 1908 Mr. McDonald finished the upstairs into four bedrooms, a hallway and a bath. Lumber for this was hauled to Trinity Center from Lamoine. The original siding was 12" boards with battens. The

Site 26. The Oddfellows' Hall as it appears in its present location in new Trinity Center. Built in 1905-06, it is an excellent example of the buildings which once comprised old Trinity Center.

Site 35. These headstones mark the grave of two small children in the Ridgeville cemetery.

Site 28. This pasture on the Norwegian Ranch had its beginnings in the 1850's and supported a flourishing cattle business for nearly one hundred years.

present shiplap siding was put on when the house was moved from its original location in old Trinity Center to new Trinity Center at the time the Trinity Lake formed. It is one of three buildings pre-dating the turn of the century which have been moved to new Trinity Center.

The house has remained in the pioneer McDonald family through the years. Pete McDonald ran the general store in old Trinity Center and was also a miner. Later, his son Elmer, together with Raymond Tapie, a stepson, ran a store. Elmer continued to do so when the new Trinity Center was established. He, like his father, also was involved with mining having worked for awhile at the famous Nash Mine. Elmer and his wife, Louise, still live in the family home.

Site 28. Norwegian Ranch (Olsen Ranch)

Isaac Cox, in his 1858 "Annals of Trinity County", describes the Norwegian Ranch as being a swampy meadow of 160 acres which, because it is "embraced by mountains on all sides without outlet, scarcely admits to further culture." It was located one and one-half miles south of Trinity Center.

The ranch, however, was a flourishing ranch in its early days. The September 15, 1871, issue of the Trinity Journal makes reference to its productivity by stating, "A large number of cabbages were brought to Weaverville by Mr. L. Olsen of Trinity Center. The cabbages . . . were of unusual size. One cabbage was perhaps the largest ever raised in the county, weighting 23 pounds."

Louis Olsen ran the Norwegian Ranch at that time. He had come to Trinity County in 1855 from Wisconsin and operated it until his death in 1883. He ran cattle and raised grain. The County Directory of 1885 refers to the size of the ranch as being 197 acres, but when his widow sold the ranch to James Ursher in 1887 the amount of acreage deeded was only 157.49 acres. The low hill over which the present highway passes in the vicinity of the Preacher Meadow Campground bears the name of Mr. Ursher. The Urshers had an important place in the history of the Trinity Center-Carrville areas. George L. Carr, the son of James E. Carr, a prominent businessman, married into the family and lived on the ranch for awhile. Mr. Ursher did not operate the ranch long for it was acquired by the Trinity Farm and Cattle Company interests in 1893 which used it for the grazing of cattle. For many years it was operated by Jake Foster, brother of William Foster, the founder of the cattle company.

Because of its strategic location, the ranch was used for many years by pack trains as a stopover place where feed for the stock could be obtained and where supplies destined for the mines located in the Forks of the Salmon area of the Salmon River could be temporarily stored. The ranch was easily accessible to the trails heading up Swift Creek toward Siskiyou County.

Site 29. The Delta Road

One of the last toll roads to be constructed in California and the last to cease operation in Trinity County was the Delta Road. It extended from Trinity Center for a distance of 28 miles to Delta in Shasta County where it connected with the railroad along the Sacramento River. The road was built in 1902 by the Northern Trinity Toll Road Company which had been granted a 50 year franchise for its operation. It was the shortest route reaching a railroad in the northern portion of Trinity County, and thus it became an important commercial link between the mines and ranches of the area and the rest of the state. Operation was discontinued in 1926 and in April, 1928, the road was purchased by Shasta and Trinity Counties which have since incorporated it into their respective county road systems. The western end of the route now lies under Trinity Lake.

Edwin Scott, who hauled freight over this road between 1915 and the early 1920's, recalls that the round trip took four days. It was a pleasant trip during the spring and fall months, but in the summer it was a hot and dirty job as the dust would sometimes be as much as six inches deep. In the winter mud holes could mire down the wagon and if the weather was very cold, ice and snow could make travel difficult.

Site 30. Covington Mill

Covington Mill is just off Highway 3 along the East Fork of Stuart Fork on Guy Covington Drive. It was one of the earliest mills to be started during the large scale revival of the lumber industry during World War II. The mill specialized in large timbers such as railroad bridge material, the demand for which was assured by a business contract with the Southern Pacific Company. Covington Mill had a reputation for producing quality lumber which never diminished. Lee Covington had purchased the skeletal remains of a prior mill in 1942 and with much hard work had put it into operation. It burned in 1950 but was replaced. At the peak of its operation the mill supported a small community of about 130 people. The mill was run by steam. Among some of its special orders were materials for Camp Pendleton, Disneyland and the elevator shaft at the Carlsbad Caverns in New Mexico. It also produced timbers for many mines.

The mill shut down around 1960 and was sold for salvage in 1976. Only the mill pond and the burner remain as reminders of this unique and prosperous mill.

Site 31. Bowerman Barn

To reach Bowerman Barn drive approximately one mile south on Guy Covington Drive from the junction with Highway 3.

According to the Trinity Journal of July 10, 1880, the Bowerman Barn was under construction at that time. It is a rare example of hand-crafted construction. It is a two-story rectangular structure, 40'x60' in size, and made of whipsawn pine lumber and hand hewn beams. It is a beautiful example of mortise and tenon construction secured with hardwood pegs. The whipsawn siding is rare and is still in good condition. Some of the flooring beams are nearly 60' long. Square nails were used to secure the flooring and siding. It was originally painted with red paint made from materials mined southeast of the barn. The color is still visible. There have been minor alterations, including the replacement of the shake roof with corrugated iron about 1940. The barn was in active use until 1974. It was acquired by the U.S. Forest Service the following year. The Forest Service has completed a partial restoration using original materials and techniques to preserve the integrity of the barn.

Some of the barn's interior lumber has been used over the years for outside fencing, one piece of which has a hand forged hinge attached to it. Two hand hewn watering troughs are in the meadow near the barn.

Alfred and Daniel Stroupe had first established claim to this land in 1853 but sold it to Albert Reinerson three years later for $250.00. A year later Christian H. Miller became the owner and paid $650.00 for it. Four years later the property changed hands again when, in 1861, John and Jacob Bowerman purchased this 160 acre ranch for $1800.00

Jacob Bowerman had come west in 1856 to seek his fortune in the gold fields but soon realized that ranching, which was a business he knew from earlier days spent in Ohio, had greater potential. His brother, John, came west to join him in this venture. They made their ranch a working and productive ranch, raising beef and dairy cattle and planting the land to hay and corn. Irrigation water for the fields came from the old Kennedy and Cox water race which circled the hill above the meadow. The brothers had purchased a half interest in this water in 1870. In 1872 Jacob married Anna Tourtellotte whose father ran a store and hotel in Minersville. John Bowerman never married. The brothers

Site 31. The Bowerman Barn, built in 1880, and now located on National Forest land, has been partially restored and is being preserved as an historical attraction.

Site 33. This Diener Mine trestle, 2500' long, was part of an eight mile water race which brought water to the Ridgeville, Digger Creek, and Chicken Flat mines.

continued to operate the ranch until their deaths: John in 1895, Jacob in 1917.

The ranch was located on what was then the main road between Trinity Center and Weaverville and so it became a major stopping place for travellers. Across the road from the barn, among some huge and graceful trees, is the site of the Bowerman's house. It burned on June 15, 1929. A small family cemetery is hidden in heavy brush nearby. Old wooden fence lines and corrals surround the barn and fields.

Site 32. Heath Ranch

The Heath Ranch, located on Rainier Road at the base of Granite Peak on the upper Mule Creek, was homesteaded in the 1860's by John W. Heath. Although Mr. Heath operated the homestead as a cattle ranch, he also served as County Coroner for a time. Mr. Heath married Helen Gertrude Tourtellotte, a member of the Tourtellotte family of nearby Minersville. The marriage was of short duration as his wife died at the ranch shortly after the birth of their son, Charles Jesse Heath, on July 21, 1882. When, about 1898, John Heath decided to leave the ranch and move to Weaverville, he sold the property to his former mother-in-law, Fannie Tourtellotte, who later resold it to Frank Russell. John Boyce, owner of the nearby Cedar Stock Farm, next acquired the property and used it to provide additional grazing land for his cattle operation. In 1939 the Heath Ranch, along with the Cedar Stock property, was acquired by Graeme Stewart and his nephew, Stewart Ralston. This 163 acre homestead has recently been divided into three parcels with the new owners being William Beatty, N. L. Bush and J. W. McMillan.

For years the ranch was accessible only by trail. It was not until the early 1920's that a road was built into the area by Arleigh Rix who had homesteaded the adjacent property to the south on what is now known as Echo Flat. None of the original ranch buildings still stand; fire destroyed them years ago.

Site 33. Diener House, Mine, and Trestle

Diener House stands near Highway 3 just north of the Estrellita turnoff. The deserted, two-story Fred Diener House was built in 1853-55. Until the construction of Highway 3 in the 1950's the house was connected to the outside world by trail only. Since that time vandals have made a skeleton of it. The Diener House is important because it was build at such an early date and was an elegant home considering the remoteness of the area. In 1855 Fred Diener began buying up the property of others nearby and retained these holdings until his death in 1881. Among the various owners since then was the Minersville Hydraulic Gold mining Company. For many years John and Henrietta Conner were caretakers of the property. They came there in 1900 as bride and groom and several of their children were born there.

All of the area below and to the side of the house has been subjected to hydraulic mining. A few stunted pines are struggling to establish themselves on the denuded soil.

Remnants of a huge wooden trestle still remain. It extended 2500' and was part of an eight mile water race which crossed the property. The water was not used for the Diener Mine but was used by the Ridgeville Water, Mining and Milling Company. The trestle carried water from the East Fork of Stuart Fork and from Strope Creek to Ridgeville and Chicken Flat. It was started by John Wright and Company and was built of heavy wooden timbers. About 1908-09, because of leakage, it was lined with sheets of heavy-gauge iron. The flume was 60" across the top, 40" across the bottom, and 40" deep. It could carry 40 sluice heads of water. In 1955 the flume was still supported by heavy timbers high above the ground. Construction of Highway 3 forced removal of the flume

Site 34. Dining room at the Trinity Alps Resort on the banks of the Stuart Fork. The 1955 flood destroyed the first dining room which bridged the creek.

Site 34. Guest cabins along a tree lined road at Trinity Alps Resort are each named for one of California's counties.

from the highway right-of-way. Taxes are still being paid on this ditch 125 year later.

Site 34. Hobart Ranch (Goetze Ranch) (Trinity Alps Resort)

For seventy years prior to its acquisition by Anna and Antone Weber in 1924 the Trinity Alps Resort was a cattle ranch under several ownerships. It was first claimed by Chambers in 1854 and was known as the Little Hay Ranch. It became the Loomis Ranch when A. J. Loomis and his brothers bought it in 1855 as part of their meat business. It continued as a cattle ranch in connection with butcher shops in Weaverville and Junction City under the following owners: Dye (1862), Watson and Brown (1871), Hobart (1876), Zarli (1884), Ellery (1913) and Goetze (1916). The ranch house, located on the hillside a distance from the creek, was built in 1905 and has been remodeled substantially over the years.

The Webers developed the property into Trinity County's first large and successful resort. Many simple, rustic cabins were constructed along both sides of the stream. Each cabin was given the name of one of California's counties. A large administration building, store, recreation hall, and dining room were also constructed. Originally the dining room bridged the creek, but rampaging waters of the stream during a heavy winter storm in 1955 took this out. Now a long swinging bridge leads from the dining hall to the cabins on the other side of the stream.

The Webers offered horseback rides and packtrips into the Trinity high mountains, and by so doing, were largely responsible for making the Trinity Alps famous. Ownership has changed several times since the Webers developed it but it still continues as a resort for vacationers.

Site 35. Ridgeville Town Site

Ridgeville is one of Trinity County's oldest, and virtually extinct, mining communities. It was settled in 1855 by Allen and Wasser, two men who did not remain in the area long. Miners, merchants and adventurers flocked to this new community and by 1856 it numbered 700 inhabitants. It was called "The Golden City" and became noted for its "beautiful women, fast horses, and lazy men." Growth was short-lived, however. The miners had gambled on a rich strike which did not materialize and the merchants had overextended credit which soon brought business failure. By 1858 the population had dwindled to 150 and in a few more years had been abandoned completely. A little cemetery with only two headstones remaining is all that is left to mark the site of this once lively mining town.

Ridgeville was located on a high ridge between Stuart Fork and the East Fork of Stuart Fork, 12 miles from Weaverville and two and one-half miles from the Trinity River. Today it is not far from the shores of the recently formed Trinity Lake.

HISTORIC SITES COVERED BY TRINITY LAKE

In 1957 the U.S. Bureau of Reclamation started construction of the Trinity Dam, a part of California's Central Valley Project. The work was completed in 1961 and water began to build up behind the dam covering forever many historic sites and ranches as the Trinity Lake formed. The powerhouse and the Lewiston Dam were also constructed at this time. The following is a brief account of many of these historic sites which now lie under Trinity Lake (refer to accompanying map).

HISTORIC SITES
COVERED BY TRINITY LAKE

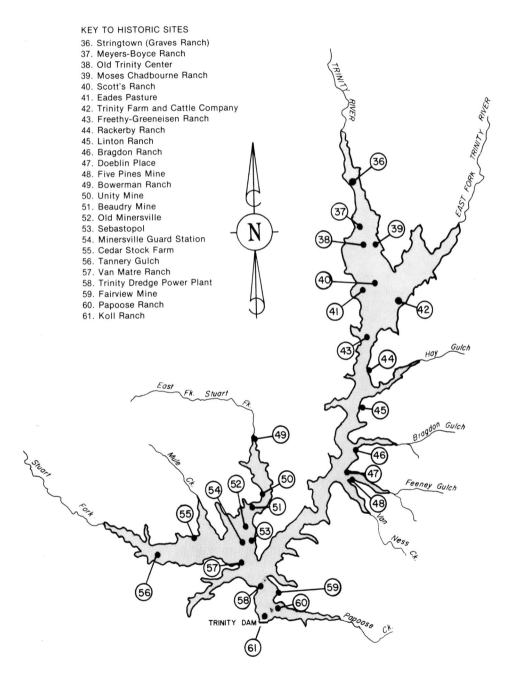

KEY TO HISTORIC SITES
36. Stringtown (Graves Ranch)
37. Meyers-Boyce Ranch
38. Old Trinity Center
39. Moses Chadbourne Ranch
40. Scott's Ranch
41. Eades Pasture
42. Trinity Farm and Cattle Company
43. Freethy-Greeneisen Ranch
44. Rackerby Ranch
45. Linton Ranch
46. Bragdon Ranch
47. Doeblin Place
48. Five Pines Mine
49. Bowerman Ranch
50. Unity Mine
51. Beaudry Mine
52. Old Minersville
53. Sebastopol
54. Minersville Guard Station
55. Cedar Stock Farm
56. Tannery Gulch
57. Van Matre Ranch
58. Trinity Dredge Power Plant
59. Fairview Mine
60. Papoose Ranch
61. Koll Ranch

Site 36. Christy Ranch (Sohm's Ranch) (Graves Ranch) (Stringtown)

This large 200 acre ranch which was located on the west side of the Trinity River was considered, in 1860, to be one of the finest ranches in the county. In 1917, its third owner, Dick Graves, sold the property to the Pacific Gold Dredging Company which had been operating in the Coffee Creek area. The dredging company had run into ground containing such enormous boulders that it decided to move its dredge to the Graves property. The dredge was disassembled, moved, and reassembled along with all of the homes and other buildings comprising the dredge camp. The new camp or settlement that arose on the site of the Graves Ranch became known as Stringtown because the homes were strung out in a long line along either side of the road. Two stores and an early gasoline filling station also served this community. The dredger worked here until 1924 destroying much of the good farming land. The remaining untouched land would have made good home sites had the Trinity Lake not covered it. When the dredge ceased operation Charles Kingsbury, together with his sister Annie and her husband Matthew MacIllawaine, purchased the former Graves home and lived in it for many years. Later, Elmer McDonald owned the property and constructed a store there.

During the 1930's another dredge known as the Carrville Dredge operated at Stringtown. This dredge sat idle from 1946 until 1965. Since it was built with a steel hull and had salvage value the dredge was purchased, disassembled, and shipped to Brazil for a mining operation in that country. This was the last of the big bucket line dredges to be seen in Trinity County.

Site 36. One of the stores which served Stringtown, a small community which arose when the Pacific Gold Dredging Company set up their dredge camp on the old Graves Ranch.

Site 37. Meyers Ranch (Boyce Ranch)

This ranch was located on the east side of the Trinity River about one mile north of old Trinity Center. As early as 1860 it was said to be one of the best ranches in the county. As with so many of the other ranches, this ranch was subjected to dredging. It was here, in 1900, that the first dredge in the Trinity Center area started operation.

Site 38. Old Trinity Center

The original townsite of Trinity Center lies under Trinity Lake a short distance north of the present town. It is believed that Trinity Center had its beginnings in 1851 when Moses Chadbourne cleared the land, established a ranch and started a trading post. Several placer mines in the area as well as its location along the California-Oregon Trail led to the growth of a small community. The community was at first referred to as Chadbournes, but as the town grew and became the principal trading center in the northern part of the county it became known as Trinity "Centre" as it was the central point along the trail from Shasta to Yreka. (Current spelling is "Center.")

By 1853 it had become the most thriving mining community in the county. About 75-80 mines had been established and the population was estimated to be about 1200. Records show that by 1869 Trinity Centre boasted two hotels, two general merchandise stores, two blacksmith shops, three livery stables, three saloons, a barber shop and a telegraph office.

Although mining was an important factor in the town's growth Trinity Centre also supported several productive ranches. The town, as well as many of the ranches, was inundated by the waters of Trinity Lake following the construction of the Trinity Dam by the U.S. Bureau of Reclamation in 1961. Trinity Centre, as it used to be, no longer exists. In 1959 a new community was established on a portion of land owned by Scott's Ranch. Because several buildings from the old town were moved to the new Trinity Center a link with its past has been maintained.

Site 39. Moses Chadbourne Ranch

This ranch was the first ranch to be established in the Trinity Center area (see old Trinity Center). As others came into the area they settled nearby and the town of Trinity Center grew. It was located about one-half mile from the ranch on its west side. The ranch land was subjected to dredging operations just prior to 1920 when the Estabrook Dredge operated on the property. It is regrettable that this productive ranch belonging to the founder of the town should have been destroyed by this dredging. The lush ranch soils were washed away and high piles of river boulders were left in their place. (See Estabrook Home.)

Site 40. Tolly Ranch (Owings', Scott Bros., or Scott's Ranch Resort)

Scott's Ranch was located two miles south of old Trinity Center on the west side of the Trinity River. It is quite probable that Wintu Indians first lived at this place. It is also probable that they did not live here peacefully. The Scott family reports have turned up so many obsidian projectile points during spring plowing that it led them to feel that the area was once a battlefield.

The first white resident of this place was Ladue Vary who came to Trinity Center in 1851 and was associated with Moses Chadbourne. In February, 1853, James Tolly settled on the ranch and made it his home until his death in 1868. During that period there was a 36-room hotel or stopping place called the Trinity House built here to accommodate travelers along the old California-Oregon

Site 38. Old Trinity Center, now covered by the waters of Trinity Lake, showing the Ellery Hotel on the right and the two-story Oddfellows' Hall in the center distance.

Site 40. The barns of the Scott Brothers' Ranch as they appeared in 1921.

Site 40. The vast fields of the Scott Ranch are now covered by Trinity Lake. An abundance of hay was raised on these fields as this 1920 photo depicts.

trail. The trail, and later the stage road, ran along the west edge of the ranch.

After Mr. Tolly's death, John Mark Owings and Davis Hall took over the ranch as well as another ranch located to the north of Trinity Center. The two men divided the properties and this ranch became the home of Owings and his wife, Mary (Diddy) Owings. The 1870 census indicated that the Owings and Diddy families had come from Ohio and it listed Mr. Owings as a farmer. Mrs. Owings' parents, William and Margaret Diddy, lived their declining years here and were buried at the edge of one of the pastures. (Their graves were moved to the new Trinity Center Cemetery before the Trinity Lake formed.)

In 1909 three brothers from Lewiston (Irvin, Stanford and Edwin Scott) purchased the property. (Irvin married Owings' granddaughter, Nova.) The Scott brothers cleared more of the land and raised beef cattle as well as quantities of hay on the vast fields. In summer the cattle were grazed in the high mountain meadows of the upper Swift Creek. For a time the ranch also kept a herd of dairy cattle and shipped cream via parcel post to the Cottonwood Creamery in Shasta County. Irvin died in 1924; Stanford sold his interest in 1926; Ed remained on the property and married Maude (Stuart) Dickey in 1927. Ed and Maude, together with their children, successfully operated the ranch as Scott's Ranch Resort until it was covered by Trinity Lake. The resort provided ranch-style meals and cabins for vacationers and provided pack trips into the high mountains.

In 1945 Scott's Ranch acquired a whole section of land from the Southern Pacific Land Company just west of the ranch. It is on this land that the new town of Trinity Center is located. The main ranch is now gone but one important asset remains that the residents of the new town are enjoying: an ample supply of water from Swift Creek. The water-right for this water dates back to about the beginning of this Tolly-Owings-Scott Ranch. Many items of historic interest that were once used on the ranch are on display at the Scott Museum in Trinity Center. The museum is a legacy that has been created and left to the community by Ed Scott who made the Scott Ranch his home for fifty years.

Site 41. Eades Pasture

What for years was known as the Eades pasture was, in the early days, a ranch with a home and farm buildings. For years this property was used as pastureland in conjunction with Scott's Ranch. Part of the western end of this pasture remains above the Trinity Lake water line and lies between the present marina and Trinity Center.

Site 42. Trinity Farm and Cattle Company

The Trinity Farm and Cattle Company which became one of the largest cattle operations in northern California once occupied extensive holdings of land now covered by the Trinity Lake. Originally the property comprised the Robinson and Hall ranches as well as the Peterson Ranch with its East Fork fields. Eventually the holdings covered 2330 acres in northern Trinity County, as well as 1800 acres of deeded land in the high mountains including Foster Meadows in the Swift Creek drainage. Prior to the formation of the company the ranch property was owned by Dr. F. Grotefend, a Redding dentist, who financed the operation. The company was established and operated by William Foster, Sr. and his five sons, William Jr., Milton, Melvin, Harvey and George.

Mr. Foster's career as a cattleman began in 1882 when he worked as a ranchhand on the Pat Larkin Ranch at $8.00 per month. On one occasion he was given two heifers and a bull in lieu of wages. From this small start he soon built a herd of 80 head. After the Trinity Farm and Cattle Company was formed the herd eventually numbered between 1600 and 2000. In 1907 Mr. Foster received one of the first permits to graze cattle on public lands. During the summer his herd grazed in the high mountains. In the winter the cattle were driven to the Bald Hil's in Shasta County where the Fosters had approximately 4200 acres of winter grazing land. It took six days to make the cattle drive. The three year old steers and any beef destined for market were driven, instead, to the railhead at Delta in the Sacramento River Canyon.

Twenty men were employed in the summer to harvest the 1200 tons of hay grown on the green fields of the Trinity Farm and Cattle Company. It took twenty head of horses to draw the mowing machines, rakes, and wagons necessary to harvest the hay crop. (See also Foster Ranch House and Foster Cabin.)

Site 43. Freethy Ranch (Story Ranch) (Greeneisen Ranch)

The Freethy Ranch was situated on the west side of the Trinity River and on the main trail to the north. In the 1850's a 20-room building on this ranch accommodated travelers along this route. A bridge which crossed the Trinity River at the lower end of the ranch burned about 1890. Soon after, a new wagon road connecting the Hall Ranch with the Bragdon Place was constructed up the east side of the river bypassing this ranch. The property continued to operate as a ranch under several ownerships: the Freethy's were the first owners, (Mrs. Freethy was the sister of Gertrude McDonald, a member of a prominent Trinity Center family); the Story family next owned it; the Scott family farmed it for a time; the last owners were the Greeneisens who were living here prior to the construction of the Trinity Dam.

Site 44. Rackerby Ranch

This ranch was a large place which lay north of Hay Gulch. At one time it had a large house and barns all of which burned in 1910. It served as a freight stop on the old stage road.

Site 45. Linton Ranch

The Linton Ranch extended along both sides of the Trinity River with the house and barns being located near the mouth of Clawton Gulch. After these buildings burned, Mr. Linton relocated his ranch on the east side of Linton Gulch along the French Gulch to Trinity Center road.

Site 46. Bragdon Ranch

The Bragdon Ranch, with Bragdon Creek flowing through it, was located along the California-Oregon stage road nine miles south of Trinity Center. It was a successful ranch and a popular scene of community dances and parties. Between the period 1898 and 1903 and again between 1914 and 1924 a U.S. Post Office was located here. During the first period it was known as the Bragdon Post Office; during the second period, it was known as the Five Pines Post Office after the name of a mine located two miles south of the ranch. (In the interim period the post office was moved to Trinity Center.)

In 1876 this 160 acre ranch was purchased from Winfield Scott Conway by Edwin Harley Bragdon and Hiram Augustus Bragdon, 18 and 19 year old brothers and sons of Hiram Higgins Bragdon, a teacher and one-time Superintendent of Trinity County Schools. In time the two brothers divided the property, but after the death of Edwin in 1909 his widow, Emily Jane (Duncan) Bragdon, purchased Hiram's parcel and the ranch once again came under one ownership. Emily and her children continued to live on at the ranch until 1924 when it was sold. The post office that was situated there was discontinued. The

Site 42. The Trinity Farm and Cattle Company harvested 1200 tons of hay grown on their large fields, now covered by Trinity Lake.

Site 42. The Trinity Farm and Cattle Company was one of the largest cattle operations in northern California during the first half of this century. Its herd numbered nearly 2000 head.

children of Edwin and Emily Bragdon continued to live on in Trinity County. One of their children, Ora, married Charles Jesse Heath (see Heath Ranch).

The John Nielson family were the last owners of the property before it was purchased by the U. S. Government in connection with the Trinity Dam construction project. A large bucket line dredge lies buried in Trinity Lake near the site of the Bragdon Ranch. It had been owned by Fairview Placers who had moved it here from its former location near Junction City in 1948. With the building of the Trinity Dam the dredge shut down and plans were made to move the machinery again. It was thought that the boat would float as the lake waters rose but sand had filled in beside the dredge and it stayed on the bottom.

Site 47. Doeblin Place (Dobelin Place)

The Dobelin place was located on what is now known as Van Ness Creek just east of its junction with Feeney Creek. (There is some question regarding the correct naming and spelling of these creeks.) Doeblin built a hotel and overnight teamsters' stop at this place. There was a large two story house as well as two large barns together with a nice field and garden spot. At the time of the filling of Trinity Lake old cabins and orchards still stood on several flat spots along the creek.

The nearby Feeney Creek was named for Richard H. Feeney, an Irishman who lived many years in the area but who moved to French Gulch toward the end of the century where he built and ran the French Gulch Hotel. This hotel is still standing today. Mr. Feeney was also involved in the toll road business between French Gulch and Trinity Center. He died in French Gulch in 1899.

Site 48. Five Pines Mine

The Five Pines Mine was discovered in 1895 by H. J. Van Ness who originally called it the Surprise Mine. Later the Five Pines Mining Company was formed with Hiram Bragdon of the nearby Bragdon Ranch as a partner and Mr. Van Ness as its president. Eventually Mr. Bragdon withdrew from the partnership and the company continued to be operated by the Van Ness family. The mine straddled the old California-Oregon Stage Road and was located about a mile from the Trinity River on what, according to a 1907 U.S. Forest Service map, was then known as Dobelin Creek, although there is some question as to the correct name of this creek. The creek has since been renamed Van Ness Creek after the founder of the mine.

The mine had three locations. The first mine was a small one with a small stamp mill. A 3-stamp mill powered by a gasoline engine was set up at the second location. An overshot water wheel was used to power the mill at the third location. The mine was at its fullest operation at the turn of the century.

Most of the mine sites and their dumps are under the waters of Trinity Lake, but some of the mining activity that was at the higher elevations is still visible where it has remained above the water level of the lake.

Site 49. Bowerman Ranch

Much of the Bowerman Ranch lands lie buried under the Trinity Lake, but their barn and the site of the ranch house remain above the water line and have been treated as a separate site. (See Bowerman Barn, Site 32)

Site 50. Unity Mine

The Unity Mine was a part of the Hayward Flat Mines. A very large boarding house and other buildings belonging to the mine lined the west side of the

Site 49. Situated across the road from the Bowerman Barn, The Bowerman Ranch house burned June 15, 1929 and is seen here as it appeared about 1892.

Site 51. The tailing flume at the Beaudry Mine at Old Minersville.

old road to Trinity Center. It was once the site of the Minersville Post Office which was moved to this location from old Minersville in 1860. The U.S. Forest Service now maintains a large public campground at Hayward Flat on the shores of Trinity Lake on an unflooded portion of the Unity Mine.

Site 51. Beaudry Mine

This mine was named for a man who was vice-president of the Minersville Hydraulic Gold Mining Company. This was a French company which, about 1895, acquired many old mining properties including the old town of Minersville. Water for their mining operation came from the East Fork of Stuart Fork via the Diener Ditch. This was sufficient to enable them to operate four hydraulic giants at a time.

Site 52. Old Minersville

Old Minersville, or Diggerville as it was sometimes called, was located on Digger Creek at its confluence with the East Fork of Stuart Fork. The town was established in the 1850's and soon boasted several business enterprises. Rev. William Morris, Pat Griffin, and Ed Foggarty, moved a store in from Ridgeville—a town which was meeting its decline. Rev. Morris, with the help of his son and a Mr. Cameron, also constructed a hotel. This building served a dual purpose as Reverend Morris also used it for holding religious services. Fred Leach from Hayfork set up a blacksmith shop and a dairy. Across the street was a two story, board and batten building that served many purposes. It was known as the Opera House for the second floor was a ballroom where dances and entertainments were held, and occasionally it served as sleeping quarters; downstairs were a stable and wagon shed. (A wagon from this shed is on display at the museum in Weaverville.)

In 1863 Jesse Hardison Tourtellotte and his wife, Fannie, also opened a hotel-stopping place here which they ran for the next 38 years. They also had a productive garden which supplied all of their produce needs. Mr. Tourtellotte had many talents for it is said that he sometimes pinch-hit as a dentist. He did not hesitate to come to the aid of a miner suffering from a toothache by obligingly pulling the offending tooth with forceps while the miner set on the porch steps! The Tourtellottes sold their property in 1898 to Fred Beaudry (see Beaudry Mine) and moved to Weaverville to live out their remaining years.

Clint and Thelma Riordan were the last people to live in this town which has since been abondoned to the waters of the Trinity Lake.

Site 53. Sebastopol

Sebastopol, located one mile downstream from old Minersville on the east side of the East Fork of the Stuart Fork, was a town started by John F. Chillis in 1853. Mr. Chillis was an enterprising man who was responsible for the establishment of a flour mill, a sawmill, a sash and window factory, and the construction of an eight mile water race (called the Sebastopol Race) which provided water and water power to an otherwise dry location. Other industries also flourished here and provided supplies to the miners and homesteaders in this remote location. Joshua Lorenz made plows and other implements which were taken by mule train as far away as Siskiyou County. Jack Mundel had a large furniture shop and made slat bottomed chairs that sold for 50 cents each. Several of these chairs are still used today in the Masonic Hall in Weaverville. Jesse Tourtellotte, who later moved to old Minersville, was in partnership with Chillis in the ownership of many of the buildings in the town including the hotel. After the coming of the California-Oregon Stage Road, goods became

Site 52. This Old Minersville street scene shows the "Opera House" at the extreme left and the Tourtellotte home to the right of it.

Site 52. The Tourtellotte family home in Old Minersville.

more easily available from other locations and the town was abandoned. It completely disappeared by 1900.

Site 54. Minersville Guard Station

This U. S. Forest Service Guard Station was located on the north side of Stuart Fork between the Cedar Stock Farm and the mouth of the East Fork. The road between Minersville and Weaverville ran in front of the station; across the road was a public campground with picnic tables and outside stoves. The station was used as headquarters for fire suppression during the summer season when the danger of forest fires was high. It was a two-story building which served as both home and office for the Forest Service Guard and his family. Barns and a fenced pasture provided facilities for pack and riding stock.

Site 55. Cummings Ranch (Boyce Ranch) (Cedar Stock Farm)

The Cedar Stock Farm was located between Mule Creek and Stoney Creek on the Stuart Fork about four miles west of Old Minersville. It comprised 1000 acres, 160 of which were meadowland. It was developed during the Civil War and comprised many buildings. There were two houses, three barns, and two shops. The largest barn was 100' x 150' in size and had stanchions for feeding 136 head of cattle. It was built of hand-hewn timbers held together with dowels.

The ranch buildings and some of the acreage of the farm were inundated by the rising waters of the Trinity Lake after the construction of the Trinity Dam. Only 17 acres of the original farmlands remain above the water line of the lake. The hand-hewn timbers from the barn were salvaged and are now part of the Cedar Stock Lodge which was constructed nearby. The holes for the dowel pins and the mortise and tenon joints of these timbers are easily visible. The only original building that was once part of this ranch is a small 13 x 13 cabin which was moved to the upper end of the present Cedar Stock Resort property. This cabin is also constructed of hand-hewn timbers that have unusual corner joints.

It is believed that the original owner of this ranch, which was located along the Stuart Fork, may have been a man named Stuart and the nearby stream may have been named for him. Whether or not this is the case is uncertain for several different spellings of this name have been in usage. Issac Cox in his 1858 Annals of Trinity County refers to the Steward's Fork; the early survey maps call it the Stewart's Fork; and present day usage is Stuart Fork. It is known, however, that two of the early owners of the property were Fogarty and Griffin; the ranch's cattle brand was first issued to these men. It consists of the letters FG marked on the left ribs. This brand has been in continuous use to this date and is still a valid brand as it has been re-registered by Cliff Johannsen, the present owner of the lodge. At the time that the ranch was forced to cease operation because of the formation of the Trinity Lake it was owned by Stewart Ralston and Graeme Stewart.

The road between Minersville and Weaverville at one time came right in front of the two ranch houses. Across the road were the barn and the pasturelands. The ranch served as a stopping place where travelers on this road could obtain meals and lodging.

Cedar Stock got its name from cedar trees which grew in the meadow. The trees were cleared from the land by the early owners. The ranch has had several owners over the years besides those already mentioned. It was known as the Cummings Ranch at the turn of the century. It was Thomas Cummings

Site 55. One of the two ranch houses on the Cedar Stock Ranch. The road between Minersville and Weaverville was directly in front. Prior to submergence by the Trinity Lake, it offered meals and lodging to travelers on the road.

Site 55. The second of the Cedar Stock houses as it appeared before it was abandoned at the time of the construction of Trinity Dam.

who had secured the first patent to the land in 1879. During the 1920's John N. and Charles Boyce were the owners and it was known as the Boyce Ranch at that time.

Site 56. Tannery Gulch

This gulch received its name from the Bartlett and Company Tannery which was built in 1856 at the mouth of the creek where it joins the Stuart Fork. It was the only tannery in the county and consisted of a water race, a bark mill, and 32 tanning vats. Bark from trees plentiful in the area was used in the tanning process.

Site 57. Bates-Van Matre Ranch (Van Matre Ranch)

Records indicate that Fordyce Bates and Peter Van Matre bought this 160 acre ranch from Harry Seeman in 1853. When Bates was elected to the State Legislature in 1858 he sold his share of the ranch to Van Matre. The property continued to remain in the Van Matre family for the next 100 years — until it was taken over by the U.S. Government to make way for the Trinity Lake. Peter and Almira Heath Van Matre had come to Trinity County from Wisconsin in 1852. They had three small children upon their arrival in Minersville; eight more were born at the ranch. Indians in the area were the children's only playmates as there were few white people living in Minersville during the early years of the ranch. Not all of the Indians, however, were friendly and did cause some trouble for the family.

The first family home was a two-story log cabin which burned in 1862. The second one which was built to replace it used lumber from the grist mill at Sebastopol. (This lumber had become available because the grist mill by that time had ceased operation.) The family cultivated the rich soil and sold garden produce, potatoes, and alfalfa seed. The ranch was also used as an inn and a halfway point between Trinity Center and Weaverville. Coming from Scott Valley many teams loaded with grain, flour, butter and other supplies for Weaverville made an overnite stop at the ranch. Beds were 50 cents, meals 25 cents, and horses 50 cents for the night. Van Matre was a rancher rather than a miner so very little mining was done by the family. One son, George, however, found a huge gold nugget in Mule Creek that was valued at $1900 (gold then bringing $19.00 per ounce).

When Peter Van Matre died in 1884, his son John helped his mother to continue to manage the ranch. Some time later Almira Van Matre moved to Weaverville, and John and his wife, Bertha (Koll) (Denison) Van Matre, acquired the ranch. In 1901 they doubled their holdings by adding 160 acres which they purchased from the Cummings homestead (see Cummings Ranch-Cedar Stock Farm).

Fire again destroyed the Van Matre home in 1902. It was rebuilt on the same site the following year. This home survived until it was torn down in 1958 as the land was being cleared for the Trinity Dam Project. Many Van Matre family members continue to live in the county.

For years the ranch remained the center of activity in the Minersville area. About 1909 the U.S. Forest Service installed a telephone at the ranch and the family relayed messages between Weaverville and Trinity Center as there was no through line. The Minersville Post Office was set up at the ranch after it was moved from Old Minersville. The ranch also became a crossroads for travelers as roads led from here in three directions — to Weaverville, Lewiston and Trinity Center.

Site 57. The Van Matre Ranch dates back to 1853. Fire twice destroyed the ranch house. This house, built in 1903, is the third house on the same site. The Van Matre Ranch was a center of activity in the Minersville area for nearly a century.

Site 59. The Fairview Mine dated back to 1900 and included a 40-stamp mill. Power to operate the mill was generated with water brought from the Stuart Fork and carried across the Trinity River by a pipeline suspended from a swinging bridge.

Site 58. Trinity Dredge Power Plant

The Trinity Dredging Company which operated a dredge in gravels along the Trinity River in the area now inundated by the Lewiston Lake built a powerhouse near the mouth of Stuart Fork. Almost 1000 horsepower of electricity was generated here with which to operate the dredge. This was unique as most dredges in the area were powered by steam. Water was brought out of Stuart Fork above the Van Matre Ranch and carried in a ditch along the south side of the river for a distance of seven and one-half miles ending in a drop of 285 feet to the powerhouse. The powerhouse was in operation between 1912 and 1922.

Site 59. Fairview Mine

The Fairview Mine was a quartz mine located on the side of the mountain on the southeast side of the Trinity River about a mile below the junction of the Stuart Fork with the Trinity River. Most of the mine site is now covered by the Trinity Lake, but some of the dumps from the tunnels located at the upper elevations are still visible.

Gold was discovered here in the late 1890's with the mine's development starting in 1900. A good road to the mine did not exist at that time, although a wagon could be driven to the mine from Lewiston by fording the river eight times. Access to the mine was made easier when the company built a road from the mine to the top of Trinity Mountain to connect with the road that went from French Gulch to Trinity Center. All the mining equipment for this mine, including a 40-stamp mill, was hauled in from Redding over this road by horse or mule-driven freight wagons.

Power to operate the stamp mill and other machinery as well as to light the camp was generated with water brought from the Stuart Fork by a ditch three and one-half miles long that contoured around the mountain to a point on the north side of the river near the stamp mill. From here the water was carried down the hill and across the river in a pipeline suspended from heavy cables. The Fairview Mine had its own sawmill to produce lumber needed for construction of the many buildings. The mine was so large that it also had its own post office which was given the name Papoose after the nearby creek and gulch of that name. The mine was operated until 1912. The buildings were demolished or moved at the time of the construction of the Trinity Dam.

Site 60. Papoose Ranch

Papoose Ranch was, at one time, the site of an Indian village. It was a fine small ranch with very fertile soil. There was also a gravel bar that was rich with gold. At the time of the building of the Trinity Dam this property was owned by Herbert S. Blakemore. Except for a period of time when he was out of the country educating himself and working for the Shell Oil Company, Herbert Blakemore spent his long life of over 90 years in the vicinity of this ranch. He had been born at the Blakemore Ranch which was located a short distance down the Trinity River. When he made his return to Trinity County after his absence, he settled on this ranch. He farmed and mined here until the ranch was taken over by the U.S. Government because of the construction of the dam. He loved this ranch; its loss made him heartbroken and bitter. His last years were spent not far away — at Posey Gulch near the shore of Lewiston Lake.

Site 61. Old Koll Ranch

The Old Koll Ranch was a hillside ranch that was wedged in between steeper hills and the Trinity River and was situated where the Trinity Dam now stands. This ranch had been deserted by the time the dam was built. The Koll family was a German family which had moved to Trinity County in 1873. One of their children, Bertha (Koll) Denison married John C. Van Matre in 1890 and lived out her life on the Van Matre Ranch in Minersville. (See Van Matre Ranch.)

The cabin shown here is very typical of early-day shelters found in all parts of Trinity before the 1900's.

This magnificent eight-horse team of white horses was driven by "Butch" Ehrman of Lewiston. This photo taken by Eugene Goodyear in about 1900 shows freight coming into Trinity over the Lewiston Turnpike road.

WEAVERVILLE

KEY TO HISTORIC SITES

1. Chaunceyville
2. Old Airport
3. Johnson House
4. Blaney House
5. McNamara House
6. Leavitt House
7. Weinheimer House
8. Gray House
9. Flagg House
10. Condon House
11. Lowden House
12. Lowden Office
13. Osgood House
14. Hagelman House
15. Clement House
16. Old High School Site
17. Vollmers House
18. Greenwell House
19. R. I. Carter House
20. Armentrout House
21. Colbert House
22. Jack Hall House
23. Hocker House
24. Hafley House
25. Hupp House
26. Esau Montgomery House
27. Sam Lee House
28. Robinson Place
29. Weaverville Cemeteries
30. Weaverville Grammar School
31. California House
32. O'Neill House
33. Forest Service Office
34. Edgecombe House
35. Weinheimer House
36. Ryan House
37. Lautenschlauger House
38. Trinity County Hospital
39. Young House
40. Isaac Woodbury House
41. Junkans House
42. Davis Barns
43. Ed Todd House
44. Goetze House
45. Schall House
46. Caton House
47. Rudy Junkans House
48. Chadbourne House
49. Colbert House
50. Blake House
51. Oberdeiner House
52. Paulsen House
53. United States Bakery
54. Hall House
55. Bowie House
56. Balch House
57. Catholic Church
58. Chapman House
59. Barnickel House
60. Abrahms House
61. Louis Todd House
62. John Meckel House
63. The Cooper's Shop
64. Henry Junkans House
65. Meckel Rental
66. Old Young House
67. Mulligan House
68. Chinese Tong War Site
69. Lowden Park
70. Costa House
71.-119. Historic District (Main Street

52

AREA **II**
WEAVERVILLE

Historical Overview

At the foot of Weaver Bally lies a basin holding the historic town of Weaverville. When James Hilton, author of "Lost Horizon", first saw the community he called it "Shangri La, that strange and wonderful somewhere which is not a place, but a state of mind". Weaverville's charm is greatly enhanced by the delightful streams that run through the basin. Formerly these stream channels were rich in gold. Early miners came to the vicinity in droves. Living quarters often consisted of cloth tents or shelters of hides stretched over four posts driven into the ground. The first log cabin was located near the present courthouse.

The 1850's were a period of great activity. For a short time Weaverville was county seat of a much larger Trinity County comprising the counties of Del Norte, Humboldt and Klamath. When the other counties were established Weaverville remained the seat of Trinity.

Women began coming to Weaverville. Mr. and Mrs. Ewing (first lady of Trinity) established the United States Hotel. Mr. and Mrs. Richard Johnson had a boarding house on Sidney Hill. James Howe, who owned the town's only ox team and cart, surveyed and built a ditch bringing water from West Weaver to Sidney Hill. Dr. William Ware bought the ditch and narrowly escaped being hanged when he took all of the water from West Weaver. James Howe was responsible also for bringing water from East Weaver Creek, which today remains Weaverville's main water supply. Water now flows in pipes. The ditch is abandoned.

Weaverville was a vigorous community with everyone building where he pleased. A few got together and laid out the main street. John Carr's claim was the first piece of land recorded north of Shasta. Mule passenger and freight trains operated over trails between Weaverville and Shasta, as well as between Yreka and Arcata (Uniontown). Trade was brisk and many business houses lined the streets of Weaverville only to be lost repeatedly to fires.

In the fall of 1851 Weaverville had a post office. The first mail was a letter brought to town in the hat of the mail carrier names Mr. Weed. A man named Becket and another named Lathrop each had whip sawmills near town to supply flume lumber as well as that needed for buildings. During the winter of 1852-53 especially heavy snows isolated the town and the residents subsisted on barley as their main food. By 1853 a school and hospital had been established. Church services were conducted in hotels or saloons by circuit riding clergymen. Traveling entertainers also came to Weaverville; Lotta Crabtree, Lola Montez and the Chapman Family to name a few.

By 1854 the town had built eight fireproof brick buildings. Two were two-story. To make the buildings even more fireproof a one foot layer of dirt was spread between the ceilings and the tin roofs. Iron shutters were attached to both windows and doors. By 1859 Weaverville had 21 brick buildings of which 19 are still standing and in use. Bricks were made locally in nearby kilns. Iron doors and building hardware were made by local blacksmiths. All lumber for the door casings, shelves, etc., was cut locally. All travel to the outside world was then by foot or horseback. In 1854 the town had 22 stores, two banks, two drugstores, six hotels, four restaurants, six saloons, three bakeries, four markets, three blacksmith and carpenter shops, seven lawyers, four physicians, and a population of 1,000 plus many Chinese.

In early days, residential Weaverville was divided into areas. Faggtown was said to be the area south of town "near Weaverville". This was what is now called Mill Street. French Town was the area northeast of where Mill Street leaves Main Street. English Town was east of what is now Highway 3 and north of Lowden Park. (Much of English Town was mined off during the 1930's by "doodle bug" dragline dredgers.) Chinatown took in both sides of Main Street near the Joss House. Irish Town was the area near the courthouse. German Town was up Taylor Street.

In 1854 the first newspaper, the "Trinity Times", was published. In 1855 the "Democrat" came out, but these papers lasted only a short time. The "Trinity Journal" published its first paper in January of 1856. This paper has served the town and county for 125 years. In May of 1858 the first wagon road was completed from the Tower House in Shasta County to Weaverville. This was the Buckhorn or Grass Valley Toll Road. A free public wagon road to Hayfork was opened to travel in 1860. A short time later the Lewiston Turnpike Road was opened, and soon a road over Buckeye Mountain to the Van Matre Ranch on Stewart's Fork (spelled "Stuart" on present day maps) was built. In 1859 fire destroyed 50 Weaverville buildings including all of Chinatown. Almost everyone immediately rebuilt. During this first decade mining was extensive along the streams of the Weaver Basin. Gold pans, long toms, rockers and ground sluicing were used. As the ground was worked out, many of the white miners easily became discouraged and left their claims, only to have the Chinese come in and re-work them.

The 1860's saw longer water ditches and the mining of higher ground. The Civil War was in progress. 150 men enlisted from the county (the Halleck Rifles and the Douglas City Rifles). Word of President Lincoln's assassination reached town by the new telegraph, "word for word". Water was carried to upper Weaverville in "wooden logs with a head so it will squirt over the houses". Some of this wooden pipe, as well as the augers used to make the pipe, is on display at the museum. The Oddfellows and Masonic lodges were very active.

By 1870 mining in the Weaver Basin changed even more. Isaac Woodbury bought a monitor (giant) which he used in his mine on Garden Gulch, thus introducing the hydraulic method of mining to the Weaver Basin. The Hupp and McMurray Mine soon installed a monitor in their mine on East Weaver. They reported $26,000 in one cleanup. Testy and Lorenz Mines below town along Weaver Creek later used this hydraulic method of mining. A mining boom was in progress which created new problems for businessmen. Usually, cleanup occurred only once a year. Men working in the mines were paid after cleanup time and retail stores were obliged to carry the accounts of the mine owners and the

This picture taken right after the fire of 1873 shows upper Main Street. The adobe building in the foreground was demolished and the lot was later used for a town plaza before the building of the present bandstand.

This lithograph of a Mai Fest (May 1, 1860) was sketched from in front of the present Weaverville Hotel. The I.O.O.F. Hall is the highest building on the right. This was before the porch and stairway were added.

This is an 1898 picture of Isaac Woodbury's hydraulic giant working in Garden Gulch. At one time Woodbury had 500 men working along Garden Gulch.

George Jumper established this steam powered sawmill four miles north of town on Brown's Creek near the present Highway 3.

workmen on their books for long periods of time. Operation of the mines, the economic well-being of the town's businesses, and the amount of snow and rainfall were all interrelated. Without a plentiful water supply, hydraulic mining seasons were shortened and Weaverville businessmen became more deeply involved in mining operations as they continued to grubstake mining ventures.

Citizens of Weaverville should be indebted to Superior Court Judge T. E. Jones, for in 1876 he established the townsite of Weaverville. Later that year William Spencer Lowden surveyed the area, which covered 516 acres. Young locust trees were planted along Weaverville streets. Many of these trees still survive today.

Quartz mining became important during the 1880's. Farming and stock raising were also important. George Jumper started a steam operated sawmill near town. The 1880 census listed 860 whites and 493 Chinese living in Weaverville. 1881 saw a fire district established. Wagon roads were dusty in summer and almost impassable in winter. Hold ups of stages made life hazardous for drivers.

In the 1890's the first electricity was generated at a plant located in Gambler's Gulch and the town received its first telephone with the establishment of the Sunset Telephone Company in the Blake and Reed store. A steam powered, bucket-line dredge commenced operating in Weaver Creek below town.

The first automobile came to Weaverville in 1901. The Trinity Forest Reserve was established by presidential proclamation on April 26, 1905, with an office established in Weaverville. Mining was still paramount and quartz mining was at its peak. Early in this decade there were 1839 mining claims in the county. 1905 was the year of another big Chinatown fire. The hand pumper fire engine was purchased the following year. The Trinity County High School was established in 1909.

Soon after 1910 the first auto stage from Redding arrived in town. By 1916 the county had a free public library. World War I brought an end to most mining. This had a disasterous effect upon the economy of the town and it did not recover for many years. The population dropped to 500. Many of the returning servicemen settled in other counties after the war. Stock raising continued in Trinity. Quite a few Weaverville businessmen ran herds of beef cattle.

In the 1920's the downriver road to Humboldt County was completed. This had a tremendous impact upon the town. It was in 1929 that the first airplane landed at the Trinity Airport.

The 1930's brought the failure of the Trinity County Bank. A few large bucket-line dredges continued along the Trinity River. Several drag-line, "doodle-bug" dredges operated along creeks near town. Highway 299 was routed up Main Street past the courthouse and on to Oregon Mountain where a large cut was sluiced out by monitors using water from the old Sweepstakes system.

The 1940's were war years and Weaverville's economy again suffered. Many people left to take defense jobs elsewhere. Five local citizens acquired a navy contract and started a small defense project (Weaverville Industries) which manufactured ship fenders from fir saplings. When young men returned from World War II many went into the logging industry which now was gaining importance in the area's economy. A number of small sawmills were in operation in and near Weaverville.

In the early 1950's the California Division of Highways decided to widen Main Street. The historic locust trees were removed, the sidewalks were narrowed, and diagonal parking was changed to parallel; this increased parking problems. Removing the trees exposed sad looking buildings which were badly in need of a coat of paint. The Chamber of Commerce appointed five women to serve as a committee to improve Weaverville's appearance. The 1957 Weaver-

Weaverville looked like this in 1950 before the trees were removed and while diagonal parking was allowed. The picture was taken from the sidewalk in front of the New York Hotel.

After the Paint-up Festival in 1957 when all buildings along Main Street were painted in two days by volunteers, wood trim was added to some of the awnings. New trees were planted at this time and utility wires were put underground.

ville Paint-Up Festival was the result. In two days all of the buildings on upper Main Street were painted by volunteers from Weaverville and neighboring communities. The project received national attention. The town was growing rapidly. Weaverville Water Works built a filtration plant and installed water meters. But higher water rates resulted in the disappearance of many of the beautiful lawns and gardens around homes. Weaverville's sewer system was constructed. The creeks smelled better and it was now safe for children to play in water along the streams. Trinity Dam was built in the late 1950's and early '60's. During the construction of the dam there were more newcomers in the area than long-time residents.

The 1960's found people wishing to change their life styles. Many former city families moved to Weaverville. Rather than wealth, they were now seeking a better quality of life. In 1961 Western Telephone Company installed the first direct long-distance dialing system without an operator in the United States. This linked Weaverville with 38 million telephones. Small sawmills closed during this period leaving but one large mill in town. Boating and fishing on Trinity Lake greatly expanded the county's recreational industry and markedly affected the economy of Weaverville.

The 1970 decade was a transition in the town's economy. Recreation and home buying and building were increasingly important. Small suction type gold mining dredges began to be used on many of the streams. The 1980 census found Trinity County the fastest growing county, percentagewise, in the state. Weaverville's population is now estimated to be approximately 3500.

The Trinity County J. J. "Jake" Jackson Memorial Museum was built in 1968 within the Historic District of Weaverville. It holds artifacts from all sections of Trinity County.

The lure of gold brought gold seekers by the hundreds into the mining camps of Trinity County. They worked their way up every creek and gulch searching for that bonanza which had lured them here. Many of these gulches bear the name of one of these early miners or prospectors. Other names are more colorful. Many of these names are recorded on present day maps but others remain only in the memories of a few old-timers. The names which general usage has assigned to the creeks and gulches of the Weaverville area are identified on the accompanying map.

KEY TO MAP SITES

1. Austrian Gulch
2. West Weaver Creek
3. Alder Gulch
4. Bear Gulch
5. Sowden Gulch
6. Goodyear Gulch
7. Grubb Gulch
8. John Undenstock Gulch
9. Mt. Safter or Mt. Severin Gulch
10. Democrat Gulch
11. Munger Gulch
12. Sidney Gulch
13. McKenzie Gulch
14. China Gulch
15. Weaver Creek
16. Ash Hollow
17. Little Garden Gulch
18. Garden Gulch
19. Nigger Al Gulch
20. Pinky Gulch
21. Dog Gulch
22. Chillis Gulch
23. Cannon House Hill
24. Ten Cent Gulch
25. Gamblers' Gulch
26. Five Cent Gulch
27. East Weaver Creek
28. Snow Slide Gulch
29. East Fork of East Weaver Creek
30. Schofield Gulch
31. East Branch of East Weaver Creek
32. Lance Gulch
33. Cooper-Watson Gulch
34. Little Browns Creek
35. Finley Gulch
36. China Gulch
37. Long Gulch
38. Last Chance Gulch
39. Union Gulch
40. Rush Creek
41. Baxter Gulch
42. Bear Gulch
43. Deer Gulch
44. Muckawee Gulch
45. Snow Gulch
46. Trinity House Gulch
47. China Gulch
48. Limekiln Gulch
49. LaGrange Ditch
50. Loveridge Ditch
51. Sweepstake Ditch
52. Howe-Ware Ditch
53. Weaver Bally—Site 120.
54. Costa Ranch—Site 121.

WEAVERVILLE AREA WATERSHED
Historic Creeks - Gulches - Ditches

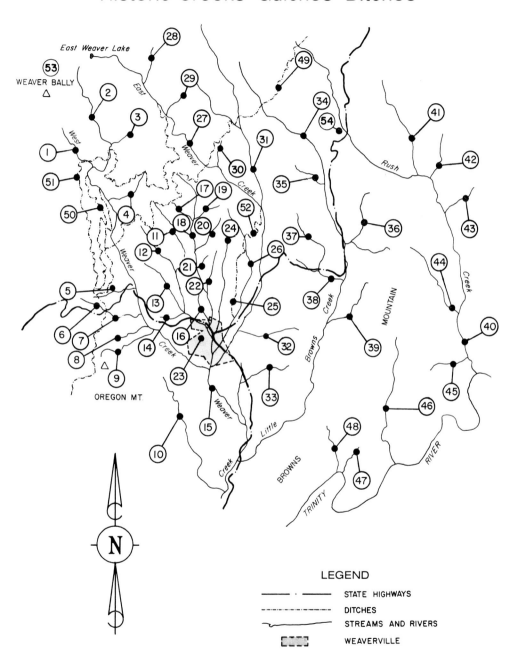

East Weaver Lake

WEAVER BALLY

West

East

Weaver

Creek

Rush

Weaver

OREGON MT.

Browns

Creek

MOUNTAIN

Creek

Little

Weaver

Creek

BROWNS

TRINITY

RIVER

N

LEGEND

—— · —— STATE HIGHWAYS

---------------- DITCHES

~——— STREAMS AND RIVERS

WEAVERVILLE

Site 1. Chaunceyville (Waldorff Place) (Junkans Ranch) (Lorenz Place) (Arbuckle Place)

The Arbuckle Place is a large plot of meadow and hillside located along Weaver Creek adjacent to Highway 299, at the southern edge of Weaverville. It was acquired by the Arbuckle family in 1932 and was occupied as a mining claim until 1980 when a patent to the land was granted to the Arbuckle family. Originally this area was known as Chaunceyville. In the 1850's Dr. H. M. Chauncey ran a small stage stop, hotel, ranch and sawmill here. The hotel must have been a lively establishment for the Trinity Journal of June 28, 1856, gives a vivid account of a dedication ball held there.

Jacob Theodore Waldorff and his wife, Maria Louise (Eike) Waldorff, acquired the property in 1860 and lived there until 1875 when they left to live in Hyampom and later at Little French Creek near Big Bar. Another owner was Henry Junkans who ran it as a productive ranch but who also mined the land extensively. In fact, his great grandniece, Karlyn Van Matre, states that it was Mr. Junkan's dream to eventually mine the entire Weaver Basin. He did not accomplish his dream but the next owners continued to mine the property. They were the Lorenz brothers who also owned a well-known ranch nearby. Tailing piles from these various mining operations are still in evidence.

The oldest building now standing on the property is a basic pioneer, one and one-half story, cross-gable house with a high-gable roof, plain boxed cornice and veranda. It was built in 1898-9 by Moore and Hanna who owned the property at that time. An abandoned shingle style, hip roof, two-story house with a one-story hip roof entry porch stands nearby. It was built about 1915 and is the only true shingle style building surviving in Weaverville. Dating from the same time is a gable, board and batten barn built on high piers as a protection from possible flooding of the nearby Weaver Creek.

Pasture land dotted with old fruit trees surround these old buildings. The old stage road from Lewiston passed directly in front of the house. A watering trough for teams using the road sat at one end of the house.

Site 2. Race Track (Old Airport) (Golf Course)

This long stretch of almost level ground was used for many years as a race track. It was the perfect place to run the "quarter mile", running slightly uphill. Horse racing was part of the excitement of the very early celebrations in Weaverville. Among horses running this track was "Hayfork Kitty", a horse named for Miss Katie Weinheimer when she was teaching near Hayfork at the Salt Creek school. Charlie Crews was always the jockey. John and Idell McDonald Rourke raised many horses to race on this track. John Van Matre of Minersville was often a contestant with his horse "Hollywood". Mart Van Matre of Lewiston ran a bay gelding that often won over "out of county" horses. Charlie Daniels, a popular young Indian, owned and rode a beautiful horse with flaxen mane and tail. Elias Ellery from Trinity Center and Mr. Porter from the Bonanza King, near Trinity Center, had race horses that frequently ran on this racecourse. The memory of these races is still enjoyed by older horse fanciers in the county.

When airplanes came into use, the old race track was the only suitable place near Weaverville to land. The first plane landed in 1929 with local businessman Moon Lee at the controls. Unfortunately, the strip was plagued by a cross-draft which caused a number of near accidents. Quite large planes, including a Ford Trimotor, were used on the strip by the U. S. Forest Service. During one plane take-off, a number of Forest Service employees were injured. After the clearing and completion of the present airport, this old field lay idle for a number of

Site 1. This old house built in 1898 is the first historic house to be seen upon entering Weaverville from the east. This stop on the old stage road was called Chaunceyville and is now known as the Arbuckle Place.

Site 1. This is a view of Weaver Bally and Weaver Basin as seen from below the Arbuckle Place. Deep ruts show the road as it was before 1915.

years. It was finally offered by the county for auction and sold to private parties. A part is now used as a community golf course, restaurant and clubhouse.

Site 3. Johnson House (Nellie Johnson House)

The Johnson House, located at 1017 Mill Street, was originally a one-story, three-room structure built sometime before 1900. The upstairs and the cross-gable were added in 1912 by Fred Johnson and Tom McNamara when it was the home of Fred Johnson and his wife Nellie. It was here that their daughter, Edith (Johnson) Smallen, was born. Edith is still a resident of Mill Street.

The house is located on what was, at one time, the main road into Weaverville. The road at first passed by the house on the west side. Later ut forked and passed on both sides. The wide area in front of the house was used as a turnaround.

There is a low-gable porch on the front of the main gable as well as three shed-roof dormers. These dormers are a prominent feature of the house because they are characteristic of the workmanship of Tom McNamara. Similar dormers are to be found on the nearby Simpson House which McNamara helped build. The board and batten siding is also distinctive for it is the only board and batten house in the Mill Street district.

Site 4. Blaney House (McKnight House) (Knight House) (Brabrook House)

The house at 1014 Mill Street, now owned by Katie (Burgess) (Knight) Brabrook, was built in 1898 by David Woodbury. Woodbury bought the lot from W. S. Lowden and sold the property including a residence and buildings to Blake and Reed in 1904. John and Bessie Blaney bought it in 1914 and lived there until 1920.

James N. McKnight bought it in 1925 and his wife Jane (Duncan) acquired it in 1926; Steve and Alice McKnight bought it in 1945 and in 1957 John and Katie (Burgess) Knight became the owners.

This graceful old house is a one and one-half story, high-gable structure with a lower cross-gable to one side. Dental molding and pediment frieze define the attic. It remained unaltered until the Knights added a shed roof extension on the south, a new shed roof porch on the north and an addition in back.

It was once thought this house had been used for prostitution, but this is not true. The original house on this lot, however, probably was. It was owned by Madam Morie Legagneur, a native of France, who died in February, 1891. A month later, someone set the house on fire in the middle of the night. It was described as one of the oldest houses in town.

Site 5. McNamara House (Simpson House)

The original part of the house at 1009 Mill Street was built in 1900 by Tom McNamara, an excellent carpenter and cabinetmaker by trade. Unfortunately, not much more than the basic shape of the original section of the house has been retained. Nonetheless, the house still has historic significance because of its age. It is a one and one-half story, high-gable structure with a hip roof screened veranda across the front. Two shed roof dormers on the front gable end are of interest as they were a McNamara trademark. Similar dormers are part of the Nellie Johnson House which McNamara helped build. The original siding has been covered with asbestos shingles and a large addition has been built at the back. These changes have depreciated the historic significance of this structure. The present occupants are William and Elnora Simpson.

64

Site 6. Neusse House (Brunken House) (Jackson House)

The Jackson House, 1001 Mill Street, dates back to the 1860's. Charles Neusse was the original owner. Later owners were Allen Butler, Nora Dannenbrink, Robert Brunken, Nettie Brunken, and Wilda Mae Dockery. In 1919, J. J. Jackson, County Treasurer and founder of the Trinity County Historical Society, acquired the property including a water right and a ditch serving it.

This house has no particular architectural significance but its overall simplicity and age give it an enduring appeal. Its greatest appeal is in its large and beautiful yard as the lot has retained its original size. Jackson's widow is a very fine gardener.

Behind the house is a medium sized barn surrounded by an old post and rail fence which is covered with berry bushes. The barn is the only barn remaining in the Mill Street area and is still in use.

Site 7. Weinheimer House (Funk House)

The house at 920 Mill Street was built about 1880 by Mr. Guthrie, the operator of a sawmill up Canyon Creek. It was owned and resided in for many years by Henry and Clara (Flagg) Weinheimer. Its present occupant is Wayne Funk. This house is the only combination Greek Revival-Gothic style structure on Mill Street. It is a one-story gable building with a hip roof addition on the north side and a small hip roof on the front. The main gable end has a gothic window with a cross pattern of panes which is distinctive. The house is essentially unaltered except for the removal of an original bay window and the installation of new windows. It still has the large yard so characteristic of early houses in the area.

Site 8. Gray House (Larkin House) (Rose House)

The house originally on this Mill Street lot was owned by George and Sarah Drake who homesteaded the land in 1871 and received the patent to it in 1880. The property has changed ownership many times. In 1899 the Unity Mining Company purchased it and two years later it was bought by Harry Lyon. In 1904 the home was owned by Herbert Gray, who was one of the partners in the Trinity County Bank. The house burned in 1905 and was rebuilt the following spring. It remained the property of Mr. Gray for 38 years after which it became the home of Elmer Larkin, County Sheriff. The present owners are C. W. and S. E. Rose.

Remodeling of the building has occurred over the years with major changes being made to the street side of the front gable in the 1970's. The house is a one and one-half story, high-gable structure with a cross-gable to the rear. Originally the street side of the main gable roof was high but a medium-gable roof has been set on top. It is possible to see a small portion of the original high-gable on the south side. The new roof was constructed so as to extend out to the two dormers facing the front which were part of the original building. Clerestory windows were placed under the eaves and a one-story, bellcap roof porch was added beneath, thus appreciably changing the appearance of the front of the building. This is the only well preserved shingle style house in town. The house is also distinctive in that it is not now, nor has it been, a white house as were so many of the older houses. The yard, which was once larger, contains large locust and sycamore trees and across the front is a picket fence with diamond shaped pickets and posts.

Site 9. The Flagg home at 914 Mill Street was built in 1876.

Site 9. Flagg House (Lucia Smith House)

This house, located at 914 Mill Street, was built by Jacob Flagg in 1876 and replaced an earlier residence which had been destroyed by fire. It occupies its original large lot and has a white picket fence across the front, both of which add substantially to the character of the house. It is an excellent example of the homes which once lined Mill Street, as its exterior remains virtually unchanged. The house is a one and one-half story, shotgun plan, high-gable structure with shiplap siding. Its open veranda which spans the entire front of the building extends around a portion of the north side. There is a lean-to across the back as well as a secondary lower lean-to serving as access to the basement.

Site 10. Condon House (Don Taylor House)

The address of the Condon House is 910 Mill Street. It is unique because it is one of the first two story houses to be built in the county. It is also one of the finest for its structural and conceptual composition. The style is early Trinity County Victorian but it has a symmetrical dignity not usually found in Victorian houses. The house is in good condition; the foundation has been maintained; the shiplap siding is intact; and a sound metal roof protects the original shake roof.

Although the land was patented by J. A. C. Goering in 1878 this house was not built on it until shortly after Mr. Goering sold the property to the Wilson family in 1896. The Condon family purchased it in 1908 and it remained their home until 1944, giving it its historic name. The Condons operated Weaverville's Empire Hotel for many years.

Site 11. The William Spencer Lowden home was built in the 1870's. Lowden was responsible for surveying and helping to build Weaverville's first road in 1858.

Site 12. This hip roof office building on Mill Street was used by both William S. Lowden and his son, Henry L. Lowden; both were surveyors. William Lowden was largely responsible for the Trinity County road system.

Site 11. Lowden House (Duncan House)

The Lowden house, 905 Mill Street, was built in 1890 immediately following a fire which destroyed an earlier house on this lot that had been built in 1876. It was built by William Spencer Lowden, one of the most important of Trinity County's pioneers. The house has an old-time formality and elegance which sets it apart from the others on the street. The following features make this one-story, high-gable house distinctive: pronounced shelf lintels, 4/4 windows, transom and sidelights around the main door, symmetrically oriented pediment gable on the entrance porch, gothic attic vent in the rear south end, a brick chimney and a wide frieze.

Mollie Lowden, spinster daughter of William Spencer Lowden, lived on alone in this large house for many years. It has since been the home of George and Beulah Waller and Howard and Doris Duncan.

Site 12. Lowden Office

Sitting flush with the street at the intersection of Mill and Washington Streets is a building which was the surveying and abstract office of William S. Lowden, the founder of Trinity County's road system. It also served as an office for his son, Henry L. Lowden, who carried on his father's business after him. This building was built in 1895. Lowden had built his home nearby in 1876. The two buildings, along with a barn, originally occupied the same lot but are now separated by a modern home which was built after the lot was divided. The Lowden office and the Lowden home are built with similar shiplap or "channel rustic" siding. The office structure looks like a commercial building since there is no yard nor are there any plants, but it does lend an historic character to the street. It is a one-story pyramid hip roof structure with a lean-to at the rear and a hip roof porch across the front. Except for a new brick chimney the building remains essentially unaltered but it is, however, now used as a residence.

Site 13. Osgood House (Cobb House)

This house at 810 Mill Street is one of the oldest houses on the street as it dates back to about 1858. It is one of the few small houses that still remains. Although it has been partially altered it retains its original shape and size. It is a medium-gable L-plan structure with a veranda across the front gable end. Another veranda on the south side has recently been enclosed to make a new room. The original clapboard siding is visible on the side gable ends. New windows have replaced the originals except on the front where the four-paned double casements are still in place.

Historically, this house is known as the Osgood House but it is not known who the original owner was. The present owner is Bud Cobb.

Site 14. Hagelman House (Spratt House)

The house at 809 Mill Street was built about 1870 by Johnny Hagelman, a blacksmith. Hagelman lived here with his widowed mother for many years. Later the house was owned by the Stephen Spratt family. Mr. Spratt worked for the Weaverville Supply Company and in later years was superintendent of the old county hospital. His wife Blanche, a registered nurse, assisted him in this job. After the death of Mr. Spratt the house had a succession of owners.

The house has been altered over the years but it still retains it shotgun plan which distinguishes it from the other houses in the area. It no longer retains its original front, for a portion of the porch has been enclosed to make a room and the location of the front door has been slightly changed. The front door is now solid and is recessed into the gable end. Except for an old apple tree, little remains of a once attractive yard.

Site 15. Clement House (Burger House)

The Henry Dix house, which was destroyed by fire, originally occupied this site at 806 Mill Street. The lot was then purchased by William Clement who, in 1914, moved this house onto it from the Day Ranch several miles outside of town. Mabel and George Burger, the present owners, have made this their home since 1943. This house is a rather complex ranch house which was built around 1890. It is a one and three-quarter story, high-gable structure with gable dormers on two sides. A low-gable porch is across most of the front and the cross-gable has an enclosed lean-to porch with a cellar below. The house originally sat on a large lot which was typical of the houses on Mill Street in earlier days. The lot has since been split to accommodate a second house next door.

Site 16. Old High School

Trinity County's young people had the privilege of a high school education offered them in Weaverville as early as 1909. Classes were first held in a spare room of the old grammar school (now Nazarene Church). In 1910, generous citizens of Weaverville purchased a large lot and building which they presented to the county for use as a high school. The building was completely remodeled, for it had been used for lumber and hay storage. In the beginning there was no inside plumbing or running water. A gasoline pump was used to obtain water from a well in the school yard. Outside toilets were in back of the school building just above a group of small hovels lived in by Chinese along the creek. When Carl Bremer's father vacated his house next to the school to go live with his son and his son's wife Edna, the house was acquired by the school. For a time it was used as a dormitory for out-of-town students. Later, use was made of the house as a music room and shop. The Bremer building partially burned and eventually was torn down.

In the early 1930's a gymnasium was started. This building stood unfinished and was condemned. Several years later a W.P.A. project fund was acquired to complete the structure. Under the direction of David Culbertson, shop teacher, and with local labor, the gymnasium was completed. A new high school was built directly in front of the former school and was connected to the gymnasium. The dedication took place in the spring of 1938. Edna Thayer Bremer served for many years as trustee, being appointed in 1920. When a playing field was acquired in back of the school, it was named Bremer field in her honor.

During the 1950's, Hayfork acquired its own high school. There had been a branch school for freshman and sophomore students in Hayfork in the 1920's. In 1970 Weaverville also acquired a new school complex at the north end of town on ground previously owned by the U.S. Forest Service. The old high school stood idle for a number of years and was finally demolished in 1972 after the lot was purchased by Continental Telephone of California.

Site 17. Vollmers House (Barber House) (Large House)

This house at 703 Main Street, now rented by the Large family, was built in 1877 and was first owned by Otto Vollmers. Mr. Vollmers, in partnership with Peter Paulsen, was a proprietor of the Union Hotel. Later the house was owned by the H. D. Barber family. Like his name, Dwight Barber was a barber by

Site 16. This building was Trinity County's first high school. The building had been used as storage for grain and hay. In 1910 it was purchased by Weaverville citizens and given to the county for a high school.

Site 16. The second high school was constructed in front of the first during the 1930's. This building included a gymnasium.

Site 17. Vollmers lived in this house after it was built in 1877. It is a good example of Weaverville homes built at that time. It is located at 703 Main Street.

trade but he also served as Justice of the Peace. The November 10, 1906, issue of the Trinity Journal made reference to this house when it ran a news item which stated " . . . repairs on Judge Barber's house have been completed . . . the house has almost been rebuilt . . . Judge now has one of the most handsome and comfortable houses in town."

This is a one-story, medium cross-gable structure which is quite similar in style to other older pioneer cottages in town. Unlike the others, however, this house has some Victorian detail. The lower peaked roof, bay window, spindle screen door, and leaded multi-paned glass in the front door are details which indicate the Victorian nature of the architecture.

Site 18. Greenwell House (Fetzer House) (Hamilton House)

The house at 705 Main Street is an extremely simple and very old house. Its construction date is estimated to have been between 1860 and 1865. It is a high cross-gable, shiplap structure with the usual pioneer style architectural details such as plain boxed cornice, 6/6 double hung windows with plain trim, and a solid wood cross-panel door with plain trim. The house is essentially unaltered and is, therefore, a better example of pioneer architecture than either of its neighbors which have been altered over the years. A small barn stands at the back of the lot.

This house has changed ownership many times. V. S. Ranier is believed to have been the first owner. At the turn of the century it was the home of Ernest A. Greenwell and his wife Emma (Todd) Greenwell. (Mr. Greenwell's life ended when he was thrown from a horse in the corral near the small barn in 1901.) Other owners have been A. J. Fetzer (town jeweler and later proprietor of the Weaverville Hotel), George Gehm, and Charles and Pat Hamilton, the present owners.

Site 19. R. L. Carter House (Brown's Ore Cart)

This house at 707 Main Street is historically known as the R. L. Carter

71

house, as it was the home of Catherine and Bob Carter for many years. Bob Carter was not only prominent in community affairs but he also served as county clerk, auditor and recorder for 42 years. The present owner is John Brown, Jr. who has his business, Brown's Ore Cart, at this place.

Historically this is an important building even though it has been somewhat altered. It is still the same basic shape and color as the other pioneer-type structures that form a row along the east side of the street. It is a rectangular, medium-gable, part clapboard and part shiplap building, with a metal roof. The rectangular shape, shed dormer, and lean-to on the north side are original, as is also the brick chimney. The date of its construction is estimated to be during the 1870's or 1880's.

Site 20. Armentrout House (Specht House)

This house was built in 1878 by the Armentrouts, an old mining and farming family from nearby Democrat Gulch. It remained in the family for many years. It is a rectangular, white shiplap, medium-gable, pioneer-type house, located at 711 Main Street. An old brick chimney in the center of the house is its most outstanding feature. This house was fortunate in surviving a destructive fire which caused the house next door to burn to the ground. Following this fire the house received a new roof and porch making its true age less apparent. The last family member to occupy this house was Effie (Armentrout) Specht, who made it her home in the latter years of her life.

Site 21. Colbert House (Curt Bennett House) (Jose's Hideaway)

The house at 719 Main Street, now a Mexican restaurant, is historically known as the Colbert House. It was at one time the home of John Colbert who used to claim that he was the first white child born in Weaverville. It is also known as the Curt Bennett residence. Bennett was a member of an early mining family, and his wife Ella was a member of the Anderline family.

This old pioneer house was built in the 1860's and retains most of its original constuction details including the shiplap siding, metal high-gable roof, plain boxed cornice, 6/6 windows with plain trim and triangular lintels, and solid wood panel front door. It is a rather austere structure but it plays an important role in the continuity of the historic character of this portion of Main Street. This continuity is enhanced by the row of locust trees which line the street in front of the house. These trees were planted between 1871 and 1875 and at one time lined both sides of the street.

Site 22. Jack Hall House (Morris Augustus Brady House)

The Brady House at 801 Main Street was built in 1876 by Jack Hall who lived in it until shortly after 1900 when it was purchased by the Morris Augustus (Gus) Brady family. The original house was a high-gable, clapboard, pioneer style structure. Shortly after its purchase by Mr. Brady the veranda was removed and a two-story, shiplap, high cross-gable addition was made to the front of the building. Unlike the older pioneer portion, the new section was modeled after the early Trinity County Victorian style of homes being built at the time, although gingerbread details were kept minimal. Asymmetry, bay windows and vertical proportions characterize this portion. This house stands as an example of additions having been made to an older house.

The Dud Brady House next door shares the lot with the older "Gus" Brady house which belonged to his father. This house is newer than the others nearby having been built in 1930 but it fits well into the neighborhood and has not de-

Site 22. This two-story house at 801 Main Street was built in 1876 by Jack Hall. Members of the Brady family have lived here for 80 years.

Site 23. This house was built by Henry Hocker in 1859 and once was the home of Judge Bartlett. The Hocker-Bartlett House is located at 807 Main Street.

preciated the historic character of the district. It is a medium low one-story structure with white shiplap siding and black plain trim. It is surrounded by a large and grassy yard.

Site 23. Hocker House (Bartlett House) (Stryker House) (Hocker-Bartlett House)

Henry Hocker built this house in 1859. He was a prominent Weaverville merchant who also built the structure which now serves as the County Courthouse. The property was later purchased by Superior Court Judge James Bartlett, who was also a noted local author, geographer and historian. The present owners, Frances H. Morris and Myska Ruditsky, acquired the property in 1978 from the Stryker family who had lived in the house for over thirty years.

This house is the only symmetrically designed hip roof and gable Greek Revival structure in the county. There is a gabled hip entrance porch across the entire front and a series of sheds and lean-tos are attached to the rear. Interesting details are the recessed and paneled door and the wide frieze and returns. Its very large and well-kept yard, as well as the excellent condition of the house itself, make this a prominent and much admired house in Weaverville. Presently known as the Hocker-Bartlett House, it is located at 807 Main Street.

Site 24. Tinnin House (Hafley House) (Shuford House)

This house, built in 1861 by Wiley J. Tinnin, was patented by him in 1877. In 1887 the house was purchased by M. H. Lowden and remained in the family until 1914 when it was acquired by John W. Shuford. At one time it is said to have been the home of Fred Hafley, Trinity National Forest Supervisor, and to have served as the forest's headquarters.

The basic house is a one-story, white shiplap, cross-gable with a hip roof veranda across the front. To the rear the gable rises to one and one-half stories. Located at 815 Main Street, the house is in an excellent unaltered condition.

Site 25. Hupp House (Sadie Day House)

This old house at 913 Main Street was built in the 1880-1890 period and originally belonged to the Hupps, an affluent mining family who ran a successful hydraulic operation at the Hupp-MacMurry Mine located on East Weaver Creek. It was later lived in by Ebenezer Flagg and Walter and Sadie (Flagg) Day. The house is cut off from the other old houses on Main Street by commercial buildings but it makes a pleasant break in the strip development which has been occurring.

In spite of its deteriorating condition the house has a homey charm which is obscured by the vines which cover it most of the year. About all that is visible from the street is a glimpse of a Victorian spindle and spool screen door and a couple of old porch chairs. It is a pioneer style shiplap with gable roof and veranda porch.

At the time of this writing the house is being torn down. An old barn is at the rear and a straggly wire fence defines the property.

Site 26. C. E. Stiller House (Esau Montgomery House) (Frush House)

This small cottage at 201 Washington Street was probably constructed prior to 1907 by Peter Hart. It was acquired by Charles E. Stiller in March 1910 and has been known, historically, as the Stiller Place. The present owners are Mr. and Mrs. A. H. Frush. Although the house has been altered it retains its original shape. It is a small sized version of a basic pioneer type

Site 24. This nice old home on Main Street was built in 1860 to 1861. It was once the home of Fred Hafley and for years it has been owned by the Shuford family. Giant locust trees planted in the 1870's frame the pleasant entryway.

house with a high-gable roof, veranda around two sides, square porch posts, 6/6 windows, metal roof, etc. It typifies the original character of the town, especially in its still "rural" setting across from the Brady House corrals and its proximity to the old Costa House and yard.

Site 27. Sam Lee House

This land at the end of Lorenz Road was originally part of the Lorenz Ranch. It was later occupied by the Sam Lee family who built this house in 1918 using some of the siding, doors and other materials from the old Ellis place on Main Street next to the art center. Sam Lee was a miner, farmer and storekeeper, as well as the first generation of the only Chinese family that still remains in Weaverville today. The old Lee House is basically a T-plan, one-story, high-gable with long cross-gable structure. It has a veranda porch across the front. It follows the building pattern of older Weaverville houses but makes use of shingle siding and contrasting trim which was popular at the time it was built.

Site 28. Robinson Place (Young Place)

The Young Place, off Oregon Road near the Weaverville Cemetery, comprises two acres of rural property in the middle of a dense Weaverville residential area. It includes a pasture, a duck pond surrounded by rushes and willows, two old barns and two newer ones, two sheds, an old rocked well, two vegetable gardens, an orchard, and a new simple gable house built over the ashes of the original house which burned in 1957. The first house was built by William Allen for his daughter Phoebe after her husband died in 1889.

The property went from Phoebe Robinson to her daughter, Mary and her husband Henry Young and is now owned by their sons, Allen and Bob, who have continued to manage it in the same manner as their parents and grandparents before them. Any changes have been kept to a minimum.

The lot to the east, now part of the large yard, was the site of the Trinity Brewery in very early times.

Site 29. Weaverville Cemeteries

Cemetery #1. Of Weaverville's six known cemeteries, the oldest is probably the one next to the Catholic Church on what was first called Graveyard Hill. George Pope Gordon was buried there in 1851 and Col. John Anderson in 1852. Later, these two graves plus those of others were moved to the public cemetery in order for the cemetery plot to be mined. When the ground was found to contain but little gold, the area was again placed into use as a cemetery. A Catholic Church was erected adjacent to the cemetery in 1853. It was destroyed by fire and was replaced by three others which also burned. The present church was built in 1924. The little cemetery on the north side of the church has remained in continuous use through all of these years. Many ornate headstones and handsome wrought iron fences still stand.

Cemetery #2, #3, and #4. The large cemetery above the former grammar school (now the Church of the Nazarene) is three cemeteries in one. The area was set aside by the county in 1856 and was laid out as a square with the public cemetery occupying the eastern half next to the school yard. The remaining half was divided between the Masonic and the Oddfellow Lodges, the Masonic Cemetery being that portion to the south and the Oddfellow Lodge having that portion to the north. At first the three cemeteries were each enclosed by neat picket fences. A stile was used to get over the fence between the public cemetery and the school yard facilitating the retrieving of baseballs.

The Masonic cemetery contains the marked grave of D. B. Logan who had died and was first buried at Logan Gulch in 1854. His body was moved as soon as the Masonic cemetery was established. His grave is the oldest marked grave in the cemetery. At one time membership in the Oddfellows' Lodge guaranteed a burial allowance and a free cemetery plot. This practice was discontinued, however, when costs became prohibitive.

The public cemetery has been expanded by the addition of ground above the west of the Masonic and Oddfellow areas. When power mowers came into use all but a few of the historic wrought iron fences were removed. The cemetery as a whole is now enclosed by a wire fence. An early provision by the Lorenz family designated for cemetery use a portion of the water from their ditch out of West Weaver Creek. It is now known as the Moon Lee Ditch. The older section of the burial ground is truly a trip through history.

Cemetery #5. An unmarked Chinese cemetery is located west of town in China Gulch. This was used by the Hong Kong Company of Chinese.

Cemetery #6. The See Yup Company cemetery has a handsome, oriental style entrance gate, erected by the "E Clampus Vitus" member of July of 1967. This leads to an area of approximately one and one-half acres which is enclosed by a tight barbed wire fence. The total plot is pocked with indentations where remains have been removed. Chinese came to Trinity County during the gold rush with the dream of obtaining wealth and returning to their native home. Living or dead, they had little desire to remain in this land. When prosperous Chinese died, their bodies were embalmed and immediately shipped home. When poor Chinese died, they were buried in the cemetery with all the customary ritual. Eventually their bones were exhumed and placed in a handsome earthenware container for shipment to China. This cemetery is a beautiful spot under many oak trees. One identifiable grave in the area is that of Joe Tuey, popular Joss House attendant, who was buried there in 1973.

Site 30. Weaverville Grammar School (Nazarene Church)

In 1878 the Ingleson and Henderson Co. of Oakland constructed the Weaverville Grammar School on this site now occupied by the Church of the Nazarene. The original building was a two-story Italianate Villa type of public building which dominated this setting overlooking the town. It served as the grammar school for Weaverville children until 1949 when the present Weaverville Elementary School was built. Primary classes continued to be held in the old building until 1952 when additions to the new school were completed and use of the old school was no longer needed. In 1961 the Church of the Nazarene purchased it, removed the top story and belfry, and remodeled it for use as a church.

On the grounds are 13 black locust trees which were planted in 1880. Originally 50 of these trees were planted around the old school building. When the trees were young each tree was placed in the care of a school boy whose responsibility it was to carry water in buckets to keep them growing. The 13 trees which remain standing a century later are a tribute to those students who cared for them so diligently.

Site 31. California House (Hanover House) (Frankie Davis House)

The house at 304 South Miner Street, now occupied by Frankie (Hanover) Davis and her husband Jack, was once known as the "California House" a house of ill repute. It was built as a rental by John Whitmore in the 1890's. Mr. Whitmore somewhat sullied his reputation as a reputable businessman and

Site 30. This picture of the Weaverville Grammar School shows it shortly after it was built in 1878. The building has been remodeled to become the Church of the Nazarene.

sawmill operator when he rented the house out for this questionable business.

It is an oddly proportioned one and one-half story gable building as the gable is wider than it is high. The original shiplap siding which has been covered with asbestos shingles is partly exposed over the front door. A low cross-gable has been added to the back and there is a small shed roof porch on the side front. Old locust trees, so typical of Weaverville, grow in the yard.

Site 32. O'Neill House (Timothy O'Neill House)

The O'Neill House is a typical pioneer cottage. It is a cross-gable structure with a veranda surrounding most of the house. The house was probably built in stages with shed roof additions being added at different times over the years. The house sits in the middle of a hillside pasture near the corner of Dockery and Miner Streets and is the only house of its kind which still sits in a large portion of its original pasture land. This house was built about 1860 by Timothy and Annie O'Neill, an Irish family who had a small dairy business. It remained in the O'Neill family nearly a century before passing to new owners.

Site 33. Forest Service Office

The U.S. Forest Service office property in Weaverville straddles Sidney Gulch on Highway 299 at the west end of town. The attractive buildings are surrounded with a profusion of native trees and shrubs, most of which were transplanted by workers of the Civilian Conservation Corps in the 1930's. The

Site 33. This picture of the present Forest Service building was taken shortly after it was built in the 1930's.

Site 34. This home across the highway from the Forest Service was built before 1862. It has been home to the Edgecombe, Dockery, Ryan, Clark and Zengel families.

main office in 1934 served as Supervisor's headquarters for the Trinity National Forest, as well as headquarters for the Weaverville Ranger District. The District Ranger's residence was west of the main office; the Supervisor's residence was directly across the highway. A C.C.C. spike camp was in back of the Ranger's residence. Truck garages and a shop were directly in back of the office building. Weaverville went to work, ate lunch, and quit work by the Forest Service shop whistle. A large barn and two horse and mule corrals were at the foot of the hill near the present high school. A large horse pasture occupied the acreage now used by the present high school complex.

Many changes have taken place during the years since these Forest Service building were first occupied. The Supervisor's office was eliminated when the Trinity National Forest was consolidated with the Shasta National Forest in 1954 and became the Shasta-Trinity National Forest. The main office building became the District Ranger's office. The former Ranger's residence is now an engineering department and the Supervisor's home is now used by the timber management staff. The number of employees has grown so rapidly that many townspeople miss the close association that once existed. Gone forever is the vision of the Forest Supervisor, under his Stetson hat, riding past on his personal horse.

Site 34. Edgecombe House (Dockery House) (Ryan House) (Clarke House) (Zengel House)

The western most house of the group of four across Main Street from the Forest Service buildings is considered to be one of the oldest houses in Weaverville, having been constructed in the 1850's. Early records show that the property was homesteaded by Dennis Carroll on April 23, 1862, and at that time the house was already there. Its next owners were the Edgecombes who purchased it in 1868. Two years latter Cecelia Dockery purchased it. The Dockerys lived there until 1899 when it passed to their daughter, Catherine (Dockery) Weinheimer, who resided in the adjacent house. From 1900 to 1924 it was rented to the Ryan family after which it became the home of the Clarke family. The Dockerys, Weinheimers, Ryans and Clarkes were all related. At the time of this 4th printing this house has been relocated to the Trinity Hospital grounds to make room for the County Library.

Although most houses built at this time were pioneer style, this house incorporates some Greek Revival features. The south gable of this T-gable structure is older than the west gable. This older, south gable has long casement windows and triangular lintels and its siding is a clapboard, whereas the newer, west gable has 6/1 double hung windows with plain trim and has shiplap siding with end boards.

The yard has a rural functional appearance with a large lawn, fruit trees, hedges of roses and grape, surrounded by a picket and decorative wire fence.

Site 35. Weinheimer House

This house, located across Main Street from the Forest Service compound and adjacent to the Edgecombe House, is one of the oldest houses in Weaverville. It was built in 1859 as a small, two-room, gable structure, but over the years many additions have been made to it and it now has three cross-gables, four shed roof additions, and a false front plus two verandas and a small porch on the back. The oldest part of the house has clapboard siding, but shiplap and board and batten siding has been used on some of the newer portions. Instead of framing, the house has vertical boards nailed to the top and bottom sills with the siding nailed to that. In spite of its poor construction it is still in good condition and has retained considerable charm.

This house was the home of Henry Weinheimer and his wife, Catherine (Dockery) Weinheimer, for over six decades. They had purchased it from P. M. Paulsen, proprietor of the Union Hotel. The Weinheimers moved into the house on their wedding day in 1869. It remained their home until Henry's death in 1930. Their seven children were all born here. One of them, Cecelia Weinheimer, was a respected school teacher in the county who served for 50 years on the Board of Education and who lived her entire life in this house. She passed away at the age of 84 in 1956. The house still remains in the family.

Site 36. (Ryan House)

Located between the Weinheimer House and the Lautenschlager House on Union (Main) Street is the youngest of a group of four early Union St. houses. During the first two decades of the 1900's new house construction in Weaverville was at a standstill. This period of economic doldrums was brought to an end in 1924 when D. E. "Ed" Ryan and his wife Annie (Weinheimer) Ryan built this house. A precedent was set and construction of other new houses followed. This house is a two-story, high gable structure with a truncated hip roof wing on one side and a one-story kitchen wing on another. The house is a good example of the architecture of the 1920's.

Mr. Ryan was owner of Ryan's Store, a well-known grocery, hardware and feed store, which he and, later, his son Vernon operated for many years.

Site 37. Valentine Lautenschlager House

The Valentine Lautenschlager house sits well back from the highway and is the most easterly of the group of four old homes located across the street from the Forest Service. This house originally was located where the Forest Service buildings now stand but was moved to its present location about 1930. Its original construction date is estimated to have been in the 1870's. The house is a simple, white shiplap, pioneer type house which has not been altered and is a good example of the simplicity and small scale of pioneer architecture in Weaverville. It is a high-gable structure with a veranda porch across the front gable, a lean-to addition on the back, and a low foundation of stone piers. It is one of five houses grouped together on approximately two acres. The houses are unfenced and share common grounds of lawns and old fruit trees giving the area a sense of open space.

Site 38. Trinity County Hospital (Trinity General Hospital)

Taxpayers of Trinity County have maintained a hospital at the present site since 1894. The first hospital erected on this site was a large, two-story, all wood frame building that stood near the present convalescent home. The well-cared-for orchard and huge vegetable garden plot was destroyed when the present Trinity General Hospital was constructed during the period of 1949-1950. A cow barn, chicken houses and pig pens had been located back of the garden plot near Garden Gulch. A large maintenance shop was located north of this area. Between the garden and the hospital stood the superintendent's home. In the lawn area to the north side of the hospital was the little cottage where elderly ladies lived. Another smaller building with a high pitch roof stood nearby and was called "The Crazy House". It was used to confine mentally ill patients. The cook's cottage stood on the hillside across Taylor Street.

Between 1894 and 1950 most patients were single, older, indigent men, numbering about twenty and, usually not more than two women. Patients who were able considered it a privilege to help with gardening and maintenance

Site 38. The former Trinity County Hospital shown here served the area between 1894 and 1950. The present hospital occupies the same site.

Site 39. The Varney home sits on the hill at the end of Court Street. The ample yard is enclosed by a handsome picket fence. The house was built in 1900 for the William Ware Young family.

chores. When D. A. Hobart was superintendent in 1898 he received $62.50 per month in addition to his meals and residence. The large 1894 building was used as a hospital as well as a home for the elderly indigents. Most doctors saw patients in their private offices or made house calls. Dr. William Ware was one of the earliest to practice in Weaverville. By 1855 there were five physicians and several dentists. They rented office space in hotels, private residences and drug stores during the 1850's. The German citizens built a hospital on the hill above the present Joss House in 1856 to care for their people. Dr. Croucher was their hospital physician. When there was no longer a need the hospital ceased to operate.

In 1859 the county supervisors purchased a residence on Court Street to care for the indigent. The facility became so crowded that land at the present site of the hospital was acquired and the 1894 building was constructed. It was used for over half a century until the present Trinity General Hospital and Convalescent Hospital were built. At a later date, additions were made and the two facilities were joined together by a passageway.

The present hospital received some of its heaviest usage during the building of Trinity Dam in the late 1950's. The present building is a great change from the 1894 building when most patients took care of themselves and helped with chores. Those patients too feeble or ill to walk up the long steep stairway to beds on the top floor had to be carried.

Site 39. Young House (Varney House)

This lovely two-story Victorian house sits on a hill at the end of Court Street where it meets Waterworks Street and commands a view of the town. It was built in 1900 for W. W. "Doc" Young who was the owner of the Weaverville Waterworks. (The waterworks had been founded by William Ware who had given the business to his namesake, William Ware Young.) The Youngs were a prominent Trinity family whose children were born and raised in this beautiful house. For a period of time the house was rented and was occupied by a succession of Forest Service families. It remained in Young ownership until 1953 when it was purchased by Fred and Lucille Varney. Since then it has become associated with the making of candy, for Mr. Varney is a well-known candy maker who has converted a portion of the house into a special kitchen for the production of fine candies.

The house is constructed of redwood lumber which was shipped down the Pacific Coast to San Francisco from Eureka. The lumber was then shipped by water up the Sacramento River to Red Bluff where it was loaded on freight wagons to be transported to Weaverville. The house is a nicely proportioned cross-gable structure with shiplap siding. Shingle work has been applied to the attic peaks. Decorative windows (one a circle and the other a triangle) are placed in the prominent gable peaks. A flat-roofed porch extends out from the front gable marking the entrance. Matching balustrades enclose this porch and its roof. A large lawn and yard with many roses and old apple trees surround the house and a lovely diamond-top, square picket fence encloses it.

Site 40. Issac Woodbury House

This house at 313 Court Street is one of Weaverville's oldest houses for it, reportedly, was built in the late 1850's or early 1860's. It was first known as the Issac Woodbury house. The Woodburys were early miners in the Garden Gulch and Ten Cent Gulch areas of Weaverville. Although the house has been extensively reconditioned, it is of importance because it is one of two old houses remaining on the upper end of Court Street. Of architectural interest is the rare stick work in the gable end as well as the large visible cellar beneath the elevated porch. The present gable porch across the front is not part of the original house and makes it less identifiable as a "vintage" house.

Site 41. Junkans House (Van Matre House)

The Van Matre House at 318 Taylor Street is one of the oldest houses in Weaverville. It was built in 1859 by F. A. Buck as his residence and soon after became the Karl Junkans house. It has remained in the family ever since. His granddaughter, Karlyn Junkans Van Matre, together with her husband W. P. Van Matre, are the present owners.

Although additions have been made to the rear of the building the original portion of the house has retained its architectural integrity. The original windows in this one-story, high-gable, clapboard structure are of 6/6 double hung sash with a complex triangular lintel above. Where windows have been enlarged these unique triangular lintels have been duplicated on a larger scale. The original shakes are still in place under a metal roof which is of interest because it is of flat, non-corrugated metal fashioned from old mining flume material.

Behind the house is a workshop building, part of an old corral, and a barn. The barn sits astride the property line for, originally, the Junkans family owned three contiguous lots and it made little difference where the barn was placed. The presence of the old corral and the barn are reminders of earlier days when homeowners in the middle of town ran cattle and kept farm animals.

The large yard and the fact that the house sits well back off the street contribute to the "old historic" atmosphere of this home.

Site 41. The Van Matre house was built in the late 1850's for Karl Junkans, grandfather of Karlyn Van Matre. The house sits back on the lot at 318 Taylor Street.

Site 42. Davis Barns (Trimble Barns)

The Trimble Barns are at 311 Garden Gulch. There is a one and one-half story horse barn as well as a two-story barn which has an attractive high, open shed across half of the front. There is also a corrugated metal shed nearby. The larger structures have vertical wood siding. These three structures were built about 1900 by Dave Davis and are crowded onto what was the back of the Davis property (the present Schofield property at 314 Taylor Street). They are typical of the small barns that went with many of the Weaverville homes at the turn of the century. Part of this complex sheltered the family cow as there were no dairies in the county at that time. The property was later sold to the Trimble family; a daughter, Dorothy (Trimble) Schofield, and her husband Glenn are the present owners.

Site 43. Ed Todd House (Nilssen House)

The Todd House, 312 Taylor Street, was built in 1880 and was owned by M. F. Griffin, one of Weaverville's most prominent citizens. He was County Clerk and owner of the Weaverville Drug Store as well as owner of a banking and brokerage business. The house was sold by Griffin's widow in 1888 to Eliza Todd who gave the house as a wedding present to her son Ed about five years later. It stayed in the Todd family until recently when it was purchased by Dr. William Nilssen.

It is basically a Greek Revival house with several special details not usually found in Trinity houses of that style. It has a recessed door with paneling on the sides of the jamb. It has molded trim detail around the windows and is the only house in the county with a full label lintel. Its porch posts have fancy capitals and a transom is above the all wood door. Unfortunately, time and neglect have deteriorated this beautiful old home.

Site 44. Goetze House

The Goetze house, 313 Taylor Street, is a large two-story Queen Anne Victorian which has remained in the Goetze family since it was built in 1897. It was built for H. W. Goetze soon after he moved to Weaverville from Lewiston, where he had been a rancher. His ranch properties included land that now comprises the Trinity Alps Resort. Besides his ranching activities, Mr. Goetze ran a butcher shop in Lewiston and operated a sawmill which was located along Grass Valley Creek in the vicinity of Buckhorn Mountain on Highway 299. Lumber from this mill was hauled by oxen to Weaverville for the construction of this house. This sawmill also provided lumber for many of the other homes in Weaverville. It is interesting to note that the contractor who built this house was paid $2.50 per day and his helpers received $1.50 per day.

This house also became the home of the Goetze's son, Bill, who brought his bride, Clara, to live here when they were married in 1905. Bill, like his father and grandfather before him, also ran a butcher shop. His bride was the daughter of John Boyce who is especially remembered because he was the stagecoach driver during the famous Ruggles Brothers holdup of the Weaverville to Redding stage in 1892. He was also a rancher and later became sheriff and proprietor of a livery stable located on Weaverville's Main Street near its junction with what is now Trinity Lakes Blvd. Clara Goetze spent many years in her lovely home. She is now 96 and was able to take care of herself in her own house until just last year (1980).

This home with its large yard and picket fence is an excellent reminder of Weaverville at the turn of the century.

Site 44. The Goetze house was built in 1897 and is a Taylor Street landmark. This house was built with lumber from the Goetze Sawmill on Grass Valley Creek.

Site 45. Schall House (John Cummings House)

This one and one-half story, high-gable structure with a veranda porch running the full length of the front was built in 1875 by Louis Schall. Mrs. Schall was a midwife in the community. Among the babies she delivered was her daughter's son, Bill Goetze, a lifetime resident of Trinity County who lived next door during the last 60 years of his life. Many well-known Trinity County families have lived in this house over the years. Among them have been the John Cummings, Larkin and Stookey families and for many years it was rented to a succession of Forest Service families. Mae (Van Matre) Browning also lived in this house for awhile. It was she who was responsible for additions to the house in the 1960's.

Sycamore trees shade the house. These contrast with the more common black locust trees which are so typical in the historic area of Weaverville. The Schall house is located at 307 Taylor Street.

Site 46. McDonald House (Caton House) (Borden House)

In 1877, the house located at 306 Taylor Street was owned by John Blackwell. It was deeded to George Blackwell in 1887 and B. M. McDonald acquired it in 1898. Louise and Antone Caton purchased the property from the McDonald family in 1917. Their daughter, Louise Caton Borden, and her husband Bill have restored the house, board by board in recent years. Tony Caton owned and operated the Mountain Market, a butcher shop located adjacent to the Court House where the state highway now runs.

The house is a low, cozy, little "T"-shaped building, a fence of diamond-top square pickets separates the tiny front yard from the sidewalk. There are old fruit trees at the rear of the house and a large lawn area stretches beyond the house in back.

Site 47. Rudy Junkans House (Paulsen House) (Lowden House)

The construction date of the house located at 302 Taylor Street is estimated to have been in the 1870's. It is a two-story gable structure with lean-to additions in keeping with other houses nearby which were built about the same time. Its original owner is not known but over the years a number of well-known families occupied the home. Among the early occupants were Rudy Junkans and his wife, Agnes (Weinheimer) Junkans. He was proprietor of one of the town's leading mercantile establishments. Superior Judge D. A. Paulsen and his wife, Jennie (Skinner) Paulsen, also lived in this house for many years. Judge Paulsen became Grand Master of the Masonic Grand Lodge of California. Following the Paulsens the house became the home of County Surveyor and Planning Commissioner Harley Lowden who lived here until his death in 1977. His wife, Irene, still resides here.

A cross-hatch lath fence in the backyard and a picket fence along the street sets the house apart from its neighbors.

Site 48. Chadbourne House (Bergin House) (Tye House)

This small residence was built sometime between March 1877 (when Clarissa Chadbourne received the patent for the land) and March 1888 (when the Trinity Journal tells of a small fire occurring at this house which is located at the corner of Court and Taylor Streets). The house was later purchased by Sheriff G. H. Bergin and his wife, Alafaire Cademartori. The Bergins renovated the house in 1927, hiring, as the Journal wrote, "a force of carpenters to renovate the old Bergin house". At this time the front gable was added.

Architecturally, the house is of importance for, in spite of its 1927 remodel-

Site 45. The Schall house with its veranda porch running the full length of the front was built in 1875. It is located at 307 Taylor Street.

Site 47. Construction of this home on Taylor Street dates back to the 1870's. It has been the home of many well-known Weaverville families. It is now the home of Irene Lowden.

ing, the middle gable section is an example of the older construction and materials. It is part of a group of houses in the Court Street district which are visually compatible and historically significant.

Other owners of this residence have been Wade Wilson (he was editor of the Trinity Journal), Harry and Lila Adams (she was County Librarian), Edwin and Julia Regan (he was District Attorney at the time) and the Van Zee family (he built Weaverville's present sawmill). In 1959 it was purchased by Fred and Elsie Tye when they moved to Weaverville from their ranch in the Big Bar area.

Site 49. Colbert House (Bowler House) (Wallace House) (Hartland House)

The house at 210 Court Street is one of few very old houses in Weaverville that has a two-story plan. It is estimated that it was built about 1856. One of the early owners was the Colbert family but by 1877 it was under the ownership of Albert Bowler who received the patent on the property in that year. Mr. Bowler was a well-known night watchman in Weaverville as well as constable. In the 1860's he was District Assessor. Over the years the house has been used as a doctor's office and as a dentist's office. For many years it was the home of the A. J. Wallace family. It was bought by Floyd and Sarah Hartland in 1956.

The predominant feature of this two-story, high-gable house is its narrow width in proportion to its height. Even a lean-to addition to the east side of the building does not appreciably affect its unique proportions. The building has not been substantially altered although changes have taken place such as the installation of metal roofing over the original shakes and the addition of a new lean-to porch on the west side as well as new sliding glass doors and a new metal frame window at the entrance.

Site 49. This house on Court Street was built before 1860. The predominant feature of this house is its narrow width in proportion to its height.

Site 50. Blake House (A. L. Paulsen House) (Brown House)

The house at 208 Court Street is one of the oldest houses in Weaverville and over the years has been the home of many of the town's most prominent citizens. It is an outstanding example of a pioneer residential house. The original hand-split plank siding is still in place in the central portion of the house. It was built between 1860 and 1863 when Dr. H. M. Chauncey had his office here. Earlier Dr. Chauncey had run a hotel and stage stop at the south end of the Weaver Basin. Dr. Chauncey sold the property to Eliza Loots, widow of a town blacksmith, in 1869. In 1883 Dr. S. L. Blake purchased the building. He was owner of the Trinity Journal, part owner of Blake and Reed Dry Goods Store, and also a practicing physician. His office was located in the present west wing which, in his time, was detached from the main building. This wing had been built between 1877 and 1883 when Dr. Blake had it moved four feet away from the main building to serve as his office.

The next owner was A. L. Paulsen. At the time the Paulsen family lived here the detached wing had been joined to the main house. In 1920 Mr. Paulsen sold to B. R. Brown who was the superintendent of the LaGrange Mine and for sixteen years a County Supervisor. John Boyce, Trinity County Sheriff, later became the owner. The present owners are Hazel Lane and Maxine Dudley who purchased the house in 1981 and have renovated it to its original style.

It is a one-story pioneer house to which additions have been made over the years. The pattern created by these additions is a unique feature of the house. Because of these various additions there is a series of roofs consisting of high and low gables—both center and offset types. Besides the west wing, the original carriage house has been attached to the back of the building. A neat diamond-top, square picket fence frames the well-kept front yard.

Site 51. Oberdeener House (Andy Moore House)

Although the exact year of construction of the house at 206 Court Street is not known, it is presumed that it dates from the 1860's since it is known that in 1868 the Oberdeener family lived in a house on this lot. There have been other owners over the years. One of its owners was Van Young who rented it to Ernest Chapman, long-time County Coroner. A Dr. Osborne used it as a doctor's office at one time, and it was used as a dentist's office by Dr. L. C. Moore in the 1930's. The present owner is Andy Moore who purchased it in 1955.

This house has not been appreciably altered and is interesting because it does not have a Greek Revival style architecture as do many of its Weaverville contemporaries. The house is built directly off the sidewalk with no provision for a front yard; however, there is a side yard enclosed with a picket fence.

Site 52. Paulsen House (Marshall House)

The Marshall House, 202 Court Street, is a fine example of the Greek Revival style of architecture. Its construction date is estimated to have been in the early 1870's, for records show that the house was patented by James A. S. Jones in March, 1877. Jones was a carpenter by trade, but whether or not he was the builder of this house has not been documented.

Peter Paulsen, proprietor of the adjacent Union Hotel, acquired the house from Jones' estate in February, 1886. The Trinity Journal of the 23rd of that month reveals that Paulsen "has been of late finishing the building he recently purchased . . . and will soon occupy it as a family residence." After Peter's death in 1913 and his wife Anna's death in 1921, it passed to C. A. and Jennie Paulsen. C. A. Paulsen was a lawyer who later became District Attorney and then an outstanding Superior Court judge. In his early years he had his office in this house. Robert and Agnes Marshall purchased the property in 1935.

This house has a symmetrical facade with the main door centered between two windows off the hip roof porch which runs the length of the west side of the building. The main doorstep to the porch is directly off the sidewalk. A new addition, in the form of an extension of the north gable, has recently been added at the rear of the house. The giant black locust trees which line the sidewalk were planted about the same time that the house was built. These and the picket fenced yard help make this a fine example of an historic Weaverville home.

Site 53. United States Bakery (Greenwood's)

Greenwood's is a one and one-half story clapboard structure with a high cross-gable roof which is met below by a lean-to veranda roof extending the full length of one side. The original building that stood on this site at the corner of Court and Center Streets was destroyed by fire on April 13, 1873. It was rebuilt without delay and the U. S. Bakery which had been in business since 1856 reopened in the new building on June 28th. Old records show that "on June 11, 1873 a fund raising dance was held in the building which still had no inside partitions." Besides the bakery the building also housed a saloon. It continued to house the U. S. Bakery until August, 1885. Mr. Fred Lachemacher was the first owner followed by a succession of owners and a variety of usages. It has been used both as living quarters and for office space. The "Trinity 1975" suggests that a Methodist Church, a school and the District Attorney's office have all occupied this property at one time or another.

Architecturally its most important features are the board and batten siding on a portion of the building, for it was unusual for any early residence in Weaverville to use board and batten siding especially in combination with the somewhat fancier shelf lintels and shipsills. Although the foundation is primarily wooden piers set on rocks, there is a section of it along the north wall where a brick foundation was installed at an early date. This is also an important feature of this house as brick foundations were rarely used for residences.

Site 54. Hall House (Given House) (Regan House)

A lithograph print showing Weaverville in 1852 shows the name Hocker on a building at this site. It is known that Henry Hocker secured the patent to the property in 1877. Francesca Clifford was the owner when a two-story house on this spot burned to the ground on May 12, 1897. Mrs. Clifford did not rebuild but deeded the land to her grandchildren, who sold it to H. W. Goetze in 1900. Later that same year Daniel James Hall purchased it and the next year built the present house on the lot which in now 217 Court Street. Mr. Hall was a lawyer and Trinity County District Attorney. He made this his home until 1908 when he sold it to Horace R. Given. Mr. Given was also a lawyer and became District Attorney. Three years after this death in 1935 the house was purchased by Julia and Edwin J. Regan. Mr. Regan, like the previous occupants, was also a lawyer and a District Attorney. He was later elected State Senator for Trinity and Shasta Counties and served as Associate Justice of the State Appelate Court.

The Givens were living in this house during the heydey of the LaGrange Mine. They gave many gala parties in this beautiful home for visiting mining executives. The Victorian loveliness of this house has been maintained over the years. Julia Regan was especially interested in retaining the early charm of the house and took great care in its restoration.

Site 51. This home which was built flush with the sidewalk and dates back to the 1860's is located on Court Street.

Site 55. The original home on this lot was destroyed by fire on May 12, 1897, along with all the other buildings on the same side of Court Street. It is now the home of the Frank Hicks family.

Site 54. The Regan House on Court Street was built in 1901 for Daniel Hall. It has always been the home of attorneys.

The house is a complex Queen Anne Victorian and is the best example of this style of architecture in Weaverville. Its complexity is indicated by the roof line which begins in the center as a truncated hip roof with a widow's walk. Gables, bay windows, a front veranda with a turret roofed gazebo built into its corner, and balustrades decorating the widow's walk and upstairs porch all contribute to the architectural complexity of this lovely home.

The lot within the ivy covered fence once was the site of the home and office of Dr. J. C. Montague. This property was later acquired by Mrs. Jennie Tatum and upon her death was purchased by the Regans.

Site 55. Bowie House (Ruhser House) (Hicks House)

This two-story, T-plan, high-gable Queen Anne Victorian house replaced the Leavitt house which stood on this lot and had been destroyed by fire on May 12, 1897, when fire had destroyed all the houses on the south side of Court Street. After the fire the land was purchased by James Bowie, then County Sheriff. He built the present house that same year, using lumber acquired from the Jumper and Morris sawmill. In 1928 it was sold to Fred W. and Ella M. Ruhser. It was while the Ruhsers lived here that the garage and woodshed were built. Mr. Ruhser died in 1932 and his widow began renting the house to whomever happened to be renting the Weaverville Drug Store. Frank Hicks, Sr. was one of the druggists who lived in this house. He eventually purchased the home that is now occupied by his son Frank Hicks, Jr. and his family.

The house, which is located at 219 Court Street, has two gable dormers facing the street as well as a square bay window and a veranda porch across the front. Geometric shingles decorate all of the gable ends.

Site 56. Balch House (Wallace House) (Jotter House) (Blaney House)

The Blaney House at 221 Court Street is a T-plan, high-gable, Queen Anne Victorian house which possesses many delightful and surprising details conceived by its builder, John Whitmore. These include the shingle pattern in the gable (a progression of geometric shapes), exquisite molding around doors and windows, and a wonderful rhythm and tempo on the long west wall with ins and outs, bay windows, and dormers all projecting at different heights and levels.

The original home on this lot was destroyed by fire on May 12, 1897, along with all of the other buildings on the same side of Court Street. It had belonged to James R. Balch, the operator of a dry goods store in the community and the one who obtained the original patent to the land. The present house was rebuilt in 1897 shortly after the fire. Mrs. Balch lived upstairs where she also ran a millinery shop. The downstairs was the dental office of Dr. W. H. LaBarre whose wife was the Balch's daughter.

In 1908 the property was purchased by Mark Manley, a mining man instrumental in attracting eastern capital to the Trinity mines. Subsequent owners have been the Wallace and Jotter families as well as the present owners, the Blaney family, for it was purchased by John and Bessie Blaney in 1922. John J. Blaney and, later, his son James were Weaverville postmasters for many years. Their daughter, Ruth (Blaney) Mitchell, is the present owner of this house in which she has lived most of her life. She was born in the Greenwood house, a few doors down the street.

The Blaney house is the ultimate in Queen Anne subtlety and dignity. It stands in marked contrast to a giant Sequoia tree growing on the east side of the house. This tree is known to have been planted in the 1920's, for it was

Site 56. The Blaney Home on Court Street is a Queen Anne Victorian house which possesses many delightful and surprising details.

planted by E. V. Jotter when he was Forest Supervisor of the Trinity National Forest during that period.

Site 57. Catholic Church (St. Patrick's)

Five Catholic churches have occupied this site. The first, built in 1853, burned in 1858. Fires in 1866, 1896, and 1923 destroyed subsequent churches built on the site. The present structure, built in 1924, is a one-story, gable building with shiplap siding behind a false front with a steeple entry. The top of the false front is formed like battlements and a gable roof covers the steeple. This is an unusual structure for it contrasts markedly with the many New England type, Greek Revival gable buildings which dominate this section of Weaverville. The land on the north side of the church has been used as a cemetery since 1851.

Site 58. Chapman House

This house was built for Ernest and Cora Chapman, respected old-timers. He was a member of the Chapman family that had mined and ranched in the Junction City area since the 1850's. Mr. Chapman, in his early years, was a well-known freight team driver and later served as County Coroner for many years.

This house, which is located at 208 Center Street, was constructed in 1930 by Jinks Wilson and his son Roy on the site of a previous house. When built this house blended in well with the older houses nearby but, as of this printing, it has been considerably remodelled and bears little resemblance to its original style.

Site 57. This 1858 Catholic Church was destroyed by fire. At least four church buildings have occupied this site. The cemetery beside it is the oldest in Weaverville.

Site 59. The Barnickel house was built in the 1880's and is located on the hill above Center Street.

Site 59. Barnickel House

The Barnickels were old-time druggists who ran the Weaverville Drug Store for two generations. Their house, located behind the drugstore at 216 Center Street, was considered one of the most fashionable in town around the turn of the century. Its construction date is estimated to be in the 1880's. It is one of three old houses forming a row on the north end of Center Street. It sits high above the street behind a fancy picket fence giving it an imposing look. In the past, its yard of old trees and lovely roses made it one of the beauty spots of the town.

Although the Barnickel house is a basic pioneer type structure, certain details such as a swagged and beaded front door, 1/1 windows, hipped picket fence and elaborate shelf lintels suggest that the building has been dressed up over the years.

Site 60. Louis Todd House (Whitteberry House)

This house, historically known as the Lou Todd House, has been known as the Whitteberry House for it was the home of Jack and Sybil Whitteberry for many years. Lou Todd, who was the first owner, was brother of Ed Todd who lived in a house on Taylor Street. His sister Emma (Todd) (Greenwell) Miller operated the Snug Restaurant at one time as well as the New York and Union Hotels.

This house is located at 222 Center Street and was probably built around 1875-1880. Although it is an unpainted structure it is probably in a better state of repair than other old houses on either side of it. It is a simple one-story, high-gable structure with a hip roof veranda across the front gable end and a lean-to porch along the south side and across the back. There is a board and batten, gable roof barn as well as a woodshed at the rear of the property. This house and the others which form a row on the east side of Center Street sit on lots which rise sharply from the street. The houses are reached by a steep climb of wooden steps.

Site 61. Abrahms House (Gribble House) (Hannon House)

The Abrahms House at 230 Center Street is adjacent to two similar houses making this a good example of what an 1870's Trinity County neighborhood must have been like. The house was built in 1878 shortly after Isaac Abrahms had received an 1877 patent to the land. Abrahms, a native of Prussia, was an early Trinity pioneer who was best known for his general merchandise business which he ran in partnership with Samuel Karsky. Isaac's son, Morris Abrahms, followed his father in the family business and lived in the house until 1905. Other owners have been the Gribble family and the Gibson family.

It is essentially a pioneer style dwelling with a cross-gable, Greek Revival wing which has been added on the south side. The house is clapboard with fine roof detailed in the boxed cornice, returns and frieze. There is a symmetrical arrangement of the doors and windows which have a continuous trim with recessed triangular lintels. Because it has not been modernized this house could serve as a prototype for the style if it is not allowed to further deteriorate.

Site 62. John Meckel House (Adams House)

This house on the east side of Center Street originally belonged the the John Meckel family who were prominent citizens and the proprietors of the famous brewery nearby on Main Street. It is the best preserved Greek/Gothic structure in the county. Construction is estimated to have been in the 1860's-1870's. Even though it has been somewhat encroached upon by new construction it remains a vintage house because of its good condition and unaltered details. Its special characteristics include a gothic lancet window in the center of the attic; original shutters, returns and molded cornice; large porch posts and capitals; and a symmetrical entry lined with boxwood.

Site 63. The Cooper's Shop (Historic District Lot 44—Block 9)

The small wooden building on Center Street behind the lot now occupied by the Montgomery Ward building is part of the complex of buildings that went with the Pacific Brewery of Meckel Brothers. The Cooper's shop was in the building and had a bedroom partitioned off at one end. The building and the locust trees shading it both probably date from right after the fire of 1874.

Site 64. Henry Junkans House (Fred Haas House)

This house on Center Street was originally known as the Henry Junkans House. Junkans was a prominent Weaverville businessman. Henry Junkans and his brothers, William and Karl, were members of an important Trinity family. Later, the house was purchased by Fred Haas, a well-known mining man and owner of the Haas Claim near Junction City.

The house was built in the 1860's-1870's and although it is still basically sound, this once handsome house is badly in need of care and maintenance. The building is architecturally significant in age and detail. It is a rectangular, Greek Gothic, medium-gable, clapboard structure with a veranda along the north and west sides. It has plain boxed cornices, returns, and porch posts with 3-tier molded capitals. The 6/6 windows and door have plain trim with triangular lintels. This building has the potential of being an historically important house.

96

Site 65. Meckel Rental (David Fields House)

The Trinity Journal of Nov. 23, 1901, reported that the "Meckel brothers have started building a house on the lot opposite the Haas residence." The Meckels, who lived nearby on Center Street, built it as a rental. Frank Smith, operator of a dry goods store on Main Street, was one of the earlier occupants, as was the Royal Trimble family. Mr. Trimble was Trinity County's first highway patrol officer. For a number of years it was the home of David Fields.

This house is a small shiplap cottage with some Victorian-type detail such as the porch posts which are carved to meet in the center with a medallion as well as the arrowhead pickets on the fence. Two gable outbuildings, one an outhouse and the other a woodshed, are located at the rear of the house. The house has not been altered.

Site 66. Old Young House (Meckel House)

This house, sitting on the hill at 502 Center Street, was built for the Frank Young family in 1876 following a fire which destroyed the original home on the property. Frank Young was a pioneer from Rhode Island who came west during the gold rush, arriving in Trinity County in 1851. He ran the Bank Exchange and served as a notary public and insurance agent. In 1861 Frank married Mary Elisa Bayles, a member of a prominent Hayfork family that operated the county's major grist mill. The Youngs had eight children, some of whom occupied important roles in the community. Descendants of this pioneer family still live in Trinity County and the house has passed from one family member to another over the years. Frank and Mary's daughter, Lucy, inherited it in 1926 after her parents had died. Upon Lucy's death in 1939 it was purchased from the other heirs by her brother, Van B. Young. After Van's death in 1947, ownership passed to his wife, Annie. It is now the home of Henry C. Meckel, Annie's nephew.

This house has a spectacular setting on a large grassy knoll overlooking the town. It is surrounded by a long hipped picket fence and shaded by giant oak trees. The house itself was modernized following a fire that destroyed the second story. Basically it is a white clapboard gable structure with 8-pane casement windows and plain trim on the surviving facade. All of the basic original structure remains but additions have recently been added to the rear. The house still maintains an important visual place among the town's historic buildings.

Site 67. Mulligan House (Marshall House)

In 1865 Michael Mulligan built this building at 216 Trinity Lakes Blvd. for the Finian Brotherhood, forerunner of the Irish Republican Army. The building later became a residence when William O. Wallace purchased it for his mother and sister. Though not outstanding architecturally, the Mulligan House is a good example of the basic pioneer style. It is a one-story, high-gable, rectangular structure with a shed roof porch across the front and along a portion of the west side. It sits in a large yard with old fruit trees and berry vines. Although its maintenance has been neglected, it has an historic appeal for it is the only old house on this stretch of the highway. Agnes and Bob Marshall are the present owners and use it as a rental.

Site 68. Chinese Tong War Site

A marker on Trinity Lakes Blvd. on the Weaverville Elementary School grounds commemorates the historic battle at Five Cent Gulch between two rival Chinese associations or "tongs"—the Hong Kongs and the Cantons. Al-

Site 43. The Ed Todd house was constructed in 1880 and was once a showplace.

Site 67. The Mulligan House on Trinity Lakes Boulevard was built in 1865 for the Finian Brotherhood forerunner of the Irish Republican Army.

though these tongs were established to offer protection and security to the Chinese in the new world, the rivalries that had existed in the old country had remained. Disputes over mining rights became especially bitter. After one of the Cantons was killed by a shot fired by a Hong Kong during an argument over the ownership of a sluice, the Cantons challenged the Hong Kongs to a battle. Many of the Weaverville townspeople became involved in this battle which took place in 1854. Blacksmiths throughout the area were kept busy fashioning wicked, barbaric weapons of war resembling an overgrown salmon spear. Bets were placed and the Chinese were encouraged and goaded into action by the "Whites" who were eager to witness a pitched battle between the two groups. When both "armies" met on the predetermined battleground neither tong was anxious to take the offensive. It was the proddings of the "Whites" which finally started the fighting which lasted but ten minutes but which resulted in the death of several Chinese from both sides. The Cantons buried their dead the next day at the south end of town near what is now the Trinity Alps Golf Course. The Hong Kongs were buried in a cemetery in China Gulch just a few hundred yards above the intersection of Sidney and China Gulches. It is believed that about 700 Chinese participated in this Weaverville "war" and that about 1200 white miners from various parts of the county and from Shasta gathered to witness the scrap. Relics of this "war" may be seen in the Trinity County Museum in Weaverville.

It is estimated that there were about 2000 Chinese in Trinity County at the time. They lived in several Chinatowns throughout the mining areas. Their homes were largely temporary shelters located along the creeks and rivers. Permanent homes were not established for there were very few women and children. The men had come to the gold fields hoping to quickly gain their fortune and to soon return to China.

Site 68. Jake Jackson, Weaverville historian, helped set up a 1920's display of Chinese artifacts from the Tong War in the old Memorial Hall. Note the vicious instruments of warfare used in this 1854 conflict.

Site 97. The Chinese Masonic Hall was crushed by snow in the winter of 1949-50. The Shell station was located north of the hall at the extreme right of the picture.

Shortly after the war the Shasta Courier received a letter from three Chinese men who came up from San Francisco to investigate the cause of this war. The results of their investigation were published in the Shasta Courier of August 5, 1854, and give a different version as to its cause:

In April of 1854 the Hong-Kong and the Canton men became the joint proprietors of a public gaming house in Weaverville. In June a Chinaman belonging to the Yong-Wa Company was playing against the bank at a table kept in this house by a Canton man when a dispute arose as to who was the winner of a small stake (less than a dollar). The Hong-Kong man snatched the money from the table and ran into the street, pursued by the owner of the table. A squabble ensued in which several engaged on each side but no considerable injury by any of them. The Yong-Wa Company took the side in favor of their companion, and the others sided against him.

From this small beginning a very serious quarrel grew up. Taunts, threats and challenges were sent by the Yong-Wa Company, and that company began to prepare arms. They frequently came in front of the houses of the Canton men and dared them to fight. The others prepared arms, and the result was the fight of which the community are already advised.

Signed by Ha-Sing, Ge-Ti, Ah-Ching

Not all of the weapons were made in Weaverville. The Sacramento Union had an article which said that several hundred of them were being manufactured there for this fight and described the weapons in detail.

Site 69. Lowden Park

The Lowden Park land of 20.74 acres was originally owned by the Lowden family and was sold to the county for $1,122 in 1937, along with an eighth interest in the town's water ditch. For years it was known only as The Ball Park. The high school used the field for track meets as well as an outdoor physical education field and baseball diamond when the school had no playing field. The town team had used the ball park for many years before that time. During the 1920's, with the building of Highway 299, most of the actual labor of highway construction was done by convicts from Folsom and San Quentin prisons. The men lived in highway convict camps that were moved as the road progressed. Many of these convicts were excellent baseball players. During the time they were camped near Weaverville, it was not uncommon for the convicts to play name teams from Sacramento and other valley towns in the field at Lowden Park on a Sunday afternoon. Ball fans from miles around gathered to enjoy these exciting games! During the depression days of the 1930's, the ball park and surrounding area became the "tent city" of Weaverville. W.P.A. jobs paid $30 a month and many people came to this county from the cities, hoping to find a job or to do a little mining. Either mining or W.P.A. work provided a family with food and enabled them to "get by" if they camped out. Whenever the Forest Service needed firefighters, the ball park residents provided a most willing crew.

During the late 1930's, the Boy Scout House was built in Lowden Park, to be followed by a community kitchen. During the 1940's and 1950's the rodeo grounds and grandstands, a caretaker's home, barbecue pit and picnic area were established. Years ago, the Cattail Reservoir was on park property and furnished water for the lower end of town. A small swimming pond was dug on one side of this reservoir around 1920. During the late 1930's, a larger, better swimming hole was dug near East Weaver Creek on the other side of the park. Finally, after the Weaverville-Douglas City Recreation District was formed, Lowden Park acquired a new, fenced-in heated pool, with dressing rooms. A Little League ball park was added, as well as tennis courts. At present, the park includes a playground for small children, a recreation hall and teen-center.

Many happy events take place in this pleasant park under the pines. It pays tribute to the foresight and generosity of the Lowden family, especially H. L. "Hank" Lowden. The park improvements have been provided by many generous and hardworking, dedicated citizens who have seen the need for this delightful area that serves all ages. The California Department of Forestry has a fire-control station at the north end of the park, adding to the park's security. Lowden Park is used all year, but the days of the Fourth of July celebration are the busiest times of all.

Site 70. Costa House

The present Costa House at 211 Washington Street was built by George and Frank Costa in 1929 to replace the old home place which had burned. The old home place had included not only a residence but a slaughterhouse and gunsmith shop as well. The present building is a basic pioneer style, high-gable structure with a veranda on two sides. An outhouse is attached to one of the

100

verandas and there are several sheds nearby. It is surrounded by a small horse pasture which is enclosed by a barbed wire fence. It is an excellent example of the rural character of so many of the early Weaverville homes.

The Weaverville Historic District

The Weaverville Historic District was added to the National Register of Historic Places on October 14, 1971. Sites beginning with the Courthouse (Site 71) and ending with Morris Hardware (Site 116) make up the Weaverville Historic District.

An early 1900's photo of lower Main Street showing the Congregational church built in 1891 and its parsonage built in 1902.

WEAVERVILLE HISTORIC DISTRICT

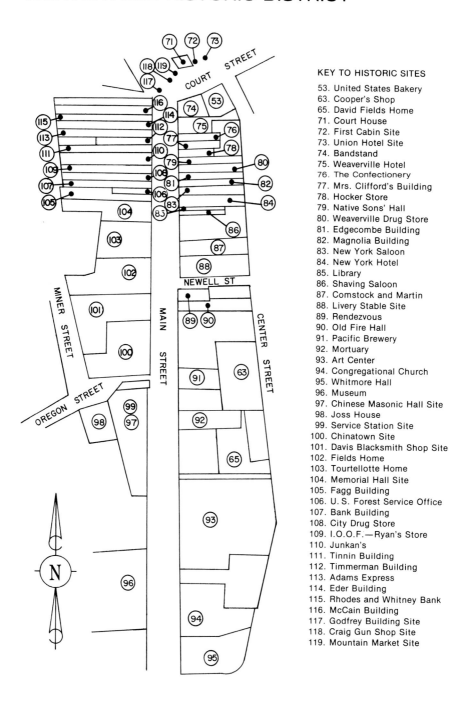

KEY TO HISTORIC SITES

53. United States Bakery
63. Cooper's Shop
65. David Fields Home
71. Court House
72. First Cabin Site
73. Union Hotel Site
74. Bandstand
75. Weaverville Hotel
76. The Confectionery
77. Mrs. Clifford's Building
78. Hocker Store
79. Native Sons' Hall
80. Weaverville Drug Store
81. Edgecombe Building
82. Magnolia Building
83. New York Saloon
84. New York Hotel
85. Library
86. Shaving Saloon
87. Comstock and Martin
88. Livery Stable Site
89. Rendezvous
90. Old Fire Hall
91. Pacific Brewery
92. Mortuary
93. Art Center
94. Congregational Church
95. Whitmore Hall
96. Museum
97. Chinese Masonic Hall Site
98. Joss House
99. Service Station Site
100. Chinatown Site
101. Davis Blacksmith Shop Site
102. Fields Home
103. Tourtellotte Home
104. Memorial Hall Site
105. Fagg Building
106. U. S. Forest Service Office
107. Bank Building
108. City Drug Store
109. I.O.O.F.—Ryan's Store
110. Junkan's
111. Tinnin Building
112. Timmerman Building
113. Adams Express
114. Eder Building
115. Rhodes and Whitney Bank
116. McCain Building
117. Godfrey Building Site
118. Craig Gun Shop Site
119. Mountain Market Site

Site 71. Hocker Building—Trinity County Courthouse (Block 12; Lots 1, 2, 3)

This three-story brick Courthouse building was constructed for Henry Hocker during 1856-57, to be used as a store, office building and hotel. The Apollo Saloon opened on the ground floor soon after the building was completed. (Trinity County's first piano, weighing over 600 pounds, was transported on a one-horse cart over the old trail from Shasta County before a wagon road was built to Weaverville. The piano was for use in the Apollo Saloon.) The Hocker building was made of locally fashioned bricks. The roof was of flat tin sheets, seamed and soldered together. Inside walls were covered with lime plaster over hand-split lath.

Trinity County's first courthouse had been a dilapidated three-story wooden structure, sitting on the hill at the head of Court Street. (The top story of that building was owned and occupied by the Masonic Lodge.) The Grand Jury decided that new quarters were needed and, in 1865, the Hocker building was purchased for $9,000. At this time the lower floor was shared by the Apollo Saloon and the Halleck Riflemen. At first, not all of the building was needed for a courthouse. In 1875 the need changed and the Board of Supervisors ordered all persons occupying the top floor as sleeping apartments and offices to immediately vacate. It was at this time that the porch balcony was added to the front of the building. In 1897 the county supervisors ordered a gravel fill be made at the front of the building, thus covering windows and doors of the lower floor facing Court Street. This fill was topped by a concrete walk. In 1979, this old sidewalk was replaced; when bulldozing was done, the old iron doors and windows were again exposed—for one day only—and immediately recovered with a new fill and sidewalk. Also uncovered at this time were the remains of a buried brick wall and stairway in front of the first story (or basement) of the Courthouse.

In 1934 Highway 299 was routed so as to connect with Main Street at the south side of the Courthouse. This necessitated removing the commercial buildings that stood between the Courthouse and Morris Hardware (then Weaverville Supply). Streetside windows were at this time cut into the south side of the Courthouse.

In 1935 the Courthouse was expanded to the rear, with the addition of new quarters for the Superior Court, Sheriff's office and jail. Previously, the iron jail cells had been in the basement. They are now on display at the Trinity County Museum. In order to remove them, they were painstakingly hacksawed apart and re-assembled in their new location by Historical Society members. In 1958 the space between the old building and the 1935 addition was filled in to provide room for the Board of Supervisors and Justice Court, as well as additional office space.

In 1976 the Sheriff's office and jail moved to new quarters and the rear of the building was again expanded toward Garden Gulch. The front of the building retains its evenly placed upper and lower sets of handsome French doors, flanked by folding iron shutters. The north side of the original building remains much as it always was. Iron shutters, flush with the outside wall, still adorn the windows. These windows now look out on a parking lot filled with cars. Years ago these windows faced Union Street and the Union Hotel. Union Street passed over a Garden Gulch bridge and ended at Court Street.

This Courthouse is one of the oldest in the state of California. It holds the complete records of the county, going back to its very beginning. In addition, it is one of the most imposing buildings of the Historic District.

Site 71. The Trinity County Courthouse is one of the fireproof brick buildings built in Weaverville before 1859. Brick buildings were covered with a foot thick layer of earth between ceiling and metal roof. For additional fire protection iron shutters were attached to the sides of window and door openings. It is not certain whether these iron shutters were made locally or at Red Bluff and packed here by mule.

Site 72. Weaverville's First Cabin Site

The first cabin built in Weaverville is believed to have been at a spot denoted by a marker located at the right of the Courthouse.

Weaverville was officially named and settled on July 8, 1850. The first cabin was built by James Howe, John Weaver and Daniel Bennett. The cabin was made of logs over a dirt floor with a fireplace on the west end. After the cabin was built one of the men wanted to name their fair city. Each wanted his name chosen. Pine needles were drawn. Weaver won by drawing the short one, hence the name Weaverville.

Another version recently came to light when Rita Hanover was researching old Trinity Journals. An article in the paper dated September 17, 1910, states that James Howe, one of the oldest pioneers, was brought to town from Mad River for medical treatment. He had first come to Weaverville in 1850 when the basin was covered with trees and there were only a few log cabins. One belonged to Matt Stewart and occupied the site where the Courthouse now stands. Stewart and Howe were great friends, and in the summer of 1850 they decided to give the place a name. Howe suggested they call it Rich Gulch City, but Stewart thought it should be named after Mr. Weaver who had been the first to enter this wilderness in 1848. Mr. Howe approved, picked up an eight foot long bark slab and wrote Weaverville thereon with charcoal. He then tacked the bark on a tree in front of his bakery shop. The christening took place on August 9, 1850, according to Howe.

Whichever version is correct, the location of the cabin must have been approximately where the marker has been placed. The marker was dedicated by the Native Daughters in 1930.

Site 73. This 1890 picture shows Court Street when the Union Hotel occupied the parking lot next to the Courthouse. The two-story building over Morris Hardware housed the Trinity Journal at this time. (This second story burned off in 1940.)

Site 73. Union Hotel Site (Courthouse Parking Lot)

The Union Hotel, which was in existence as early as 1852, was located next to the first cabin (Site 72.). In 1866, Otto Vollmers, Peter Paulsen and Peter Weise took over the business. In the next two years the hotel was remodeled and enlarged. According to the Trinity Journal, "A fine parlor was added, the table will be well supplied with everything the market of this section affords." The Union Hotel's large dinner bell was given additional use when it was rung as a fire alarm for the town.

After several years P. M. Paulsen bought out his partners. Although Paulsen owned the building, many others took a turn at running the business. In 1908, Bremer and Ackerman, the next year W. A. Neilson, then O. O. Brown, and later W. W. Pitney; each had their turn, P. M. Paulsen died and his son, C. A. Paulsen, took charge and remodeled it in 1914. Between 1917 and 1919, the Union Hotel Moose Club held meetings in the lobby.

Shortly after World War I Sam and Emma Miller bought the place. Sam Miller was killed in 1927 and Mrs. Miller ran the hotel until her death in 1938. The hotel burned the following year, leaving only memories of the grand place it had once been. Several years after the fire the property was purchased by Trinity County from Mrs. Miller's children for use as a parking lot to serve the Courthouse.

Site 74. The Bandstand (Block 9—Lot 40)

The bandstand, located across Court Street from the Courthouse, was built in 1901 with funds raised by public subscription. It was constructed by Thomas McNamara and Edward Yount (who later became head of the State Polytechnic Institute at San Luis Obispo). The bandstand was first painted by Yount's father, George W. Yount, photographer and artist. Before 1853 a saloon occupied this lot. Two years later that building was destroyed by fire.

As early as 1856 a brass band was formed to help fill a need for music in the

Site 74. The Bandstand, built in 1901, is located across the street from the Courthouse. The restoration of this building became Trinity County's official bicentennial project.

community. J. E. Sediak, C. Lenz, J. F. Long, Henry Hoehn, A. M. Kruttschnitt, L. B. Thorp, Fred Walter and Charles Hosp, all members of the Brass Band were becoming well-known for their fine music. There was a building in back of the present courthouse known as the "band room"; they may have met there.

The Trinity Journal carried articles of "a disgraceful hole being left since the fire of 1873 burned the building which covered it". The hole was finally filled with sand and gravel from Woodbury's mine sluice which was then operating in Garden Gulch. In 1877 the county purchased the lot for a public square. Trees were planted and temporary platforms were used. The plaza was soon the focal point for the town's summertime musical and social activities.

It became evident that a permanent bandstand should be built. In 1900 the Ladies' Eltapome Band, under direction of Albert Paulsen, was formed. Paulsen was a grandson of Kruttschnitt, a member of the 1856 Cornet Band. The Eltapome Parlor #55, Native Daughters of the Golden West, sponsored the group. The bandstand was built and the Ladies' Eltapome Band continued until their leader moved away in 1914. During that same time, Paulsen directed the all-male Weaverville Silver Cornet Band. Needless to say, the bandstand was in constant use.

106

During the 1930's the lower portion of this structure was covered with stucco which was popular at that time. Several other buildings in town received this treatment at the same time. Gradually the little bandstand received less use and became neglected. The roof sagged and leaked until it became apparent it would be lost without immediate attention. The Trinity County Historical Society, in conjuction with grants from the Board of Supervisors, sponsored the restoration of the building. This became Trinity County's official bicentennial project. A re-established ladies' band performed in the bandstand on July 4th, 1976. One member of the original Ladies' Eltapom Band (Agnes Weinheimer Junkans) and two members of the Weaverville Silver Cornet Band (Ray Jackson and Clifford Harding) took part in the re-dedication ceremonies that day. Each year since its restoration this building in the Historical District receives more use. It is part of the courthouse complex and the property and surrounding lawn is carefully maintained by Trinity County.

Site 75. Empire Hotel (Weaverville Hotel) (Block 9—Lots 38 and 39)

Weaverville Hotel was originally the Empire. It is an interesting building because fire has played such a role in its history and it is Weaverville's only old hotel still in operation. The ordeal of this building will be recounted to show how it came to be as we see it today.

William Condon, after successfully mining on Sidney Hill above Weaverville for about ten years, started Condon's Saloon here in 1861. After his marriage the enterprise shifted its emphasis and became the Empire Hotel in October, 1863. For a short time Maurice Condon was in partnership with his brother but he soon left and moved to San Francisco.

In April of 1873 a fire started in the hotel kitchen which destroyed the hotel and practically all of upper Main Street, spreading also to Court and Center Streets. The rebuilt Empire burned again in 1880. Condon bought the lot next door so that he had a 45 foot frontage and could have space between the new hotel and what is now The Confectionery. This hotel was a two-story wooden building, 24 by 80 feet, with porches on the first and second stories along the Main and Court Street sides.

There was hotel fire damage again in 1881; Condon was forced to borrow. When Condon died in 1888 Henry Junkans, who held the mortgage, bought the hotel at auction and sold to John Bergin in 1889. Bergin had done very well mining on Oregon Gulch. He left the mines to his three sons, and ran the Empire Hotel. He bought the land where Greenwood's is located from Newman and improved the hotel, squaring the front and digging a cellar. The Empire had a narrow escape from a roof fire in 1890. In 1894 John Bergin died and Mrs. Margaret Bergin managed the hotel. Her daughter Lizzie married J. J. Murphy in 1895 and the Murphys helped her. In 1900 Mrs. Bergin sold to Mrs. George Leavitt of Deadwood. Under the obligation of a four-year mortgage, the hotel reverted to Mrs. Bergin and J. J. Murphy who took over management in 1904. Mrs. Leavitt crossed over to the Union Hotel, which had recently been only a rooming house, and opened up a rival hotel across the street.

In 1907 Mrs. Bergin deeded the hotel to the Murphys. The Murphys had financial troubles, and Murphy went to try the Tonopah Mines in 1910. Foster was manager when a roof fire gutted the top floor. A metal roof was put on and the first floor put back in operation in 1911.

In 1914 Mrs. Bergin died and Murphy's debts were cleared. They then sold to A. J. Fetzer. Fetzer, who had come here as an infant, was a jeweler and watch repairer. He had his home and shop where the Trinity County Title Company is now located.

Site 75. This is an excellent view of what Weaverville looked like at the turn of the century. Weaverville Hotel, on the left, was at the time of this picture the Empire Hotel.

Fetzer and a Chinese carpenter cleaned up the second floor and remodeled the building. The name was changed to Weaverville Hotel in 1916. Fetzers moved into the hotel when Fetzer gave up leasing in 1917. The dining room was abolished and the jewelry shop took the place of the bar. The front door was moved to the center, and show windows resembling four pane bay windows were added.

During thirty years of operating the hotel the Fetzers closed in the Court Street balcony to provide bathrooms for the 12 bedrooms, added steam heat, built a new section on the south side and put in a new lobby. The fireplace in the lobby came from the LaGrange mansion. In the 1930's the front porch roof was removed, the front was squared up hiding the gable, and stucco was added to the Main and Court Street sides.

The building we see now is essentially the Weaverville Hotel of A. J. Fetzer. He sold to the Claude Hollands in 1944. When he gave up his jewelry business, the Hollands put in a sport shop. In 1957 the Ralph Walters became owners, and in 1972 Dave and Emilie Brady took over this fine old building.

Site 76. Nonpareil (Young's) (The Confectionery) (Block 9—Lot 37)

The first recorded establishment on this location was Hart's and Lang's Ten Pin Alley in 1851. The fire of 1853 destroyed the building, and two months later Lang sold the lot to A. G. George who sold to J. B. Karnes. After Karnes' shop burned in 1855 he sold the property to Henry Junkans. Stone's Shoe Shop occupied this lot in 1856 and by 1860 Krohm and Co. had a shoemaker shop here. In 1866 Junkans sold to A. G. Clark. At that time John Wales' shoe shop (known as the Pioneer Shop) occupied the premises. W. L. Hudspeth purchased the property from Clark in 1867. Hudspeth had a tailor shop here until his death in 1891. A. W. McLean bought the building when the estate was settled and opened a confectionery; milkshakes were advertised among the offerings. McLean went out of business in February, 1900.

Site 76. This picture was taken of The Confectionery and the spiral stairway in 1950 just after a run-away lumber truck lost its brakes on Oregon Mountain.

Site 79. The two-story brick Clifford building was built in 1855. This picture was taken in 1933 when the post office occupied downstairs space and the Native Sons and Daughters Hall was upstairs.

In February, 1900, W. W. Young and Mary E. Young, his mother, purchased the building from A. W. McLean. In June, 1900, H. H. Noonan purchased the business and operated a variety store for nearly three years. In January, 1903, the building was deeded to W. W. Young by his mother. It then became known as the W. W. Young Building and had a new roof and new proprietors. The Blaney girls, Rose (Mrs. A. C. Meckel) and Nora (Mrs. D. B. Fields) opened the Nonpareil, selling candy, citrus fruits and toys.

In June, 1904, Charles S. Wilson bought the Nonpareil and moved his one-year-old candy store across from the west side of Main Street, combining the two businesses. In 1906 Henry Young, W. W. Young's youngest brother, joined Charles Wilson as a partner. In 1909 the firm became the agency for Edison Phonographs. In 1912 Wilson drowned in Canyon Creek Lake, and Henry Young continued the business alone. Young's attracted great attention with the addition of a new soda fountain in 1913.

Young's, later known as Henry's Place, had a marble counter and big back bar. It sold candy, tobacco products and notions, and was noted for its ice cream and milkshakes. Young made his own ice cream using a five gallon copper freezer driven by a small gasoline engine.

Henry Young died in 1949 and his wife, Mary, and son, Bob, took over the operation of the store. Soon after, in March, 1950, a runaway lumber truck hit this and four adjacent stores late at night, destroying the front of the seventy year old building. By June, 1950, the Youngs were back in business as Young's Confectionery in a cinder block building with a brick front. The wooden building with its gabled roof, rustic front, and small projecting show windows was gone forever.

After nearly sixty years in business, the Youngs sold the confectionery to

Mr. and Mrs. Elwin Bagley in 1965. In 1966 Fred Varney leased the business. As a former forest fire control officer trained in the family craft of candy-making, Fred's candies had been sold there since 1950. In 1972 Varney decided to retire to his candy kitchen at home. The Bagley's sold to the John Browns, and the business has changed hands twice more, to Angells and then to Carole Vincent and Sandy Tilden.

Site 77. Mrs. Clifford's Building (Blaney Building) (Block 9—Lot 36)

The buildings on this site have been frame buildings; it is probable that this is at least the fourth building on this site, as it is known that the fires of 1873 and 1880 destroyed the Clifford buildings. In 1854 John Adams, watchmaker, was located here. In June, 1857, Richard Clifford moved into his "new store". Clifford was one of Weaverville's leading citizens, a merchant, Wells Fargo representative, sheriff, district attorney, and builder of the two-story brick building two doors down the street. After Clifford died in 1879, Mrs. Francesca Clifford carried on, finally leaving the building to her grandson, Joseph Hocker, in 1914.

In the 1860's the building had been divided into two shops, and seems to have been leased out that way for most of the time. Barbers were frequent users of one of the shops. After the rebuilding in 1873 (with a "modern glass front") Mooney and Smith, harness and shoemakers, were tenants. Barbers included: Thomas Belden, 1879; Benner, burned out in 1880; Adam Klimm, 1881; Weaverville Shaving Saloon sharing with A. Cochell's variety store until 1883; J. A. Wallace, 1913-c.1920; and H. D. Barber, 1923-1928. H. D. Barber, Justice of Peace, purchased the building from the estate of Christian Meckel in 1923 and moved his barbershop here. Judge Barber left the building to the children of his daughter, Mrs. John Blaney.

For about the last fifty years the building's two parts have severed several functions. The left half was occupied by the Weaverville Electric Company and then its successor, California Pacific Utilities. When Cal Pac moved down the street, the Thrift Shop of the American Field Service moved in. The right half was the telephone office for many years. It was first Barnickel's little company and then Snyder's Western Telephone Co. When the telephone company moved to the Magnolia and Edgecombe Buildings, a gift shop (Heffington's), then two jewelers (Roundy's and Rhoades' Gold Nugget), and now an attorney (Gene Maxwell) have used the space.

Site 78. Hocker Building (Title Company) (Block 9—Lot 35)

This building, one of a group of brick buildings to be constructed here in 1854-55, was built by Henry Hocker, who opened his store in the building in June, 1857. By 1861 Cahnbly and Junkans were occupying the property and Hocker had moved to his three-story building up the street (the present Courthouse). In 1863 Junkans and Schuyler were the proprietors here together with Krohn and Company, shoemakers. Then, in 1868 Hocker again moved back into this building.

In 1878 Judge T. E. Jones granted a deed to Henry Hocker, establishing his legal ownership, but by 1881 the property had been acquired at auction by Henry Lorenz. By 1883 the building had been partitioned; Cochell's notions were in the left half and Lefren the jeweler, was in the right half. Morris A. Brady replaced Lefren in 1886 and remained until 1892.

In 1902 A. J. Fetzer, watchmaker, was in the building with his brother, August, a photographer. The building was also the A. J. Fetzer residence until the family moved to the Weaverville hotel in 1917.

In the next fifteen years the building filled three functions. There was a Bigelow butcher shop there for a time. It was used as a movie theater around 1920. The post office, which moved many times, was also in the Hocker store building, probably from 1923 to 1932.

Weaverville had been without a bakery for sometime when Walter Davenport moved here in 1931 and established a bakery in the Hocker building. Later the bakery was sold to Earl Acton. After Acton moved away in 1957, the Leo McGlynns moved their Trinity County Title Company into this building from across the street. Mr. and Mrs. Scott Barrow later purchased the business, and in 1981 sold to Forslund. Dero B. Forslund is the fifth generation of this family to reside in Trinity County. John and Henrietta Conner of Lewiston were his grandparents.

Site 79. Clifford Hall (Lorenz Building) (Native Sons) (Block 9—Lot 34)

This two-story brick building was built by Richard Clifford in 1855. In 1856 the tin, stove and hardware store of S. Markewitz and Bros. was on the lower floor. Later, December, 1856, the county clerk and sheriff had their offices in the Clifford Hall. In February, 1859, the I.O.O.F. moved their meeting place to Clifford Hall from the Magnolia, which may date the time of the erection of the outside spiral stairway to the second floor (it was there in May of 1860). The Oddfellows moved across the street to their present location several years later. The history of the second story of the Native Sons Building is fairly simple: the Sons of Temperance and their successors, The Good Templars, met there for many years and in August, 1893, the Good Templars' Hall was sold to Karsky who sold to the Native Sons of the Golden West.

The two parlors, Native Sons and Native Daughters, met in the hall until the Native Sons became inactive and the Native Daughters' Parlor went out of existence. The hall was bought by Mr. and Mrs. Richard Morris in May, 1970. The Native Sons have become active again, but now meet in the Oddfellows' Hall. After being used for a time as an office, the hall in now vacant.

The history of the ground floor is much more complicated. By 1878 ownership was in the name of Henry Hocker. In 1879 Balch's Store and Wells Fargo Express were located here. Henry Lorenz bought the first floor building in 1881. Balch was still in business in 1893, but in 1896 Blake and Reed installed their warehouse here. The post office made one of its many moves in 1918 and took the ground floor. They remained there until 1923 when the Knights of Pythias purchased the building from Lorenz.

The space was remodeled and large windows put in when F. M. Smith moved his business up from the Edgecombe Building. The post office was back from 1932 until 1941 when it moved to the new Knights of Pythias Building across from the courthouse.

Mr. and Mrs. Richard Morris bought the ground floor from the Knights of Pythias. When they later purchased the Native Sons' Hall in May, 1970, the entire building came back into single ownership. David Hammer is the present owner.

Since 1941 there has been a variety of tenants: a sheet metal shop, Trinity Gas, women's dress shops (Lilyan's and Staircase Fashions), and now the legal office for David Hammer.

Site 80. Weaverville Drug Store (Block9—Lot 33)

This one-story brick building was constructed in 1855 by Wilson Bray for Davison and Harris, two physicians. D. W. Anderson was the first to conduct a drug store in the building. By 1858 the business became Anderson and Seaman's and a soda fountain was installed just inside the entrance. By 1862, under new ownership, the business was known as Weaverville Drug Store. Five years later "and Weaverville Book Store" was added to the firm's name. In 1870 the business and building were sold to John Jacob Barnickel. He and his son were to continue the business for the next 58 years. George E. Noonan rented space within the building for his Notary Public office in 1884. J. Barnickel died in 1884 and was succeeded by his son Bernhard (Ben) Barnickel, who ran it until 1921 when he died suddenly of diphtheria. Adam E. Brandes of Alameda purchased the Barnickel Drug Store and operated it for eight years when he sold it to Fredrick William Ruhser of Anderson. In 1932, W. G. Downing and his wife, Lorene, of Chico purchased the business and building and renamed the business Weaverville Drug Store. He also remodeled the building, removed the iron shutters and replaced the windows with plate glass. Downing sold to Basil R. Gillett who kept the store only one year before turning it back to Downing. In 1941 Frank E. Hicks, Sr., bought the business and in 1956 he purchased the building as well. In 1962 Frank Hicks, Jr. returned home after finishing pharmacy school and military service and assisted his father in the business. When Frank, Sr. retired in 1967, the Weaverville Drug Store was purchased by his son, Frank Hicks, Jr. and his wife, Patricia J. Hicks. Many relics of the store's early days are on display within the building which has housed a drug store during its entire 126 years.

Site 81. Edgecombe Building (Schall) (Trinity Mercantile) (Western Telephone) (Letton) (Block 9—Lot 32)

The American Hotel first occupied this lot and the one next door, the building burned in 1853. In 1854, Lot 32 was known as the northern half of the former American Hotel lot. At that time the property (Lot 32) was owned by Charles G. Kopp and John Foster. By 1855 it was owned by Jeremiah and Daniel Callahan who sold to Thomas Magnier. The Callahans had been using a building on this property as a storehouse for their business in Shasta. Magnier then sold it for $1,100 to B. Gettleson for the same amount he had paid for the property when he purchased it four months earlier. The following year (1856) it was purchased by James Edgecombe.

The drug store brick building next door was completed in 1855. H. B. Davison and James S. Harris, the owners, sold "one half of the brick wall on the south side of the drug store, together with the ground on which the wall was built, twenty inches in thickness" to James Edgecombe for $375. Edgecombe agreed to erect a brick building on his lot and also agreed to erect the southern wall to a thickness of twelve inches and extend it four inches upon the inside studding of the adjacent Magnolia building. The owner of the Magnolia paid half the cost of the wall with the provision that the wall could have an additional story added at no cost to Edgecombe. If he should wish to own half of the upper wall, he would have to pay for half of it. Edgecombe erected his fine "fireproof brick" building between the drug store and the Magnolia during 1856. Edgecombe sold his building and a year later the building was purchased by John Louis Schall for $600 in gold coins. Samuel Loffman had the New York Clothing Store here from 1858 to 1864 followed by Karsky and Co. In 1870 the Schall and Dam Shoe Store opened in the building. In 1871 this building was lighted by gas. The building was shared between 1870 and 1890 with jewelers: E. T. McCausland in 1876, P. A. Lefren during 1879 and M. A. Brady in 1886.

By 1890 Schall and his wife Magdalena sold to Louis Frederick Timmerman for use as a furniture and carpenter shop. Timmerman had just lost his business in a fire. In 1893 Timmerman and his wife, Emilie, moved their business back across the street to their former location and sold this property to Pauline Abrahms and Samuel Karsky. Abrahms and Karsky connected this building by an archway to the downstairs of the Magnolia next door. Plate glass doors and new bay windows were installed in the building front. One building was used for men's wear and the other for ladies. An ad stated "Three languages are freely spoken."

In 1917 F. M. Smith, one of the members of the Trinity Mercantile Company (see Magnolia) bought the business. In 1923 Warren Leach and Charles Kreiss bought this building from the Abrahms and Karsky heirs. This had been a clothing, dry goods, boot and shoe store from 1856 to 1923. It now became a meat market, but Kreiss and Leach dissolved their partnership the next year. Four years later Leach sold his share of the building and business to Charles Kreiss and Ed Norgaar of Hayfork. In 1930 J. J. Jackson leased the business and ran the meat market. In 1932 W. R. Bigelow and his wife, Maude A. Bigelow, owned the property and in 1934 they transferred it to their children prior to Mr. Bigelow's death in that same year. The next transfer of the Edgecombe building was to Don and Connie Creath by the ten Bigelow children. In turn, they sold to Ida Mae Davenport, a sister-in-law of Mrs. Creath. In 1951, the Western Telephone Company became the owners. The property was again—for the third time in a century—joined under one ownership with the adjacent Magnolia lot (Lot 31), the two lots having comprised the original American Hotel property.

The telephone company completely remodeled the two buildings, but later, needing more space, built and moved to their new quarters on the old high school property. The Edgecombe building (Lot 32) and the two-story Magnolia building (Lot 31) were sold to John Letton and his wife, Sara Letton, in 1979.

Site 82. Magnolia Building (Abrahms & Karsky) (Trinity Mercantile) (Masonic Hall) (Western Telephone) (Letton) (Block 9—Lot 31)

This structure has always been known as the Magnolia since the first floor of the building was erected in 1855. The lot is 23x120 feet and runs between Main and Center Street. At first, lot 31 and the lot next door (Lot 32) contained the American Hotel which was destroyed by fire in 1853. James Stanmore owned the land in 1851 and Mary Kopka owned the lot in 1855. It was S. D. Kreider and Company who advertised in the Trinity Journal "The Magnolia Bowling Alleys". It is known that Kreider was postmaster in 1856 and the post office was moved to this building for a short time. It was during 1856 that the second story was added to the Magnolia. The two-story building was described as being 22x60 and built at a cost of $8,000. North Star Lodge of the Independent Order of Oddfellows moved into the upper floor as soon as it was completed. In 1857, the Magnolia was advertised as being for sale plus "tenpin alleys, billiard table, restaurant, barroom with all furniture, mirrors and paintings. In the second story is a large hall and two rooms suitable for offices. Also a small dwelling house on the same lot". Mr. Kreider wished to sell so he could return to the east. In 1857 William Todd purchased the Magnolia and leased the bottom floor to W. S. Moore. The Oddfellows moved to the Clifford building (Lot 24) north of the drug store. The Masonic Lodge (Trinity Lodge #27) bought the second floor of the Magnolia. The Masons had previously occupied the top floor of the courthouse, located on the hill at the head of Court Street. This building had recently burned.

In 1867 Todd sold the lower floor of the Magnolia to I. Karsky and Company for 1,200 gold coins. Karsky died later that same year. The Masonic Lodge held

Site 82. This is a late 1930's view of the Magnolia building which was build in 1856. a meat market occupies the Edgecombe building. At left edge of the picture is the Weaverville Drug Store.

possession "to the door and stairway leading to their upstairs building". The next year Karsky's widow sold to M. Karsky and Isaac Abrahms, for $7,000, the lot and lower story of the Magnolia and they used it for a clothing store. Abrahms and Karsky also bought the Edgecombe building next door. The double original American Hotel lot was again under a one firm name, with the two buildings joined by an archway (see Edgecombe).

When Abrahms and Karsky retired the Trinity Mercantile Company purchased the property. In 1917 F. M. Smith, one of the owners of that firm, bought out his partners. In 1923 S. C. Miller, owner of the New York Hotel next door, bought the lower story of the Magnolia. The Magnolia had been an elegant saloon from 1856 to 1868, a clothing store from 1868 to 1923, and now it became a part of the New York Hotel. Samuel C. Miller had purchased the New York Hotel in 1911. In 1927 Mr. Miller was riding his horse on Center Street and was thrown to the ground and killed. In 1935 his widow, Emma Todd Miller, remodeled the lower floor of the Magnolia for a restaurant and the Masons had a spiral stairway placed in front. The old interior stairway was removed and the space was added to the restaurant. When Mrs. Miller died in 1938, a daughter Birdie, and husband Frank Newell, bought the property from other family members. In 1967 the Masons moved to their new hall in the southern end of town and Western Telephone Company bought the upper and lower stories of the Magnolia as well as the Edgecombe building next door. The Western Telephone Company became Continental Telephone of California and the three buildings were remodeled to hold their offices and equipment. Eventually, Continental Telephone purchased, built, and moved to the old high school site. In 1979 John and Sara Letton purchased the property on lots 31 and 32, the original American Hotel property. Letton has a law office on the upper floor of the Magnolia and the lower floor is rented to Western Title Insurance Company.

Site 83. New York Saloon (Gem Saloon) (Elite Saloon) (Block 9—Lot 30)

In July, 1856, Mary Kopka, owner of the Magnolia, deeded to Farrell the right to use the south wall of the two-story Magnolia Building. In October of 1856 Michael and John Farrell were operating the New York Saloon between the Magnolia and the New York Bakery and Restaurant. In December, 1856, F. W. Blake and S. D. Kreider sold the lot to A. Mitchell, and in December, 1857, it went to William Todd for a general merchandise store.

In July, 1859, this building was destroyed, and again in October of 1863 the site was burned out. In 1864 Cantorowitz had his tobacco shop here. Richard Clifford bought the building as a site for his Wells Fargo Express Agency in 1870. In 1873 the building was torn down and the Justice office was moved on to the lot.

When William Todd displaced The Bank Exchange Saloon in 1879 with his own saloon (located two doors down the street), the Bank Exchange business was sold and the new owner moved into this building. Wells Fargo moved up under the spiral stairs sharing Balch's Store. In 1882, the saloon located here was known as The Gem and was operated by Sam Hensley. In 1883 The Gem was run by William Woodbury; J. C. Wood bought the business in October, 1883; in 1886 Newman and Jackson took over; and four months later Jackson sold his interest to Newman.

Ownership passed to Jacob Paulsen in 1886, and he sold it to William Clement in 1888. As The Gem, it went to C. W. Smith in 1891, and in 1893 to Walter Baker, who changed the name to The Elite. In 1895 O. E. Lowden bought from Baker, and in 1896 rented to J. H. Levick and H. H. Lyon. In 1902 H. H. Lyon was the new owner of the New York Hotel. He had an archway cut through connecting the saloon. From this time on the building has been tied to the hotel and its history.

Site 84. New York Hotel (Block 9—Lot 28)

Before 1854 Barney Brady had a New York Bakery and Restaurant here. In 1854 Tom Morris, brother of James Morris, built a hotel for the partners, Morris and Brady. It was a frame building which included a bakery. When the big fire of July, 1859, burned up the street to the Magnolia building, sparing the Carr brick building on the way, Morris and Brady started immediately to rebuild in brick. They moved in November of 1859.

Another fire in October 1863 burned this part of Weaverville, gutting the New York Hotel; the next year it was again rebuilt. Brady died in 1867, and Morris formed a partnership with Silas Rule (who later married Brady's widow). Rule sold his share to Morris in 1874. James Morris operated the hotel, Weaverville's official stage stop, through the remainder of the century. In 1894 electric lights were added. (This dates the beginning of the local power company.) In 1902 the New York was sold to H. H. Lyon.

In 1911 Sam C. Miller bought the hotel, and in 1913 the Journal tells us the hotel was "modernized". The Millers were already running the Snug Restaurant down the street. In 1923 the Millers bought the ground floor of the adjacent Magnolia building (formerly half of Abrahms and Karsky's dry good store) to be part of the New York Hotel. In 1927 Sam Miller was thrown from a horse and killed. Emma Miller, his wife, carried on the business which at that time also included the Union Hotel.

In 1931 the New York Hotel underwent a major remodeling, said to be in the Mission style like the Redding Hotel. J. P. Brennen built the two big arches: one across the "card room" and one across the hotel entrance. The "card room", or old Elite Saloon, was one-story, so two rooms were built above and the

Site 84. This 1910 picture shows the New York Hotel and the Elite Saloon next door as they appeared at that time.

whole front squared off. Twelve rooms were available for guests, six with bath. Mrs. Miller gave up the Snug Cafe to concentrate on the two hotels in 1932.

The last big change came in 1935. Emma Miller's daughter Birdie, and her husband Frank Newell, converted the first floor of the Magnolia which was adjacent to the New York Bar into a restaurant. It became known as the New York Coffee Shop. This was connected with the old bar, now known as the New York Cocktail Lounge, and also with the hotel lobby. In this conversion the Masonic Lodge above the coffee shop lost its inside stairway, so Weaverville's third outside stairway was built to provide access to the second story.

The New York Hotel was Weaverville's stage stop until the stages ceased operation. Today it is no longer a hotel. In 1974 the lobby was made into a liquor store. The sleeping rooms are no longer available to guests.

The New York is changed as much in appearance as any old building in town. To get an idea as to what it looked like in 1890, one needs but look at the two-story I.O.O.F. Hall and store across the street. This is a building without added show windows and modern doors; it retains the old iron doors and shutters as well as its second story veranda. All of the buildings looked like this after the fire of 1863. The verandas were limited to the two-story buildings, of course.

Site 85. Carr Building (Ozark Saloon) (Library) (Block 9—Lot 27)

This building has been on this location since 1856. It is one of the second set of original Weaverville brick buildings. John Carr and Frost built the building and leased it in May, 1857, to James Hamilton to be used as a saloon and billiard parlor. In 1857 the business was sold to Frank and John Young and was known as the Bank Exchange Saloon. John Carr was a blacksmith; there is some question as to whether or not Carr may have first used this building for his shop. Scraps of metal found in the cellar under the building might indicate that this is the case. The question, however, is really of little importance since the building became a saloon within a few months of its completion.

The fire of 1859 seems to have spared Carr's building, but the fire of 1863 gutted it. Through the years Frank Young continued business here as proprietor of the Bank Exchange Saloon and as an insurance agent. His brother John left the partnership after several years and moved to Eureka.

Carr sold to William Todd in 1875. In 1879 when Todd established his own saloon, Frank Young sold the Bank Exchange Saloon business and the new owner moved it two doors up the street (see Site 83.). The Bank Exchange of Hanna and Carter, however, was again in this building in 1895-97. In 1898, H. H. Lyon was operating the Ozark Saloon there and in 1902 B. R. Brown became the owner of the Ozark, a name which, in the news of the day, also was given to the building.

It is likely that the building sat unused for much of the next few years. In February, 1913, Paulsen and Carter leased the building to operate a theater named "Recreation". In March, 1913, Dr. D. B. Fields bought the Ozark building from Abrahms and Karsky who were then the owners; Recreation closed three months later. Dr. Fields sold the building to Trinity County when he went into the Army Medical Corps in 1917. The Trinity County Free Library was moved into the building and has remained at this site since that time.

Site 86. Shaving Saloon (Davenport Barber Shop) (Gold Nugget Jewelers) (Block 9—Lot 26)

This site was undoubtedly occupied through the 1850's. The first reference is to an Isaac Dixon's Humboldt Shaving Saloon at this spot in 1854; Dixon sold it to Hickman in July, 1857. Two years later, July, 1859, Edgecombe is the seller of the lot and the right to share the south wall of Carr's building (the Library today) to Matthew Griffith.

The fires of July, 1859, and October, 1863, destroyed the frame buildings that were on the lot. In 1874 a new building was back in use again as a barber shop, known this time as the Union Shaving Saloon. For a short time, however, in 1862-1863 Cantorowitz's tobacco store was housed here. The building seen today is the one rebuilt after the fire of 1863. It has living quarters in the rear.

In the late 1870's purchases by William Todd caused considerable shifting of businesses. His purchase of this building and the present library building resulted in Frank Young's selling of the Bank Exchange. The Bank Exchange was moved to the north side of the New York Hotel, making room for Todd's Saloon, and the Union Shaving Saloon moved up the street, making room to move Todd's meat market in this building. The market was leased to Jose and Dix in 1881, and went out of business sometime after 1886. In 1893 the building was repaired and set up as a butcher shop again; its function is unknown after 1895 when Eliza Todd died. For a time in the early part of this century the whole building was used as a residence by the Whitchurch family.

In 1917 E. A. Urban purchased a share of the building and again it was used as a barber shop. Frank Davenport took over the business in 1928, purchasing the building in 1929. Frank and his son, Dean, operated Davenport's Barber Shop here until Dean retired in 1976. At this time the new owners, Gold Nugget Jewelers, moved down from the Clifford Building (Site 77.), thus ending about one hundred years of barbering at this location.

Site 87. Comstock and Martin (Lang's Store) (Snug Restaurant) (Western Auto) (Block 9—Lot 24)

Comstock and Martin built a two-story brick building on this lot in 1856. It was one of a group of brick buildings constructed at that time. The firm of Pierce, Church and Co., general merchandise agents, occupied the lower floor. When the fire of July, 1859, damaged the building, the County Treasurer's office and the Trinity Journal occupied the second floor.

In 1861 Pierce, Church and Co. sold out; Max Lang moved in from the west side of the street forming Goldstein and Lang. The fire of October, 1863, gutted the building and John Martin covered the remains to rebuild. In the following spring, he built the one-story building of today. (In 1878 John Martin received the deed as legal owner.) Lang returned in 1864 and continued to use the building. In June, 1889, Max Lang sold his business to W. F. Smith and Co. (composed of W. F. Smith, S. L. Blake and H. R. Given). A few months later Lang moved to Portland. In 1892 Blake and Given bought out W. F. Smith, and moved up to their new store on the west side of Main Street in the present Morris Hardware building in December of 1892.

Meanwhile, John Martin, perhaps Weaverville's richest man, continued to direct Comstock and Martin, the successors to Pierce, Church and Company (forwarding and commission agents), the livery stable, and various other mining and business endeavors. John Martin died in 1892; his widow, Isabelle, sold this building and the livery business to D. G. Reid in December, 1894. That fall Goetze and Junkans had opened a meat market in the store. Soon after, Reid sold "Max Lang's Store" to Goetze and Junkans. In 1897 Goetze and Junkans sold their meat market business to James Dockery who operated the Mountain Market at the upper end of Main Street. The store was then leased to Robert Moss to be a saloon. In 1900 Moss opened the Snug Restaurant.

In 1902 Ford and Cochran opened the Mint Saloon next to the Snug. In May the Snug burned and Ford and Cochran leased the Snug, built a separate kitchen, and put in new fixtures, combining all of it into the Snug Cafe and Bar. Ford then sold out the business to the S. C. Millers in 1906.

For years the Millers operated the restaurant and saloon, both of which were reputed to have been outstanding establishments in Weaverville. In 1913 they had also acquired the New York Hotel. Bill and Clara Goetze used the brick building for the Snug Ice Cream Parlor beginning in the summer of 1922. The Millers bought the lower part of the Magnolia adjacent to the New York Bar in 1923 to join to the hotel (see Site 83.).

Ownership during the next few years is somewhat confusing. The "Lang" store building housed a store of the Purity chain in 1935. Later the building was Dan Miniere's Weaverville Cafe. Harvey Arbuckle started Western Auto in 1952. In the meantime a creamery occupied the wooden section along the side, and an ice plant operated in the rear on Center Street. Larkin's Variety Store was in this wooden section from 1936-1941 (until it moved to a Lee building down the street). Goetzes sold the pair of buildings to Dan Adrian in 1947. The wooden building went back to restaurants for a time as the Busy B, and Pick and Shovel. Several years ago the wall was cut through combining both halves into Western Auto.

Site 88. Livery Stable Site (Block 9—Lot 23)

This location is one of several ghosts included in this book. The livery stable occupied the large lot between the old firehouse and the Comstock and Martin brick building and had a narrow passage down the side giving access to Center

Site 88. The old livery stable was located just south of the present Western Auto Store.. Highway 3 is on ground once occupied by this once important business.

Street. It was vital to life in this part of Trinity County.

Comstock and Martin were associated with Pierce, Church and Co. working between Weaverville and Red Bluff expediting trade. Pierce, Church and Co. were also general merchandisers who first occupied the Comstock and Martin building in the 1850's.

The big barn of the Martin stable dated from the fire of 1863 and sat back on the lot along the north side. The two-story depot with living quarters upstairs sat up by Main Street. Sheds and stables were in a row along the south side, in the present parking area behind The Kreiss building (Site 89), and dated from the rebuilding which followed the 1905 fire.

The John Martins lived in the livery stable's apartment; he died there in 1892. Isabelle Martin sold the livery and equipment to D. G. Reid in 1894. Klein and Frye owned the stables in 1898.

In the early 1900's, John Boyce, the driver of the Ruggles hold-up stage, owned the livery stable and sold it in 1907 to the Vitzthum brothers. The big Martin stable was torn down and a new one built on the south side of the lot in what later was Mulligan Street. Ten years later, in 1917, Walter Day purchased the livery stable and rebuilt the barn forward and over to the north side. Here it evolved into Weaverville's garage.

After several changes of ownership, "Hap" Miller bought what had been known as The Pioneer Garage in 1934. Miller's Garage used the old barn until 1956. Moving to a new location, Miller left the barn and it was demolished in 1969 to make way for Trinity Lakes Blvd. in the development of Highway 3.

Site 89. Kreiss Building (Rendezvous) (The Shoe Tree) (Block 9—Lot 23)

In early days this lot was the south side of the large livery stable lot. Since it was not a brick building site, the big fires on lower Main Street in 1859 and 1863 wiped it clean of its previous buildings. Here the stables for the livery teams were located; it also provided a narrow passage from Main Street to Center Street. The town's long-lived principal livery stable was located on a large lot between this site and the brick building that is now Western Auto. Later the livery barn became a garage, and Mulligan Street was cut through from Main Street to extend up the hill as the route to the East Weaver and Minersville areas.

Removal of the stables opened space where Charles Kreiss built his butcher shop in 1930. Later, a small addition was built along the south side to hold the butcher shop, and the main building became a lunch room. Within the decade the building became the Rendezvous Cafe and Bar; Kreiss intended that this would become the night spot of Weaverville. For years the building continued to be a restaurant with a bar in the rear. Hanlon's Cafe was here for awhile and William Jackson and others have operated the business. Generally, older Weaverville people still refer to the building as the Rendezvous.

Since its days as a restaurant, the building has been a nursery and gift shop and now a shoe shop. Offices and shops have occupied the barroom section and have completely changed the role of the building. The name Rendezvous still shows in the paint along the back side of the building.

Site 90. Old Fire House (Block 9-Lot 22)

In the very early days this lot probably held a saloon. In 1855 Blake and Rowe built the Weaverville Theater here. The fires of 1859 and 1863 burned the site clean. After the 1863 fire, four rammed earth buildings were built in a row in this location by the Chinese. This building technique was used on several buildings in Weaverville's Chinatown. After the loss of its three neighbors (demolished since a fire in 1977) this and one other are the only rammed earth buildings left in Weaverville. Heffington's gift shop is a younger building of the same type. The buildings had thick walls, iron doors, and a very heavy ceiling with a foot of earth on top. As a result, the four buildings and their contents survived the September, 1874, fire in Chinatown with only the loss of their roofs.

The 1877 survey records show that this land was owned by John Bartlett. In 1896 John Bartlett sold three of the lots (#22, #21 and #19) to Sarah A. Stone of Beloit, Wisconsin, and Lot #20 to Charlie Ah Get. In 1898 when the livery stable next door belonged to Klein and Frye, a fire started inside but was confined and snuffed out after burning the partitions. The Chinatown fire of 1905 was the worst in Weaverville in 30 years but the adobe buildings escaped again.

When the Weaverville Fire Department bought the old hand pumper in 1906, the Department rented this old building, at that time a dwelling, to shelter it. Later they voted to buy the building, and received title in 1910. The front earth wall was demolished and a wooden front added with double doors. The fireman put a steel bell tower and bell on the roof. The building served as the main firehouse until 1949. A hand drawn chemical cart was kept in a shed in Faggtown and later under the bandstand.

After thirty years, community effort and a state grant have provided shelter for the earthen walls and restored the front. These are believed to be one of two remaining examples of exposed rammed earth walls to be seen in California.

Site 90. This old firehouse is believed to be one of the two remaining examples of exposed rammed earth walls to be seen in California. It is located just north of the new North Valley Bank.

Site 91. The Pacific Brewery building was constructed in 1854-55. The wooden shed addition was rebuilt after a fire in 1950. This is the only survivor of a number of Weaverville brewer buildings.

Site 91. Pacific Brewery (The Brewery) (Block 9—Lot 16)

The brick building at this location was built by Frederick Walter and Co. in 1854-1855. It was built along with others in the first group of brick buildings to be built in Weaverville. Pacific Brewery's fireproof building is the only survivor of at least three breweries that were in Weaverville in early days.

In 1861 the Brewery caught fire, probably from the drying of barley. Finding the fire too big to extinguish, the firemen closed the iron doors and shutters to confine it. They tore down the wooden out-buildings and Kruttschnitt's building to the north and let the fire burn out, gutting the building. This use of the building design to control fire was also used in the old firehouse adobe in 1898.

In 1865 Frederick Walter sold an interest in the business to Lorenz and Hagelman. Following this the business was operated by various partnerships involving Lorenz, Hagelman, Jacob and Stiller. In 1883 the Brewery was bought by John Meckel of Helena. Upon his death in 1889 the Pacific Brewery became the Meckel Bros. and remained in business until Prohibition stopped brewing operations in 1917. The brick building and its equipment then sat unused for many years. A wooden wing attached to the south side of the building enclosed the horse-powered brewery machinery. The monthly meetings of the Volunteer Fire Department were held here for years. It also served as the Humboldt Motor Stage office. On an October night in 1950 the wooden structure was destroyed by fire but the iron shutters again saved the brick building and its contents. Fullerton and Jarrett operated a feed store in the building for a time starting in 1953. Later Trinity Market had its feed department here. In the early 1970's it was remodeled into a restaurant. An outdoor eating area and a kitchen were added to the south side of the building. The Brewery continues to operate as a restaurant with Gerard and Dale Kaz, the present owners.

Site 92. Mortuary (Heffington's) (Block 9—Lot 15)

The early history of this site is very sketchy as is the history of all of Chinatown. Most of what happened here was not considered to be newsworthy. The deed for this lot was granted to Jane Golden (Dibbins) in 1878. On this side of the street, Chinatown extended from the old livery stable down to this point and beyond, with the Brewery like an island within. The building is two rammed earth buildings, one behind the other. The adobe buildings may date back to the time of the group up the street. There is an 1894 news item about an adobe being rebuilt to replace one damaged by snow several years earlier. It may refer to one of these. However, Chinatown below the Brewery burned in 1878 and in 1896 and there is no reference in Trinity Journal accounts to adobe buildings.

Like the other buildings, this adobe structure probably was a store with living quarters behind. In 1905 it was the residence of the Guoy family. They are said to have survived the Chinatown fire of 1905 within the building protected by the earth walls, the earth layer above the ceiling, and the iron shutters. It is not certain whether the 1905 fire involved all the surrounding wooden buildings, however. The Trinity Journal report refers to only one Chinese wooden building being spared.

In 1912 the new partnership of Anderlini and Miller moved from upper Main Street into what had been the home of Mrs. Mar Guoy. The firm advertised a tin shop, shoe repair shop and mortuary. In those days there was a frame building on the right with a narrow alley separating the two. The mortuary was in this wooden building.

In 1916 J. A. Anderlini left the firm, and Frank Miller's father-in-law, C. E. Goodyear, became a partner. When Goodyear died in 1922, Miller carried on alone until 1932 when his nephew, Hal Goodyear, joined him. Miller died in 1934 and the enterprise split up; Hal Goodyear continued the sheet metal, plumbing and shoe repair portion of the business until he sold out to Don Creath in 1938. The mortuary was taken over by McDonald and Scott (Stanford Scott) of Redding with Ernest G. Chapman as their Weaverville representative. The mortuary was moved into the adobe building in 1938 as Creath moved his stock and equipment away when he bought the plumbing business. McDonald bought the property from the Meckel family in 1943.

George Files bought the mortuary in October, 1955, and tore down the wooden building in 1956. The adobe buildings were remodeled in 1960 with an apartment added above. The earthen walls are now almost entirely concealed by stucco. When George Files moved to a new location in 1971, the building was modified for Heffington's Flower and Gift Shop, which moved down from the Fagg building next to the Mountain Marketplace.

Site 93. Jackson House (Meckel House) (Young House) (Snyder-Highland Art Center) (Block 9—Lots 2-7)

The main art center house was built in 1893 as a residence for his family by the Reverend A. T. Jackson who was a carpenter as well as a minister. In 1902 the house was purchased by Helena Josephine Meckel. In 1915 the adjoining property to the north containing a large barn was purchased at auction from the Henry Junkans estate. Also in 1915 Mrs. Meckel purchased the adjoining property to the south from the estate of Eli E. Ellis. The house on the Ellis property was torn down in 1918 and the lumber used by Sam Lee to build his home on Lorenz Lane. In 1934 the property was purchased from Helena Meckel's estate by Van and Annie Meckel Young. Annie Young died on December 31, 1951, and her nephew, Frederick A. Meckel, inherited the property. In 1953

Site 93. The Snyder-Highland Art Center is located on Main Street in an old home built in 1893.

W. Gilman and Lucille Snyder who formed a non-profit foundation to establish the Highland Art Center.

The barn now serves as a studio for resident painter and sculptor, Stephen Hubbell. Attached to the barn are three garages which have been made into a studio for pottery. On the hill, in the hayloft of what had formerly been the Ellis cow barn, is the studio of Lillian Godbe, weaver. The original woodshed is now a display and sales area for the "Porch and Pantry", a craft group.

This place, including the outbuildings, is typical of many early Weaverville homes. It accommodated every family need. House, woodshed, barn, pigeon loft, chicken house, large garden plot and orchard were all enclosed within a neatly painted white picket fence.

Site 94. Trinity Congregational Church (Block 9—Lot 2)

The first church on this site was completed in 1881. It apparently was the third or fourth Protestant church in Weaverville; a building of 1855 and one of 1870 were both destroyed by fire.

In September, 1890, the Congregational Church Chapel was destroyed by fire. As the fire swept through four nearby buildings there was time to save the contents and even the doors and windows. The present building was erected on the same site and was completed in December of 1891. This building is about the same width but ten feet longer than the first.

Through the years the building has been improved by the addition of a choir loft, an organ, and a general re-doing of the interior. The exterior is practically as it was in the 1890's. Shrubbery and new steps in the front and replacement of the authentic colorless glass by colored panes are the only apparent changes.

The congregation has bought property on both sides. The lot to the left side was bought in 1902 and the present parsonage was built and furnished. In 1917 a stairway was built to the attic floor of the parsonage by a minister who had eight children. The exterior of the house has changed little in over 75 years.

The first lot to the right of the church was purchased in 1910. It had two houses on it, and the larger one in front was moved back to the rear of the church to serve as a Parish House. The second lot to the right was occupied by the Whitmore Hall when it was purchased in 1920. The hall was torn down and the materials used to build the Congregational Church in Hayfork.

The present Parish House was built and dedicated in June, 1950. It occupies part of the two lots and replaced the old Parish House of 1910. This building, like the church building, was a result of community effort, gifts and fund raisers, especially by the Ladies Aid Society.

In 1961 the congregation voted to adopt the constitution of the United Church of Christ, thus uniting with that church. The three-building unit, however, is known as Trinity Congregational Church.

Site 95. Whitmore House (Griffith House) (Larson House) (Block 9—Lot 1)

In 1877 Henry Hocker owned this property. In May of 1878 he sold most of it to John Martin, a Weaverville businessman. Martin built his home on the site. In September, 1890, Mrs. Martin (Isabelle) had an accident with a lamp in the middle of the night and ignited packing materials and household goods not yet unpacked. The fire burned the house and the three neighboring structures including the church and Whitmore's Hall.

In 1893 Isabelle Martin, widowed in 1892, sold the property to John Whitmore. He had a house built in 1895 by A. T. Jackson next to his new Whitmore Hall and retail lumber yard. This large house with attached woodshed and large yard is a good illustration of the kind of home a prosperous Weaverville businessman built one hundred years ago.

After the death of John Whitmore, Catherine Whitmore and her daughter, Ruby, sold the house to John Griffith in June, 1917. The Griffiths spent the rest of their lives in the house, and sixty years later the heirs sold to Dale and Lesley Larson, the present owners.

Site 96. J. J. "Jake" Jackson Memorial Museum and Historic Park

The museum property was acquired in 1964 and by June 23, 1968, the museum had been built, dedicated and put into operation. Funds for construction came from several sources: $60,000 from a State Historical Park grant, $35,000 from county funds, and many dollars from public donations. The design for the museum was one of a number of plans submitted in a contest. The one used was chosen because of it similarity to that of the original Weaverville brick buildings dating back to the 1850's. The museum front is of used brick from the old Carnegie Library of Redding. All assembling and displaying of historic material was done by volunteers. All museum cases and artifacts were gifts to the museum from people who cared.

Before World War I Harry H. Noonan and Ray Jackson had collected a number of guns and other historic relics and displayed them in the Weaverville Supply Store where both young men were employed. When Ray Jackson entered the armed services to serve in World War I and Harry Noonan left the county, they turned the collection over to Ray's brother "Jake" Jackson. The collection was then placed on display in the Native Sons Hall. When the Memorial Hall was built a place was provided there for the exhibit. All articles were

Site 95. This beautiful Whitmore home, built in 1895, is within the Historic District.

saved from the Memorial Hall when it burned in 1944. Jake Jackson was then instrumental in obtaining room in the courthouse basement for a small museum. J. J. "Jake" Jackson donated countless hours to the preservation of county history and died before this building, which bears his name, was constructed. The museum and park are under the management of the Trinity County Historical Society.

Site 97. Chinese Freemason Hall Site

The old Chinese Freemason Hall was located where the Joss House parking lot is now situated. Some say that they remember the building being spared in the 1905 fire but others think that it was lost and immediately rebuilt. In either case, it was to be the last two-story Chinese structure in town. Several others had succumbed to earlier fires. The Chinese Freemason Hall was a long, narrow, two-story wooden building with a steep, narrow stairway leading to the top floor. Many tiny rooms were at either side of a narrow hallway that ran the full length of the building. The whole building smelled of the punks that were always kept burning. Even though this building was known as the Chinese Freemason Hall, there was no association with the real Masonic Lodge and it was considered a clandestine order. This building was torn down after the roof caved in from the weight of heavy snow in January, 1950.

The Chinese Freemason Hall was at the south end of Chinatown which, at the turn of the century, occupied much of the area on both sides of Main Street between the present museum and the Trinity Theatre. The Chinese lived in tiny shacks and hovels with sewers dumping into the creek or outhouses hanging out over the creek. Pigs, ducks and chickens roamed freely among the houses.

It was not uncommon for as many as twenty Chinese to be living and sleeping in a little one-room cabin. Most men worked from daylight to darkness in the nearby mines. They possessed little of worldly goods; they hoped to accumulate enough gold to permit them to return to their native land to live out their remaining days comfortably. Many a dream was shattered because one of their failings was gambling. Fortunes were gained by back-breaking labors in the mines, only to be lost over the gambling table. Smoking opium was a constant pastime, perhaps to "cushion" their loneliness and miserable existence. There were few Chinese women in Weaverville and few family homes such as the "Whites" had. Because of the terribly crowded living quarters and constant opium smoking, their cabins frequently caught on fire. These fires often raged out of control and were responsible for burning half the town, including homes and places of business. Early accounts in the Trinity Journal repeatedly refer to the determination of the "Whites" to eliminate the Chinese population from the town of Weaverville. Each time that Chinatown burned it was immediately rebuilt, except after the fire of 1905. Judy Davis Moore remembers her mother saying that several hundred Chinese lost their homes that night. This 1905 fire started in the Chinese section and burned in all directions destroying everything in its path. To the north it destroyed the Davis Blacksmith Shop and burned as far as the Fields' residence. After the fire most Chinese left the county. In looking at the area today it is hard to realize that the population of Chinatown in the 1860's was over one thousand. Today, only one descendant of these early Chinese inhabitants remains (see Site 100.).

Site 98. Weaverville Chinese Joss House

The characters over the door of the Weaverville Joss House, the oldest continuously used Chinese temple in California, mean "The temple of the forest beneath the clouds". A creek ripples along between the temple grounds and the administration building. Lacy locust trees shade the Joss House at the back and on each side. A pleasant walkway through a nicely kept lawn area invites visitors. The well-kept appearance of the entire complex is in marked contrast to the run-down appearance of this landmark before it was acquired by the state of California as an historic park.

Hundreds of Chinese, along with many other gold seekers, came to the Weaverville area during the early 1850's. Soon after their arrival in 1852 or 1853, the Orientals erected a church for Taoist worship. Their church burned to the ground in 1873. A Doctor Croucher, at one time a physician at the German Hospital on the hill, lived in a cabin at the rear of the Joss House. He had become the "town drunk"; one night in 1873 his cabin caught fire and spread to the Joss House. The cabin, Dr. Croucher and the Joss House were all consumed in the flames. Although some of the priceless temple hangings and carvings from China were saved, many were lost in the fire.

In October, 1873, the Chinese purchased the lot adjoining the site of their church which had burned and proposed to erect another Joss House. Between February and April of the following year, the present Joss House was erected. This great accomplishment was the result of the combined efforts of over two thousand dedicated Chinese whose names are recorded on the walls of the conference room adjoining the temple. In April of 1874 the new temple was dedicated with a great celebration by both Orientals and Whites. Firecrackers, bombs, and the pounding of drums, gongs and cymbals made the town very aware of the happy occasion.

Gradually, as mining decreased, the Chinese left Weaverville and the once colorful Joss House became neglected. Many townspeople became alarmed over

A general view of Weaverville showing Chinatown. Chinatown was located at the lower end of Main Street in the vicinity of the Joss House. The buildings in the lower right show Chinatown as it was before 1900.

Site 98. This Weaverville Joss House was constructed in 1874 to replace an earlier temple lost by fire. It is the oldest continuously used Joss House in California.

the possibility of losing this landmark. Largely through the efforts of Moon Lee (whose grandfather had contributed to the building in 1874) the Joss House was accepted into the State Division of Beaches and Parks system in 1956. A complete restoration of the building has taken place and an administration and parking area has been added.

The knoll in back of the Joss House was known as Chimney Point in early days. At one time it was the site of a Protestant church and was also the site of the town's first school for primary grades. This knoll is now within the park.

As one enters the temple an ornate wooden gate to the porch and fanciful gables and cornices on the building set the Oriental theme. The front is painted bright blue with white lines to resemble Chinese tiles. Spirit screens keep out evil spirits. Ornately carved wooden images of gods stand along the back wall and in front of them is an alter. The temple has been in continuous use as a place of worship since its construction. Worshippers visit the temple alone, with their families or with friends. Moon Lee is the only descendant of a pioneer Chinese family living in Weaverville, but many Chinese come from far away places to visit and pray at this temple.

The Weaverville Joss House is one of the most complete in the Western Hemisphere. It draws over 20,000 visitors a year from all over the world.

Site 99. Old Shell Station (Joss House Administration Building)

Between the old Chinese Freemason building site and the corner of Oregon Street is a narrow strip of land where the present Joss House Administration building now stands. After the 1905 fire Charles Newell (father of Frank Newell and Carrie Newell Davis) had a cabinet shop, undertaking business and coroner's office in a building on this strip of ground. In the 1920's C. J. "Collie" Mead remodeled the building and it became Weaverville's first service station.

In 1925 Mead purchased land across Oregon Street, known then as the China Garden, to be a campground. (It is now Trinity Market's parking area.) In 1928 Joe Harrington and his wife, Winnie Koll Harrington, leased Mead's Shell Oil Service Station and, in 1934, purchased it. In 1932 the Harringtons bought Mead's land across Oregon Street and Rayce Altermatt built for them a one and one-half story family residence on the corner as well as several small rentals behind their home. Altermatt also remodeled the service station in the then popular "Spanish Mission" style, finishing it with stucco.

Harrington owned and operated the station for many years. During this time he was Chief of the Weaverville Volunteer Fire Department. Later Robert L. Marshall rented the station. Marshall is a member of an old-time Trinity family of Douglas City. In 1954 Joe Harrington sold the station, as well as the property across Oregon Street, to Horace Westmoreland. Later the station was torn down to make way for the Joss House Administration building and Westmoreland moved his Shell business to the site of the former Carl and Edna Bremer home near the intersection of Mill Street with Main Street.

Site 100. Part of Chinatown (Trinity Market and Trinity Theatre)

In 1938 Moon Lee purchased from Carrie Newell Davis the property where the Davis Blacksmith Shop had been located, as well as the land between that and the Harrington home. Moon had for many years assisted his father, Sam Lee, in a grocery business directly across Main Street. Lee built a new, larger store on the lower part of his new property and called the business "Lee's Supermarket". Because Weaverville needed a theatre, Lee sold the land that was to be used as the store's parking lot to Ken and Helen Loomis for the Trinity Theatre. The Loomis family lived in the apartment above the theatre prior to building a residence on Miner Street. Ken Loomis was active in civic affairs and was County Supervisor for fourteen years. Trinity Theatre is now owned and managed by Mr. and Mrs. Thomas R. Miller. The building front and the lobby have been remodeled. Side and front windows were added to the lobby and the front entrance has been covered with rustic board and batten.

In 1954 Moon Lee sold his grocery business to Mr. and Mrs. Charles A. Hood and Hood's daughter and husband, Patricia and Guy McTimmonds. The business was then known as H and M Supermarket. John and Shirley Fields purchased the business in 1959. In 1964 they consolidated this market with their Trinity Market which had been located up the street. The store then became Trinity Market. After John Fields' death the store was sold to George and Mickey Halcomb. Halcomb had been store manager for a number of years. Though George was not raised in Trinity County, his grandfather, Walter Day, was the original owner of the former garage located across Main Street (see Site 88.). Under Halcomb's ownership, Trinity Market was enlarged and a new front and side entrance were added. The Harrington-Westmoreland property was purchased; the buildings were moved; and the lot was leveled for parking.

After selling the grocery store, Moon Lee returned to a business in the Chinese rammed earth building across the street where he had formerly worked with his father. This new venture was conducted as a paint, appliance and hardware store. Over the years, Lee served on many Chamber of Commerce committees for the betterment of north state highways. In 1967, while Ronald Reagan was governor of California, he appointed Moon Lee as a member of the California Highway Commission. Lee served for over eight years. The Lee family property on both sides of the street was part of the Chinese settlement which extended from approximately the present intersection of State Highway 3 to the Snyder Highland Art Center.

Site 100. This Chinese parade and celebration in 1903 could have been for Chinese New Year. The picture was taken from the hill above the Joss House.

Site 100. Jack Lim, cook for the Snug Restaurant, stands in front of one of the Chinese rammed earth buildings destroyed by fire in 1977. This is the site of the new North Valley Bank.

Site 101. The Davis Blacksmith Shop stood on ground now partially covered by the Trinity Theater. The photo shows Griff Davis and his partner Hagelman in their shop about 1913.

Site 101. Davis Blacksmith Shop

The Davis Blacksmith Shop was located on ground now partly occupied by the Trinity Theatre and included the lot to the north of the theatre building. The business was started in 1890 or 1891 by Dave Davis. His brother, Griffith T. Davis came to Weaverville from New York in 1888 to work with his brother and to learn the business. He was 18 years old at the time. Although the shop was lost in the big fire of 1905, it was immediately rebuilt and the business continued. When Dave Davis died three years later, Griffith Davis carried on the work for his brother's widow, Ida Junkans Davis. Griffith became the owner in 1913 and took on as a partner a man named John Hagelman. (Hagelman's parents were early owners of the brewery across the street.) Davis and Hagelman had the equipment and the skills to build fine wagons. This they did during the winter when horseshoeing and other business was slack. The wagon wheels were immersed in the creek behind their shop in order to shrink the hot iron tires onto the wooden wheels. With the decline of horse and wagon usage and the coming of the automobile, Hagelman quit the business and moved away. When Griffith Davis died in 1936 his widow, Carrie Newell Davis, had the shop torn down. In 1938 she sold the south portion of the property to Moon Lee; she retained the north portion now owned by her daughter, Judith Davis Moore.

Site 102. Dr. David B. Fields Home and Office

It is a surprise to find this beautiful old home in the center of the business district. The exterior has not been altered since 1905 when it may have been partially rebuilt because of fire damage. Firemen and neighbors worked frantically to save this house in the 1905 fire which burned so much in the area.

The building's most distinguishing features are the fish scale shingle siding and the intricate diagonally paned windows. The house was built as a residence for the Fields family as well as an office for Dr. Field's medical practice. The rear of the house is two-storied to fit the drop-off at the rear of the lot. Rooms downstairs provided a kitchen and dining room for the family as well as living quarters for a cook and housekeeper.

Fascination with gold mining brought Dr. David B. Fields from Texas to Trinity County. He was involved in many mines throughout the county. In 1899 he was public health officer. He married a local girl, Honora Blaney, and they raised six children. He was a doctor of the horse and buggy days; his rustic weathered barn sits on the creek bank at the rear of the lot and is the only one left in this section of town.

In 1930 Dr. Fields hired "Jinks" and Roy Wilson (father and son) to build a new office building on the lot to the south of the house. Lumber for this office was sawn at the Schaffer Mill on Oregon Mountain. When Dr. Fields became ill, the family left Weaverville and the property was rented to Dr. C. H. Law. He used the new office building for his office and the downstairs rear of the Fields' home for a hospital. After the death of Dr. Fields, Mrs. Fields and some of the children returned to occupy the house. Since Mrs. Fields' death, about 1956, the home has been used as a home, a business office and as a lunch room. The garage downstairs has been remodeled into a craft shop and recently has been turned into a shoe repair shop.

Site 103. Tourtellotte Home (Jepsen Building)

The big Tourtellotte home on Main Street barely escaped the fire of 1905 which burned from Chinatown to Dr. Fields' house next door. Jesse and Isa-

Site 102. This house, built about 1905, was a combined home and medical office used by Dr. David B. Fields and his family.

Site 102. This barn on Miner Street at the rear of the Fields' lot was used by Dr. Fields for his horse and buggy.

bella Fox Tourtellotte purchased the property in 1898, when they moved to Weaverville from Old Minersville. Mr. Tourtellotte later became Trinity County Assessor.

The home has been drastically remodeled. During the 1930's Dr. Wilson had his offices in the building which also served as a hospital. It was used as an apartment house when Frankie Davenport Hammock owned it. At one time, the Fred Howells and then John and Shirley Fields were owners. John was a son of Dr. David B. Fields and his wife, Honora Blaney Fields. It was John Fields who replaced the picket fence in front. John's daughter, Nora, and her husband, Ernest Jepsen, purchased the property in 1976. It is now rented as an apartment and office building.

The small wooden building in the rear of the Beauty Boutique was a part of the original Tourtellotte property. For many years it was used as an attorney's office. During the 1920's Dr. Fields had his office there. At present it is occupied by Jepsen Printing and Supplies.

Site 104. Gibson Hall Site (Memorial Hall Site) (Bank of America) (Block 10 —Lot 16)

An early building on this large lot, now occupied by the Bank of America, was Gibson Hall, a one-story frame structure. The Pastime Movie Theatre operated in this hall which had a complicated slanting floor that could be removed for dancing. Saturday night dances were held almost every week at Gibson Hall and were the favorite social event of young and old alike. Before Gibson, the hall was known as Todd Hall (the Todd family lived in part of the building). Gibson Hall was torn down to make room for the new Memorial Hall which was built just after World War I "to honor the services rendered by soldiers, sailors, and citizens in the war effort". The lot had been donated to Trinity County by the citizens of Weaverville. The 40'x70', one-story concrete building was built and paid for by the county and dedicated in 1922. It was destroyed by fire in 1944 in what was the biggest fire since 1905. The lot stood vacant for a number of years. The present Bank of America was built on the lot and dedicated in 1958. An earth fill parking lot was added at the back.

Site 105. Fagg Building Site (Legion Hall Site) (Bank of America Driveway) (Block 10—Lot 17)

R. A. Fagg, in 1854, constructed a 20'x70', two-story brick building on this lot. Mrs. James Barkla later owned the building and lived in a portion of it. At this time the building was connected by a doorway to Gibson Hall next door so that the downstairs kitchen and dining room could serve both buildings. In 1922 when the Memorial Hall replaced the Gibson Hall these rooms continued to serve the new building. In 1923 Trinity County purchased the Fagg building. The upstairs was used as office space for the Trinity County Development Association as well as a general meeting place for the American Legion. This building was demolished in 1957. It was one of two original brick buildings constructed in the 1850's that no longer stands. The Bank of America driveway now occupies the lot.

Site 106. F. W. Blake Bank (U. S. Forest Service Office) (The Diggins) (Block 10—Lot 18)

This is a very early one-story brick building with a dominant brick trim across the top of the front. In 1860 an awning covered the sidewalk but is no longer there. The building dates back to 1856 and was built by Moss, Mabie

Site 104. The Memorial Hall was built after World War I and was lost by fire in 1944. The two-story brick building to the right was built by Fagg in 1854. Originally it had an upstairs balcony like the I.O.O.F. Hall.

Site 106. The Trinity National Forest had its headquarters in this 1856 building (now The Diggins) for many years before moving to their present location in 1934.

and Company for the F. W. Blake Bank and Wells Fargo Express. By 1877 it was owned by Isaac Pincus. After the death of Pincus, his widow sold the building in 1901 to Louis Lewis for $1,750. Subsequently it was sold to Becky Karsky, wife of S. Karsky, then to James Barkla, then to the Trinity County Bank. In 1933 it was sold to W. R. Bigelow, former Trinity County Sheriff. From about 1909 until 1934, the building was the headquarters of the Trinity National Forest. It was used as the Supervisor's office, as well as an office for the Weaverville Ranger District. The Forest Service had only two or three trucks at this time and most of their work was in the field on horseback. Goetze's large barn and corral, situated at the site of the present post office and shopping area, was rented by the Forest Service. Mules and horses, their hay and feed, and all gear were kept there. A storage shed at one side was for Forest Service tools and the equipment for sharpening the tools. After the Forest Service moved into their present building in 1934 the building became a pool hall run by Merris Heaton, and later, Russ Chancellor. Bassic and Driscoll opened the Detroit bar in 1943. Dan Adrian is the present owner of the building and bar, now known as "The Diggins".

Site 107. Solomon Building (Bank Building) (Western Shop) (Block 10—Lot 19)

This 21'x56' building was built in 1854 by A. Solomon. In 1858 it was used by the Greenhood and Newbauer Bank. In 1877 it was owned by M. F. Griffin and in 1889 by Champion Smith, a banker. Trinity County Bank purchased it in 1900 for $2000. This bank failed in 1932; four years later Bank of America moved into the building and stayed there until their new building was ready in 1958. It then became office space for a succession of people: Stennett Sheppard, Dr. John Herring, Hill and Lowden, Griffith Associates and Western Title Company. It is presently owned by Leonard and Florence Morris who installed the awning across the front. The Western Shop includes this building as well as the one on the adjoining lot (Lot 20). The buildings were connected in 1980 by an inside archway. The Western Shop maintains a stock of western saddles and horse gear, as well as western clothing. It is operated by Judy Carter Siefkin who came to Weaverville from Sacramento where she had served as private secretary to Edumnd G. "Pat" Brown when he was governor of California.

Site 108. Fagg Building (City Drug Store) (Trinity Journal) (Heffington's) (Western Shop) (Block 10—Lot 20)

This one-story, 20'x60' brick building was erected in 1854 by R. A. Fagg. In 1856 it housed the City Drug Store which was purchased two years later by James Barry. The business was sold to the Weaverville Drug Store across the street, and by 1877 the building was in use as a warehouse in conjunction with Hansen's Store next door. During the time that the U. S. Forest Service was occupying the building two doors down the street (Site 106.), they had a cache of groceries in the front of this building ready for emergency fire fighting use. During the 1940's the building housed the Trinity Journal, followed by a radio shop, and then for a short time Moderne Pharmacy, before becoming Heffington's Gift and Flower Shop. When Heffington's moved, it was purchased from a descendant of the Todd family by Leonard and Florence Morris and is now rented to the Western Shop. The front awning was replaced by the Morrises in order to help restore the building's original exterior appearance. The interior of the building was stripped to expose the beamed ceilings and natural brick walls.

At the rear of this one-story brick building is attached a simple gable, two-story wooden structure which, about 1900, was used as an exercise spa while the front building was being operated as a confectionery. Ryan's store used both of these buildings for warehouse space; Vernon Ryan remembers old exercise bars and equipment being taken out when they moved into the space.

Site 109. Buck and Cole (I.O.O.F. Hall) (Ryan's Store) (Block 10—Lot 21)

A general provisions store occupied this site as early as 1852. F. A. Buck sold his one-half interest in the lot to John Cole on January 11, 1856. The present two-story 20'x57' fireproof brick building was constructed during the summer of that year. The John Cole family resided in the rooms above the store that now comprise the lodge hall of the North Star Lodge #61 of the Independent Order of Oddfellows. In 1860 Ira and Mary A. Howe owned this building which had been known as the Einfalt and Hoslinger brick building. In that same year the present spiral staircase was erected to the second story of the building. William Kolb, former brewer at the Bavarian Brewery, operated a general merchandise store in the lower story at that time. In 1862 Henry Overmohle bought out Kolb. The Oddfellows, who had occupied the second floor of this building since 1862, were able to purchase from Howe the second floor in 1865 for $650. In 1867 Howe sold the lower story to Overmohle who, a year later, sold his part of the building and his business to Detlef Hansen. Hansen continued in business until 1908 when he sold the business and fixtures to Charles Hanna and Rudolph Junkans, retaining the building himself. In 1909 Junkans and Hanna took in an additional partner and the firm became Junkans, Hanna and Ryan (all brothers-in-law). This partnership lasted until 1919 when D. E. Ryan became sole owner. Ryan sold to his son, E. V. "Vernon" Ryan in 1945. All goods were delivered free of charge with delivery being made by pack horse or with horse and wagon. The store maintained its barns, stables, and corrals in the location of Alward Court below the museum. Regular trips were made weekly to deliver to the mines on Canyon Creek and to other customers along the way. When the Globe and other mines closed down during World War I, it was a bitter blow to this business as well as to the other stores in Weaverville. In 1915 a gas pump was installed in front of the building with a gas storage tank placed under the street in front of the store. Groceries were now delivered by pickup truck. This service to customers continued until Ryan sold the store in 1970. This was the last store in Weaverville to provide such a service.

Ryan's Store was sold to Mike and Hilma Harris in 1970. Detlef Hansen died in 1914 and his wife in 1916; they deeded the lower floor of the building to their niece, Louisa H. Brady. In 1980 the Brady family sold the building, and Harris dissolved his business. The building has been purchased by the Mountain Marketplace, a store specializing in natural foods. Two couples own the land, the lower floor of the building and the business. Arnold and Susan Ann Whitridge and Walter and Emily Robb are the new owners. They stripped everything out of the old building and completely restored it before stocking it with groceries. Beautiful handmade bins and fixtures were made locally. Pine and madrone from the area of Junction City and oak from Zenia were used. The wooden floor was stripped and repaired. The building was extended 26 feet at the back and the windows and rear entrance of the old building were enclosed. This old grocery store that saw foodstuffs arrive and leave in bulk has gone full circle and customers may again purchase groceries that are not pre-packaged. The Oddfellows still retain ownership of the second floor. This is the only case of dual ownership of a building remaining in Weaverville.

In the years between 1856 and 1981 the brick building front has changed very little. The original doors and windows have been left as they were. The two-story porch with hip roof was probably added when the spiral staircase

136

Site 109. This stable was used by Junkans, Hanna and Ryan in 1907. In about 1920, it was used by Alward and Root for horses, hay and grain when they had the stage contract between Redding and Weaverville. Roads were impassable for car travel in winter, making horse stages necessary.

Site 109. This is how the Buck and Cole building looks today. It is the last building under dual ownership in Weaverville.

was built in the summer of 1860. The geometric stick railing surrounding the upper porch was skillfully replaced during the 1970's by members of the Oddfellows' Lodge. F. A. Buck, one of the first owners and the author of "Yankee Trader in the Gold Rush", would be pleased with the beautiful condition of this handsome building which occupies land he once owned.

Site 110. Junkans (Trinity Market) (North Valley Bank) (Block 10—Lot 22)

In 1890 Henry Junkans covered the space between the wall of his big brick building (the Tinnin building) and the wall of the Hansen building with a roof. This provided him with warehouse space. This was later used by Blake and Given and Weaverville Supply Company for storage. When the Weaverville Supply took on the Dodge agency, this former warehouse was transformed into a display area for cars and trucks. This is a fine example of an unusual building that really wasn't a building—only a closed-in area between two brick buildings. It is now in fine condition and the area to the rear that was once Junkans' pack station for his general merchandise store is now a parking lot. The building was used at a later date as a secondhand store. About 1946 John Fields purchased the grocery department from Weaverville Supply Company. At the same time he purchased this building and the Tinnin-Junkans brick building next door. After much remodeling, the space became Trinity Market, a grocery store. When Trinity Market moved to its present location, the property was purchased by Mr. and Mrs. Horace Stevens who remodeled it to accommodate North Valley Bank. The 1860 lithograph of the "Mai Fest" shows the New Orleans Bar occupying a double two-story frame building on this site.

Site 111. Tinnin Building (Junkans) (Abrahms & Karsky) (Trinity Market) (North Valley Bank) (Block 10—Lot 23)

This one-story brick building was built in 1856 for W. J. Tinnin. Tinnin, an attorney, later became the twentieth Grand Master of Masons in California. He also served as a member to the State Assembly in the early 1870's. W. J. Tinnin operated a hardware and tin shop in this building which is the longest of any of the brick buildings. The front remains as it was when first constructed. Two sets of narrow, high French doors are recessed into the brick front. Heavy iron shutters flank their sides. The rear of the building is two-story and has easy access to the downstairs by two iron shuttered doorways of unequal size. Above them are two iron-shuttered unequal sized windows. Two doorways along the south side of the long building show that they were intended to open out to the spacious courtyard at the side and to the back. Vernon Ryan remembers that this area was used as a pack station about 1910. There were sheds and barns to house horses and mules as well as their hay and feed. Also in this area there was a sawdust-filled ice house.

Between 1867 and 1895 Henry Junkans was the owner of the business and building. He operated an extensive hardware and general merchandise business as well as several mines and thirty-five or forty miles of mining ditches. After the Junkans ownership, the building was used by Abrahms and Karsky. They continued the same type of grocery and general merchandise business as was carried on by Junkans. At this same time Abrahms and Karsky had a clothing store across the street. The building was later used as a warehouse in conjunction with the Blake and Reed store, the Weaverville Supply Company, and more recently the Trinity Market. In 1964 it was leased by Mr. and Mrs. Horace J. Stevens and purchased by them in 1970. This building is beautifully kept and is one of the finest examples of the fireproof brick buildings of the 1850's.

Site 85. The present library building was constructed in 1856 by John Carr who was a blacksmith. He may have used this for his shop.

Site 111. This is a 1981 photo of the rear of the Tinnin building which was constructed in 1856. It is the longest of the fireproof buildings.

Site 112. Timmerman Building (Mint Saloon) (LaGrange Office) (Brandes Realty) (Block 10—Lot 24)

An 1860 lithograph shows that at that time the two-story Miner's Hotel occupied this site. Timmerman, a maker of cabinets and fine furniture as well as an undertaker, had his business here. (In the I.O.O.F. Hall, at the time of this writing, there is a large oak desk built by Timmerman over a century ago.) The main Timmerman building was used as a showroom with a carpenter shop connected at the rear. In 1887 this 20'x60' frame building caught fire and was destroyed, taking the post office next door with it. Timmerman rebuilt and restocked, only to have another devastating fire three years later. The fire started both times in the shavings of the carpentry shop. The post office survived this time. Timmerman then purchased J. L. Schall's brick building across the street (formerly used as a shoe store) and moved his remaining stock to Schall's building. S. J. Turner purchased Timmerman's lot and built this one-story building. The building housed the Mint Saloon until prohibition. In the 1920's, during the time he was undersheriff, Judson Van Matre and his family lived here. Later the LaGrange Mine had an office in the building, and Margaret and Dr. Lyman Stookey (Superintendent of the LaGrange Mine) used the front as an office and the rear as living quarters. In 1946. Vincent and Marie Brandes Ryan occupied the office and home. Robert Brandes is the present owner and has used the building as an insurance and real estate office.

Site 113. Adams Express (Post Office) (Law Offices) (Wilkins) (Block 10—Lot 25)

The lot now occupied by Wilkin's law office has had on it several buildings over the years with many uses. The Hope Restaurant may have been the first. Adams and Company Express was another. Between 1876 and 1878 a business directory lists Charles Harmouth, postmaster and hairdresser, at this location. In 1887 Alex A. Stiller was postmaster when Timmerman's building, next door, caught fire. The post office was also destroyed. The next day a new building was started, and within a week the post office was back in business. Three years later Timmerman's new building burned and this time the post office was spared. Snow covered the roof and the side wall was kept from catching fire when townspeople threw snowballs and shovelled snow against it. Fortunately, a narrow alley has always run between this building and the one to the south. Judge Threshie had his law office in the building in 1922. It was used as a beauty parlor by Mrs. Russell in the 1930's and early 1940's.

For some time the building has been occupied by attorneys. The tenants have been Edwin J. Regan, Donald S. Kennedy, E. Richard Walker, James J. White, and Alfred S. Wilkins who is the present owner. The one-story building has its original horizontal wood siding. Two twelve light windows replace earlier six light double hung windows. One of the original windows remains in the old front portion on the alley side. Two added-on sections extend the building in the back. An enormous locust tree shades the rear office space.

Site 114. Eder Building (Weaverville Supply Company) (Van Matre's) (Block 10—Lot 26)

This one-story, 20'x70' building was built in 1854 and was the first of the brick "fire proof" buildings constructed in Weaverville. By 1857 D. M. Eder had sold his building to Joseph Kahn who operated a clothing store in it for a short time before selling to E. Neblett. In 1870 Alex Love purchased it for a town hall. In 1893 it was used as a warehouse. In 1895 Blake and Reed Company expanded their business and used this building for "gents" furnishings. This use has continued to the present day. In 1925 the front was modernized by the Weaverville Supply Company. The iron shutters were removed and plate glass show windows were installed.

In 1945 W. P. "Pete" Van Matre and his wife, Karlyn Junkans Van Matre, purchased the business from the Supply Company. Albert and Rose Blaney Meckel owned the building at that time. The following year they sold it to Van Matres. This couple, both descendants of pioneer Trinity families, continued to operate the store for the next thirty years. In 1975 the building on Lot 26 and the building on Lot 27, as well as the business known as "Van Matre's", were sold to Thomas Jerome Ludden.

Luddens, like "Pete" and Karlyn Van Matre, are not newcomers to Trinity County. Tom's grandparents, Thomas Jefferson and Emma Adell Ludden, moved to Buckhorn Mountain in 1904 to establish a homestead and timber claim. His father, Chesley D. Ludden, was born there in 1908. Tom has taught in the local elementary school for many years and currently serves on the Shasta College Board of Trustees.

This store is truly a "family" store. In addition to Tom and his wife Joanne, daughter Kimberly and son Patrick T. Ludden, together with Patrick's wife Cindy, also work in the business.

Site 115. Rhodes and Whitney Bank (Blake and Reed) (Weaverville Supply Company) (Van Matre's) (Block 10—Lot 27)

This one-story, 21'x70' brick building was constructed for Rhodes and Company for $7,000. Rhodes and Whitney, a bank and exchange office, was the first to occupy it. Jessee Rhodes sold it to James and Peter McCain; in 1867

140

Site 114-115. This street scene is in front of the Weaverville Supply Company after 1901. "Gents Furnishings and Dry Goods" is now Van Matre's. Morris Hardware is to the right.

they were advertising their dry goods and clothing business here. When the next door business of Blake and Reed was expanded in 1895, it expanded to include this store. The Weaverville Supply Company became the successor to Blake and Reed in 1901. Their grocery department occupied this building. When the Weaverville Supply Company dissolved its business in 1945, Albert Meckel, a partner in the company, was the owner of the building. He retained ownership of the building and sold the grocery department to John Fields upon his return from military service in 1946. The next year John and Shirley Fields moved the grocery business a few doors to the south (see Sites 110 and 111.). Albert Meckel died a short time later; his wife, Rose Blaney Meckel, willed this building to her nephew, Henry Fields. It was rented for a time to Trinity County Title Company. When the Title Company moved, Van Matre's dry good business next door, expanded into this store space. They purchased the building from Henry Fields in 1968.

This portion of Van Matre's, as well as the store on Lot 26 next door, was sold in 1975 to Thomas L. Ludden. Van Matre's name was retained. The business continues to be a ladies' ready-to-wear department. The front window in this store was the first on the street to be remodeled when a bay window was installed. This was later removed and replaced with a window flush to the wall. An original iron-shuttered entry door remains to the right of the window. The four buildings of Van Matre's and Morris Hardware are connected inside by beautiful old archways, bringing back the former department store charm from the turn of the century when the business operated as Blake and Reed, and later as the Weaverville Supply Company. On the outside the buildings are connected by an awning.

Site 116. This is the Blake and Reed Store in 1894. Successors to this store were the Weaverville Supply Company (1901-1945) and Morris Hardware (1945 --). Pictured here are (left to right) H. R. Given, Dr. S. L. Blake, Frank T. Blake, Carl W. Bremer and William Condon.

Site 116. McCain and Company (Blake and Reed) (Weaverville Supply Company) (Morris Hardware) (Block 10—Lots 28 and 29)

James S. McCain and Thomas Gallagher of Weaverville bought the land for what became McCain and Company on August 2, 1852, and started a hardware and general merchandise business. In 1854 McCain hired Francis W. Blake to construct a one-story fireproof, 21'x40' brick building on the upper lot (Lot 29). Later the same year McCain commissioned J. M. Rhodes to erect a 20'x70' brick building south of the first (Lot 28). This building was destined to be used as a hardware and general merchandise store for the next 127 years. An advertisement in the Trinity Journal of September 28, 1861, refers to the following: "James S. McCain and Company, groceries, clothing, oilcloth, hardware of every variety, crockery, codfish and mackerel, cigars, tobacco, mining and blasting powder."

Max Lang owned the building between 1869 and 1890. (His advertisement gave special attention to the manufacture of hydraulic pipe, tin ware, etc.) Lang then sold to W. F. Smith, S. L. Blake and H. R. Given for $11,000. The firm name was Blake and Given. They also owned the Trinity Journal at the same time. A wood frame, second-story was added on the brick saloon building next door (Lot 29) and this became the new home of the newspaper. On May 15, 1895, Blake and Reed Company, a corporation, took possession and expanded to include the building next door (Site 115.) and the Eder building (Site 114.) as well as a warehouse (Sites 110. and 111.).

Blake and Reed continued until 1901, when the firm became the Weaverville Supply Company, a corporation with the following owners: Carl W. Bremer,

Albert C. Meckel, Adolph N. Meckel, George F. Gehm, Frederick C. Meckel and David P. Davis. The first two named owners worked in the firm continuously from 1901 until 1945. They were old men by the time the business was sold. The Weaverville Supply was a general store selling almost everything. They occupied not only most of the buildings in the upper west side of Main Street, but the whole area between the buildings and the creek as well. There were wagon sheds, horse stalls, corrals and warehouses in back. The business made weekly deliveries with wagons pulled by both two and four horse teams to Junction City and Helena, as well as up the North Fork to the Enterprise and Keystone mines. The LaGrange Mine on Oregon Mountain was one of their best customers. Blasting powder was an important item in the store when the mines were in operation. A "powder house" was kept a short distance from town in Ash Hollow. Deliveries included blasting powder along with other items. After the Weaverville Supply Company acquired the agency for Dodge cars and trucks, they changed from horse delivery to truck delivery. A gas pump was installed at the edge of the sidewalk, with a large gas storage tank buried under the street. This was before the advent of service stations. In 1945 the large business was divided and sold to various parties. The buildings on Lots 28 and 29 were purchased by Leonard M. Morris and Harold F. Sebring as partners.

The building on Lot 29, constructed in 1854 for McCain, had many business tenants over the years. After McCain moved to the larger building next door, Gettleson may have been the first firm name. For years this building was the home of the Corner Saloon and later the Challenge Saloon. With the advent of prohibition in the 1920's it could no longer be used as a saloon, so for a time Frank Searles, who already had a popcorn machine in his building, served soft drinks. Later Mr. and Mrs. Wm. Seeman operated a tailor shop there, and after that the Raleigh Carrico family operated The Sahara Cafe for several years. In 1940 a fire broke out in their kitchen located in the wooden frame building behind the dining room. The fire consumed not only their kitchen but also the former Trinity Journal office on the top of the brick building in front. Fortunately, the Journal had recently moved to the building south of Ryan's store. The brick saloon which Carrico's used as a dining room was not seriously damaged. The Weaverville Supply Company owned the property at this time and replaced the wooden structure in back, but not the former second story. During World War II the front brick building was used as a draft board office; the building in the rear was occupied by the Red Cross and later became a dental office. The rest of the building became part of Morris Hardware. Today, the exterior front looks much as it did when first built. The windows and doors have not been changed. From 1949 to 1974 the business and buildings were owned by Leonard and Florence Scott Morris and became known as Morris Hardware.

In 1957 Morris Hardware tore down the old sheds in back of the store (except for one warehouse) and a new two-story steel building was joined to the rear of the 1854 brick. In 1974 the business and buildings were sold to a son, Richard L. Morris, who had worked as a partner in the store since finishing college. In 1979 Dick Morris restored the inside of the brick building (Lot 28) to expose the original brick walls, beamed ceiling and fir floors. A back porch and entrance from the parking area were added at this time. The horse and wagons are gone from the back area; there are Honda cycles and pleasure and fishing boats to take their place. Deliveries continue from the store as they have in years past, but delivery is often of fine furniture. The rock powder house in Ash Hollow was torn down when it was no longer safe to store Hercules blasting powder in an area now grown up with family homes. The hardware store on

Lots 28 and 29 is one of the oldest, if not the oldest, hardware store in the state of California.

Leonard Morris served for twelve years as Trinity County Clerk, Auditor and Recorder prior to going into the store. Leonard and Dick Morris are both past presidents of the California Retail Hardware Association.

Site 117. Godfrey Building Site

Originally there were three buildings at the head of Main Street between the Courthouse and Morris Hardware. In the 1930's it was decided to change the main highway to Junction City from its former route up Oregon Street to be an extension of Main Street past the Courthouse. This necessitated the removal of these three buildings. The Godfrey building was a wooden frame structure, two-story in the back and one-story in front. Mrs. Godfrey had lived in the upstairs after her home on lower Main Street burned. After her death in the 1920's the upper floor was used by various businesses. At one time it was Weaverville's principal "boot-leg" shop. Mr. Barber had his barber shop there for a time. The lower floor of the building was used as a stage office when Goetze had the contract between Weaverville and Junction City. The drivers used this downstairs space for their quarters and gear. A narrow alleyway ran between the Godfrey building and the then Weaverville Supply Co. store.

Site 118. Craig Building Site

The Craig Building was the center building of the three that originally closed off Main Street at the north end. Joseph Craig was the maker of the famous Craig Rifle. (There is a 44 Caliber target rifle made by Craig on display at the museum.) Craig's home and gunshop were located in this building. Vernon Ryan remembers hearing about Craig "sighting-in" his guns from a narrow balcony that ran the length of the back of the upper story of this building. Craig would shoot over to a big white rock on the hill above the present Ryan home (Site 36.) on Union Street. Christian Wolf Craig, son of Joseph Craig, was publisher of the Trinity Journal from 1877 until 1887, when he sold the newspaper and moved from Weaverville. Later the post office was located in this building. At one time Tony and Sara Dickey Anderline conducted a leather shop and repair business here. The building was destroyed in the 1930's.

Site 119. Loomis and Huscroft (Mountain Market Site)

The Loomis and Huscroft building was built as a two-story brick building at the head of Main Street. As early as 1856 this building was known as the Mountain Market and it always remained a butcher shop. Loomis and Huscroft ran the business in 1856. In 1897 James Dockery had the market; by 1905 H. W. Goetze was the owner. Between 1908 and 1909 their ad listed the business as "Butchers and Teaming". Bigelow Bros. Butcher Shop was here in 1917 and by 1922 it was Antone Caton's. Warren Leach and Charles Kreiss purchased the meat market from Caton and remained here until they moved the Mountain Market to the Edgecombe building prior to highway construction.

The picture of the big white steer which hung in Mountain Market from the time Goetze owned the business may be seen at the museum. This picture was painted by George Yount, Weaverville artist. Children sent to the butcher shop for meat remember this picture as well as the slice of bologna they received as a gift from the butcher, who for years was Louis Schall.

Meat was purchased only in butcher shops, not in grocery stores, during the time of the Mountain Market. This market was an open market on the street

Site 118. The area between the Courthouse and Morris Hardware was occupied by three buildings before the 1930's when they were removed to make room for the highway. The Mountain Market was a brick structure.

Site 119. This freighter turning in a 55' circle on upper Main Street was driven by Harry Larrison, "King Pin" of the early freight team drivers.

Site 116. This ancient powder house was built in Ash Hollow for Blake and Reed (now Morris Hardware). It was abandoned when residences were built nearby.

Site 120. The first lookout on Weaver Bally was set up in 1912 "at the spring". This structure was built later in order to obtain better visibility of the Trinity River canyon.

side. Two big arches in the brick wall were covered at night by heavy iron shutters. At the back of the building was a walk-in cold storage room, kept cool with a big refrigeration plant. A huge belt ran the compressor for an ice plant as well as the walk-in box, where as much as a ton of ice would be stored. The belt also ran meat grinders and a sausage stuffer. Goetze also had a bottling works and manufactured creme soda. The east wall of the main shop had huge hooks where halves and quarters of fresh meat were hung from which the butchers cut meat to order. It was not uncommon during cooler weather to see a whole veal carcass hanging in front of the market overnight.

This two-story brick building was the first of the "fireproof bricks" to be lost; the second was the two-story Fagg building which was demolished to make way for the Bank of America. Eighteen of the original twenty remain.

Site 120. Weaver Bally Area

Weaver Bally is an historically significant mountain ridge which rises 5000 feet above Weaver Basin. Three dormant mining ditches traverse the side of the mountain. The oldest one, the Chaumont Quitry Ditch, was built prior to 1894 and was named for the father of Baroness De LaGrange. Baron De La-Grange, a French nobleman, was the president of the LaGrange Hydraulic Mining Company that constructed the second and longest ditch. The LaGrange Mine, at its peak production, was the largest hydraulic gold mine in the world. To supply sufficient water for this operation, located at the head of Oregon Gulch at the southern end of Weaver Bally Mountain, it was necessary to obtain additional water. In 1898 construction of a 29 mile-long series of flumes, siphons, ditches and tunnels were added to the Quitry Ditch and combined to form the LaGrange Ditch which brought water from the headwaters of Stuart Fork to the mine site. The ditch started at the mouth of Deer Creek and extended along the east side of the Stuart Fork drainage. A large part of this section was flume. It crossed Deep Creek on a high trestle where it also picked up water from a smaller extension of flume. The water was siphoned across the Stuart Fork at a point near Bridge Camp, using a 30-inch steel pipe with a drop of more than 1,000 feet. Alongside this pipe was another 18-

Site 120. This pretty little lake sits in a basin on the east side of Weaver Bally and is a source of Weaverville's water supply.

Site 120. This is Ed Blunden beside the ditch tender's cabin of the LaGrange ditch on Weaver Bally. This cabin will soon be reconstructed on the museum grounds.

inch pipe. From here a ditch took the water for about two miles to a tunnel, 9,000 feet long, cut through solid rock and which extended from Van Matre Creek to Rush Creek. At Rush Creek additional water was picked up. There were two other tunnels in the system: the so-called Mud Tunnel which extended from Little Brown's Creek to the East Branch of East Weaver Creek, and a tunnel from Sidney Gulch to West Weaver. A number of ditch tender's cabins were established along the ditch which contoured around the side of Weaver Bally at about the 3500 foot elevation. Water from the ditch was collected in a reservoir at the top of Oregon Mountain.

Contouring the mountain at the 4000 foot elevation is the third ditch, the Sweepstake. It is a ditch and pipeline constructed in 1901 to bring water from East Weaver Creek to the Sweepstake Mine site located at the head of Dutton Creek on the west side of Oregon Mountain. The previous year, the Sweepstake Gold Mining and Ditch Company had purchased a large acreage of land in the area. The land was reported to contain huge deposits of gold-bearing gravel. The Sweepstake ditch system was intended to not only bring water from East Weaver Creek but there was to be a branch ditch and tunnel which was to bring water from Canyon Creek as well. These two branches of the system were to come together at Glennison Gap. Glennison Gap is a low point or gap at the southern toe of Weaver Bally where it meets Oregon Mountain. In early days the main trail for foot and horse travel from Weaverville to Canon City and the upper Canyon Creek area passed through Glennison Gap as did a trail to Junction City down Clear Gulch. The Canyon Creek branch of the Sweepstake ditch system was started but never completed. Besides the abandoned mining ditch, there still remains today a portion of a narrow guage road or trail over which the pipe for the siphon portion of the Sweepstake system was transported. This "Dolly Road", as it is known, roughly parallels the ditch and pipeline.

The Sweepstake mining venture was of short duration. Frought with difficulties and disappointments, the mine closed after only one year of operation. In 1908, however, the LaGrange Company acquired the Sweepstake holdings including the ditch system. For awhile a small amount of water from West Weaver was used for domestic purposes by the LaGrange Company and for a short time this water was used to power a sawmill. In the late 1920's the line from West Weaver to East Weaver was reactivated; a greater volume of water became available and was used for mining purposes.

In 1933, as the result of an agreement between the LaGrange Company and the state of California, the LaGrange hydraulic equipment and the Sweepstake ditch were used to cut through Oregon Mountain for the location of the State Highway. In making the highway cut, 10,748,000 cubic yards of material were moved. To make such a highway cut using the hydraulic method was an unusual undertaking.

The East Weaver drainage on the side of Weaver Bally not only supplied water for the LaGrange and Sweepstake mines but it is also the source of domestic water for the town of Weaverville. East Weaver Lake at the head of the drainage was also the first source of ice for the town. Before the advent of mechanical refrigerators, ice was cut at the lake and packed to Weaverville by horses and mules.

The story of the significance of Weaver Bally is not complete without reference to the Forest Service lookout which is located on its crest. The first lookout post for the detection of forest fires was set up in a tent located "at the spring". In 1912 a permanent structure was erected at a spot 200 yards north of the present U. S. Forest Service lookout. It was moved to its present location in order to obtain better visibility of the Trinity River canyon and more especially the Junction City area. During the Depression years a rash of incendiary fires occurred and better fire detection was needed. The new lookout was built in 1936 by Jim Everest with the help of men from the Civilian Conservation Corps. For many years the lookout could be reached only by trail. In 1955 the Southern Pacific Land Company built a road as far as Low Gap in order to log their holdings on the mountain. At that time the Forest Service, under the direction of Jim McKnight, extended the road to the lookout for a cash outlay of $865.00. The original single wire ground line still provides telephone service to the lookout.

Site 121. Junkans Ranch, Barn and Sawmill Site (Costa Ranch and Barn)

The Junkans Ranch, later known as the Costa Ranch, is located just west of the intersection of Highway 3 and Rush Creek.

William Junkans, Sr. owned the 520 acre ranch during the 1890's. He ran cattle, as well as operated a sawmill at the ranch. The sawmill was situated just south of the barn and the old road to Minersville passed near the mill.

This first sawmill was run by water power from nearby Rush Creek. A later mill was powered by steam. At that time Bill Carr of Lewiston was fireman and J. J. Jackson was sawyer. Lou and Ed Todd of Weaverville worked in the woods and used oxen to skid logs from forest to mill. Later, horses were used. Although a plentiful supply of timber grew on the ranch property, the operation was unsuccessful as there was little sale for lumber at that time. Frank Costa remembers huge stacks of sawed boards lining both sides of the road. Some boards measured as much as twenty-four inches across. The mill eventually closed and nothing remains today.

Junkans built an enormous barn with lumber and timbers from the mill. The barn measures 60'x70' and is 50 feet high. Two huge double doors opening on the south side enabled large pieces of equipment and wagons to be drawn in for winter storage. Stanchions to hold 150 head of cattle, as well as space for 150 tons of loose hay fit comfortably within the structure. There were stalls for the horses used in logging as well as those for running the beef cattle. This large barn covered with weathered wood is in good condition today, partly due to the corrugated iron roof over the original wood shakes. The area around the barn is neat and orderly and many old fruit trees are still growing nearby.

The lower forty acre ranch was the first home of Jesse and Joaquina Costa and was purchased in 1885 from a man named McBride. At first it was a mining claim and was patented in 1906. Jesse Costa then purchased the upper 520 acre Junkans Ranch from the Junkans estate, as well as 160 acres from Godfrey and 156 acres from Blake and Reed. Frank Costa was born on the lower ranch when it adjoined the Junkans Ranch. He and his wife, Maida Hafley Costa, now live in a cottage to the north of the enormous barn. Although Jesse and Joaquina Costa had other children, Frank is the last to live on the place. Frank and George Costa, brothers, mined along the creek below the fields for a number of years. George left to mine in Alaska and other places; Frank remained and mined above the ranch opposite the Rush Creek Campground. He may have operated the last hydraulic mine in Trinity County.

HELENA - JUNCTION CITY

KEY TO HISTORIC SITES

1. Junction City Hotel
2. Meckel House
3. Enos House
4. Junction City Mining Ditches
5. Bergin Gulch-Bergin Mine
6. White Oak Gulch Mine
7. Big Gulch
8. Chapman Mine-Ranch
9. Evans Bar
10. Indian Rancheria (site)
11. Myers Ranch
12. China Hill Mine
13. Maple Creek Mines
14. Dutch Creek Ranch
15. Soldier Creek Road
16. Carter Ranch
17. Colonel Seelye Grave
18. Mun Loa Spring
19. Sturdivant Ranch
20. Junction City Cemetery
21. Arkansas Dam (site)
22. Felter's Ranch
23. LaGrange Mine
24. Sweepstake Mine
25. Altoona Ranch
26. Cie Fse Mine
27. Hocker Ranch
28. Davy Evans Grave
29. McGillivray Ranch
30. Jim Dedrick Home
31. Clear Gulch
32. Butler's
33. Lizard Point
34. The Steps
35. Reservoir Hill
36. Pennsylvania Bar
37. Gold Dollar Mine
38. Conrad Gulch
39. Pioneer Trail Crossing
40. Rarick Gulch
41. Clark Mine
42. Dannenbrink Mine
43. Gwinn Gulch-Burger Home
44. Canon City Cemetery
45. Guthrie Place
46. Hayes-Cie Fse Mine Dam (site)
47. Canon City
48. Fisher Gulch
49. Early Hydraulic Mines-Tunnel
50. Murphy Ranch
51. Canyon Creek Placers Community
52. East Fork Road
53. Dedrick
54. Old Adams Place
55. Ackerman Homestead
56. Chloride-Bailey Mill (site)
57. Globe Mill
58. Schlomer Brick Building
59. Meckel Brick Building
60. Currie House
61. Schlomer Feed Stable
62. Helena Cemetery
63. The Spring
64. Ritterbush Gulch and Cove
65. Durkee's Sawmill (site)
66. North Fork Bridge
67. Brock Gulch
68. Annie Slide
69. Buntain Ranch
70. Peter Zuella Place
71. Tolin Place
72. Rich Gulch
73. Hobo Gulch Road
74. Alex Pelletreau Home-Mine
75. Engle and Ozark Mines
76. Barney Gulch
77. Oklahoma Bar
78. North Star Mine
79. Lone Jack Mine
80. Enterprise Mine
81. Cliff House
82. Coleridge and Yellowstone Mine
83. Yellow Jacket Mine
84. Keystone Mine
85. Bob's Farm
86. Molitor Mine

LEGEND

- - - - - - - - - - ROADS

~~~~~~~~~~ STREAMS AND RIVERS

● HISTORIC SITES

AREA **III**
JUNCTION CITY-HELENA

Junction City
Historical Overview

It is historically useful to think of Junction City not just as a small village, but as a community covering the region along the Trinity River from Dutch Creek to Lime Point. The pioneer Junction City school house, where community dances were held, was symbolic of the regional nature of the community. It was located a mile from the village and just off the Weaverville road on a small flat near Oregon Gulch. Here it could be accessible to pupils from up and down both sides of the Trinity River and from Oregon Gulch and Canyon Creek. It is interesting that the site of a new Junction City community park should be near the old schoolhouse site — just across Highway 299.

Historical changes in the Junction City area should be thought of in terms of the river, in terms of the methods of transportation at a given time and in terms of the routes that developed as the modes of travel changed. The travel routes from Weaverville in the first years of the 1850's were of course by trail, on foot or horseback. The main route was from Weaverville to Douglas City, from Douglas City to Steiner Flat, from Steiner Flat to Evans Bar, from Evans Bar to the Sturdivant Ranch, from Sturdivant's past the Felter Ranch on Oregon Gulch and thence to the mouth of Canyon Creek, where in the early 1850's there were a sawmill and a small settlement called Milltown. The bluffs beyond the mouth of Canyon Creek on the north side of the Trinity River were impassable until the 1930's when Highway 299 was constructed. Early down-river travel went down the Red Hill or south side of the river. Issac Cox, following the route just described, reports that he crossed the river near the mouth of Canyon Creek on a ferry operated by John Hocker and then traveled down the Red Hill side to the Hocker Ranch, where John Hocker also had a trading post and facilities for overnight guests. From there Cox went past the Red Hill mines and crossed the river on a bridge at the McGillivray Ranch (near the present location of the Big Foot Campground).

In the early 1850's the settlement at the mouth of Canyon Creek had a gold rush and then for a period of time apparently declined. Cox reports that there were in 1852 two or three cabins, the Henry Seelye and Dowles sawmill, a trading post, one blacksmith shop, one butcher shop and a hotel. Cox estimated that there were between 150 and 200 miners at work. In addition he reported 70 to 80 Chinese.

151

In the middle 1850's Joseph Sturdivant put a toll bridge near the mouth of Oregon Gulch. Travelers coming over the trail from Weaverville via Oregon Gulch or following the river route could cross the river on Sturdivant's toll bridge and go down the river on the Red Hill side. The Sturdivant bridge apparently had the effect, for a time, of putting Milltown off the main travel route. The Red Hill area, with John Hocker's Ranch, trading post and mill as a center, seems to have been the scene of the greatest human activity; the Arkansas Dam area (between Chapman's Ford and the Sturdivant Ranch) and lower Oregon Gulch were probably next in importance.

There was a period during the 1850's when, for election purposes, the Board of Supervisors designated the polling place at the junction of Canyon Creek and the Trinity as the "Mouth of Canyon Creek," a name to which the Trinity Journal took a marked dislike. Events were occurring to bring about changes, however. Weaverville was connected with Shasta by a wagon road in April of 1858. In May of 1859 the Oregon Gulch Wagon Road was opened. That same year a road was built from McGillivray's Ranch to the North Fork. In 1861 a Canyon Creek road was started to connect with the road at McGillivray's, circumventing the formidable bluffs along the Trinity. As the age of horse and wagon travel arrived in Trinity County, the Mouth of Canyon Creek was becoming a junction point in the newly developing transportation routes. The Trinity Journal editorialized that the settlement should be called Junction City. On August 19, 1861, a post office called Messerville in the Oregon Gulch area was closed and a post office established at the mouth of Canyon Creek. The town of Junction City officially came into being.

The year 1861, which brought the official naming of the community, also brought the disastrous great flood of the century. It was in the Junction City area where the effects of the flood were most dramatically evident. The Trinity Journal's December 21, 1861 edition published an hour-by-hour account of the destruction. Here at the confluence of the Trinity River and Canyon Creek the river "became an ocean, spreading from mountain to mountain, sweeping in its furious current farm houses, miners' cabins, mills, men, women and children; in very truth all that was animate and inanimate." Besides homes, sections of bridges and flumes were destroyed. Everything within one hundred feet of the river was washed away. While the flood of 1861 was unique in its fury, Junction City suffered periodic rampages of the river, including the one in 1955 pictured in this book, until the construction of the Trinity Dam.

Although the economic condition and the optimism of many of the most prominent citizens became markedly altered as a result of the flood, Junction City, during the next three decades, became more and more of a town. It was during the 1860's that Junction City's most famous hotel, the Carter House, was erected by John W. Carter, whose son, Robert H. Carter, was later county clerk for many years. It was located on a site in the upper part of the town just beyond the building now known as the Enos House. Among the owners were Gottlieb Baumgartner and Gustav Thede; Richard M. Stone; C. W. Day and G. W. Todd; John C. Wallace; and Josephus Bradbury. Also after the flood, Louis Raab, one of Junction City's most famous Germans and about whom old timers told tales, built a new home, store and saloon in town. The home stood about where the Junction City Cavern is now located; the saloon was on the opposite side of the street. Many years later, the Raab home, with a rooming house added, became the John Bartlett Hotel. A notable older home was the house of the William Cushman Given family located on a lot just up the street (in the direction of Dedrick) from the present tavern. Adjoining the Given property further in this direction was a saloon with a residence in the

Old Junction City before the great fire of 1897 destroyed the north end of the town. The photograph shows the location of the famous Carter House, the two-story town hall (at the left), the Louis Raab house (about the middle of the picture), the Reed warehouse and barns on the bedrock, and Chinatown in the right foreground near the river.

The Carter House, Junction City's most famous hotel, at the first centennial celebration, July 4, 1876.

During the 1870's the hillside point at the south end of Junction City was mined by George P. Chapman and his brother-in-law W. C. Given, creating the bedrock flat now occupied by the elementary school, the North Fork Grange, and the U. S. Forest Service. Given is standing to the right of the rocker. His nephew, Fred Gross, is at center.

Junction City about 1918, showing one of the two suspension foot bridges across Canyon Creek; the home of Edgar Reed, Jr., in the lot to the right of the bridge; the Cummings store (later the Enos House); the alfalfa fields of Fritz Meckel at both the upper and lower ends of the town; and the white house of James C. Given in the field at the far right.

rear. It was first operated by Peter Verstegen, a pioneer German miner, and later by John Bartlett. Another house erected in the period after the flood was Heinrich Schneider's home on Main Street. Of the several buildings just described, this house is the only building still standing today.

Mining, as has already been suggested, played a central role in the history of Junction City. In 1867 the editor of the Trinity Journal observed that there were more good-paying mining claims in the vicinity of Junction City than in any other place in the county. By the 1870's hydraulic mining was coming into vogue and the sluiced-off red mountain sides and exposed bedrock surfaces on both sides of the Trinity River testify today to the extent of the hydraulic mining during the last part of the nineteenth century and the first two decades of the twentieth. In fact, if one judges by the large amount of sluiced-off sections of red earth, the exposed bedrock, the deep gashes and cuts and the tailings of mines such as those from the LaGrange, then hydraulic mining in the greater Junction City area appears to have been of greater extent than in any other part of the county.

More details on Junction City mining appear later in this account. Two mining operations, however, should be mentioned at this point. During the 1870's the hillside point at the south end of the town was mined off by George P. Chapman and his brother-in-law, W. C. Given. The bedrock flat that resulted is now occupied by the Junction City Elementary School, the North Fork Grange, and the U. S. Forest Service, as well as by the homes of the Harold Smiths and the John Mikkolas. (This information was obtained from Mrs. Elinor McCartney, granddaughter of Chapman.) The township survey of W. S. Lowden, recorded September 16, 1896, and made for the purpose of patenting the properties, included lots. on this bedrock as part of the town. In fact the accompanying map indicated that Main Street of Junction City was partly located on this bedrock area and made approximately a ninety degree turn to the right before going down the hill to the main part of the old town.

A second important development in the history of Junction City's hydraulic mining took place in the 1880's. Previous to this time hydraulic mining in the area had been carried on by families or partnerships, with a few extra men hired when necessary. Later hydraulic mining was done on a larger scale and was financed by outside capital. In the 1880's, for example, Albert H. Hayes, of Boston, purchased all the mining property on the Red Hill side of the Trinity River between the Bergin Mine and Hocker Gulch. Under the management of E. M. Benjamin extensive work was done to bring water from Canyon Creek near Canon City. The Trinity Journal in 1892 reported that this mine employed 92 men. In 1894 Hayes sold his mining interests to a group of French capitalists who operated the mine under the name Compagnie Francaise des Placers Hydrauliques de Junction City. Locally the mine became known as the Cie Fse Mine. During the time of the operation of the mine, Junction City was at the height of its development.

In 1876 a young man twenty-two years old by the name of Edgar L. Reed came from New Hampshire to Junction City. For thirty years, until his death in 1906, Edgar Reed was a leading figure in the affairs of the town. Reed first engaged in ranching and lumbering with John Whitmore. In 1878 this particular business was dissolved and Reed and Whitmore purchased the mercantile business of Kuper and Karsky Company in Junction City. Two years later, in 1880, Reed married Whitmore's daughter, Mathilda, who had been educated in a private finishing school in the San Francisco Bay area. The Edgar Reed home was on the east side of Main Street and was the most comfortable and most fashionably furnished house ever erected in the town. Adjoining the home property on the same side of the street was the store building, which still

155

stands and which today is known as the old Junction City Hotel building. The Reed home no longer exists. Whitmore continued in the lumber business and operated steam saw mills on Oregon Mountain and Brown's Creek. He moved to Weaverville where he built a home on the corner of Main and Center Streets, This building, which still stands today, is one of the very nicely proportioned Victorian houses in the town. Edgar L. Reed for a time operated the mercantile business in Junction City under his own name. With S. L. Blake he founded the firm of Blake and Reed Company, which was incorporated on May 7, 1895, to do general merchandise business both at Weaverville and Junction City. Reed was in charge of the Junction City branch of the business.

In August of 1895, the Trinity Journal called Junction City "the liveliest town in the county". Not only in the area near the town, but on Canyon Creek and the Helena area, mining was flourishing. The LaGrange Mine between Weaverville and Junction City employed a large force of men and the Cie Fse Mine across the river in the McKinney Gulch and Benjamin Flat area was at the height of its operation. In addition to the Blake and Reed mercantile business there were two other merchandise stores carrying on business in Junction City. The town had its own butcher shop. A Catholic Church had been built on the bedrock area of the town. The community had a town hall which, in addition to other functions, served as a place for Protestant religious services. From the time of its founding the town had several saloons. To counteract their influence, the village had a strong and active temperance union supported energetically by a number of wives. From the time of its naming until the end of the century, glimpses of life in Junction City are often delightfully recounted in the Trinity Journal. The following issues are suggested to the reader: March 14, 1863; February 13, 1864; November 3, 1867; July 29, 1870; February 11 and June 10, 1871; May 30 and August 1, 1874; April 2, 1892; August 16, 1895; and September 25, 1897.

In September of 1897 fire broke out in the store of Abrahms and Karsky and destroyed all buildings on both sides of Main Street in the upper third of the town, the section which today includes all of the modern buildings in the village. The famous Carter House and the town hall both burned to the ground.

Scarcely two months later the Trinity Journal reported that the majority of those burned out by the fire were rebuilding and would soon be in a position to resume business. Josephus Bradbury was building a hotel on the property formerly owned by both Bradbury and Hagelman. South of Bradbury's hotel, C. W. Day was erecting a store building. A. A. Flagg had a new dwelling on his lot. Joseph Smith had erected a new blacksmith shop and was already doing business again. Henry Hutchins and his partner Murphy were putting up a two-story building on their lot. More precise locations can be determined from the accompanying map.

In March, 1908, the Journal again reported that fire had devastated one half of the pioneer town. The very same area destroyed in 1897 was once more leveled to the ground. This time the fire started from the barroom stove in the Bradbury Hotel. A heavy wind was blowing and most of the men were away working in the nearby mines. The Bradbury Hotel, the Gribble Hotel, the Post Office, the blacksmith shop, the Douglas residence, the two-story Forestry Hall and the Gribble barn were all destroyed. Only by the hardest work were the Cummings store and the barn opposite it saved. For several years charcoal timbers, twisted water pipes and other debris from the fire littered the ground in the north part of town. This time almost all the individuals and families who had owned the burned buildings moved away and for a time there was no one to take responsibility for cleaning up the lots in the burned section.

In addition to the second fire, the town suffered another set-back. The extent of operations in the Cse Fie Mine proved not to be justified by the amount of gold produced. The mine closed down and the loss of the large payroll had an adverse economic effect on the community.

In January of 1901, six young Weaverville men organized the Weaverville Supply Company, purchasing the general stock of merchandise of the Blake and Reed Company in Weaverville. Blake and Reed retained all of their real estate and Edgar L. Reed retained and continued to operate his store in Junction City. But in 1906 Reed died suddenly. His son Edgar, Jr. carried on the business until the death of his mother, Mathilda M. Reed, in 1908. In the settlement of the two estates, the Weaverville Supply Company purchased the stock of the Reed store and arranged to lease the store building, warehouse and barns. In 1909 Frederick C. Meckel, one of the six owners of the Weaverville Supply Company, was assigned to manage and operate the Junction City Branch Store and in September of that year moved his family from Weaverville. Meckel lived most of the remaining years of his life in Junction City, renting the home of Edgar Reed, Jr. until 1918 when he purchased the Schneider home across the street. (These homes occupied Lot 12, Block 2 and Lot 9, Block 1 as depicted on the accompanying township map.) Having a vital interest in the political and economic affairs of Trinity County, Meckel, at different times, served five terms on the Board of Supervisors as representative of District IV. After moving to Junction City he became interested in the cattle business and in this connection had a marked influence on the appearance of the town. He secured water rights to the old Henry Hocker ditch out of Canyon Creek and used it to bring water from Canyon Creek for the raising of alfalfa. He planted Lots 19 and 20 of Block 2 in alfalfa and the resulting large green field on the west side of the street made a pleasant introduction to the tree-lined lower section of Main Street. He also planted alfalfa on Lot 12 on the north side of the house he rented from Edgar Reed. The greatest improvement of all occurred when he cleaned up the debris left from the great fire of 1908 and also planted Lots 11, 12 and 13 of Block 1 in alfalfa. His barns and corrals were on the opposite side of the street in the burned area.

Another man who came into the town of Junction City about the same time as Meckel was John H. Bartlett, who had been born and raised at Red Hill. Bartlett and his wife Mary took over the old Louis Raab property, which the Reed family had purchased from Raab's estate, built a rooming house on the southeast corner of the property near the street and operated a hotel. Bartlett also leased the saloon on Lot 13, Block 2 from the Reeds. For much of the time during the first two decades of the century, the Bartlett saloon was the male social center of the town. During the late spring, summer and early fall the barroom chairs on the porch and on the street in front were places which invited both townsmen and visitors to exchange news, gossip and stories. The Bartlett's bartender, Fred K. Reed, was much beloved by the children of the town. Miners in the summer would come to town for a week or two, eat and sleep at the Bartlett Hotel, socialize and drink or play cards at the saloon and put in their orders for winter supplies at the Weaverville Supply Store or the store of R. F. Cummings (Lot 10, Block 1). The town well covered with ivy and still existing today, was just to the right of the saloon.

The Bartlett Hotel caught fire in March of 1919 and the main building and lodging house burned to the ground. The life-style of Junction City was never the same thereafter.

In its earlier days the population of Junction City always included Chinese. Cox, as indicated earlier, reported the population of Milltown as including 70-80

157

In 1891, the Edgar L. Reed house on the east side of Main Street was the most comfortable and fashionably furnished home in Junction City.

Built in an architectural style reminiscent of the Maine Coast from which he came, the home of William Cushman Given was a familiar landmark in old Junction City. It was sold by Mrs. Caroline Augusta Given to James Mullane in 1910.

The James E. Given meat market at Junction City. Mr. Given stands in his butcher's apron with Sam Jackson to the left and Edgar Reed, Jr. to the right.

Built originally by E. M. Benjamin, Junction City mining engineer for the Albert Hayes' Mine, this house was later purchased by the Reed family and remodeled as a home for Edgar L. Reed, Jr.. For nine years it was the home of Fritz and Mary Meckel.

The Catholic Church at Junction City was erected after the tailings from the La Grange Mine made the church at Oregon Gulch inaccessible.

JUNCTION CITY, 1896

PROPERTY OWNERSHIP
(based on patent survey)

BLOCK 1.
Lot
1. John Reed
2. F. G. Haas
3. John Reed
4. Catholic Church
5. E. L. Reed
6. L. F. Raab
7. Mrs. Edgar L. Reed
8. Blake & Reed Company Store
   Weaverville Supply Company
   Junction City Hotel
9. Heinrich Schneider
10. Robert Cummings
11. Bradbury & Haselman Hotel
12. J. W. Smith
13. Robert Flagg

BLOCK 3.
E. L. Reed

BLOCK 4
Lot
1. James E. Given
2. Foresters
3. E. L. Reed
4. John Reed

LEGEND

- - - - — STATE HWY AND CO. ROAD
- - - - - — LOT BOUNDARIES
————— — BLOCK BOUNDARIES
● — HISTORIC SITES

KEY TO HISTORIC SITES

A. James E. Given Home
B. Bartlett Hotel and Lodging House
C. Given Butcher Shop
D. William Cushman Given Home
E. Bartlett Saloon
F. Edgar L. Reed, Jr. Home
G. Town Hall
H. Carter House
I. Cummings Store
   Enos House
J. Meckel House
K. Blake & Reed Store
   Weaverville Supply Company
L. Edgar L. Reed, Sr. Home

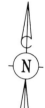

BLOCK 2.
Lot
1. E. L. Reed
2. Mrs. G. W. Todd
3. Karsky & Abraham
4. George F. Douglas
5. Town Hall
6. A. A. Flagg
7. J. W. Smith
8. E. W. Treloar
9. Henry Hutchins
10. Bradbury & Hagelman
11. Blake & Reed
    Robert Cummings
12. E. L. Reed, Jr.
13. E. L. Reed
14. W. C. Given
15. W. C. Given
16. W. C. Given
17. L. F. Raab
18. W. C. Given
19. Bradbury & Hagelman
20. Heinrick C. Schneider
21. Chinese
22. Chinese
23. W. C. Given
    Slaughter House

Chinese. In 1886 the total Chinese population of the county was reported by the Trinity Journal as being 426. Of these, 51 were in Junction City. The Chinese mined, some owning mines and other property; some worked as laborers in mines; some were cooks; some raised and sold vegetables. In June, 1889, a Chinese child in Junction City, playing with matches, started a fire and the entire Chinese section burned to the ground. One Chinese went by the American name of Limpy, having been shot and seriously wounded in one leg for having robbed a flume. A much younger Chinese of the same era was named Wah Sing. Besides gardening and selling vegetables, Wah Sing cooked at the Bartlett Hotel and also at some of the mines. Limpy and Wah Sing were the last Chinese. When they departed to their celestial rest, Junction City children no longer received packages of candies, peanuts and leche nuts on Chinese New Years and mothers no longer were given Chinese bowls and China lilies growing in water amongst white quartz pebbles. The third shack in the Chinese section at the time of Limpy and Wah Sing was situated on a slightly more elevated location in the Chinatown section. This little building had red curtains at its windows. From time to time it housed a traveling lady of very easy virtue.

In the 1920's C. W. Mead and his wife Susan took over the remaining Reed properties and made considerable alterations. The house which had been the residence of young Edgar Reed (Lot 12, Block 2) was made into two rental units; a small store and gas station were built in front; the old saloon was torn down; and the old Blake and Reed store building became the Junction City Hotel. There was still some hydraulic mining going on in the area and there were surveying crews working on the construction of the state highway to Eureka. As one can see from the township map, this state highway right-of-way cut through several lots in the south section of town. By the time the highway

Junction City suffered periodic floodings from the Trinity River and Canyon Creek, this one in 1955.

Lower Main Street, Junction City, about 1895.

Sites 1, 2, 3. Street scene in Junction City today showing the Enos House; the Meckel House, next to it; and the Junction City, Hotel beyond.

was completed in the 1930's the old pioneer town of Junction City had almost completely disappeared. With paved roads and high speed automobiles there was no longer need for a hotel. Junction City became a place that people passed through.

In the 1940's as a result of dredging operations from Hocker Flat to the Chapman Ranch, the banks of the Trinity River were completely altered, leaving piles of rock where once were gentle natural banks and giving Junction City a stark and desolate appearance.

In more recent years the mining claims patented by pioneer families have become subdivisions of new settlers seeking escape from urban environments. In a sense the life of the community has gone full circle; Red Hill again has become a center of population and Junction City has become the Mouth of Canyon Creek.

Only three of the old historic buildings remain in Junction City today: the buildings known as the Junction City Hotel, the Meckel House and the Enos House. These buildings are side by side on the east side of Main Street, occupying Lots 8, 9 and 10, respectively, of Block 1. A more detailed account of these buildings follows.

Site 1. Junction City Hotel (Weaverville Supply Company Store) (Edgar Reed Store) (Blake and Reed Store) (Whitmore and Reed Store)

This building on Lot 8 is the first building on the east side of Main Street as you enter the town coming from the direction of Weaverville or Red Hill. Near it today is a corral, a shed barn and a trailer home. These three structures occupy Lot 7, the site of the former Edgar Reed, Sr. home. The "hotel" is a rectangular building with shiplap siding, gable roof, false front and a shed-roof porch attached to the false front. The roof is metal over wood shingles, with one terra cotta chimney and exposed rafters at the eves. The building rises almost from the street itself and extends to the side of the hill at the back of the lot. It rests on an exposed wooden pier foundation and is in poor condition. The building at one time contained a wine cellar.

As has been previously noted, prior to the 1920's and the era of C. W. Mead, the building had always been a merchandise store and not a hotel. It is uncertain exactly when the building was built, for it is difficult to trace ownership from the property descriptions prior to the time that the town was surveyed and lot and block numbers assigned. Before Collie Mead made a hotel out of it, the building was rented by the Weaverville Supply Company. Before that, Edgar L. Reed, Sr. conducted business there under his own name, under the name of Blake and Reed (this name can still be seen on the north side of the building) and under the name Whitmore and Reed. Whitmore and Reed, who had been operating a sawmill together, purchased their merchandise business in 1878 from Kuper and Karsky. Kuper and Karsky, in turn, had purchased the business from Louis Raab. Legal records show that Louis Raab had obtained his merchandise business from Tinnin and Owen and before that C. W. Craig had transfered the business to Tinnin and Owen. (Craig at one time was editor of the Trinity Journal and Tinnin and Owen were businessmen in Weaverville.) A smaller building on the bedrock, which Reed and the Supply Company used as a warehouse, may have been the Raab store and Reed and Whitmore, since they owned a lumber mill, may have built a new building in the center of town after purchasing the Kuper and Karsky business. If so, the building would have been built soon after 1878; if not, it is much older.

During the time it was leased by the Weaverville Supply Company, the

Site 1. Exterior view of the Blake and Reed store in Junction City, made into a hotel by C. W. Mead in the 1920's.

Site 1. The interior of the Edgar L. Reed general merchandise store in 1895. Left to right, Edgar Reed, William Reed, John Reed, George Wallace, Joe Van Zile, Jack McGovern and Joe Pontrey.

building housed the Junction City Post Office. For a good many years it contained the only telephone in town. The store sold everything: picks and shovels and gold pans; shoes and hip-height rubber boots, rain gear and clothing of all kinds; canned goods and groceries; wines and liquors; an assortment of candies, cookies and crackers; fishing tackle and shells for guns. The store opened early in the morning, closed at 9 or 10 o'clock at night and was open seven days a week.

Horses, wagons and buggies were kept in a large barn and adjacent corrals on the bedrock. Here hay was stored for the stock and was also for sale. This barn was erected by Edgar Reed in 1897. A stock of merchandise was also stored in a good-sized warehouse nearby. Powder used for blasting in the mines or by the county for road work or trail construction was kept in a powder house considerably removed from the other buildings.

When the Weaverville Supply Company leased the building, four men operated the business: Frederick C. Meckel, the manager, known all over the county as Fritz; William F. Flowers, Joseph Schaffer and James E. Given, clerks. All four men came from well-known pioneer families. Jim Given's main responsibility was taking care of the horses and wagons and the delivery service. Occasionally, however, other members of the staff might assist with the delivery service, depending upon whether deliveries were being made to places where the fishing was good or whose turn it might be to go fishing! The present owners of the property are Ross and Joyce Edwards.

Site 2. Meckel House (Vandeford House) (Heinrich Schneider Home)

Situated on Lot 9 of Block 1, the Meckel house is a two-story, shiplap, high-gabled rectangular structure. On the front and side is a shed-roofed, one-story veranda supported by square, beveled posts. The house is a full two-story structure and above the second story is an attic. The front part of the downstairs was divided by a hall which opened to the outside at one end and to the kitchen at the other. Doors on the right and left sides of the hall opened to front rooms. The room at the right, for a time, housed the Junction City Post Office, the arrangement of the hall making it possible to enter the post office without entering any of the family rooms in the house.

The house was built by Heinrich Schneider, one of Trinity County's German citizens, who came to Junction City in 1864, becoming naturalized in 1869. In the first part of the present century it was occupied by Irving Vanderford, a son-in-law of the Schneiders. Frederick Meckel purchased the house in 1918 shortly before he married his second wife, Mrs. Edna May Wilson, and did considerable redecorating and remodeling. Mrs. Meckel died in 1946 and Meckel continued to live in the house until 1952, when he sold the house to C. A. Luckett who did further extensive remodeling. The house is presently owned by Mrs. Linda Printy McFarland.

Site 3. Enos House (Cummings Store)

The Enos House was built in 1897. It is a basic one-story rectangular building with a high gable roof and usable attic and is constructed with clapboard and endboard siding and a plain boxed cornice. A lean-to porch with square beveled corner supports surrounds the front and north sides. Two metal chimneys indicate the kitchen and living rooms. A metal roof covers the original shingles.

Occupying Lot 10 of Block 1, the house is set close to the street, its front porch rising almost from the pavement. The location and design of the house arise from the fact that the building was originally built as a store. Patented title to the property was obtained in 1897 by C. W. Day, a county pioneer who came to Trinity County in 1852. For nine years he mined on Canyon Creek. Later he engaged in an express business between Junction City and Canon City. About 1876, in partnership with G. W. Todd, he purchased the Carter House and after Todd's death in 1878 continued to operate the business with Todd's widow. When the hotel was sold to James C. Wallace, Day made an extended visit East and to Oregon, but returned to Junction City and established a merchandise business, which he sold in 1895 to Abrahms and Karsky. Fire broke out in the building in 1897 and the building burned to the ground along with every other building in the north end of the town. Day erected the present building after the fire.

Robert F. Cummings first came to Trinity County as a young man in his twenties, did some mining, then returned to Illinois, the state of his birth. He returned to Junction City in 1894. It is likely that he started his cash store when C. W. Day erected the building after the 1897 fire. Day died in 1899 and Cummings was a co-executor of his estate. The Junction City property was sold at auction to C. W. Smith in 1900 and was bought by Cummings in 1901. In 1903 Cummings bought the lot directly across the street from Edgar L. Reed, Jr., a lot which contained a barn which he used as a storehouse.

When Cummings owned the building, it contained a storeroom directly behind his salesroom and living quarters behind that. Cummings conducted his business strictly on a cash basis, allowing no unpaid accounts to accumulate. A spacious corner in the rear right-hand section of the store contained a large wood stove surrounded by captain's chairs where Cummings and his friends would relax in the winter time between customers. In summer he and his friends sat on the front porch. Cummings was a very dedicated member of the Masonic Lodge and his closest friends were Masons. In October of 1938 he left Junction City and went to West Chicago, Illinois. He died the following March.

Cummings left his property to Jesse Tourtellotte, a fraternal friend and the property eventually passed to George Herron, who made two apartments out of the building. Marvin Enos and his wife Esther Chapman Enos acquired the property in 1945 from Herron's daughter, Mrs. Hazel Turner and her husband Andrew W. Turner. Mrs. Enos died in 1969 and her husband sold the property to James and June Heath in 1972. The present owner is Mrs. Joyce Lenihan.

Site 4. Junction City Mining Ditches

Junction City's mining ditches are visible on the hillside as one looks up Canyon Creek. Cox's Annals reports that in the early 1850's there were three ditches, all from Canyon Creek: two belonging to Henry Hocker, about two miles in length; and one belonging to Ray and Company, one half mile long and which had an aggregate capacity of thirty sluice heads. Judge Bartlett regarded these as among the first ditches constructed in Trinity County. According to Bartlett, in addition to these ditches, the Seelye-Dowles sawmill was powered with a ditch that was later extended to Eagen's Flat.

At the present time, as one looks up Canyon Creek, four ditches are in evidence, three on the hillside along the east side of Canyon Creek and one high on the mountain on the west side. Of the east side ditches, the lowest ditch, probably originally Hocker's, ran through the property of F. C. Meckel, past the Reed home, and then under the wagon road from Weaverville. It was used by Meckel to irrigate the family garden at his home and his alfalfa fields at the south end of town. According to C. H. McCartney, the next highest ditch on the east side was probably used by George Chapman and Cush Given in mining off the bedrock where the Junction City School is now located. The highest ditch on the east side, which ran from Clear Gulch and also from Canyon Creek in the Lizard Point area, was used by Fred Haas in his mine on the hill above the south end of town. It had at one time been utilized, according to McCartney, by Cush Given for his ranch and for mining, the water crossing Oregon Gulch on a trestle.

The ditch on the west side of Canyon Creek was constructed originally by the Hayes Mining Company and was later purchased by the Cie Fse Company, a French corporation which obtained water rights not only from Canyon Creek but from the Canyon Creek Lakes as well.

Trinity River Up-river from Junction City

The search for gold during the 1850's led to the exploration, mining, or agricultural development of every mile of the Trinity River. The sites of historical interest along the Trinity River upstream from Junction City in the direction of Steiner Flat are described in the following two subsections.

Subsection 1: West Side of the Trinity River
Site 5. Bergin Gulch and Bergin Mine

The Bergin placer mining property was slightly less than a mile from Junction City. It included 600 acres of patented land which previously was part of the Hayes-Cie Fse Mine, portions of the Joe Sturdivant property and property of the Laws family, to which Bergin was related. Bergin Gulch, near the beginning of the property, is now the site of the home of Jack Bergin. Part of the mining on the property was done by the Gilzean and McGovern families, to whom the Bergins were also related. A mile and one half from Highway 299 is Mill Creek, which was a source of water for the hydraulic mines. Two-tenths of a mile beyond Mill Creek and on the right side of the County road is an enormous cut 60-70 feet deep — an impressive sight. A deep tunnel under the county road conducted tailings from the sluicings down a gulch to the Trinity River. A zig-zag trail on the left side of the road, built as part of the movie set for the picture "Gold is Where You Find It," leads down the mountain. From this trail the cut on the river side of the tunnel is visible, which increases one's amazement at the power and extent of early-day hydraulic mining.

Site 6. White Oak Gulch Mine

This mine, two miles from Highway 299, was one of the smallest mines in the Junction City area. It is located about one-tenth of a mile from White Oak Gulch from which the mine derived its name.

Site 7. Big Gulch (Deep Gulch)

The gulch, one half mile beyond White Oak, was generally known by early residents as Big Gulch but was sometimes called Deep Gulch or Davis Gulch. (In a state publication on Trinity County Mines and Mineral Resources the name appears as Deep Gulch.) Beyond this gulch, about two-tenths of a mile is a side road to the old Gribble Mine and ranch located about a half mile up the mountain. The Gribble family was especially prominent in the Junction City area before and after the turn of the century. The family, in the 1890's operated a hotel at Junction City. Richard Gribble and his sister, Mrs. Peter Jensen, made their home for a number of years at the junction of the Canyon Creek and old North Fork roads. Richard Gribble farmed the old Felter Ranch on Oregon Gulch and his son, Loren, still lives on the old Felter property.

Site 8. Chapman Mine and Ranch

The Chapman Mine, four miles from Junction City, was perhaps the most prominent family mine in Trinity County, both in productivity and in length of ownership. It is also a prominent feature of the landscape as one drives west along the lower end of Oregon Gulch on Highway 299. These red banks are the last red banks that are visible as one looks south far up the Trinity River.

The Chapman mining claims were located in 1871 by George Phelps Chapman and John Stuart Fisher and the property was first known as the Chapman and Fisher Mine. Chapman bought Fisher's interest in 1882.

Born in Big Hollow, Green County, New York, Chapman came to Trinity County from Utica, Michigan, in 1853. He was associated in earlier mining activities with his brother-in-law, Cushman Given, in mining off the bedrock at Junction City. He was married to Sarah Small of Bath, Maine, in San Francisco, on New Year's Day, 1879. Two sons, prominent in the activities of Trinity County where born of this marriage: Ernest Chapman and George Phelps Chapman II. Chapman died when the boys were 18 and 16 years old, respectively, and the young men from then on took over the family mining activities. Ernest married Stella Crofer, who died in childbirth. He was later married to Cora Gorham, who survives him and still lives in Weaverville. George married Elsie Luman and ten children born of this marriage survived to adulthood. The Chapman Mine and Ranch has been owned by, and been the home for, three generations of the same family. Frank, the youngest son of George and Elsie, is the present owner of the property. Interestingly, each succeeding generation of the family has had a son who bears the name George Phelps.

The Chapman property originally included two large fields near the Trinity River, where alfalfa was raised for cattle and where there were orchards with apples, pears, peaches and plums. The family also raised gardens which produced a generous amount of corn, beans, squash and other vegetables. On the ridge near Soldier Creek was another field with an orchard and a house which at one time was the home of Ernest Chapman and his wife Stella. Over the years the hillsides have been washed away to the bedrock by the extensive mining activities. Water for this hydraulic activity came from Soldier Creek.

The old Chapman home dates back to about 1860. It was first built as a one-room cabin. It still stands today but many changes have been made. The original part of the house has become a kitchen; a living room and bedroom have been added; and upstairs there are two dormitory-type rooms. The original rock fireplace rises prominently on the outside of the house but above the first story height the native rock has been replaced with a large mining pipe. In the yard are two old pear trees and a large mulberry tree. Also in the yard is a huge boulder — one so large that the hydraulic monitor could not budge it. It has stayed in the same relative position even though much of the ground has been washed away from beneath it.

Not far from the house is a deep gully that is the result of mining activity. Also on the bedrock property is another deep, gorge-like cut which ended in a tunnel through which the washed out earth was sluiced over riffles in a flume that carried the tailings to the river level. Near the northern limits of the property there is an enormous slide area on the side of the mountain. This occurred in 1933 when the earth was sluiced away by hydraulic monitors.

The Chapman Mine was a profitable family mine, producing not only gold but also platinum. Some of the largest and finest gold nuggets produced in Trinity County came from the property. The Chapmans always employed a number of men to work as miners. Among them were Tom Dawson, George

Site 8. The Chapman Ranch and Placer Mine, showing the location of the Trinity River, the upper field, the mined-off bed rock, and the lower field which was turned into a gravel pile by dredging.

Gregg and George Barker, well known young miners in Junction City in the early part of the century. The last mining on the land was done by Earl Phelps Chapman (known as Sonny Chapman) and his brother John. They stopped mining in 1945.

The river-level fields were sold to the United Grocers Dredging Company and were dredged out in the 1930's. The sales agreement provided that George and Ernest Chapman were to be paid a percentage of the gold obtained. Ironically, this river land proved to be much less rich in gold than had been expected. Today only piles of gravel and rocks remain of the land that for so many years produced hay, vegetables and fruit so abundantly.

The Chapman property on the river included Chapman's Ford, a major non-bridge crossing that was recognized on official maps and used by up-river school children when the Junction City School was located one mile from Junction City near Oregon Gulch.

Site 9. Evans Bar

A tenth of a mile beyond Chapman's the up-river county road makes a sharp turn to the right and a side road turns down the hill to the mouth of Soldier Creek and the river. Here the latter road proceeds along the tailings to a private foot bridge over which people owning land on Evans Bar may reach their property.

Evans Bar figured prominently in the early history of Trinity County, as it was one of the first areas to be mined. According to Cox's Annals, a Frenchman named Gross came to Evans Bar in 1849 to mine and built the first log cabin in the county. In 1851, a company of nine miners succeeded in augmenting their water supply by bringing water from Evans Creek to the head of the Bar in what was one of the earliest ditch systems in the county. By 1858 Evans Bar boasted 20 homes, a store, a boarding house, a blacksmith shop and even a few women. During the late 1850's a group of men headed by Peter Verstegen, a German, built ditches and flumes to bring water from Dutch Creek across the Trinity by trestle. The project was demolished by the great flood of 1861, and Verstegen, in his attempts to meet the financial responsibilities of the group, lost heavily. He later conducted a small store in Junction City, where he spent the last years of his life at the home of his daughter.

Before the development of the wagon road over Oregon Mountain from Weaverville to Junction City, Evans Bar was on the main-traveled river road from Weaverville to Junction City and Helena. Early mail and express service regularly followed this route.

By 1865 the bar was worked out and miners began working bodies of gravel on higher grounds and hills. Gradually the miners left; the process of deterioration began and eventually all signs of early mining had disappeared except for the extensive piles of rocks left as mining debris from the activities of the sluice boxes. The section of river between Steiner Flat and Evans Bar is today an area of very little habitation.

Site 10. Site of an Indian Rancheria

Above the Evans Bar turn-off, the road forks. The up-river road turns to the left. Four and one half miles from Junction City is the Green Campground, located on the left side of the road. On the right side is a fenced property with a house and small orchard. Both the campground and the fenced area were the site of an important pre-pioneer Indian rancheria. Adjoining Soldier Creek, the rancheria was relatively accessible to the Trinity River for salmon and trout fishing, was located in good game country and was on an Indian trail that led into the Hayfork Valley. An important Indian burial ground was nearby on what was known as Georgie Ann Ridge, now heavily covered with manzanita. This burial site contains the graves of two Indian women who played a prominent progenital role in the early years of this century: Georgie Ann Setti and Lucy Scott. Georgie Ann married Fred Setti, also an Indian. He was also known as Fred Tye. Children from this marriage were Archie, Erwin, Fred and Tommy Tye. Georgia Ann later was married to George Barker and was mother to Buck Barker and Amos Barker. Additional information concerning this prominent Indian family can be found in the 1970 edition of The Trinity, published by the Trinity County Historical Society. Lucy Scott was married to Bob Scott, an Indian also well known in the Junction City area. Previously Lucy had been married to a white man named Dawson and by him gave birth to Thomas Dawson, Ruth Dawson Gregg, Frank Dawson and Marissa (also known as Mary). Her son Tom married Hettie Hailstone and was father of the Dawson family, a well-known Junction City family in the early years of the century. Lucy Scott was skilled as a mid-wife, and a number of up-river children, now senior citizens, came into the world through her special skills.

Site 11. Myers Ranch

This pleasant property, five and one half miles from Junction City and watered by several springs, was located and developed by a German sometimes called John Munster, but generally known in Junction City as John Myers. Of interest here are some of the people who were directly or indirectly associated with Mr. Myers. It was his daughter Gussie who had a daughter named Viola

170

who married John Martin, known in Weaverville as "Baby John". Baby John was the son of Isabelle Martin and John Martin (the brother of Henry Martin who made a fortune in the Brown Bear Mine at Deadwood). Before her marriage to John Martin, Isabelle had been known as Belle Hoffman and, for a number of years both before and after her connection with the Martins, had provided colorful social copy for the newspapers of San Francisco, most of which was reprinted in the Trinity Journal. Isabelle Martin at one time caused considerable consternation in Trinity County by threatening to poison the town water system.

Gussie Myers later married Esau Montgomery by whom she had two daughters, Hazel and Lola, who were educated in the public schools of Weaverville where the family made their home. Esau, who was born on the coast, was half Indian and during his life was a colorful figure in the Junction City, Canyon Creek and Weaverville communities. A man who endured work as something one had to put up with, he enjoyed drink and had a reputation of being popular with women. Old Junction City residents take special delight in recalling his escapades and adventures. He was known everywhere by his first name and there was general and genuine community regret when he lost his life in a fire that destroyed his home. Both Esau and Gussie are buried in the public cemetery in Weaverville.

The Myers Ranch, which is patented land, has recently been parceled.

Site 12. China Hill Mine

After rising gradually from the Myers Ranch, the county road goes over a low gap and starts down the hill. To the left of the road was the China Hill Mine, once operated by a group of San Francisco investors who with ditches and siphons brought water from Maple Creek. Some of this ditch system is visible further along and below the road. China Hill received its name from the fact that the area between the hill and the river had been extensively mined by Chinese.

Site 13. Maple Creek Mines

Maple Creek is six and one half miles from Highway 299. Much mining has been done in the Maple Creek area, utilizing both water from Maple Creek itself and water from Dutch Creek. At one time Dan R. Perroh mined a gravel bank twenty five feet high above the bedrock using water he brought through a three mile long ditch out of Dutch Creek.

Site 14. Dutch Creek Ranch

The Dutch Creek Ranch, slightly over seven miles from Junction City, is situated along the north bank of Dutch Creek at the end of the road. The ranch comprises a pleasantly situated fenced field, with ancient fruit trees, that is about one mile up Dutch Creek from its confluence with the Trinity River. The land has never been patented; it is, therefore, part of the public domain. Many people, impressed with the charm, beauty and relative remoteness of the place, have, however, filed a mining claim, lived there for a while, added some improvements and then moved on. A recent location, designated as Dutchman No. 1 and Dutchman No. 2, includes a total of 160 acres of land. Among the well-remembered owners was Jim King, a large and impressive man, who mined on the creek, was an outstanding gardener, raised and sold strawberries and later patented a homestead on the Trinity River which is today Del Loma. Another well-known owner was George Lewman, who married Annie McKay, a widow with three children, Myrtle, Warren and Frank, all of whom grew to adulthood in the Junction City area. As Mrs. Lewman, Annie also had a daughter, Leola.

Site 15. Soldier Creek Road

Four and one half miles from Highway 299 a Forest Service road goes up Soldier Creek, crosses the ridge into Big Creek, and follows Big Creek down into Hayfork. This general route was followed by both Indians and early pioneers. Two early-day events are associated with this route. It was on this old Indian trail that the white men tracked and followed the Indians prior to the Natural Bridge Massacre. And John Carr reports that as he was attempting to go home by this route to Hayfork after a Board of Supervisors meeting in Weaverville, the great flood of 1861 washed out the Sturdivant Bridge across the Trinity making it impossible for him to get home for several days.

Site 16. Carter Ranch

The Carter Ranch is reached by a side road that turns right off the Forest Service road up Soldier Creek, about a mile beyond the Chapman Mine. The ranch is a beautifully situated piece of mountain property, well-watered by springs. The ranch has special climatic advantages, being situated well above the fog level and consequently enjoying a generous amount of sunshine during much of the autumn, winter and spring months.

The property was originally located and patented by James Alonza Carter, a Cherokee Indian, who came from Iowa, and his wife Margaret (Maggie) Nichols, part Indian. Carter was a hard-working man who engaged mostly in raising cattle, which he grazed on adjoining government land. He at one time served on the Junction City School Board. Maggie Carter was a woman especially well thought of in the Junction City area. She was a woman of great integrity, hard working and practical, with great family loyalties. The couple had three children: Enid, Everett and Margaret.

The Carter ranch is now owned and operated by Fritz and Margaret Loegering and supplies fine produce to the citizens of Weaverville. The old Carter house still stands on the property, but the Loegrings have erected a larger modern house that stands at the opposite end of the ranch, overlooking the property and the mountains beyond.

Subsection 2: East Side of the Trinity River
Site 17. Colonel Seelye Grave

Henry Seelye (the name also occurs as Sealy), with a man named Dowles, operated a sawmill in the early 1850's in what is now Junction City. Because of this fact, the place, for a number of years, was called Milltown. The remains of Seelye are buried in a grave just off a road that goes up Bergin Gulch (also called Ryan Gulch) near the mouth of Oregon Gulch. The grave has a coping and once contained a marker, which has been removed by vandals. Seelye, according to Trinity County Library files, died September 12, 1857 in Junction City. He had been born in St. George, New Brunswick, and at one time had held the title of colonel. The present grave represents a reburial necessitated by mining operations near or on the original gravesite.

Site 18. Mun Loa Spring

Located between the mouth of Oregon Gulch and the Sturdivant-Cush Given Ranch (now popularly known as the Skyranch), this spring, whose water gushes forth from a pipe on the hill side of the road, runs with a heavy flow even in years of extreme drought. Oldtimers in Junction City tell us that in early days a Chinese by the name of Mun Loa had a productive garden watered by this fine spring and sold vegetables to all the countryside. Citizens began to give his name to this prolific spring. That this account may not be completely accurate is indicated by the fact that court house records show that in 1867 Alexander George sold to Al Fin and Company all the ground below the Leon Ola claim on Dacy's Bar on the Trinity River, 500 feet fronting on the Trinity. Dacy's Bar was near the mouth of Oregon Gulch.

Site 19. Sturdivant Ranch (Cush Given Ranch) (Skyranch)

The Sturdivant Ranch is an extensive and beautiful ranch that stretches along the Trinity River above Junction City and near the mouth of Oregon Gulch. The largest and most fertile part of the property, lying along the River, was dredged in the middle 1930's. The land that is left possesses many large graceful oak trees and open fields, now unworked, covered with grasses. The property has been parceled and there are a number of newer houses on the ranch. None of the original buildings remain. The ranch ditch is still clearly evident. This ditch brought water out of Canyon Creek and used a trestle to take the water across Oregon Gulch.

The Sturdivant Ranch was located on March 24, 1853 by Joseph Sturdivant. Even before this date, however, the place was a noted mining camp, according to Cox. Sturdivant developed it into one of the outstanding ranches of the county, putting 300 acres under fence and 200 under cultivation, as well as maintaining an orchard and vineyard. The rich soil yielded 35 bushels to the acre in grains. Sturdivant also had a flour mill, a sawmill and water races for mining, employing 20-30 men in the 1850's. In addition, the ranch lay on the main travel route down the Trinity River as well as the route from Weaverville to Hayfork via Soldier Creek and Big Creek. It was thus an important stopping place. Sturdivant built a toll bridge across the Trinity River. This was an important crossing when the road down-river was on the Red Hill side. Sturdivant owned the ranch with Jerry Whitmore between the late 1850's and the late 1880's. Both were leading men in the county. Later the ranch was purchased by Cushman Given of Junction City and Given's brother-in-law, George P. Chapman.

Located near the site of the old ranch house is a large oak tree which is one of the largest Canyon Live Oaks in the state and is estimated to be nearly 900 years old. The massive trunk of the double tree measures 34 feet in circumference 4½ feet from the ground. The tree is one of three large oaks which provided shade for the ranch house. The Trinity Journal describes one Fourth of July that was celebrated by the community in the shade of this great tree. The ranch was for a number of years the site of the Junction City horse races, a popular competitive sport of the area.

Site 20. Junction City Cemetery

The Junction City Cemetery, plotted and fenced in 1895, is located on the hillside off the Skyranch road that goes up the southeast side of the Trinity River to Chapman's Ford. It is accessible from a side road that turns toward the hills near the Great Oak. This cemetery is the resting place of many old Junction City residents, among them James A. Carter, C. W. Day, Cushman Given and his family and members of the Chapman, Dawson and Wolff families.

Site 21. Arkansas Dam Site

The Arkansas Dam Site is located just below Chapman's Ford on the Trinity River approximately two miles above Junction City. One of the first attempts at large-scale mining, the Arkansas Dam was designed to change the course of the Trinity River so as to expose the gold-bearing gravel of the river bed. In the summer and fall of 1851, a group of men, largely from Arkansas, formed a joint stock company and constructed a dam across the river and a race through the bar large enough to divert the river around a stretch nearly three-quarters of a mile. Washed out by a flood, the dam was rebuilt, standing for a longer time than the first, but it also was destroyed by flood. It was built for a third time in 1854, lasting until 1857. The builder of the third dam was Jerry Whitmore, prominent sawmill operator and Junction City businessman, who was praised by Cox for building "positively the greatest (work) that ever has been executed on the Trinity River". The principal stock holders in the company were Joseph Sturdivant, John Carter, Jonathan Logan and Whitmore, all leading men in the Junction City area. Monetary returns from the project were disappointing. The area in the vicinity of the dam was a site of a trading post and small community of settlers and miners. The settlement was well enough established to be used for some years as a dateline for the Trinity Journal. C. H. McCartney of Junction City recalls that when a dredger worked through the area in the 1930's, it uncovered portions of logs used in the construction of the dam.

Oregon Gulch Area
Historical Overview

In his memoirs David R. Gordon, co-publisher of the first issues of the Trinity Journal, describes Oregon Gulch as a "stream with deep and swift running water". From the summit of Oregon Mountain to Felter Gulch, the stream was, he said, "literally lined with miners". In the earliest days of the 1850's the area was accessible only by trail. By 1859 a wagon road had been built.

With the beginning of the operation of the LaGrange Mine, the gulch began to be filled with tailings which now extend to its mouth at the Trinity River and which have completely changed the character of the once wild and beautiful stream.

Early accounts of Oregon Gulch in the Trinity Journal treat the entire gulch as a single community with activity centered at the area where Slattery Gulch flowed into Oregon Gulch. There was no Slattery Pond until LaGrange tailings created it. Oregon Gulch as a community was predominantly Irish. There was the Slattery family with ranches on both sides of Slattery Gulch. John Colbert operated the Oregon Gulch Hotel and Saloon. Frank Harris operated another saloon. The Ryan family mined and farmed at Bergin Gulch (sometimes called Ryan Gulch) further down toward the Trinity River.

Oregon Gulch had its own Catholic Church, and many Catholics born on the west side of Oregon Mountain Summit were baptised there. Schooling, however, took place toward the mouth of the Gulch, where the Junction City School was located on land adjoining the Felter Ranch. The school served pupils not only from the Gulch area, but students from the country up the Trinity River and from Red Hill, Junction City and lower Canyon Creek as well.

Two German families were closely associated with Oregon Gulch history. August Schaffer had a mine, ranch and later a sawmill at the Schaffer Ranch somewhat east and south of Slattery Gulch and raised a family of three sons:

Arthur, Fred and Joseph. Nicolas Wolff of Canon City later raised his family on the Wolff Ranch across from Slattery. The upper Wolff property had formerly been an Indian Rancheria. Also on Oregon Mountain was the ranch of Alexander George, a Pennsylvanian who had come to Trinity County in 1850.

Site 22. Felter's Ranch

Felter's Ranch was located at the lower end of Oregon Gulch approximately one mile from Junction City. Today the property is bounded by Highway 299W on the north, Oregon Gulch on the south and Felter's Gulch on the east. None of the original Felter buildings any longer exist, but the property today includes the home of Loren Gribble and a large barn, further east, constructed by the Gribble family.

In the 1850's and 60's it was the home of Andrew J. Felter, a leading man of the county. The property is described in Cox's Annals as including 250 acres, 300 fruit trees, 20 grape vines, an extensive vegetable garden and two acres of strawberries. For a number of years the ranch supplied Weaverville with fruits and vegetables. It was the strawberries, however, that contributed to the early reputation of the ranch. Especially in the early 1860's, Felter annually held a strawberry festival at his ranch, widely advertised and attended by people from all parts of the county. A main feature of the festival was a dance that lasted all night, with strawberries a special part of the refreshment. During the strawberry season it was fashionable in those early years to ride horseback from Weaverville to Douglas City and down the Trinity, stop for strawberries at Felter's and return home on the trail over Oregon Mountain.

Felter was highly influential in getting the wagon road constructed over Oregon Mountain in 1859. He read law, became an attorney and was prominent as county judge. His son, J. R. Felter, in partnership with E. P. Lovejoy, became publisher of the Trinity Journal in 1870. Judge Felter left Trinity County and moved to San Bernardino, where he played an important role in the affairs of that part of the state.

The fate of the Felter property as a ranch depended partly on its water rights. Felter obtained his water out of Oregon Gulch. After Felter moved to Weaverville Joseph Sturdivant and John Whitmore obtained Felter's Ranch and mined a portion of it. The Trinity Journal in 1875 mentioned that James T. Anderson had the Felter property and had discovered on it a number of interesting Indian artifacts which were on display at the Challenge Saloon. In 1913 the property was generally referred to in Junction City as the Jim Anderson Place. By that time, however, the LaGrange Mine had been operating for a number of years and Oregon Gulch had been receiving a deluge of tailings and debris. Sufficient water was not available and the fruit trees on the property died. It was in 1919 that the LaGrange ceased operation. In 1921 Richard Gribble acquired all the Felter property and other adjoining property by purchase from the Trinity County Bank and from C. H. Edwards and C. A. Paulsen, trustees in liquidation of the Trinity Gold Mining Company. Among the properties involved were the Dedrick Homestead, the Tipperary Placer Claim, Oregon Gulch Placer Claim and the Wheaton and Stewart Placer Claim. This gave Gribble ditches and rights to the water of Clear Gulch (sometimes called Wolff Gulch and Church Gulch), Slattery Gulch and Oregon Gulch. Gribble developed a first-class water system out of Slattery Pond. When the Stookeys', who had purchased the LaGrange Mine in 1927, wanted to dredge along Oregon Gulch it was necessary to secure title to adjoining land. (The old LaGrange had had only dumping rights along the Gulch.) Gribble sold them the title to his land but retained the right for him and his heirs to use the property until the year 2014. In recent years Richard Gribble's sons, Loren and Leonard, have raised family gardens but the property does not aspire to the agricultural pretensions which made it famous in the days of the Felter Strawberry Festivals.

Site 23. LaGrange Mine

At the height of its production, the LaGrange Mine on Oregon Mountain was regarded as the largest hydraulic mine in the world. Today the entire west side of the mountain, along Highway 299, serves as a visual reminder of the extent of the mining operations. Starting from the top of the mountain to the bottom of the draw, the earth has been sluiced away, exposing either the bedrock or a heavy blue clay and leaving little or no vegetative cover. Piles of tailings, part of the 100,000,000 cubic yards of earth and gravel that were moved from the face of the mountain, extend all the way down Oregon Gulch to the Trinity River. It has been estimated that these tailings are 40 feet deep at the mouth of the gulch, 100 feet deep at Slattery Gulch and 120 feet deep above the mouth of Poison Gulch.

In its days of operation, an entire community existed on the forested mountainside east of the mining pit. The buildings included the boarding house and bunk house, houses for families of miners and a school house. On the west side, on a knoll overlooking the mine, was the spacious and impressive manager's house, known as the Castle.

The history of the mine goes back to 1851 and 1852, when it became recognized that a large deposit of gold-bearing gravel extended from the Weaver Creek side of the mountain to the Oregon Gulch side. Various individual mining claims were located on both sides of the mountain and were worked during the 1860's. In 1873 Peter M. Paulsen and Orange Merwin Loveridge consolidated these mines and formed the Weaverville Ditch and Hydraulic Mining Company, constructing two ditches from West Weaver. In 1879 they sold to a group of stockholders made up of leading businessmen of Weaverville, who reincorporated as the Trinity Gold Mining Company. In 1892 a French nobleman, Baron LaGrange, founded the LaGrange Mining Company and purchased the Trinity Gold Mining Company for $250,000. Baron LaGrange brought to the mine a French engineer, Chaumont Quitry, who extended the LaGrange ditch to Rush Creek. Finding that the mine needed still more water, the engineer recommended extending the ditch to the Stuart Fork. Later the capacity of that stream was increased by raising the level of the Stuart Fork Lakes with dams. (It is interesting to note that the development of this water system represented the fulfillment of the dreams held by pioneers in the 1850's, who wanted to bring Stuart Fork water to the Weaverville Basin to enable mining, and consequently the County economy, to flourish during the summer months. Their plans for a much publicized Trinity Canal were never completed.)

When completely constructed, the LaGrange water system consisted of 29 miles of ditch, flume and pipe. (For a more complete description of this water system the reader is referred to a description of the LaGrange ditch on Weaver Bally Mountain appearing in Area II.) Water from the ditch was collected in a reservoir at the top of Oregon Summit south of Highway 299 and north of the old Weaverville-Junction City road. From there it was delivered by pipe to giants in the mine pit. Because of successive break-offs of earth caused by the sluicing below, a new reservoir was later built further down the saddle of the ridge on the south side of the old Junction City road. These holding reservoirs can still be seen. Humphrey (Jack) Tudor was in charge of the reservoir for a number of years and lived with his family near the site of the old reservoir. The Tudor family consequently became closely identified with operation of the mine.

Site 23. The La Grange Mine Community. Prominent in the photograph are, from left to right, the bunk house, the boarding house, and the elementary school. Other buildings are homes of employees.

Site 23. The residence of the general manager of the La Grange Mine symbolized the aristocratic elegance of its French connections.

Site 23. The pit of the La Grange Mine showing two monitors in operation.

Baron LaGrange was drowned on his estate in France in 1899. He was succeeded by his father. In 1901 Pierre Bouery became general manager in residence and directed operation of the mine through the days of its greatest success. In addition to being an effective manager, Bouery was also a local social figure. He remodeled and refurbished the Castle and its grounds. He installed fireplaces with imported tiles, sent to France for special wallpapers and made use of stained glass. The residence became famous for its wine cellar and gourmet food. The Castle with its cupola on the hillside, high above the mine pit, and removed from the quarters of the mine workers on the opposite side of the mountain, thus symbolized the aristocratic elegance of its French connections.

Association with the greatest hydraulic mine in Trinity County added a certain distinction to the lives of a number of local men who were directly responsible at operational levels. These men thus became identified with the history of the mine. In addition to Humphrey Tudor, they included B. R. Brown, who had managerial responsibilities; John Griffith and Peter Jensen, mine foremen; Levi P. Poage, superintendent of the entire ditch system; William Condon, in charge of the boarding house; Joseph Britten; Charles and Carl Van Cleave; and Katherine (Katie) Weinheimer and her sister Celia, the two teachers of the 17-22 children who attended the LaGrange public school.

In 1905 eastern United States capitalists bought into the mine, providing $425,000 of added capital. In 1908 the LaGrange Company bought all the holdings of the Sweepstake Mine. In 1919, because of economic factors related to World War I, the mine was forced to close. It has been estimated that by this time the mine had produced $3,500,000.

In 1927 the mine was sold to Dr. Bryon Stookey, a New York brain surgeon, and his brother Dr. Lyman Stookey, professor of biochemistry at the University of Southern California Medical School. The Stookeys reactivated the old Sweepstake pipeline out of East Weaver Creek and mined on the south rim of the old mining pit near the old road.

In 1934 the California State Highway Department arranged to lease water from the Stookeys in order to sluice out a cut 210 feet deep to create a low pass over Oregon Mountain for Highway 299W. Engineers estimated that the route of the highway through the cut would reduce the distance from Weaverville to Junction City by two and a half miles. This operation required the movement of 10,748,000 cubic yards of earth and took six years to complete. All the earth was sluiced down into the old mine pit and no attempt was made to recover gold.

In 1940 the Stookeys attempted to clean up the bottom of the pit. They used the hydraulic method with moderate success. Further down, tailings were mined by doodle-bug dredges. This operation was highly successful. In an attempt to recover the fine gold that was known to exist in the lower end of Oregon Gulch they used a large bucket-line dredge. This part of the mining venture proved ineffective in recovering the extremely fine gold. Mining operations ceased in 1941, brought to an end by the beginnings of World War II.

In 1960 the LaGrange properties were acquired by Edwin J. and Julia Regan and Robert and Ruth Brandes of Weaverville. They sold the property to Paul Edgren of Redding. Present owner of the mine is the LaGrange Aggregates Corporation, the two principals of the corporation being Larry E. Yingling and James Grigsby.

Site 24. The Sweepstake Mine

The Sweepstake Mine was located on Oregon Mountain at the head of Dutton Creek, which flows into the Trinity River near Steiner Flat. Sweepstake Flat is a place name appearing on most maps of the Oregon Mountain area and is a pleasant flat on the southeast slope of the ridge. Multiple springs here supply water to Dutton Creek. Sluiced-out ground below the flat and the reservoir area near the top of the ridge are all that remain at the site of one of the most fabulous, astonishing, and short-lived hydraulic mining operations of Trinity County.

On June 29, 1901, the Trinity Journal reprinted a story from the San Francisco Examiner reporting the rumor that the Sweepstake Mine near Weaverville had been sold for $6,000,000. Further investigation by the Examiner, however, revealed that the selling price was only $1,500,000 and that the buyer was the Consolidated Lake Superior Company, with head offices in Philadelphia. Plans for the property, according to the story, included an additional expenditure of from $720,000 to $1,000,000 to construct a twenty-six mile ditch around the side of Mt. Bally to bring water from Canyon Creek. An additional ditch was to be constructed to bring water from West Weaver and East Weaver Creeks. One hundred men had already been hired to clear the rights-of-way and the company expected to put 1500 men to work to get the ditch completed by the end of the year.

A week later the Journal carried a story to the effect that the Sweepstake contained the richest known body of gold–bearing gravel in the world and that the eastern capitalists had sent a noted mining expert to California who employed 26 men to prospect for nine days. They reported fabulous gold deposits, with gold particles varying from minute sizes to nuggets worth $10.00. The mining expert estimated that the gravel deposit was 350 feet deep, 1000 feet wide, and 10,000 feet in length. With gold at $19.75 an ounce and the lowest test value 45 cents per cubic yard the mine should yield $58,500,000. Three members of the eastern company and another mining expert came to Trinity County and confirmed these findings and estimates.

During the remainder of the year the bonanza possibilities of the Sweepstake Mine affected all aspects of Weaverville life. Real estate values increased, merchants were filled with optimism, employment increased, and on Oregon Mountain activity at the famous LaGrange Mine was eclipsed by all the projects at the Sweepstake. Sawmill machinery was being hauled in; a large camp of expert machinists was set up at the Ward place on the Weaverville side of the summit to rivet pipe; 300 men were working on the ditch; men were opening up the mine; still others were erecting a sawmill on Dutton Creek. By September ten miles of ditch had been dug: seven miles on the Canyon Creek side and three miles on the Weaverville side. Three and a half miles of pipeline had been laid and covered. By November ditch and pipeline had been extended to East Weaver Creek but work on the water line to Canyon Creek had been postponed until the following year.

By January of 1902 the Sweepstake was ready to work with water from East and West Weaver Creeks. Difficulties developed, however. Portions of the ditch slid away in February. The company decided to tunnel from Garden Gulch to Munger Gulch, then decided to use trestle and pipe instead. By April giants were working again, but the total working season was short. A blast in the mine drove a big rock through one of the bunkhouses. When clean-up time came, results were deflating, and before the year was out mining operations ceased. The great expectations generated by the promotors and prospectors came to an ignoble end. There were rumors that the old original mine had been salted with nuggets; there were rumors of a law suit; there were claims that the mine had been badly worked and that the property did not have a fair test. But once the eastern capitalists closed down operations there was no capital available to complete the 26 mile ditch that would have brought the waters of Canyon Creek to Oregon Mountain. Sections of the Sweepstake ditch and pipe line are still visible on the mountain especially in the vicinity of Glenison Gap. An incomplete tunnel can be seen around the hillside toward Clear Gulch.

Several of the mining claims comprising the Sweepstake group were owned by John Whitmore, some in partnership with other persons. Whitmore's share of the sales agreement was to have been $100,000, payable in four installments; a down payment of $2500 and three payments of $31,666 each. The first of these payments was to be made within one year from the time the waters of Canyon Creek were brought to the properties and the remaining payments, one and two years later. Since the ditch, flumes, and pipelines to Canyon Creek were never completed, Whitmore and his co-owners received little money. A-vailable records do not indicate the amount of fees received by the promotors, Senator John F. Davis and Frank H. Hall.

Site 25. Altoona Ranch (Alex George Ranch) (John Souza Ranch)

High up on the mountain on the ridge that stretches westward to the Trinity River was the ranch of Alexander Cummings George, a Pennsylvanian who crossed the plains and came to California in 1849. The ranch is just west of the old Sweepstake mining property and is reached by a private road that intersects the old Junction City-Weaverville road on the summit of the mountain. The ranch is 2.8 miles from the junction of these two roads. Blessed with one of the most beautiful views in the county, the ranch faces Weaver Bally mountain to the north and the peaks of the New River-North Fork divide to the northwest. The property is watered by a series of mountain springs.

Alex George was well known both in Junction City and Weaverville. When he first came to Trinity County, he engaged in various mining ventures, but in later years devoted himself to farming. He apparently was a farmer at heart. He had farmed at one time at the Dacy Ranch on Dacy Bar which was located near the mouth of Oregon Gulch and between the Gulch and the Weaverville-Junction City wagon road. (The Dacy Ranch property was later mined and is today largely bedrock.) George was born in Altoona, Pennsylvania, and named his ranch on Oregon Mountain the Altoona Ranch. For him, giving the name "Altoona" to his ranch, with its beautiful mountain views, must have symbolized a "homecoming". He was 23 years old when he came to California and 86 years old when he died. Horace R. Given, district attorney, delivered the eulogy at his funeral. Given, who was one of the owners of the Trinity Journal at the time, probably also wrote his obituary. In it, George is described as a man of sound judgment, wide reading, active in his younger days in local affairs, and socially one of the most companionable of men. He never married and left no known relatives.

Courthouse records on the Alex George property are incomplete, partly because some of the key deeds apparently were never recorded. A patent on the property was issued in 1919, seven years after George's death. Ownership to the property later passed to the Schaffer family, who owned adjacent properties. In the 1960's the Altoona Ranch was acquired by the U. S. Plywood Corporation which, in turn, traded it to the New Covenant Church of Bellflower, receiving from this religious group, in exchange, other land on Oregon Mountain which possessed more valuable timber. Through several later transfers of property rights by individual members of the church, the ranch has been acquired by its present owner, John Souza. Souza also owns a six-acre meadow, further west, historically known as the Bunker Ranch, and which at one time was part of an old Indian allotment. Souza has transferred George's Altoona Ranch into an attractive mountain property with sturdy fences, an attractive mountain home, commodious out-buildings, and a small lake.

Red Hill and the Trinity River Area Down-river from Junction City
Historical Overview

Red Hill was the site of some of the earliest mines of the Junction City area and was consequently the site of very early settlement. The position of the region in relation to early down-river travel has already been mentioned. It is next to impossible to trace the dates of location and transfer of the various mining operations, evident though these are today in the exposed red clay earth and hillsides, which nature has still not been able to cover. Cox mentions the Hocker Ranch and Placer Mine. Judge Bartlett, Cox's annotator, born in the area, mentions his father's mine known as the David Evans and Bartlett Mine. He mentions the operations of Gerald O'Shay, who, with others, at one time operated the Montezuma, as well as the other Red Hill properties; the Jacobs family, of whose home only one heroic fig tree survives; and the mining activities of J. A. (Bert) Gilzean and his brother Warren. In connection with Red Hill one thinks of the John Day Cut, visible from the Jacob's fig tree; the North California Mining Company; and of the activities of Goldfield Consolidated. Probably the last Red Hill mining was done in the 1930's and early 40's by a group of local men: Bert Gilzean, manager; Charles Adduce; James Brown; Marion (Smoke) Hackler; Clarence Kunkler; C. H. McCartney; Warren McKay; and Albert Noble. These men leased from Goldfield Consolidated and used water from the McGillivary-Heurtevant Ditch, carrying the water across the Trinity by a pipe bridge constructed by North California Mining Company.

The McGillivray Ranch was one of the most noteworthy agricultural sites on the Trinity River. The McGillivray Patent, which included mining claims as well as the ranch, extended from the settlement surrounding the present Elkhorn Motel and Trailer Park (the old Stoddart Placer Mine) to Parks Bar, two miles below Junction City. The ranch house, located in about the center of the Cooper's Bar property, was three and a half miles from Junction City. A considerable part of the mining property was on the Red Hill side of the Trinity.

Site 26. Cie Fse Mine (Albert Hayes Mine)

The old town of Junction City reached its zenith in the 1890's. Hydraulic mining in the area reached the highest point of its development approximately at the same time with the purchase of the Albert Hayes mine on Red Hill by a group of French capitalists acting under the name of a corporation known as the Compagnie Francaise Des Placers Hydrauliques de Junction City. The words Cie Fse were abbreviations for Compagnie Francaise.

The general importance of the Cie Fse Mine in the history of Junction City has already been described. The elaborate ditch and flume system, amazing siphons and pipelines, and the piers for the suspension bridge across the Trinity have also been mentioned. Other information about the mine is set forth in two portfolios of documents and photographs recently received by the Trinity County Historical Society from Paris, the gift of Madame Emile Rabut. Mme. Odette Saladin Rabut, now in her eighties, made a trip from France to Junction City in 1978 to see the site of the mine, of which her father, M. Edouard Saladin, had been general manager from 1895-98. Born Odette

182

Site 26. The house of M. Edouard Saladin, manager of the Cie Fse Mine at Junction City, in 1896. The house stood on the upper west corner of Benjamin Flat. The child in the photograph is Saladin's 3½ year old daughter Odette.

Site 26. The north Mountain power house below Junction City, after purchase by the Pacific Gas and Electric Company. Using the water rights purchased from the Cie Fse Mine, the dynamos generated electricity for the city of Eureka. Not anticipating the energy problems of today, PG and E later destroyed the power house and the dam at the head of the ditch at Canon City.

Site 26. The pipe-line of the Cie Fse Mine dropped almost perpendicularly down the bluffs just below the mouth of Canyon Creek at Junction City, then crossed the Trinity River on the pipe-line bridge.

Saladin, she had lived in Junction City as a little girl. To those who received her at the historical society, she brought not only information about the famous mine, but also a story of human sadness, the story of the death of her mother in childbirth, of her broken-hearted father, and of the sad return of the family back to France with the body of her mother, who, from the point of view of the family, had lost her life in a frontier wilderness far removed from the expert medical care that she might have had in France.

The manager's home, in which the Saladin family lived, was located on the upper western corner of the large field directly across the Trinity from Junction City. This field is on Benjamin Flat which was named for E. M. Benjamin who was the engineer who designed and supervised the development of the remarkable water system from Canyon Creek for Mr. Hayes. Only a few locust trees among the native shrubbery remain today to indicate the site of the elaborate house with its verandas and grounds.

Mr. and Mrs. Hayes sold their mining property for $250,000, the sale being arranged through Fred Beaudry of Weaverville, a mining promoter, and Francis Heurtevant, a French mining engineer and promoter, who later acquired the McGillvray Ranch and who was afterward murdered and thrown into the Trinity River.

The location notice of the Cie Fse, dated April 5, 1894, included over 1200 acres of land. The following historic Junction City mines were encompassed in the sale: the McKinney Placer Mine, Bakers Bar Placer Mine, Benjamin Placer Mine, Keno Bar Placer Mine, Picket Placer Mine, Keno Placer Mine, Lion Placer Mine, Boston No. 1, 2, 3, 4, and 5 Placer Mines and the El Dorado Placer Mine. The location apparently also included all of the property from what became known later as the Montezuma Mine to the corner of the Hocker Placer Mine and the Last Chance Placer Mine. The water rights on Canyon Creek included not only the Hayes rights to the creek water and the ditch systems, but also the water of Canyon Creek Lakes; the waters of McKinney Gulch and all ditches leading from that stream; and an undivided half interest in the waters of Mill Creek obtained by virtue of an agreement with John Whitmore. The scope of the sale by the Hayes family is further indicated by the fact that it included all tools, houses, blacksmith shops, barns, fences and sheds, horses, cattle, sawmills, milling machinery, logs, lumber, hydraulic pipe and giants owned by Hayes.

A special feature of the Cie Fse mine stressed in the press and in mining reports was its electric lighting system, by means of which mining was possible during the night as well as by day.

In the portfolios received by the historical society from France was one coupon bond certificate. Only two coupons were ever clipped: that for December, 1901, and for the one for June, 1902. The property did not fulfill the expectations of the capitalists who purchased the mine and sold bonds to back large-scale operations. In 1904 a group of San Francisco and Eureka businessmen organized the North Mountain Power Company, capitalized for $500,000. They purchased the water rights and ditches of Compagnie Francaise, built a power house on the McGillivray property below Junction City, and for a number of years, until they sold to the Pacific Gas and Electric Company, furnished power for the city of Eureka.

Site 27. Hocker Ranch and Placer Mine (Hocker Flat, Gulch and Meadow)

The Hocker Ranch was an over-night stopping place in the days when gold seekers and miners going from Weaverville to Helena followed the river route that went along the west side of the Trinity below Junction City, avoiding the impassable bluffs on the east side of the river just below the mouth of Canyon Creek. The ranch in those days also functioned as a kind of community center for the Red Hill area.

The property was located on January 25, 1853, by John Hocker, brother of Henry Hocker, early Weaverville merchant and builder of the Trinity County Court House. Both Hocker men had been born in Hanover, Germany, and came to the United States with their father and mother and three sisters as part of a historic group of Catholic immigrants who settled on farming lands near Jefferson City, Missouri. The brothers left the family farm and came to California when news of gold discoveries reached the Middle West, and both spent the remainder of their lives in Trinity County.

The Hocker Ranch and Placer Mine is located approximately two miles from Junction City on the present Red Hill County Road. Hocker Gulch, also named for John Hocker, runs along a portion of the southwest boundary of the property. Located for many years on county maps as Hocker Flat, the property can be seen as an open flat across the Trinity River from the public campground just below Junction City on Highway 299.

In addition to farming and housing and feeding traveling gold seekers, John Hocker is also reported in the Trinity Journal at different times as operating a ferry across the Trinity, conducting a trading post, and operating a mill. In the days when horse racing was a popular sport in Junction City, his horses were vigorous contestants. He was a man who was especially fond of dancing, gave dances at his residence, and was frequently asked to be responsible for the sale of tickets in the Junction City area for important county-wide balls. On Christmas Eve of 1881, at the age of 50 years, he died of a sudden heart attack, which occured while he was dancing at a community holiday party on Red Hill. He was buried in the Catholic Cemetery in Weaverville. Following his death, his cattle, horses, wagons, poultry, farm produce, and farm equipment were sold at auction by his nephews, John Henry Hocker and Joseph M. F. Hocker. The inventory of this sale indicates that he had a well-equipped and productive ranch.

John Hocker was accustomed to driving his stock up a steep mountain trail to a pleasant mountain meadow cradled in a draw at the head of one of the branches of Conner Creek. This meadow became named for him and Hocker Meadow now appears on all county and Forest Service maps. For many years it was a favorite hunting ground and camping place for deer hunters. The site of the meadow and the area surrounding it have been logged twice, however, and much debris now litters a region that was once exceptionally beautiful not only for its trees and shrubbery and fine springs, but also for the magnificent view of the Trinity Alps that greets the eye of anyone who ascends the mountain. This is now very easy to do in the summer time, for a Forest Service timber access road now makes the area easily accessible.

The Hocker Ranch was patented by Mary Elizabeth Hocker, a niece, January 23, 1893. Known by the name of Lily Hocker, she was for a number of years the postmistress of Weaverville until her marriage to Lawrence Ecklon of San Francisco. Before her death in 1905, Mrs. Ecklon deeded her interest in the Hocker property to her husband, who later deeded the Ecklon interest to his sister-in-law, Mrs. Mary Teresa Hocker Meckel, prominent in educational activities of the county, especially with the establishment of the Trinity County High School. On Mrs. Meckel's death, her ownership passed to her husband, Frederick, and her children, Henry, Lily, Teresa, and Frederick. The other owner of the property at this time was Joseph F. M. Hocker of San Francisco. The property passed out of the ownership of the Hocker heirs in 1918, when it was sold to Jafet Lindeberg, mining promoter. In later years the portion of the property which was not mined or dredged has been subdivided, and a number of homesites now occupy the land which in the early years of the county was one of the well known historical sites along the Trinity River.

Site 28. Davy Evans Grave

On Red Hill, on one side of the pond which is fed by a ditch out of Conner Creek, there is a lone grave surrounded by a scattering of manzanita and other bushes. The grave is enclosed by an iron pipe railing. At the head of the grave is a red rectangular gravestone three or four feet high. This marks the grave of David Evans who was born May 24, 1861, and died September 7, 1892. Below this identifying information are the following lines:

As you are now once was I
As I am now you soon shall be
Now you prepare to follow me.

From the grave site there is a commanding view of Weaver Bally, of the Trinity River and Junction City, and of the hills and mountains in the direction of North Fork. Mr. Evans had done extensive mining in the Red Hill area and, according to the Trinity Journal, had selected this grave site himself.

David Evans had been a native of Wales. He was believed to be a man of considerable wealth. Several stories were current, during his life and after his death, of gold which he had supposedly buried. One such story was that Evans, because of the heaviness of his pack, had buried 40 pounds of gold near a large pine tree in the vicinity of a cold spring on the divide between the South Fork of the Salmon River and Grizzly Creek on the North Fork side. There was another story that he buried gold on Red Hill and for years miners there were constantly on the lookout for it.

After Evan's death, a small envelope, marked as his will, was found among his possessions, but was empty. A typewritten will, signed when he must have been very ill — for his signature is scarcely legible — left equal shares of his estate to John Dixon Cope Day and Theodore Begel. Two reliable men had witnessed his signature. The inventory of his estate shows that at the time of his death Evans had $4531 in cash; Red Hill mining properties, ditches, and water rights appraised at $6700; Canyon Creek mining properties and water rights appraised at $1500; five tons of hay; one cow and calf; powder, caps and fuses; and one stove.

Site 29. McGillivray Ranch

McGillivray's Ranch was dredged out in the early 1920's and so today appears largely as piles of dredge tailings along a flat across from Highway 299 below Junction City. Some brush and timber have since grown. The patent filed with the County Recorder has a color drawing of the claim with the location of the house, roads, and ditch. The McGillivray ditch can still be seen along the west side of Canyon Creek.

Originally known as Cooper's Bar, the McGillivray Ranch became one of the finest agricultural establishments in the county and perhaps the state. Joseph McGillivray, from Scotland, first came to Vermont where he learned the stonecutter's trade, and then to Cooper's Bar in 1851 after news of California's gold reached the East. He decided to give priority to farming rather than to mining, acquired rights to the Conner ditch on Red Hill, and hired a trained horticulturist from New York named William H. Berber. Berber went back East for the leading varieties of fruit trees, shrubs, and flowers. By 1864, when McGillivray considered offering the ranch for sale in the Trinity Journal, he had 10,000 hop vines and 20,000 fruit trees, the largest and best assortment of budded and grafted stock in northern California. His distribution of fruit tree stock had an immeasurable effect on the agriculture of the county.

McGillivray also constructed a toll bridge across the Trinity River which was part of the road system from Junction City and Red Hill to the North Fork. He was also instrumental in the building of roads from his ranch to Helena (labeled McGillivray's road on the patent); to Butler's place on Canyon Creek and on up to Canyon City; a road upriver to the Chapman ranch; and the road from the Felter Ranch on Oregon Gulch to Weaverville. According to Judge James H. Bartlett these roads "made great changes in living conditions in the area". McGillivray later decided that parts of his land could be more profitably mined than farmed. The McGillivray ditch, taking water from Canyon Creek about four miles above the mouth, was fed by a dam below Reservoir Hill. McGillivray proposed to cross the river with the water by means of a siphon pipeline which he himself designed and engineered. Judge Bartlett credits him with an invention which had tremendous impact on mining all over the world.

McGillivray sold his ranch to Henry Lorenz and Jacob Leibrant and left Weaverville in 1872, going to Oakland. The ranch was again sold to Francis Heurtevant, a French mining engineer. Heurtevant later helped organize the Valdor Dredging Company which turned the ranch into a rock pile.

Canyon Creek and Dedrick
Historical Overview

In the early days of the 1850's, pioneers recorded that it was impossible to take a mule through certain of the narrow rocky sections of the canyon. Consequently in the earliest pioneer days, miners came to the Canyon Creek mines by way of two trails from Weaverville: one trail route was from Weaverville to Glennison Gap, to Clear Gulch, to Conrad Gulch; the other was from Weaverville up East Weaver Creek over East Weaver Bally and thence down the East Fork of Canyon Creek. The wagon road from Junction City was first built in 1867. Until the development and use of heavy equipment in the last half of this century, the Canyon Creek road had a reputation for being one of the most narrow and hazardous roads in the county.

The history of Canyon Creek from the boundaries of the present primitive area to its mouth at Junction City has been a history of mining. The first mining by pan and rocker, sometimes called drift mining, was extensive, and up and down the creek are immense piles of boulders on what remains of the old bars. Hydraulic mining later had its day, as one can see from the red side of mountains sluiced away by monitors. Quartz mining became important after the turn of the century and high up on the mountain sides are the dumps from tunnels that produced ore for the Globe, Chloride and Bailey, and Mason and Thayer stamp mills.

In places along the creek were a few family mines, where men like Adam Burger or Conrad Dannenbrink staked out claims, married, raised families, eventually patented their claims and passed on, their patented land now owned by newcomers who wish to live away from the complications of urban environments. Eventually mining activities came to an end, the population declined, cabins and houses fell down and scarcely little remains today in testimony of the vitality and activity of one of the busiest mining areas of pioneer days.

(Note: The following historical sites located along Canyon Creek road have been further identified in terms of their mileage from Highway 299 in Junction City.)

Site 30. Dan Dedrick Home (1.1 miles)

To the left of the road at this point is a small flat with a few old apple trees. On the banks of Canyon Creek, the flat is covered with sand from the big flood of 1964. Popularly known as The Apples, and occasionally a stopping place for people driving campers, this was the site of the Daniel C. Dedrick home. Dan Dedrick was a miner and skillful prospector, who is reported to have discovered many of the important quartz mines of Trinity County. The town of Dedrick is named for him.

Site 31. Clear Gulch (1.3 miles)

An old pioneer trail which connected Weaverville and Canon City follows up Clear Gulch. By means of this trail a hiker can ascend the west side of Weaver Bally Mountain to Glennison Gap and then follow a Forest Service access road down to Highway 299 near the Oregon Mountain summit. The old homestead ranch of Frank Coppins is near the head of Clear Gulch. About a mile above the ranch on a small branch of Clear Gulch is a landmark known as the Onion Patch. Here, a spring arising in a small mountain meadow has been used by hunters over the years and has supplied water for some mining activity.

Site 32. Butler's (2.0 miles)

In early days the property at this point was called Butler's, after the owner, Allen Butler, who mined, had a trading post, a home, an extensive orchard, gardens, and fields sufficient to support stock. Butler was born in Albion's Mill, England, in 1818, and came to Trinity County in 1852. He died in Weaverville in 1900.

Butler's was a pioneer landmark for several reasons. Here was the intersection of an old road to Helena, completed in 1866 and the wagon road to the Canyon Creek mines. The old Helena road crosses the creek, proceeds right, through a lane between two houses, makes a hairpin turn to the left, and proceeds to a low gap known in the last century as Butler's Saddle. The old Helena road then proceeds along the hillside at a gentle downgrade and joins Highway 299 near the Bigfoot Campground. Another road goes over the hill with a steep downgrade to Highway 299. In the first part of this century, this road was the only access to the North Mountain Powerhouse, which supplied the city of Eureka with electric power.

Butler's Saddle was an important point in connection with two historical ditches out of Canyon Creek, each of which can be clearly seen as one drives up the Canyon. The lower ditch, built by Joseph McGillivray and known later as the Heurtevant Ditch, went through a tunnel under the road at Butler's Saddle. Higher up on the mountain side is the ditch that carried water to the Hayes Mines at Junction City, later purchased by a French company and known as the Cie Fse Mine. At Butler's Saddle the water in this ditch came down the mountain through a siphon and on up the other side to a ditch which carried the water on toward Junction City. Here it was dropped through pipes several hundred feet down a cliff and then conducted across the Trinity River to the mine via a suspension bridge. While the LaGrange Mine water system was more extensive, the Cie Fse water system out of Canyon Creek was a much more complicated engineering project. The Cie Fse ditches and water rights were later purchased by the North Mountain Power Company.

The two houses on either side of the lane formed by the old Helena road have been familiar landmarks for over fifty years. The larger of the houses on the right was the home of Peter and Minnie Jensen. It is now owned by Mrs. Irene Root. The house on the left was for many years the home of Mr. and

Mrs. Richard Gribble. It is now owned by William Jones of Redding.

Site 33. Lizard Point (2.6 miles)

Canyon Creek and the road make a sharp turn at Lizard Point, which received its name because the warmth of the sun made it a favorite place for lizards. Across the creek are huge wash-outs from the old ditches, both the Cie Fse ditch and the McGillivray ditch being very prominent landmarks at this point.

Site 34. The Steps (2.8 miles)

In early days this section was one of the impassible sections of the canyon. The roadbed at this point was on bedrock and exceedingly rough, some of the rock having the appearance of steps. On the cliffs above, in the early spring, grows the very pretty flower, *Lewisia cotyledon*, which locally is known as the "step flower".

With modern road-building equipment the road through this part of the canyon has been regraded and greatly widened, so that none of the roughness and rocky primitive quality remain. The roadbed has been filled and raised, and the periodic flooding that occurred in the winter no longer takes place.

Site 35. Reservoir Hill (3.8-4.3 miles)

At this point the road begins to climb what is known as Reservoir Hill, though here again the road has been regraded so that one is no longer very conscious of the grade. About one-tenth of a mile up was the site of the McGillivray-Heurtevant Dam and the beginning of the famous ditch. The dam, some years ago, was destroyed by dynamite to facilitate the migration of fish, which previously could navigate the stream only by fish ladder. Recent mining has been done in this area, which was also one of the sites used for filming the motion picture, "Gold Is Where You Find It".

Reservoir Hill has an interesting geological history. The natural reservoir at the top of the hill was formed by a gigantic slide from the side of the mountain across the creek, which occurred many years before the advent of the white man. The growth of timber and other vegetation on the mountain side obscures the extent of this event of nature, which is more evident to an observer who notes carefully the soil formation as he proceeds down the road on the other side of the summit.

Site 36. Pennsylvania Bar (4.7-4.9 miles)

Here in early pioneer days was an extensive mining settlement named in honor of the Keystone state. Close to the road on the right is a tree with a signboard reading "No Trespassing Area Patrolled". Underneath are the remains of a cellar and a stone fireplace. Across the road, approximately 30 feet, are the remains of another stone fireplace. The road crosses Pennsylvania Gulch approximately one-tenth of a mile farther.

Pennsylvania Bar was for some years the home of Mrs. Ola Sward Peterson, the author of "Mountain Musings," a feature of the Trinity Journal. Mrs. Peterson's life here has figured prominently in her column.

Site 37. Gold Dollar Mine (5.2 miles)

Along the next half mile are the Gold Dollar Placer Mining Claims, owned and worked intermittently by a number of different people. At 5.2 miles from Junction City is Gold Dollar Gulch, 0.1 miles farther is Forty Dollar Gulch, 0.1 miles beyond is the mine residential building. The mining property includes approximately 100 acres along Canyon Creek. Extensive mining was done across the creek as well as in the area through which the road passes. Water for the mine was brought from Conrad Gulch through approximately 2700 feet of ditch. A portion of the pipeline is visible from the road. The mine was leased and operated for a number of years by Hipolito Espinosa. Among its owners and operators have been S. F. Gambell, members of the O'Neil family of Weaverville and their descendants, and Bert Gilzean and Herbert W. Day. The mining claims are presently owned by George Griner, who lives on the property.

Site 38. Conrad Gulch Area (5.6 miles)

Conrad Gulch is located on the Canyon Creek side of Weaver Bally and over the years has been an important source of water for several mines. On the mountain above the gulch was the Canyon Creek portal of the Sweepstake Mine Tunnel. This tunnel was never completed but it had been planned as part of a system of ditches, flumes, and pipelines which would have conveyed water from Canyon Creek to the Sweepstake Mine on Oregon Mountain.

Off the road to the right is a field known as the Major Price Claim on which once stood buildings, long since gone. A jeep road runs partly up the mountainside and an old pioneer trail goes over the ridges into Clear Gulch and thence over Glennison Gap to the Weaverville Basin.

Site 39. Pioneer Trail Crossing (5.8 miles)

At this point the old pioneer trail from Weaverville to the mines crossed the road. The trail proceeds across Canyon Creek and goes over the mountain on the left to Rich Gulch on the East Fork of the North Fork. From here it went on until it intersected the Back Bone Trail, which was the main trail out of the North Fork into Siskiyou County.

Site 40. Rarick Gulch Area (6.3-6.8 miles)

The field on the other side of Rarick Gulch is known as Slack Field. This at one time was cultivated land with a house on it.

Site 41. Clark Mine (7.1 miles)

Arthur Clark, who mined this property for a number of years, was married to Julia Burger, whose father, the older John Adam Burger, originally located the property. Clark also purchased additional adjoining mining property from Louis Heimburger.

Site 42. Dannenbrink Mine (7.3 miles)

The Dannenbrink Mine and homestead were developed by Conrad Dannenbrink, a Hannoverian German, who came to Trinity County in 1852, settling early in Canon City. Dannenbrink acquired the mining property in 1862, the same year he married his wife Augusta, a sister of Henry Junkans, a prominent pioneer merchant of Weaverville. Ten children were born to the couple on this property.

The original Conrad Dannenbrink home, built in the 1860's, was destroyed by fire in 1911, and the present house was built shortly after by Carl and William Dannenbrink, who were living on the property with their sister Gussie. Lumber for the house was milled by the two brothers, who, at the time, operated a sawmill in Dedrick.

The Dannenbrink Mine, like so many other placer mines along Canyon

Creek, was a family mine which provided income for the same family for almost two generations. The mining property later became part of the Canyon Placers. The homesite is now owned by James Curran. A second building was erected on the property in recent years.

Site 43. Gwinn Gulch and the old Burger House (7.6 miles)

The old homestead on the other side of Gwinn Gulch was originally a mining claim located by John Adam Burger and his friend Louis Heimburger. John Adam Burger was born in Urweiler, Alsace, in 1854 and came to Trinity County with his wife Elisabeth Fichter Burger, also from Alsace. He was a second cousin of an older John Adam Burger who came to Canyon Creek about 1854 and lived further down the canyon. Four of the couple's children lived to become adults: Elisa, a set of twins — John and Adam — and George, who now lives in Weaverville. Characteristic of Alsace, the Burger home had chestnut trees and grapes for wine. Burger and Heimburger mined by drifting, digging tunnels at the creek level for gravel deposits under the bedrock. The old Canon City School was across the road from the Burger home. The building, added to, still stands.

Site 43. The Canon City school, across the road from the John Adam Burger home at Gwinn Gulch. Among its teachers were Emilie Meckel McAfee and Nellie Scott Pattison.

Site 44. Canon City Cemetery (7.8 miles)

The old Canon City cemetery on the hillside above the road contains the remains of James Gilzean, pioneer miner from Scotland and grandfather of James Albert (Bert) Gilzean and Warren Gilzean, very well known in mining activities around Junction City during most of the century. Also buried in the cemetery are some members of the Nicolas Wolff family. Vandals carried off grave markers, but the cemetery was fenced during recent years by the county.

Behind the cemetery is a spectacular example of hydraulic mining. The great hole, reported to have been sluiced out by a man named Chris Wolfiski, involved an outlet tunnel under the road and another huge sluiced-out cut below the road.

Site 45. Guthrie Place (8.0 miles)

In earlier days this flat was a mining claim owned by William Guthrie and was known as the Guthrie Place. It is located near the head of the ditch and dam that were built for the Hayes-Cie Fse Mine at Junction City. A sawmill on the site provided timbers for the construction of the flumes along the water way, and the Guthrie house became a residence for the ditch tenders. The North Mountain Power Company later acquired the water rights and ditches and also utilized the house as a ditch tender's residence. John Adam Burger of Gwinn Gulch and his son George acquired the property from a member of the Mansfield family, demolished the building and used the lumber for the construction of a shed and utility building on their Gwinn Gulch property. The large building, now on the site, was built by Burger's son John and his wife Ellen.

Piles of rocks between the Guthrie Place and the bridge beyond give mute testimony to the great amount of mining done in this part of Canyon Creek. Just above the Guthrie place were extensive Chinese mines. C. H. McCartney of Junction City, in search of old bottles and other artifacts, did considerable digging in the area, where he noted the remains of old cabins and found many remains from the Chinese miners: pottery, implements, opium pipes and other paraphernalia.

Site 46. Hayes-Cie Fse Mine Dam Site (8.4 miles)

At this point on the road the site of the old Hayes-Cie Fse Mine Dam can be clearly seen. The dam was demolished after the Pacific Gas and Electric acquired the North Mountain Power Company and the dynamos in the power house below Junction City ceased to operate.

Site 47. Canon-City (8.6 miles)

Although the section from Gwinn Gulch to the bridge was generally thought of as the Canon City area, this location was the "heart" of the early-day Canon City mining community, as the rock piles and sluiced-away hillsides testify. According to Cox's Annals, the locality was first discovered in 1851 by J. W. Statler, from Ohio. During the hard and snowy winters of 1852 and 1853 extraordinary riches were discovered and miners flocked to the area in great numbers. Cox designated the population of the community as about four hundred in the later part of 1855 and as about two hundred fifty in the first part of 1857, when the Fraser River gold discoveries were beginning to provide competition. The extent to which pioneer miners made use of the water resources of Canyon Creek is indicated by the fact that water for the Canon City diggings was provided by six different water ditches.

Prominent among the later residents of Canon City was Ellis Flowers, whose residence stood on land now occupied by P. W. Fullerton, and whose water ditch can still be seen on the hillside to the right of the road. Fullerton has developed a family museum of artifacts gathered up and down the Canyon.

Across from the Fullerton home are two out-buildings, one of which during the early part of the present century was the Canyon Creek business location of a lady known as Glass Eye, an itinerant prostitute who for several years came by stage to service lonely men in the canyon and Junction City.

192

Site 48. Fisher Gulch (8.9 miles)

The name Fisher was well known in the Canyon Creek area in the 1850's. L. G. Fisher and his brother J. M. Fisher were both born in Tennessee. L. G. came to Trinity County in 1852 and in 1853 he and his brother were issued a license for selling merchandise at Canon City. Cox refers to L. G. Fisher as head of the Canyon Creek Water Company, owner of the principal water ditches on the creek. According to Bartlett's annotation, the ditch extended from a short distance below what was later the town of Dedrick down as far as the Dannenbrink Mine, a distance of about five miles. Fisher Gulch has been the site of a sawmill, operated by water power from the Gulch. An old road branches off the county road to the left and goes a short distance up Fisher Gulch to the site of an old sawmill.

Site 49. Early-day Hydraulic Mines and Tunnel (9.2-9.9 miles)

As one leaves Fisher Gulch and proceeds around the rocky points ahead, he traverses what in earlier days was the narrowest and most precarious sections of the old Canyon Creek road.

To the careful observer the next mile of the road is full of both grandeur and mining history. Two-tenths of a mile from Fisher Gulch on the left hand side of the road is an old mining tunnel, which goes directly into the rock, the mouth of the tunnel partly obscured by falling rock. Directly across the creek was the Wallace Mahoney Placer Mine. Half a mile further on is a magnificent view of the Trinity Alps, the impressive peak in the center of vision being Sawtooth Mountain. Across the creek, further on, one can see where whole mountainsides were washed away by hydraulic mining, water being carried in ditches from both Canyon Creek and its East Fork. At one time Davey Evans had extensive interests in ditches and mines in this area. During the late 1920's, Canyon Creek Placers, Inc., a company made up of General Motors stockholders, acquired all the placer mining claims from Dedrick to and including the Dannenbrink Mine. The California Division of Mines and Geology (County Report 4, page 85) lists these mines as including the following claims: Ackerman, Comstock, Dannenbrink, Henry Junkans, Hikes Hill, Oswald, Pittsburg, Prussian and Heimburger, Red Flat, Rough and Ready, Sidney Smith and Wilt.

Site 50. Murphy Ranch (Grasshopper Flat) (Heavenly Hill) (10.2 miles)

At this point a side road to the left goes to property first known as the Murphy Ranch. Later, and on maps, it became known as Grasshopper Flat, named by fishermen who in days past found this flat an excellent place to catch bait before proceeding to the creek to fish. From this hillside area one can enjoy a magnificent view of the Canyon Creek side of Monument Peak. A religious colony now finds inspiration in this scenic grandeur and refers to the site as Heavenly Hill.

Site 51. Site of Canyon Creek Placers Community (10.7 miles)

One cabin is all that remains today of the community of cabins, bath house and other living quarters built in the first part of the 1930's by Canyon Creek Placers, Inc., for its miners. On the right hand side of the road stood the neatly fenced house of the superintendent and the company office. Below this house, toward the creek, in still earlier times was a sawmill.

Site 52. East Fork Road (10.8 miles)

The road to the right is a Forest Service access road which climbs the mountain for several miles in the East Fork and Bear Gulch drainages. In days past this road provided access to the Green Placer Mine on the flat and hillside immediately above, to the Hikes Hill Hydraulic Mine across the East Fork and along Canyon Creek, and to the Mason and Thayer Mine on the mountainside, whose stamp mill still stands. Up on the mountain also were the Maple, Ralston, Annie, and Buck's Ranch mining claims. Accessible by a trail further up the mountain, near the top of the ridge, is East Fork Lake.

Site 53. Old Townsite of Dedrick (11.1-11.4 miles)

Canon City was the major community on Canyon Creek in the days of the sluice box and rocker and hydraulic mining. The town of Dedrick developed with the quartz mining on the mountains. All of the land is part of the National Forest, all the houses and gardens and fences that made up the town of Dedrick having been built on mining claims. The town developed about 1890 and was named in honor of D. C. Dedrick, original locator of the Chloride Mine. The post office was established May 4, 1891. The first reference to the community in the Trinity Journal was in the May 23, 1891 issue. Men and women who knew the town when it was one of Trinity County's most flourishing mining communities find it difficult today to adjust to the present complete absence of human habitation. The post office was closed December 31, 1941. The few remaining buildings in the townsite gradually disintegrated or were torn down. Only a few rock cellars and foundations remain as evidence that human beings once lived here

On the right, as one entered the town, was the home of Peter and Pauline Smith, a neatly kept vine-covered house with vegetable garden and flowers, where one could arrange to stay overnight after the two-story hotel at the other end of town burned. Across the street from the Smith's stood a well-constructed house with fenced garden, which was one of the last residential structures to disappear. Originally called the Travelers' Hotel, this house was for a number of years lived in by Riley Raglin, his brother Elmer, and their mother. At the upper end of the town, left of the road, was a store with barn and other outbuildings. Across from the store was the Gribble Hotel, operated first by William and James Gribble and their wives and later by James and his wife Susan. The main building had an upstairs dance hall. The Gribble property included not only the hotel buildings, but a saloon, dwelling house, stable and other buildings. In front of the hotel site today is the beginning of a jeep road to the Globe Mine up on the mountain. Dedrick, in its prime, even had a resident physician. Other buildings in the townsite were the residences of J. W. Shuford, Joe Gore, Joseph and Kathleen Morris, Michael Birmingham, and in later years Fred Ourth, one of the last postmasters. The town contained several saloons and in 1905 the Forest Supervisor, much to the chagrin of miners, reported that the Forest Service was considering closing all saloons not on patented land, thereby putting all Dedrick bars in jeopardy. A well-remembered bar was located near the site of the old store. It was operated in the 1950's by Tex Willburn, a thoroughly western type of woman, whose cold beer was much prized by backpackers on their way home from a trip to the Canyon Creek Lakes.

Site 54. Old Adams Place and the Little East Fork (11.6 miles)

At this point on the road there is, to the left, a bridge across the creek and a road that leads to a pleasant little flat, which in earlier times was known as the old John Adams Place. Adams was a skilled packer who packed lumber up the

Site 52. The five-stamp mill of the Mason and Thayer Mine still stands at Bear Gulch on the mountain side above the East Fork of Canyon Creek.

Site 56. Offices and living quarters for workers at the Chloride-Bailey quartz mill once stood at the upper end of what is now the Ripstein Forest Service Campground.

Site 56. The Chloride-Bailey Stamp Mill near Ripstein Gulch. Part of the concrete foundation still exists.

Site 57. The Globe Quartz Mill was an impressive sight on the steep mountain side approximately ¼ mile south of the trailhead to Canyon Creek Lakes.

Site 53. A street scene in the lower part of Dedrick. Mr. and Mrs. Pete Smith are standing at the gate of their home on the right-hand side of the street. The man with the beard on the left is Mike Birmingham, prominent early-day Dedrick miner.

Site 56. The Chloride-Bailey Mine on the mountain above the town of Dedrick.

Site 53. The upper section of the town of Dedrick in 1904. Prominent in the photograph is the three-story Gribble Hotel. The one-story building at the extreme left is the Gates Saloon, the foundation of which still exists.

mountain for the Globe Mine. Little East Fork, a small stream, can be seen somewhat farther up the road to the right.

Site 55. Ackerman Homestead (12.0-12.2 miles)

The field to the left of the road was part of the John Quincy Ackerman Homestead, patented in 1918. With neatly kept buildings and fenced garden and hayfield, the property enjoyed a plentiful water right out of Canyon Creek; the water ditch and intake pipes are still visible. The property was later acquired by Grover D. Fullerton and the Fullerton family maintained a pack station on the site for several years. Fullertons sold the property to the Kimberly-Clark Corporation, which later traded the land to the Forest Sevice for land elsewhere. The property is again part of the public domain.

Site 56. Site of the Chloride-Bailey Mill (12.6 miles)

About a tenth of a mile from the Ripstein Gulch Public Campground can be seen excavations for the site of the Cloride-Bailey Quartz Mill and remnants of concrete pillars and timber. The Chloride Mine was two and one-half miles northeast of Dedrick at about the 5000 foot elevation. Ore was carried by traveling buckets on cables from mine to mill. In 1896 the Chloride was owned by S. L. Blake, C. W. Smith, and H. R. Given of Weaverville.

Site 57. Globe Mill and Mill Workers' Community (13.1 miles)

The Globe Mine was up on the mountain at an elevation of 5500 feet. Tunnels of the mine ran clear through the mountain and dumps of these tunnels are landmarks both on the Canyon Creek and Stuart Fork sides of the mountain. The mill covered the side of the mountain below the road and office buildings, bunkhouse, dining room, and workers' residences were on the flat below the mill. This flat was completely washed away by the flood of 1964. Nothing at all remains today except the foundations of the electric plant which are visible on what remains of the flat on which it was located.

Townsite of Helena
History

When white men first came to the Trinity River, what is now called Helena was an Indian campground. Archeological excavations have recently been made in connection with the building of a new bridge over the North Fork of the Trinity River. Remains of arrowheads and grinding utensils suggest human habitation in the area as long ago as 4000 years.

The earliest description we have of North Fork in the time of the white man is that of John Carr in his "Pioneer Days of California". Carr tells how he sailed from San Francisco to Trinidad Bay, attempted without success to mine on the Klamath and Salmon Rivers, and set out over the Salmon Mountains to reach Weaverville by way of the North Fork of the Trinity. He found near the mouth of the North Fork a trading post "in a large tent stretched on four logs". Four men were in the tent playing cards. A few goods and supplies were in one corner. A keg of whisky was set on a log beside them. It was the month of February, 1851.

Where was this trading post? Modern road building equipment can very much change the original and natural character of the land. Even today, however, anyone who walks over the area near the confluence of the North Fork and East Fork is impressed by the bluffs on both sides of the North Fork. As a consequence of these bluffs, the early-day trail went down the east side of the

NORTH FORK OF TRINITY RIVER
showing
LOCATION OF 1882 TRAILS

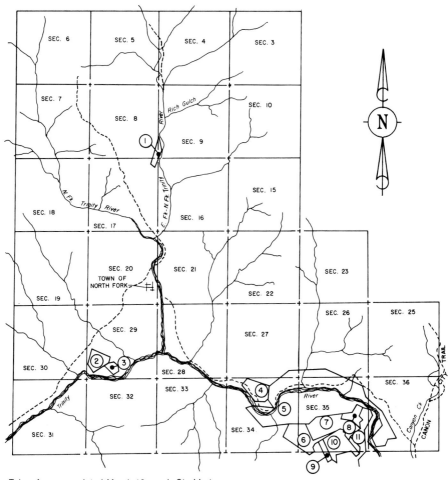

Taken from map dated March 12, 1883, showing Public Land Mineral Claims in Township 34N, R11W, Mount Diablo Meridian

KEY TO MINERAL CLAIMS

1. Peron & Dyer
2. Hydraulic Hill
3. Osborn
4. Stoddart
5. McGillivray
6. Jacobs
7. Mammoth
8. Hansen
9. Happy Jack
10. Evans & Bartlett
11. Barthel Jacobs

LEGEND

------- TRAILS & WAGON ROADS

~~~~~ STREAMS, RAVINES AND GULCHES

The above map, based on a survey made by the Surveyor General's Office in 1881-1882, shows that the old trail to the East Fork proceeded up the North Fork on the east side of the stream and not on the west side where the road is located today. The down-river trail, to avoid the bluffs on the Trinity below the mouth of North Fork, went high up on the mountain and came down to the North Fork near Ritterbush Gulch and the Cove, crossing the North Fork in the vicinity of the Meckel spring and an old campground.

North Fork and not on the west side where the road is located today. A recently discovered map of the area, made in 1882, shows that the old trail crossed the North Fork just below Ritterbush Gulch and connected with the old down-river trail, which went up the ridge at this point and down the Trinity high enough on the mountain to avoid the bluffs at the mouth of the North Fork and those down the canyon on the route to Big Flat. A likely location for the trading post would have been near the trail crossing just below the Cove and the mouth of Ritterbush Gulch. Here there is an excellent spring. In earlier days there was an excellent campsite here which has since been obliterated by bulldozers when the old road was widened. Just above this campsite, the North Fork could have been crossed on a log, as Carr mentions, except in times of very high water. The Cove, which received its name because it was a sheltered place would have been a good winter site for a trading post designed to serve travelers coming from the upper North Fork and East Fork areas as well as from the lower Trinity country and Trinidad Bay. It is important not to forget that the trading post was housed in a tent. It was therefore a temporary business.

In January of 1852, eleven months after Carr's visit to the North Fork, a young man named Craven Lee filed a land settlement claim in the courthouse in Weaverville. The Trinity County census report for 1852 indicates that Lee was a native of Massachusetts who had come to California from Indiana. He was 23 years of age, and judging by his short-time accomplishments as narrated by Issac Cox, apparently full of energy. Postal records show that he became the postmaster of a ghost post office called Trinity.

Lee's land claim included the flat on the east side of the North Fork between that stream and the Trinity. Highway 299 now passes through this property. The claim, moreover, also included the entire larger flat on the west side of the North Fork, the location of the present townsite of Helena.

Another young man at the North Fork was David Weed, who had crossed the plains in the spring of 1850 with a party of gold seekers which included John Meckel, who, with his brother, was later to play an important role in the history of the area. According to Cox, Lee and Weed erected a hotel and boarding house in 1852. A hotel in the 1850's might mean only a structure with dormitory facilities for miners. It might mean also just a house where a miner might get a bed and a meal. It is impossible to establish beyond doubt the location of the "hotel". It seems probable, however, that at that date it would have been on the east side of the North Fork, a site which miners and travelers coming down the Trinity River would reach first. In such a location a traveler would not have to cross the North Fork, for it was impossible to ford the stream near its mouth at all times of the year. Henry Weinheimer Meckel in later years was drowned attempting to do so. There are no impassable bluffs on the east side of the North Fork between the Trinity and Ritterbush Gulch, so that by trail one could proceed up that side of the North Fork and either continue on the trail to the East Fork on the same side or cross the stream and continue on the trail down the Trinity. According to Weed's obituary in the Trinity Journal, Lee and Weed also opened a butcher shop. This business, according to the Trinity Journal, was on the east side of the North Fork. That Lee owned developed property on the east side of the North Fork is indicated by a deed of his to A. F. Billay in 1859. According to the deed this property was fenced and contained improvements. The fence can be clearly seen in the photograph of the Schlomer toll bridge included in this book. Today one can still see old fruit trees in the area. The east side of the North Fork at that time would, therefore, seem a logical and practical place to start a business.

The Schlomer toll bridge before the great flood of 1861. In addition to Schlomer's first blacksmith shop and original home buildings at the left, the photograph shows the Schlomer Brick Building (Site 58) and the Meckel Brothers' Brewery to the right of it. The fence in the foreground is historically significant. It surrounded improved property on the Bagdad side of the North Fork which Craven Lee sold to A. F. Bilay in 1859.

The Meckel Hotel at Helena in 1897.

Helena Josephine Hall Meckel, for whom the town of Helena was named.

In 1852 rich gold deposits along the Trinity River and its gulches began to draw hundreds of miners to the area. One can imagine that suddenly tents, shacks, and camps of various kinds appeared in the vicinity of Lee's preempted land on the east side of the North Fork. There developed, also, another kind of gold rush. Ladies of accommodation came, seeking whatever gold dust or nuggets or coins they might obtain from the miners. Cox referred to them as "mademoiselles, senoritas, and jungfraus" to dramatize the international character and infinite variety of these feminine gold seekers. The character of life seems for a time to have been giddy. Craven Lee had a reputation as a great practical joker and the young miners on the North Fork were constantly playing jokes on one another and harassing unsuspecting newcomers. It is quite likely that he was responsible for the name "Bagdad," which he and other young miners humorously gave to the goldrush settlement on the Trinity. It was as fabulous and bizarre a place in its own way as that great glamorous and ancient city on the Tigris for which it was gleefully named. When Lee filed his settlement claim, however, he used the place-name "North Fork". The Trinity Journal in 1860 referred to "North Fork, until late years known as 'Bagdad.' How it earned, or who gave it that title," said the Journal, "we can't say." Second generation Meckels and Schlomers, however, born on the North Fork in the 1870's, must have heard glamorous tales from their fathers and old timers. They seemed to understand clearly that Bagdad was a name given to the goldrush settlement on the east side of the North Fork in the early 1850's and that the name did not also apply to the town that developed on the west side. The mining claim, later owned by the Schlomers on that east side of the stream and which included property originally claimed by Craven Lee, was consequently called the Bagdad Placer Mine. It is presently part of the DiNapoli property in Helena. (Note: This detailed discussion has been included here because of apparent confusion that has arisen in recent years between the names "North Fork" and "Bagdad".)

Issac Cox called Craven Lee "a proprietor of the Land", and mentioned that Lee had about 200 acres of land under cultivation, also a garden and orchard, a water ditch, and a number of mining claims. The Trinity Journal's obituary of David Weed stated that the Lee and Weed store business and butcher shop failed. A number of events now occurred which led to the development of the town on the other side of the North Fork, the site of present day Helena.

Trinity County Courthouse records show that on November 24, 1855, Craven Lee mortgaged his ranch at North Fork to John Follinsee, borrowing $1500 at two and one-half percent interest for nine months. In February of 1857 minutes of the Board of Supervisors indicate that Craven Lee and John Hawk had been appointed "to view out a trail from Hamilton's bridge across the North Fork to the mouth of Rattlesnake". Lee apparently was being forced to turn to labor away from his property in order to earn money. In November of the same year Craven Lee began to sell all his North Fork property, a process which continued through 1859. By 1860 Lee had left North Fork and had gone to Callahan in Scotts Valley, Siskiyou County. He later joined the Confederate Army.

A life-long friendship had begun between David Weed and John Meckel while the men were crossing the plains and was undoubtedly responsible for Meckel's coming to North Fork. John Meckel first came to Trinity County in 1851. He had heard that there had been important gold discoveries in Siskiyou County on the Salmon River. He set out to reach the Salmon mines by way of the trail up the North Fork, but he turned back after meeting a group of returning and discouraged prospectors at Grizzly Creek. He went back to Sacramento Valley, met his younger brother Christian, and the two young men mined successfully at Newcastle. It is very likely that the business failure of Weed and Lee provided the commercial opportunity for the Meckel brothers. In the fall of 1853, with the money they had made mining, they were able to start their general merchandising and packing business on the North Fork. Their business thrived. They were able to buy land from Craven Lee. As more and more miners came to the mines back in the mountains, John Meckel opened a trading post at Rich Gulch on the East Fork. The Meckel brothers kept from 50-60 mules and operated pack trains to bring merchandise from Red Bluff and Shasta, and even after a wagon road from Weaverville to North Fork was built in 1862, their packtrains continued for many years to supply miners on the North Fork, East Fork and Grizzly Creek. Their mule trains often went over the divide to the Salmon River and on to Scott Valley for agricultural products and flour from the Etna Mills.

An especially important event in the history of North Fork was the establishment in 1855 of Durkee's Sawmill, up the North Fork above the present village of Helena. Frank Buck, Durkee's partner, states in his book, "A Yankee Trader in the Gold Rush" that at first the mill did not prosper but by the summer of 1856 the mill was working day and night. As additional discoveries were made and a mining boom developed, lumber was needed for flumes and other mining purposes. As Craven Lee began to sell his land, a building boom started and the town of North Fork rapidly developed on the west side of the North Fork at the present site of Helena.

In 1855 an energetic young German by the name of Harmon Schlomer made his appearance on the North Fork. Within the next few years Schlomer, in addition to mining, had started a blacksmith shop, erected a toll bridge across the North Fork, and built a three-story brick building, which still stands. John Meckel and Harmon Schlomer married sisters. During the rest of the nineteenth century, the history of North Fork was closely connected with the activities of the Meckel and Schlomer families.

The development of a town on the west side of North Fork was further facilitated by the building of Schlomer's toll bridge which made the west side of the stream easily accessible at all times of the year, even when the stream was too high for fording. The construction, soon after, of Daniel Hamilton's bridge across the North Fork near the mouth of East Fork put the town on the west side of the North Fork on the main route to the East Fork mines. The old trail on the other side of the river, formerly the main route, eventually fell into disuse.

The business district of the new village developed along the embankment of the river, which in early days was the main street. The enterprising Meckel brothers started a brewery and imported a brewer from Germany to supervise production. By 1860 North Fork was thriving. The Trinity Journal describes the town in that year as "a rich mining locality" and as "a thriving village destined to be second to Weaverville in point of business." Special features of the community, according to the Journal, "were the toll bridge of Harmon Schlomer; the brick store of Meckel and Company; the North Fork Hotel of H. O. Adams; the North Fork billiard saloon, post office, drug store and express office of Rudolph Bock; Schlomer's brick building with a saloon in the lower story; Phillips and Day's market; Meckel, Bender and Company's Brewery and Saloon on Main Street, a new Masonic Hall, and several neat cottage residences."

The year 1861 was the peak year of pioneer mining in the North Fork area. Men were young, full of energy, optimistic, and expectant. Not only in the vicinity of the community, but up the East Fork and down the Trinity men were making money and constructing ditches and flumes to further increase their

HELENA TOWNSITE

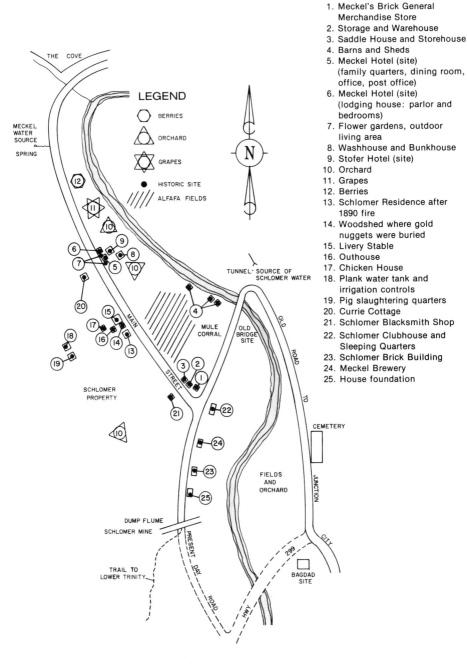

KEY TO HISTORIC SITES

1. Meckel's Brick General Merchandise Store
2. Storage and Warehouse
3. Saddle House and Storehouse
4. Barns and Sheds
5. Meckel Hotel (site) (family quarters, dining room, office, post office)
6. Meckel Hotel (site) (lodging house: parlor and bedrooms)
7. Flower gardens, outdoor living area
8. Washhouse and Bunkhouse
9. Stofer Hotel (site)
10. Orchard
11. Grapes
12. Berries
13. Schlomer Residence after 1890 fire
14. Woodshed where gold nuggets were buried
15. Livery Stable
16. Outhouse
17. Chicken House
18. Plank water tank and irrigation controls
19. Pig slaughtering quarters
20. Currie Cottage
21. Schlomer Blacksmith Shop
22. Schlomer Clubhouse and Sleeping Quarters
23. Schlomer Brick Building
24. Meckel Brewery
25. House foundation

gold production. Down the river to Big Flat numerous companies, mostly Chinese, were fluming and wing-damming the river, which had been especially low during the summer. Before the end of the year, however, the greatest flood of the century wrought catastrophic destruction along the Trinity and its tributaries.

In spite of the damage done by the flood and the financial havoc resulting — the Durkee Sawmill was completely destroyed, for example — mining continued along the streams and new gold discoveries were made in the back country. During the 1880's gold deposits in quartz were discovered and a quartz mining boom developed on the East Fork with mines such as the Ozark, the Enterprise, the North Star, the Lone Jack, and the Yellowstone prominent in the news.

Toward the end of the 1880's hydraulic mining developed. Hydraulic mining in the Helena area and down the Trinity River tended to be family projects or projects with very modest payrolls. Men mined in the winter, planted gardens in the summer, raised hay as winter feed for cattle that grazed on government land in the summer, kept chickens and frequently pigs. In Helena, Harmon Schlomer's sons, for example, mined on the various mining claims which the Schlomer family acquired over the years, but they also tended their orchards and fields during the summer and operated a feed and livery stable. Schlomer himself carried on a thriving business in his blacksmith shop.

In 1870 on a trip to Germany, Christian Meckel married Helena Josephine Hall, a young woman from his native village. In 1878 he and his brother John dissolved their partnership and John purchased the Pacific Brewery in Weaverville and moved his family to the county seat. The agreement made at the end of the partnership provided that Christian would no longer make beer at North Fork and that John would no longer engage in the mercantile business. During the remainder of the century, activities on the North Fork very much revolved around the activities of Christian and Helena Meckel. Christian continued to operate his store and the couple opened a hotel which became famous in Trinity County for its hospitality and service. For several years a grand ball was given each autumn, attended by people from all over the county. Colorful accounts of Meckel Hotel balls may be read in the Trinity Journals of August 29, 1885, September 30, 1893, and July 9, 1898. During the 1890's, as travel became easier, North Fork became a favorite place for young men and women from Weaverville to spend a Sunday. In 1891 the name of the post office was changed to Helena to avoid confusion with another North Fork in the state, the name honoring Christian Meckel's wife.

The accompanying map represents Helena during the first decade of the present century. It shows the Meckel property on the east side of the main thoroughfare and the Schlomer properties on the west side. It also shows that the water for the Schlomer gardens and fields was piped out of a tunnel on the east side of the North Fork. From here the water was brought to a large covered wooden reservoir in the rear of the Schlomer property and distributed over the garden and orchard through an intricate system of small ditches and flumes developed by Harmon Schlomer. Water for the Meckel properties came from Ritterbush Gulch and the spring which can still be seen on the left side of the road south of the field known as the Cove.

The Meckel hotel stood directly on the front street with a lodging house nearby to the north. One stepped directly from the street onto a low porch and from the porch into the hotel office and village post office. To the left from the porch was the door to the dining room, which opened on the opposite side to a garden path that led to a two-story lodging house with sleeping rooms on both stories. This building contained a parlor with a piano, which was the first piano

Street scene in Helena in the first decade of this century showing a hunting party about to depart from the town. The two-story white building in the foreground is the lodging house of the Meckel hotel. Warehouse and saddle house and Meckel store building are at the end of the street on the left. The Currie cottage and Schlomer livery stable are at the end of the Schlomer field on the right.

The Adams Hotel at North Fork was purchased by George Yohe and Bestider in 1861. It was operated by Yohe for many years. The building to the left was at one time the billiard parlor and drug store of Rudolph Bock, notary public.

brought into Trinity County. This piano had been originally purchased for the Apollo Saloon in Weaverville. (See Site 71, page 103.) The piano is now on display at the Trinity County museum.

On the south side of the hotel building, the porch continued the length of the house and around to the rear of the building. Off the porch were the Meckel family quarters, consisting of living room and sleeping rooms. One stepped from the porch into the family gardens, with gravel paths, flower beds, hammocks and outdoor furniture. Cherry trees, planted by Helena Meckel, and spreading locust trees provided shade in summer. Beyond the hammocks toward the end of a space of green lawn was a fig tree, prized by the family as a testament of the benign winter climate of the area. Farther back toward the fields was a wash house where miners and other guests washed up before meals and bathed.

The Meckels and the Schlomers received a patent on their land at Helena in 1900, the property previously having been mining claims. The patent covered 130 acres.

Christian Meckel died in 1904. His wife Helena moved to Weaverville into a house on Main Street which she previously had purchased. She leased the property at Helena for a number of years to Lin and Lilly Knowles. In 1924 the property was sold to Harvey Stofer. Stofer in 1930 tore down the Meckel hotel building and lodging house and began construction on a new building back from the street—a building with shingled siding. In 1932, the Trinity County Bank, which had financed Stofer, closed and went into receivership. Stofer's project was never completed. In 1939, H. G. Schlomer, the surviving son of the Schlomer family, acquired what had previously been the Meckel property from the Bank of Eureka, the entire village of Helena now becoming the property of Schlomer and his sister Lou. Schlomer died in 1956 and his sister Lou in 1957. The property was inherited by William Jennings Bryan Hinters, a nephew, and his sister Lulu Hinters Stevens, a niece. Mrs. Stevens deeded her interest in the property, including buildings, furniture, and equipment to her brother in 1959. After the death of Bryan Hinters, his wife Janice sold the property in 1966 to F. L. DiNapoli, owner of the Sun Garden Packing Company of San Jose, the Redding Searchlight reporting the sale under the headline: Historic Trinity town sold for $50,000.

Mrs. Hinters's deed to DiNapoli included not only the patented land of the Schlomer and Meckel Placer Mining Claim, but the following mining claims as well: North Fork Placer Mining Claim, Bagdad Placer Mining Claim, Osborn Hill Placer Mining Claim, Ritterbush Placer Mining Claim, Ohio Placer Mining Claim, Hydraulic Hill Gold Placer Mine, and the Osborn Placer Mine.

Mr. DiNapoli did extensive remodeling to the Stofer Hotel Building. In 1969, he constructed a large fireplace in the main reception room; remodeled the kitchen, installed modern hotel equipment; and built a small and complete private apartment in the northeast corner. On New Year's Day 1971, during the absence of the caretaker, the Stofer Hotel building was completely destroyed by fire and now only the foundation, concrete steps and ruins of the 1969 fireplace remain. Mr. DiNapoli died in 1974. The property is presently owned by the F. L. DiNapoli family with W. L. Battaglia, as trustee.

Until the construction of Highway 299 through the Trinity River Canyon to Eureka, Helena was at the end of the road. Necessarily it was the stopping place for all travelers who wished to go down the river or travel the trails up the North Fork, the East Fork, or to the New River and Siskiyou County. In 1931 the State of California completed the highway bridge across the North Fork. No longer did a main road go directly through the town. Helena was off to one side and reached by a spur road off the main highway. Instead of stopping at least overnight, the traffic of the world went whizzing by and the heyday of Helena as a town came to an end.

Of the various buildings standing in Helena today, five are historic: Schlomer's brick building, the post office (originally the main building of the Meckel Brother's store), the feed stable, the Currie house and the Meckel barn.

Site 58. Schlomer Brick Building (Brewery Building)

The Schlomer brick building is the first building one sees when approaching Helena on the present paved road. The building was constructed by Harmon Schlomer in 1859 out of bricks made of local clay on the site. Schlomer forged metal braces in his blacksmith shop which provide decoration to the masonry. There are large S's on each end of the building and the date of construction is in large numbers on the river side. The building was erected for income purposes and contained three stories. French doors let in light and provided access into the building in front and at the back, the doors opening onto a deck on the river side. The lower floor opened to a garden. Over the years the building has served a number of contrasting purposes. In 1861 there was a saloon in the basement and the Schlomer family lived in the upper stories. The oldest son Charles was born there. The flood of 1861 brought the waters of the North Fork up into the basement and there is still a mark in the basement showing the height of the flood waters. Next to the building, toward the town, was the Meckel, Bender and Company Brewery, which supplied beer to the town and the lower Trinity area. Today only the foundations and retaining walls remain. The brewery ceased operation in 1878 when John Meckel moved to Weaverville and purchased the Pacific Brewery there. However, in 1885, during the quartz boom on the New River and East Fork, John Meckel brought beer from Weaverville and reopened the basement saloon in the Schlomer brick building. From then on this building became known as The Brewery. Catholic Mass was sometimes celebrated in the building and two of the Christian Meckel children were baptised there. The building at one time also served as a schoolhouse. During the last years of the 1920's the North Fork Placers used the building as an office and residence of the manager. Partitions were installed to make an office, a modern bathroom and bedrooms. The basement was made into an attractive kitchen, family room, and dining room complete with an old bar and antiques.

Site 59. Meckel Brick Store Building (Post Office)

This building is one of the oldest buildings in Trinity County outside of Weaverville. Originally the main building of the Meckel Brothers general merchandise store, it was constructed in 1858 of native brick. It and Schlomer's brick building, constructed the following year, are the only two surviving pioneer brick buildings in Trinity County outside of Weaverville. Another brick building was erected in Trinity Center, but it now lies at the bottom of Trinity Lake. According to an article printed in the Siskiyou News and reprinted in the Trinity Journal of October 16, 1897, the Meckel building cost $4500 to build exclusive of iron doors, which cost $500. Bricklayers at that time received $8 per day, and lumber was worth $70 per thousand. Next to the brick building on the north side was a warehouse and a saddle house. Barns and corrals were over near the river, where from 50 to 60 mules were kept. The building was recently restored with the aid of a government grant and a new slab porch was added. It is a somewhat awkward looking addition in relationship to the well-proportioned original building with its lovely windows and doors. The iron doors were long ago sold and removed.

Site 58. Schlomer's Brick Building in Helena as it looks today.

Site 59. Constructed in 1858, this brick store was the main building of the Meckel Brothers' merchandise business at Helena, which included also a warehouse, a saddle house, and mule and horse corrals.

Site 60. Currie House

The Currie cottage was built by Algernon S. Currie and his wife Rebecca, both of whom are buried in the Helena cemetery. The house is located to the northwest of Schlomer's Feed Stable, and is shaded by a giant walnut and protected by a post and wire fence. The orchard is its backyard. The house was at one time lived in by Adam Lytle McWhorter and his family. The McWhorter daughter Pauline, later McDonald, was an especially well-known pioneer woman in the lower Trinity area. After it was acquired by the Schlomer family, the Currie House was used as rental property.

Site 61. Schlomer Feed Stable

The original sign still hangs over the door of this stable, where horses were boarded or rested. The stable stands south of the Currie House. A huge walnut tree shades it to the north. In earlier days a long watering trough stood in front. The feed stable is symbolic of the fact that Helena was a town that flourished in the days of horse, buggy and stage travel.

Site 62. Helena Cemetery

The Helena Cemetery is located across the North Fork from the Helena townsite. The cemetery was ordered surveyed by the county Board of Supervisors in 1965. An interesting aspect of this cemetery is the plot of the Harmon Schlomer family. The entire family, with the exception of the older daughter Barbara, is buried here. The plot was fenced with an ornamental iron fence forged by Harmon Schlomer, himself, in his blacksmith shop. Unfortunately, half of the fence was recently stolen by vandals. Among those buried in the cemetery are Algernon S. Currie and his wife Rebecca; members of the Alexander Pelletreau family; Mr. and Mrs. James E. Given; members of the Gribble family; Mrs. Edna May Meckel, second wife of Frederick C. Meckel; and Mrs. Isabella Thomas Hayes.

East Fork of the North Fork of the Trinity River
Historical Overview

Beginning about 1853, the East Fork of the North Fork became one of the most active early-day mining areas of Trinity County. There were so many miners on the East Fork that the Meckel brothers established a trading post at Rich Gulch, where there was an especially concentrated mining population. Rich Gulch at that time was at an important pioneer trail intersection. A trail westward over the mountain to the North Fork intersected the Backbone Ridge Trail to the upper North Fork, Siskiyou County, and the New River. Another trail went up the East Fork itself, started climbing the mountain opposite the East Branch of that stream, and on top of the ridge intersected the Backbone Trail. Southeastward a trail led over the mountain to Canyon Creek and from there to Weaverville.

The East Fork area experienced another mining boom between the 1880's and the first years of this century. Promising quartz discoveries were made and rich pockets of ore found. Mines such as the North Star, the Lone Jack, the Enterprise, the Yellowstone and the Yellow Jacket were prominent in Trinity County news. The Trinity Journal of June 6, 1889, reported that all but 30 feet of the road was completed to East Fork and that the stage-run from Weaverville to North Fork was to be extended to the East Fork the following week. The stage was to arrive at North Fork for dinner (probably noon) and would stop at East Fork overnight. In the same issue it was reported that Ed. L.

210

Newman (later a county assessor) was erecting a building for a hotel at East Fork. In the Yellowstone area a post office named Coleridge was established July 22, 1889. The minutes of the Board of Supervisors indicate that the county road was established to that point in January of 1891. The rapid rise and decline of pioneer mining populations is indicated by the fact that the Coleridge post office was discontinued in 1907.

Since so many changes have taken place over the years — in some cases an entire settlement has disappeared — speedometer mileage figures have been included after the site name to assist the reader in locating the significant historical sites along the East Fork county road. The mileage figures are measured from the Helena Post Office.

Site 63. The Spring (0.2 miles)

This spring at one time furnished water for the Christian Meckel family home until a more extensive water system was developed out of Ritterbush Gulch. The old county road was very much narrower and between that road and the river was a very attractive campground shaded by alders and frequently used by Weaverville people. The spring formerly ran with a more abundant supply of water and gained fame as a place of refreshment for men and packers coming off of the Backbone Trail. It is possible that the campground may have been the site of the "trading post" described by John Carr in Pioneer Days in California. (See Helena Townsite Historic Overview.)

Site 64. Ritterbush Gulch and Cove (0.3 miles)

Ritterbush was a German who lived in Helena in early days. The fields beyond the gulch on the side hill, left of the road, were known as The Cove and were part of Meckel's property, producing hay and fruit. The term Cove symbolized the sheltered character of this area situated on a bend of the North Fork.

Site 65. Durkee's Sawmill Site (0.6 miles)

Built in 1855, the sawmill, furnishing lumber for buildings and flumes, is described by Franklin A. Buck in "A Yankee Trader in the Gold Rush". It was significant in the development of North Fork as a town, as has been indicated. In July 1856, Buck reported that the saw was kept running day and night, that the owners had sold 25,000 feet of lumber that last fortnight, and that they had orders for 25,000 feet more.

Site 66. Bridge across the North Fork (0.9 miles)

At this point the North Fork enters a rugged canyon: here also the East Fork empties its waters into the North Fork. Up the North Fork a short distance, and accessible by a very inadequate trail along the steep hillside and cliffs, is a swimming hole that has given pleasure to several generations of young swimmers.

Not only the bridge but the topography of the banks of the North Fork and East Fork should be carefully noted in this area. The original Indian trail, later followed by the first miners, went down the east side of the North Fork, as has been mentioned. The bluffs on the west side were too formidable for a crossing. Daniel D. Hamilton constructed the first bridge across the North Fork in this location in the late 1850's so that travelers could go down the west side of the stream following approximately the route of the present road. Pack trains, however, were still using the old trail in the 1880's. Remains of other bridges are evident today, and up the stream a short distrance, anchors for the cables of a former suspension bridge can be seen set firmly in the bedrock. There is also evidence of older roads.

Commenting on this area in the Trinity Journal of September 22, 1860, the writer reports: "Here the new flume of Everest and Company, conveying water from the East Fork to their extensive hill claims above Durkee's mill, crosses the North Fork at a height of one hundred and forty feet. It is a noble structure and was built at a cost of nearly $4000. Following up the line of their ditch we see mining everywhere, and everywhere evidence of prosperity."

After crossing the bridge, a reader interested in history will find on his left the beginning of the Backbone Trail, famous route of pioneer packtrains to Rattlesnake and Grizzly Creek mines, to old Denny and the quartz mines of New River, to the Salmon River mines, and to Callahan and the fertile Scott Valley.

Site 67. Brock Gulch (1.3 miles)

On the opposite side of the East Fork is the mouth of Brock Gulch. Jeeps and trucks and sometimes cars may drive far up this gulch and along the ridges to the Canyon Creek divide on the Brock Gulch forest access road that branches off from Highway 299 near the Helena Cemetery.

Site 68. Annie Slide (1.4 miles)

The narrowness of the road at this point and the precipitous descent to the stream below are reminders of the hazardous nature of the East Fork wagon road years ago. At this slide in August, 1898, Annie Marie Meckel, while driving the family horse and buggy back from a visit to friends at the Enterprise Mine, went over the bank. The horse was killed, the buggy smashed to shambles, and Miss Meckel, age 25, crawled up the mountainside and walked home to Helena with only minor bruises and scratches.

Site 69. Buntain Place (1.6 miles)

This property was developed by Benjamin Buntain during the days of the Great Depression. Buntain carried on extensive mining here in the 1930's. His wife, Doris Chapman Buntain, died in January of 1973 of injuries sustained from slipping off the precarious frosted footbridge which provided access to her house.

Site 70. Peter Zuella Place (2.0 miles)

At this point there is an access road to the old Peter Zuella property on the banks of the East Fork. Zuella, an industrious Austrian miner, located and patented this property and kept it neat and immaculate for years. He planted a sizeable grape arbor, raised excellent strawberries and other fruits in addition to garden produce, and mined for gold during the winters. He made excellent wine and was generous to the traveler who stopped to visit him. During the days of Prohibition, Pete gained a wide local reputation for his wine, his specialties including wine from strawberries and wild blackberries as well as from his grapes. Peter Zuella's homestead has changed ownership a number of times in recent years; for older residents, however, his gracious and amiable Austrian spirit still pervades this small parcel of ground that he loved so much.

Site 71. Tolin Place (2.4 miles)

The hillside above the road near this property is among the few places in the county where "step flowers" grow in the springtime. These delicate pink and

212

white flowers are called "Lewisia" and were named for Meriwether Lewis, leader of the Lewis and Clark Expedition. Lewis was a botanist who made note of these flowers in his journal.

Site 72. Rich Gulch (3.3 miles)

Rich Gulch was the scene of extensive pioneer mining operations, especially during the last years of the 1850's. It was also an important pioneer trail intersection. A side road leading to the mouth of the gulch turns off at 3.3 miles from Helena, and to the right of this road is quite an extensive flat with several nondescript buildings. During the era of the Great Depression so many people came here to eke out a living mining for gold that a schoolhouse was built on the flat by the Works Progress Administration and then abandoned when the population moved away. In recent years, as the price of gold has risen, more people have relocated mining claims in the area.

The historical Rich Gulch mining area encompassed considerable territory, most of it on the eastside of the East Fork. The territory included an old arrastra site. The Trinity Journal in 1860 made reference to the rich mines of this area when it reported that the old Meckel trading post was four miles from Helena and that a short distance from the trading post were the rich mining claims of the Kuper Brothers and of Brix and Lightner, all of whom were Germans.

Considerable mining was also done in the area by Chinese. Two Chinese, called Auk and Suey, lived to an old age there.

Site 73. Hobo Gulch Road (3.6 miles)

At this point a road branches off to the left. This is a Forest Service road on which one can drive to the Hobo Gulch Public Campground on the North Fork near the trailhead to the main trail up the North Fork. From this road, another Forest Service road branches off to the right and goes down to Todd's Cabin on the East Fork, passing near the mouth of Yellow Jacket Creek on the way. At the point where this road crosses on a log bridge, now very flimsy, the East Fork flows through a small, very narrow and rocky gorge. The stream here is impassible except by wading, which can only be done in the late summer when the creek is very low. The road here also intersects the old pioneer trail that follows up the creek from the Yellowstone Mine.

Site 74. Alex Pelletreau Home and Mine (3.9 miles)

Sluiced-off red banks and a few elderly neglected fruit trees are the only remains of a once well-tended plot of land with a neat cabin, the property of a son of one of the early pioneers of the Lower Trinity River area. Alex Pelletreau, named for his father, spent most of his life here, his house by the side of the road a stopping point for old friends and East Fork neighbors. From 1899-1903, Pelletreau, as a young man, mined with his friends, Fritz Meckel and Lin Knowles, at Kuper Point at the mouth of Rich Gulch and later at Red Point, encountering rich and encouraging pay dirt that eventually was worked out.

Site 75. East Fork Bridge and the Engle and Ozark Mines (4.3 miles)

The older road continued up the creek and vestiges of it are still evident. On the far side of the present bridge a Forest Service access road branches to the right. About a mile up the ridge is the Ozark Quartz Mine, one of the well known early mines in the area. The present owner is Marvin McQuown. Throughout its history the mine has had a number of owners. The Trinity

Journal of 1867 reported that Henry Engle and Christian Meckel had made a rich quartz discovery at the head of Rich Gulch. The Engle tunnel is one of the several tunnels included in the Ozark set of claims. Engle recorded a notice of location on July 6, 1868. On April 2, 1873, the mine was sold for $5000, the money to be paid out of profits. In 1890, records show that a relocation was filed by John Day. In 1896 J. W. Moore of Coleridge became the owner. Dan Dedrick also did considerable prospecting in the area. Perhaps the Ozarks most famous owner was Isabella Noyes Thomas Hayes, an intrepid and remarkable Chinese woman, now buried in the Helena cemetery. Isabella and her husband, George Samuel Hayes, probably acquired the mine in the 1930's. After the death of her husband she carried on the mining entirely by herself. On the hillside below her cabin are grape vines and fruit trees and the garden plots which this remarkable Chinese woman planted and cared for in her busy and energetic pursuit of a miner's dream. The Ozark Mine has produced pockets of rich ore, but the deposits have not been consistently rich or continuous.

Site 76. Barney Gulch—Meredith Ranch (Remick Ranch) (4.3 miles)

Barney Gulch is one of the larger gulches which empty into the East Fork. It has a length of approximately two and one-half miles. How the gulch was named is not known, but old-timers in the area believe that an early-day prospector with the given name of Barney (surname unknown) met a premature and untimely end while prospecting in the gulch.

Mining activities in the early days involved placer and lode claims. The main lode claims in the area were the Thanksgiving Lode Claim and the Fountain Lode Claim. The Thanksgiving Claim was first located and filed on by George L. Bailey in 1885. The claim was again filed on by John Bergin in 1889. "Mineral Resources of Trinity County", dated 1896 and published by the California State Mining Bureau, reports the utilization of a five-stamp mill in connection with the Thanksgiving-Fountain claims, capable of processing six and one-fourth tons of ore per day. The owner of the claims at that time was Henry Junkans of Weaverville. Location notices show that El Thurston located and filed on two lode claims farther up the gulch in 1885. It is believed that Thurston Peaks of Limestone Ridge were named after this man.

Oliver H. Meredith, a native of Wales, came to Trinity County in 1896. The Trinity Journal of April 20, 1901, mentions that Meredith and his brother were working on Barney Gulch and the North Star mine for Fred Haas, brother-in-law of Henry Junkans, who at that time had charge of mining operations. Meredith acquired the mines sometime prior to 1909. Meredith's main interest, however, was in farming, and he developed a small ranch for which an agricultural and homestead patent was granted in 1923. Meredith, however, was found dead on his place by his neighbor Alex Pelletreau on March 1, 1919, the death being attributed to a heart attack. Probate records of Meredith's estate show possessory interest in certain mines and a stamp mill. Ownership of the property passed to James Meredith, a relative, who sold to John Walter Roberts in 1936. Possessory rights to the mines had been allowed to lapse, however, and George L. Bailey, the original locator, had again filed on the Thanksgiving Claim in 1932.

John Roberts sold the patented, homestead property to Russ Keeney in 1946 and Keeney, in turn, sold to Arne Salvig in 1947. Salvig then sold the property to Harold Cox in 1951, who filed a notice of location on the Thanksgiving Claim in 1953. In 1954, Cox sold the property, including possessory rights to the Thanksgiving Claim, to Mr. and Mrs. Edwin E. Remick, both of whom are now buried in the Weaverville Public Cemetery. The property and rights are now owned by Remick's daughter, Mrs. Ruth C. Smothers of Las Vegas, Nevada, and Remick's two sons, David H. Remick of Tacoma, Washington, and Richard D. Remick of Weaverville. None of the old Meredith buildings any longer exist, nor is there visible evidence of their remains. The original home built by the Remicks is still habitable. In 1971, a new A-frame type house was erected in the apple orchard area of the property.

Of current interest is the fact that the Smothers Brothers, well-known television and stage stars were grandsons of the Remicks and both men have spent considerable time as boys and as men at Barney Gulch. Father of the Smothers brothers was Major Thomas B. Smothers, Jr., a West Point graduate, who was stationed in the Philippines at the beginning of World War II and was taken prisoner when Corregidor fell. Major Smothers was a participant in the infamous Bataan Death March and died later while a prisoner-of-war of the Japanese.

Site 77. Oklahoma Bar (5.0 miles)

The terrain here gives ample indication of the extensive mining done on this bar in early days; piles of rocks are everywhere and show that every inch of dirt probably has been turned over and sluiced. Two houses still stand here, both on mining claims. Looking upstream, the property on the right is known as the Carl Howard house; that on the left is known as the Jesse H. Pitzer house. Lewisia grows in the spring behind the Howard house and on the cliffs to the right of the road.

Site 78. North Star Mine (5.4 miles)

A short distance above Oklahoma Bar an old road turns ŏff the county road to the left. This road goes to the North Star Mine. This mine was first located and owned by Christian Meckel and his friend Valentine Lautenschlager, a German pioneer well known in the North Fork and Weaverville communities. The mine was originally located in April of 1883, and after a survey to more particularly describe its boundaries, was relocated in January, 1885. In April of 1889, Meckel and Lautenschlager sold their property to Henry Junkans, Weaverville merchant. The deed indicates that their mining interests included not only the North Star property but the Linnie Quartz Mine, the Fresh Water Mine, the Comet, the Clear Creek Quartz Mine, the North Star Mill Site, water rights out of Know Nothing Gulch, and water rights and ditch out of the East Fork about one-third mile above Know Nothing Gulch. Regarded by geologists as an extension of the Enterprise lode, the mine over the years has had a number of owners. County Report No. 4 of the California Division of Mines and Geology mentions that the mine, with an ore shoot 300 feet long, developed by drifts and stopes, is said to have produced $300,000.

Site 79. Lone Jack Mine (6.3 miles)

From this point on the county road, a tunnel of the Lone Jack Mine, also a part of the Enterprise lode, can be clearly seen across the East Fork on the hillside above the flat where the Enterprise buildings are located. According to Stephen W. Bradford, mining engineer and son of Julius Bradford (see Site 80), tunnels into the mountain at the Lone Jack in some cases are over a quarter of a mile in depth and in some cases 20 minutes were required for miners to get to the working space. According to the 37th report of the state minerologist (California Journal of Mining, January 1941), from a level 147 feet higher than the creek, the main vein had been stoped out for a length of 1600 feet and some stoping had been done on a branch vein also. At a level 75 feet higher than the creek, a tunnel had been driven for a distance of 2000 feet and the vein had been stoped out to the level above for a length of 350 feet. From this lower level, a winze had been sunk for 180 feet. Crosscutting to a distance of 100 feet had been done at the 50 foot level.

Site 80. Enterprise Mine (6.5 miles)

The old Enterprise tunnel can be seen below the county road on the upper side of Noonan Gulch. A steep access road beyond Noonan Gulch goes down the hill to a small parking lot connected by a footbridge to the flat across the East Fork on which are a number of the old mine buildings in a relatively well-preserved state: a two-story bunkhouse; the cookhouse (to the right of the bunkhouse); the stamp mill (below one of the Lone Jack tunnels); and the superintendent's house. A 15-inch pipeline and a flume, taking water out of the East Fork above the Yellowstone Mine, provided hydro-electric power for the buildings and for the stamp mill in which the ore was crushed. Today, P. G. and E. power is available. Remains of an old arrastra are still visible to the careful observer near the site of the bunkhouse.

The Enterprise was first located by F. A. Moor and W. I. Day under the name of the Pioneer Mine. It was relocated by survey and notice on December 13, 1884, by Francis A. Moor, James M. Moor, John H. Day and W. I. Day. November 22, 1902, the Trinity Journal reported that the mine was bonded to a syndicate of Boston operators headed by George R. Woodin after an examination by Mark Manley, a Boston mining engineer, well-known in Trinity County in the days of quartz mining on the East Fork. At the time of the sale, the mining claims consisted of the Enterprise, Enterprise Extension, Lone Jack, Cleveland, Hendricks, Live Oak, the Boss, the Backbone and the Sunnyside. The sale also included the ten-stamp mill, water rights, blacksmith shop, messhouse, bunkhouse and other buildings. At that time, also, according to the Journal, the property had already produced $500,000. The sale of the mines to Boston capitalists, arranged by Mark Manley, resulted in the formation of the Enterprise Mining Company.

The Enterprise operated over a period of 57 years. Among its operators, in addition to those mentioned, have been Robert Skinner and Frederick (Fritz) Meckel, W. R. Bigelow, Julius Bradford, and Dean Love. Bradford and Love operated the claims under the name of the Chiksan Oil Company from 1930-41. (Chiksan is a Korean word meaning gold mountain.) The company also included H. G. Henderson and C. M. Truby. R. H. Shaw was superintendent for a large part of that time. While the Enterprise facilities were the center of the company's activities, mining was done principally at the Lone Jack and the Yellowstone. Equipment of the North Star was taken to the Enterprise, including the stamp mill and the two very heavy mortars involved. On November 1, 1938, operations were started by six lessees: Al Hansen, Earl Chapman, Joe Tuey, Jack Olson, Fred Smart and W. D. Shippey. In 1941 the Chiksan Company was dissolved and Dean Love and his wife took the mines as part of the settlement. The present owner of the Enterprise is Emery Beattie.

Site 81. The Cliff House (6.7 miles)

A wide turn on the road just above the turn-off to the Enterprise Mine is all that remains today of one of Trinity County's famous saloons, named with wry pioneer humor after San Francisco's celebrated Cliff House. The overhanging cliff has been leveled off by modern road construction, but in earlier days a house with a porch perched on this cliff overlooking the East Fork. Below was the Enterprise flume, from which could be drawn buckets of water. Across the road was an old tunnel driven into the bank where kegs and bottles of beer could be kept cool. The "Cliff House" was a last commercial outpost on the East Fork for alcoholic beverages.

Site 82. Coleridge and the Yellowstone Mine (7.2 miles)

It is difficult today, as one comes to the flat at the end of the county road, to realize that there was once a mining settlement here known as Coleridge. The Yellowstone Stamp Mill was located directly across the East Fork from this flat. Coleridge, as has been indicated, had its own post office. It also, at the height of its development, had a private school with Katherine (Katie) Weinheimer as teacher. Until a few years ago there was a bridge across the East Fork at the upper end of the flat and there were mine buildings and houses of miners across the creek and on the hill as well as on the flat. Just beyond the bridge site is the trailhead for the old pioneer trail up the East Fork.

News items in the Trinity Journal pertaining to the Yellowstone claims first appear in 1888 and only rarely after 1904. The Coleridge post office was discontinued in 1907. These years, then, were the memorable years in the history of the mine. One of the earliest owners of the Yellowstone was William T. Coleman. Coleman sold the mine to Niagara Mining Company, a Shasta County mining group located at French Gulch. The company employed too many men to make an adequate profit. Robert A. Skinner was the mine superintendent and, for a number of years, it was his faith in the mine which kept it operating. He leased the mine and mill, sometimes in partnership with others, and from time to time would encounter encouraging pockets of ore. Early in 1903 the mine was bonded to eastern capitalists. At that time the Journal reported that the property consisted of 16 locations, several of which were patented. It also included a ten-stamp mill, 800 feet of tramway, ore carts and an ore bin, blacksmith shop and other buildings, and an excellent water right. Apparently the New Jersey capitalists decided not to purchase, for in 1904 the mine was bonded to Mark Manley. Ownership of the Yellowstone is presently in the name of Mrs. Rex McGee and Edwin J. Regan.

The tunnels of the Yellowstone Mine, now caved in, give no evidence to the casual visitor today of the adits, drifts, raises and stopes that marked the extensive development of the Yellowstone claims. The production record of the mine has been reported as being between $160,000 and $190,000. Today only a very careful observer can find at the site of Coleridge and Yellowstone any evidence of its past history. On the north side of the creek is a small pile of stones which once outlined the grave of a child of Robert and Minnie Skinner, until some unknowing stranger, finding the stones so amazingly handy, used them for an impromptu camp fireplace.

Site 83. Yellowjacket Mines

The Yellowjacket Mines were prominently in the news between 1908 and 1910. They were located on Yellow Jacket Creek, a tributary of the East Fork, about three miles up the trail from Coleridge and the Yellowstone Mine. The area is one of the most rugged in the county and is best reached today on the spur road to Todd's cabin which takes off to the right from the road to Hobo Gulch Campground. The property sprang into prominence in 1908 when rich ore containing free gold, telluride, and sylvenide was discovered and located by H. L. Boyd, A. H. Wolfe, R. L. Carter, and Jesse F. Tourtellotte. Their property included nine claims. Other mines in the group were owned by the East Fork Development Company and managed by W. S. G. Todd. These mines included the Blue Jacket Group and the Bonanza, the Standard Quartz Mine owned by Condon and Weedman, the Alaska Quartz Mine owned by Henry Junkans and Peter Zuella, and the Golden Chest belonging to Laingor, Rockford and Behrmann. The Journal of October 3, 1908, referred to the Yellow Jacket Mines as the "most promising mining camp in the county". Ore from the Boyd and Company claims was assaying from $1000 to as high as $30,000 a ton. Of all the quartz mining properties on the East Fork, however, the Yellow Jacket mines seem to have been the least productive. They were also situated in perhaps the most rugged areas of the East Fork and for many years were accessible only by trail.

Historical Sites in the North Fork High Country

For many years three mines have appeared as place names on county and Forest Service maps of the high wilderness area in the headwaters of the North Fork and its tributaries. These are the Keystone, Bob's Farm and Molitar.

Site 84. Keystone Mine

The Keystone Mine was an old hydraulic mine on the North Fork of the Trinity River seven miles north of Helena. The mining claim at one time included 320 acres. Water for the mine came from White's Creek, flumes for the ditch system having been cut in a small mill on the premises. The mine at one time was owned by George W. Wilson. The Keystone cabin was a familiar landmark on the upper North Fork trail for many years.

Site 84. The old Keystone Cabin on the North Fork of the Trinity River.

Site 85. Bob's Farm

Bob's Farm is located on the Specimen Creek trail between Rattlesnake Creek and Grizzly Creek at an elevation of between 5000 and 5500 feet. It is located at the headwaters of a branch of Mill Creek, on the south side of a rounded ridge where the slope is relatively gentle. The area is characterized by a series of out-croppings of quartz rock. A portion of the area with water is frequently used as a camping site for hikers and packers.

None of the old-timers who know the Bob's Farm area well are able to explain why the place received its name. Small sections of the land might have lent themselves to some early day summer gardening by the prospectors and miners, but one cannot escape the conjecture that the word "farm", for this locality, arises out of the same kind of wry pioneer humor that attached the name "Bagdad" to the earliest settlement on the North Fork. Bob's Farm, as a name, therefore, may originally have been coined facetiously.

In the first years of this century, especially between 1900 and 1904, Bob's Farm was very much in the mining news of the Trinity Journal. In February of 1901, the Journal reported that the Bob's Farm Mine was owned by W. W. Montgomery of Woodland and J. A. Byers of Colusa County, that a crew of men were working, that a tunnel on the ledge had been driven in about 15 feet, that plans were being made to install a two-stamp mill, and that the snow in the area was 18 feet deep. By December, the small mill had been installed and six men were employed. In April of the next year it was reported that the Bob's Farm Mines included seven claims, the best developed being called the Wild Denver. By December of the same year, 16 claims had been located and a Bob's Farm Mining Company had been incorporated in Sacramento. By June, a Huntington mill from the Loftus Mine on Coffee Creek had been purchased and packed in by mules a distance of about 75 miles. There was talk that a wagon road was being planned for the mine. In the summer of 1904, twenty men were working, the mill had been operating, and work was reported as progressing satisfactorily.

It was a problem for management to feed a crew of miners at a location so far from roads and at an elevation where winter snows were deep. The Bob's Farm Mining Company attempted to face the problem by hiring a young man named Bert Gilzean as a hunter. (Bert was the son of a pioneer miner and, as an older man, active in hydraulic mining in the Junction City area.) A herd of elk grazed at the time in the vicinity of Papoose Lake and Gilzean kept the mining crew at Bob's Farm supplied, at least for a time, with meat from this herd.

Site 86. The Moliter Mine

The Moliter Mine was a small hydraulic mine on Grizzly Creek about 19 miles north of Helena. Its owner and developer was Fred Moliter, born in Alsace in 1862 and well known in the Helena and Junction City areas. Moliter was typical of the back-country, small-scale miner who operated either by himself or with a partner. Old-timers recall that during the period from about 1910 to 1920 Moliter was in the habit of coming to town in the summer when the water was too low in the stream for his mining activities. He would come with his burro and stay for two or three weeks at the Bartlett Hotel in Junction City, visiting with his friends who sat in their barroom chairs in the shade of the locust trees outside the Bartlett Saloon. While he brought himself up-to-date on the local news, his burro foraged back of the town along Canyon Creek and the Trinity River and occasionally would come into the village to make sure that his master was still there. Moliter was fond of children and permitted some of the village youngsters to ride his donkey, but the animal had a reputation for being either immobile or of suddenly running fast so as to dislodge its rider, much to the delight of Moliter and his Bartlett Saloon friends. After Moliter had completed his yearly visit, he placed an order for his winter groceries at the Weaverville Supply Store. These were delivered by wagon to the head of the Backbone trail from where Moliter would pack them on his burro and on his own back, to the mine.

When the Valdor dredger began operation below Junction City, Moliter got a regular job on the dredging crew. Then the dredger ceased to operate, he worked for a time on the Lewiston dredge. From that position he was dismissed. Despondent over the loss of his job and the state of his health, he committed suicide on the top of a bluff overlooking the Trinity River near Helena. He was 65 years old at the time. The Trinity Journal reported that Moliter was a frugal man, had saved his money, and that his financial condition should not have been cause for suicide.

LOWER TRINITY - NEW RIVER

1. Logan Gulch
2. Eagle Ranch
3. Sailors Bar
4. Big Flat
5. Old Big Bar
6. Trimble Home
7. Tinsley Place
8. Manzanita Flat
9. Price Home
10. Price Creek Cemetery
11. Willshire Placer Mine
12. Cox's Bar-Pattison Place
13. Vance's Bar (Big Bar)
14. Corral Bottom
15. White's Bar
16. Little Prairie
17. Dahlstrom Ranch
18. Williams Ranch
19. Lower Waldorff Ranch
20. Upper Waldorff Ranch
21. French Creek Tunnel
22. Taylor's Flat (Del Loma)
23. Canadian Bar
24. Hayden Flat
25. Don Juan Bridge
26. Don Juan Point
27. Cedar Flat
28. China Slide
29. Dixon's Bar
30. McDonald-McWhorter Ranch
31. Hennessey Road
32. Burnt Ranch Store
33. Gray Ranch Site
34. Bill Jackson Bridge
35. Salyer Community Wayside Chapel
36. Fountain Ranch
37. Irving Ranch

38. Five Waters Ranch
39. Hoboken Site
40. The Dailey Ranch
41. Denny Historic District
42. Francis Townsite
43. Miller Ranch and Cabin
44. Jake's Hunting Ground
45. Lake City Site
46. Mullane Corral Site
47. Election Camp Site
48. Old Denny-Mary Blaine
    Mountain Mining District
49. Old Denny Site
50. Marysville Site
51. White Rock City Site
52. Mary Blaine Meadows

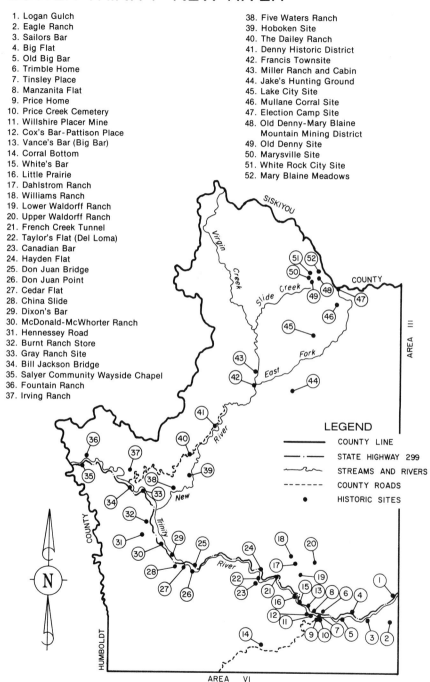

LEGEND

———————	COUNTY LINE
—— · ——	STATE HIGHWAY 299
∿∿∿	STREAMS AND RIVERS
- - - - - -	COUNTY ROADS
•	HISTORIC SITES

222

AREA IV
LOWER TRINITY RIVER - NEW RIVER

ACCIDENTS SOMETIMES HAPPEN

Historical Overview

The earliest residents of the lower Trinity-New River area were Indians. Stephen Powers, writing about the California Indian tribes in 1877, suggests that the upper New River as far down as New River City was held by Shastan Indians. Roland Dixon visited the lower New River and Lower Trinity River areas in 1906 and identified the early Indians occupying those areas as Chimariko. The Chimarikos are considered to be one of the smallest and most distinct tribes in America.

One of the first white men to enter the region of the lower Trinity River was Francois Payette in 1827 followed by Jedediah Smith in 1828, although some white men who were exploring the coastline by schooner may have anchored in Humboldt and Trinidad Bays and ventured inland a short ways before those dates. By the 1850's white miners were in the area. Many of them took Indian wives. Today there are no full blooded Chimariko Indians left.

Major P.B. Reading's discovery of gold in the Trinity drainage in 1848 led to an influx of miners and the establishment of settlements in the lower Trinity area. Confrontations between the Indians and the newcomers followed the influx. Travel in the area became hazardous. Pack trains were often accompanied by United States troops for protection. In the October 30, 1875 edition of the Trinity Journal a reporter from the lower Trinity area stated, "Indian troubles from

1861-1865 unsettled the value of property and drove many inhabitants of the frontier region away, never to return." The August 8, 1863 issue of the Trinity Journal reports that because of these conflicts "the Trinity River is totally deserted from Taylor's Flat to its junction with the Klamath." It was during this period that all buildings were burned from Big Flat to Burnt Ranch. These bloody conflicts resulted in some of the Indians emigrating to the north over the mountains, thus bringing to an end the aboriginal way of life in the area.

Prospectors and miners came from far and wide following Major Reading's discovery of gold. The bars and flats all along the Trinity River were rich in gold and were mined and settled early. Chinese soon followed the white miners. They reworked the bars and patiently extracted more gold after the whites had moved on. By 1900 the number of Chinese miners along the Trinity had dwindled and by 1925 no Chinese remained in this part of the county.

A major fork of the lower Trinity River is New River. By 1851 mining operations were spreading up this fork. Issac Cox wrote that the region was extraordinarily rich. A rush to the area began. By 1855 some 300 Europeans, Anglo-Americans and Chinese were mining on New River. But the New River gold rush subsided and by 1875 only 15 miners were still working there. However, prospecting activities slowly increased during the next several years; and by the early 1880's major gold deposits had been located which caused a second gold rush. Three towns sprang up, and a whole series of support industries including stores, saloons, post offices, sawmills, stamp mills and stopping places came into existence. Hay and grain, food, mining supplies and ore were transported by pack trains plying the three major trails which gave access to the area. The mines were gradually worked out, the miners moved on and finally in 1920 the last of the three towns was abandoned. Sporadic mining continues there as it does along the Trinity River itself.

Lack of access was one of the major problems confronting early settlers in this part of the county. Until 1924 the entire lower Trinity River drainage was accessible only by trail. All supplies and mail came into the area by pack trains. It is a steep and rugged country and in many places the trail was around rocky bluffs, high above the river. Cox wrote of these narrow trails which overhung the river. He describes the assortment of items scattered along the river bottom, the result of packs and pack animals falling from the trail—such things as "the skeleton of a mule, merchandise boxes, saddle trees, saddle pads and even a human skeleton."

The trail downriver from Helena followed the north side of the Trinity River as far as Cox's Bar (now Big Bar); here it crossed to the south side where it forked. One fork turned towards Corral Bottom and the Hayfork-Hyampom trail which went on to Korbel in Humboldt County. The other fork continued down the south side of the river to Cedar Flat and on to the coast. This trail had been cut through by 1850. The residents of the lower Trinity have always been inconvenienced by the lack of bridges across the river. As late as 1900 there was a ferry in operation at Big Bar. Soon after, however, suspension mule bridges were built at Cox's Bar, Don Juan Point, Hawkins Bar, and the mouth of the South Fork.

In the 1920's State Highway 299 was finally completed along the river from Helena to Humboldt County. Much of the construction work between Helena and the South Fork was performed by convict labor from the prisons at Folsom and San Quentin. The first road was high above the present highway and was much narrower than it is today.

Although gold seekers were the first to settle along the lower Trinity, several homesteads were developed. The farmers raised crops and stock to supply the

The New River Bridge was built across the Trinity River at New River by John and James Larson. This photo was taken at the dedication ceremony in 1914.

miners with food. Other support industries arose. The operation of pack trains was a big business and numerous stopping places were opened to accommodate the many people travelling in and out of the mining areas. As the area became more populated with families the need for schools arose and, thus, in 1875 a school was opened with 17 pupils enrolled. In time, several communities became established, lumbering became an important industry and fishing along the Trinity River attracted vacationers. It remains a growing and active area.

The following site descriptions are but brief glimpses into the history of this portion of Trinity County.

Site 1. Logan Gulch

Logan Gulch is at the mouth of Logan Creek a short distance below Helena on Highway 299.

Logan Gulch was settled in 1850 by a man named McKenlin. He mined at this location with unusual success, extracting $250 per day. He left the area as a rich man. At about the same time two brothers, J. and Boone Logan, erected a trading post and also made a fortune mining here. Boone Logan died November 27, 1854 and was buried at this location, but later, in 1858, his remains were removed to the Masonic Cemetery in Weaverville. The gravels at this place were so rich that they were turned over three times in about as many years, but by 1858 the white miners had moved on and the area was being mined by the Chinese. By using wing dams they were able to work the river more thoroughly.

Site 2. Eagle Ranch

Eagle Ranch is in the Eagle Creek drainage about a mile south of the Trinity River.

The historic Eagle Ranch in the down river area traces back to at least the 1870's. Two buildings still stand on the site, one of which may have been the original ranch house. Remnants of approximately two miles of cedar rail fencing bound and criss-cross the large meadows, which were at one time irrigated by the ditches still in evidence. Fruit trees—apples, plums and pears—are scattered throughout the meadows and two graves rest along the edge of one meadow.

The ranch was occupied from the early 1870's to 1939. It was patented as a homestead in 1909 but in recent years, through a series of events, it reverted back to National Forest land. During its entire active life of producing hay and raising cattle and hogs, the Eagle Ranch was accessible only by trail.

The ranch holds significance not only as a unique example of an isolated mountain ranch but also as a home and means of existence to early day Trinity County residents. The two graves reportedly hold Adam Guth and George Frickinger, early day immigrants from Bavaria. Guth is known in Trinity County at least since 1858 when he was listed on a military roll and Frickinger was recorded in the county's 1860 Census. From November 1929 until 1939 the Ray Howard family worked the ranch, surviving through the Great Depression. Ray Howard was born just a few miles from the ranch in 1895. Ruth (McKnight) Howard was born in Utah but came to Trinity County to join her father's family in the Mad River area when she was two years old. Right after her birth in 1902, her grandparents named the town of Ruth in southern Trinity County after her.

The above information is from the files of the U. S. Forest Service at Big Bar, California. The Forest Service recognizes the possible significance and impor-

Site 2. Old newspapers on the walls date the Eagle Ranch back to the 1870-1875 period although the patent on the property was not granted until 1909.

tance of this site and is setting up procedures for its management and protection. The site is being nominated for the National Register of Historic Places.

Site 3. Sailor Bar

Sailor Bar Creek enters the Trinity River from the south side forming a gravel bar in the river about five miles below Helena.

Sailor Bar may have been the site of the first gold discovery in California. The area had been mined successfully by Bill English and a crew of fugitive sailors in 1842, long before the pioneers of the 1850's commenced operations in other parts of Trinity County.

Site 4. Big Flat

Big Flat is on the Trinity River along Highway 299 several miles downstream from Helena.

In 1850 John Weaver who had been mining in the Weaver Basin (Weaverville) decided to branch out in search of easier diggings. He settled at Big Flat where he and his friends mined along the river. Water for this activity reached them via a flume out of Little Weaver Creek (now Big Bar Creek) which they had constructed at a cost of $10,000. With it they were able to take out $100,000 in gold in a short season. The population at the flat grew and the area has since been repeatedly mined. By 1855 there were 255 inhabitants; a year later they numbered "400 men, nine married women and three marriageable women". The settlement had two hotels, two stores, a butcher shop, a blacksmith shop and a shoe shop. A 45 foot waterwheel was erected at this place in 1855 by another Mr. Weaver (this one J. T. Weaver) and Dove and Company constructed a two mile water race out of Little Weaver Creek.

An interesting vignette in Trinity County's history took place here. During the election of 1851 the voters of Trinity County were to decide upon the loca-

Site 5. This cable car crosses the Trinity River at Big Bar Creek, providing access to the Old Big Bar site.

Site 6. The McMorrow house is located near Big Bar. It was constructed in the early 1900's. Whipsawed lumber was supplied by a local mill. Descendants of the pioneer Trimble family presently occupy the home.

tion of the county seat. Trinity County included Humboldt County at that time. The choice was between Weaverville and Uniontown (now Arcata). Weaverville was much easier for the miners along the upper Trinity River to reach. Since no voter registration was then required, a band of youthful politicians in the large village of Big Flat decided to vote early and often. They voted first at Big Flat, then Helena, then Junction City and on to Arkansas Dam where they deposited their fourth and final ballot. Weaverville won, but when the voting was challenged it was found that the same thing had occurred down river in favor of Uniontown. The fraud being even, the decision held firm. But due to this and another irregularity, a second election was held in 1852 which finally settled the matter. In May of 1853 Trinity County was divided and Humboldt County was created out of the western portion.

Site 5. Old Big Bar

The original community of Big Bar was at the mouth of Big Bar Creek (formerly Little Weaver Creek) across the river from Big Flat and Highway 299. No buildings of the original community remain. Hundreds of low tailing piles of rock were left by early miners and show the extent of their activities. In order to reach the site today one must wade or cross the river by cable car. Modern suction dredges are now operating along the river in this area. Big Bar was settled by a man named Jones. Little is known of him for he quickly got rich and left the locality. Others were drawn here also. By 1855 the community had a store, a blacksmith shop, a butcher shop, and the other usual establishments found in a community where fifty miners had gathered together. Big Bar and Weaverville were the first towns in Trinity County to have a post office. After the bar was worked out, the post office was moved down the river to Cox's Bar. A successful enterprise at this place was the Yankee Sawmill which, except for the saw blade, was built completely of wood. It cut 75,000 to 100,000 board feet of lumber annually in the early 1850's. Lumber produced here was used for mine flumes and for a bridge across the Trinity River which was built by the owner of the mill, a Mr. Warriner. The flood of 1861-62 carried away this bridge as well as all of the waterwheels along the river. (These enormous wheels were not rebuilt after the flood.) Mr. Warriner's mill was later replaced by an improved mill. For many years it was the property of William Willshire and William A. Pattison, Sr.

The first load of supplies which arrived at Big Bar from Shasta was carried by oxen that earlier had been driven across the plains by a Mr. Van Dyke, a Mr. Brown, and William S. Lowden, a gentleman who played a very important role in Trinity County history.

Issac Cox tells of two interesting personages who lived here. One was Big Bar's first woman miner, Elizabeth Walton, who settled here in 1850 and distinguished herself by probably baking the first "johnnycake" in Trinity County and by skillfully warding off a party of Indians who were bent on robbing her husband. The other was "Commodore" Line who sold mining claims to Chinese and to others. After collecting payment, he would run them away with a shotgun. The Commodore was eventually apprehended by Deputy Messic and sent to San Quentin.

There is a soda mineral spring near this first location of Big Bar. A more recent owner of property on Big Bar Creek, Ed Hostetter, maintained that this spring flowed from a deposit of lithium. Old time residents considered these waters a remedy for digestive ailments.

Site 7. The Tinsley store at Big Bar as it looked before it was destroyed by fire in 1920.

Site 7. The Tinsley house was constructed in 1920 and was used as a store and post office. It is located near the mouth of Price Creek on the south side of the Trinity River.

Site 6. Trimble Home (Keeley Place) (Vaughn Home) (McMorrow Home)

This home which is located just east of the Big Bar Ranger Station was first known as the Keeley Place. It later became the home of Pierce Trimble and his wife Rebecca who were originally from Hyampom where they had conducted a trading post. They had left Hyampom in 1870 to move to Big Flat, but eventually they had moved on to Cox's Bar in order to be nearer a school. While living at Big Flat, it had been necessary for their children to walk two and one-half miles by trail to school as well as to cross the oftentimes treacherous Trinity River by row boat. When a ferry at Cox's Bar was begun, the river crossing became not only easier but safer as well. Pierce Trimble did some mining but he was most highly recognized for his skill as a packer. He kept his pack string near his Big Bar home. Mule shoes and ox shoes have frequently been upturned in the garden plot by the present occupants.

Pierce Trimble's daughter, Belle (Trimble) Vaughn, made this her home. Today it is the home of Belle's daughter, Mildred (Vaughn) McMorrow and her husband Don. Mildred is the only remaining descendant of early Big Bar pioneers still residing at Big Bar. It is significant, indeed, that she lives in the same house that was occupied by her early pioneer grandparents.

The house is a fine example of a pioneer Trinity County home. The original portion is of board and batten construction with whipsawed lumber from the local mill. The unpainted natural wood has taken on a beautiful dark brown color as it has weathered. At first, this one and one-half story home had a roof of hand split shakes. Frequent fires, however, caused the shakes to be later covered with corrugated roofing. A pleasant porch stretches across the front gable end and one side of the house. A vine covered arbor greets the visitor before he reaches the porch entry. Several trees stand between the house and the steep hillside. A vegetable garden is behind the house. In one corner of the garden is a smoke house which received heavy use when salmon and steelhead used to be plentiful in the Trinity River.

Site 7. Tinsley Place (Kennedy Place)

This attractive house, located near the mouth of Price Creek and across the Trinity River from the Big Bar Ranger Station, was built in 1920 by George Tinsley on the site of the original hotel and trading post which was destroyed by fire. This building was constructed and used as a store and post office. The most unique feature of the building is the partly enclosed porch and its openings. The wide porch borders the simple gable structure on two sides. The outside walls of both the house and porch are neatly covered with wooden shingles.

A suspension mule bridge crossed the river at the foot of the hill just below the present home. The place is now the vacation home of Mr. and Mrs. Richard Kennedy of San Francisco. Saddle horses graze on the hillside meadow next to the house.

James A. Tinsley (Alex) and his wife, Mary, lived at Gray's Flat near Burnt Ranch in the early 1850's. While Mr. Tinsley was away from home on a pack trip to Scott Valley in Siskiyou County, Indians engaged in a major raid on the Burnt Ranch area. Tinsley's home and store were burned to the ground. Mrs. Tinsley and their two children escaped. The Tinsleys then moved to Cox's Bar (Big Bar) and established a trading post at this site (about 1871). Alex continued his packing business and expanded the post to include a hotel and tavern. It was Tinsley's son George who continued to run the business after his father's death.

Site 7. This suspension bridge crossed the Trinity River at Big Bar near Tinsley's store.

Site 9. The Price house was originally constructed in the mid-1800's, of whipsawed lumber. It is being restored by its present owners, the DuBay family. The house is located up Price Creek.

Site 8. Manzanita Flat

Manzanita Flat is located on the north side of the Trinity River along Highway 299, west of Treloar Creek and the U.S. Forest Service Ranger Station.

Joseph S. LaRocque, a French Canadian and former Hudson's Bay Company trapper, and his wife, Marianne, a Cayuse Indian, together with four other Oregonians, settled at Manzanita Flat in 1849. Mining on this flat was limited, as Issac Cox reports that not more than ten miners were working here in 1858. In 1854 a water race out of Manzanita Creek was built which carried water to this flat. The Treloar homestead belonging to Thomas Treloar was located here. The site is near the present U.S. Forest Service Ranger Station.

Site 9. Price Home (Sid Campbell Home) (Fugate Home) (DuBay Home)

This home, about three-fourths of a mile up Price Creek, contains much of the original material. The present owners are proud of the home and appreciate and respect its age. In many places they have exposed the walls of whipsawed boards. The house is long and narrow with a simple gable roof. It is given balance by the ample deck running the full length of the house front. The house is set off by a well kept lawn; ancient, neatly pruned, fruit trees are still bearing fruit as is an English walnut tree. In the back a green hillside meadow lies, sloping towards the river.

Thomas Boles Price, the first owner, arrived in Big Bar in 1852. He was a miner and, in 1868, operated the ferry across the river at Manzanita Flat. Price is buried in the Price Creek Cemetery near his home.

During the 1920's, this was the home of Sid Campbell. He was a lonely man and decided he should marry. He sent for a mail order bride (which was not uncommon in the 1920's). All went well with preliminary arrangements between him and his bride-to-be. When she arrived he found, much to his surprise, that she had many children from a former marriage. Sid Campbell's house had but one bedroom!

More recently the Fugates occupied the home, but it is presently owned by members of the DuBay family who are restoring it.

Site 10. Price Creek Cemetery

The Price Creek Cemetery is located at the left side of the road going up Price Creek. Thomas Price is buried there and his grave is marked by a neat headstone which reads: T.B. Price 1824-1911. Also in the cemetery are Sidney and Sadie Campbell's graves, as well as that of Edward Treloar, another Big Bar pioneer. This cemetery is well cared for and is enclosed with a wire fence. Four locust trees stand in a row within the enclosure.

Site 11. Willshire Placer Mine

The Willshire Placer Mine was located west of Price Creek on the south side of the river a short distance below the Tinsley place and was said to be on ground of the very oldest and richest gravel deposits in the state. Coal was also found at the Willshire Mine. It was shipped by pack train to the blacksmiths up and down the river. This mine and the LaGrange Mine were two of only a few mines in Trinity County which were granted a ditch right by the Department of the Interior. This right has remained valid through the years.

Site 12. Cox's Bar—Pattison Place

Cox's Bar was located across and slightly up river from Vance's Bar and

233

Site 12. This is the only headstone in the Pattison Cemetery located on the hill behind the former Pattison home. William Willshire was a lifelong friend of William Pattison, Sr.

Site 16. The Mortimyer house is located on the south side of the Trinity River across from Prairie Creek. Several old cherry trees at this place mark the old settlement site of Little Prairie, a stopping spot on the old down-river trail.

Site 15. Convict labor from Folsom Prison provided labor for road building along the lower Trinity River. This is how the prison camp at White's Bar appeared in the 1920's.

across from Denny Creek in the vicinity of what is now the Duncan place.

In 1852 Major Abraham Cox took up a land claim at this place. Cox built a house, kept a store, got rich, then departed in 1857. Before he left these parts he deeded the land, buildings and a ferry he had established to Amos T. Smith. Smith developed the ranch and orchard, acquired a herd of fine cattle, operated a dairy and had a stopping place here. In 1871 William A. Pattison, Sr. purchased the holdings for $400 gold coin. The property remained in his family until the 1940's. Pattison had come to Trinity County in 1853. He was a charter member of the Old Settlers Society and faithfully attended the meetings in Weaverville, a considerable distance away and reached only by trail. In 1860 he helped build the first school at Cox's Bar, served as a school trustee and was postmaster for a time. His wife was Sally McCullom, a Chimariko Indian. Eight children were born to the couple. Pattison lived to be 91. He and many members of the family are buried in the Pattison Cemetery that is located on the hill behind the former Pattison home. Also buried in this cemetery are members of the Waldorff family as well as others. The only grave with a headstone is that of William Willshire, Pattison's lifelong friend.

William A. Pattison, Jr. and his wife, Nellie (Scott) Pattison, also made this ranch their home and lived here until the home burned. After this the property was sold and during the 1940's was mined.

Site 13. Vance's Bar (Big Bar)

Vance's Bar is located where the Big Bar Post Office now stands and was named for a man named Vance who settled here in 1850. Alex Pelletreau established a store and a hotel here in 1858. Cox writes that at that time the bar seemed to contain great riches, but that mining activity was dependent upon the availability of water. The only water on the bar for mining purposes was provided by the Manzanita Water Race described above. In 1918 Thomas C. Pattison patented most of the flat and farmed the land adjacent to the present highway. At the present time Vance's bar is again a busy place; it is the location of a store, restaurants, homes and the post office.

Site 14. Corral Bottom

Corral Bottom is reached by the road from Big Bar to Hyampom. It is located over the mountain from Big Bar in the upper part of the Corral Creek drainage.

Corral Bottom was first settled by John Sanborn, but it was James Mullane, the next owner, who received the patent to 160 acres of this land in 1895. Mullane lived here with his wife, Lucy (Keeley) Mullane, who was a native of Big Bar. Mullane ran cattle and operated an extensive butcher business serving customers along the Trinity River and New River (Old Denny). In order to supply his Denny customers, Mullane would drive his cattle by trail to a holding enclosure up New River. Here he would slaughter as the demand required. This enclosure was known as Mullane Corral. In 1901 Mullane sold the Corral Bottom Ranch to William A. Pattison, Jr. and his brother, Tom Pattison. The brothers continued to run cattle on the ranch. The two worked the ranch together until Tom Pattison tragically lost his life in a deer hunting accident. William (Billy) Pattison married Nellie Scott of Lewiston in 1907 and together they built the home that still stands at Corral Bottom. The picturesque one and one-half story house remains preserved much as it was when first built. Covered with hand split, weathered shakes, with a porch on three sides, it looks out over the barns, pasture lands and forested mountains beyond. The water ditch still runs

Site 14. This is an overview of Corral Bottom Ranch as it now appears. The ranch, located on the road between Big Bar and Hyampom, was first settled by John Sanborn in the 1800's.

Site 14. This one and one-half story house was constructed at Corral Bottom by William and Nellie Pattison in the early 1900's.

in front of the house and trickles under a narrow foot bridge leading to the entry walk. The garden patch which was established by Nellie before 1910 is still in use and producing, as are a few old fruit trees. The barn, shed, and some of the original fences are still in use and cattle and horses graze in the meadow. Nothing remains of the first home built by the Mullanes; it was located farther down in the pasture.

The Pattisons did a great deal of heavy packing while at the ranch. They packed for the Great Western Power Company while the line was being constructed between Junction City and Eureka via Corral Bottom. They also packed for years for the Forest Service as well as for others. In later years Billy was assisted by his son Lloyd. Their pack stock was pastured on the ranch. Many of their outbuildings were used in conjunction with the packing business. The main trail from Big Bar to Hyampom and on to Korbel in Humboldt County went right past this Corral Bottom home. The ranch was eight miles from Big Bar and was reached only by this trail. The Pattisons sold the place in 1940. A road has since been built from Big Bar and the surrounding area has been logged. In some places it has been relogged as many as three times. The ranch has had a number of owners since the Pattisons sold. Some of the owners have been Fowler, Chastain, Elmer Kelly and Glen Mitchell. The present owners are Evelyn and James Harrigan who have owned it since 1971. The Corral Bottom Ranch is still a lovely secluded spot.

Site 15. White's Bar

Located on Highway 299 three-quarters of a mile east of Prairie Creek, the White's Bar area was one of the sections along the Trinity River which was heavily mined by the Chinese. Cox wrote that in 1858 there were two large waterwheels in the river at this location. Many old mining tunnels were exposed when the highway was constructed through this area. A prison road camp was located here in 1921-1923 and is now the site of a picnic and rest stop.

Site 16. Little Prairie

The bar across the Trinity River from Prairie Creek is known as Little Prairie. It consists of approximately eight acres of rich farming land and contains a big spring which produces two miner's inches of water. The bar was first an Indian village. After the coming of the white miners, one of the early settlers refused to permit the bar to be mined off because it had such high agricultural value. The miners had to be content with driving tunnels into the hillside at the back of the property; there are still many tunnels in evidence. The down-river trail passed by this place. Travelers on the trail would frequently stop over here. Charlie Dedrick was the owner of this property in the 1920's. Later the Mortimyer family built the two story A-frame home that is visible from the highway. Several ancient cherry trees left from the old settlement still stand near a former cabin site.

The Trinity River as it goes by this place has been the scene of two tragedies. At the time Charlie Dedrick was trying to establish the validity of his homestead at Little Prairie the first one occurred. Earnest Waldorff drowned as he was crossing the river on horseback to serve as a witness at the prove-up. The second tragedy happened May 19, 1963, when William Monte Keenan and his two teen-age daughters had gone over to Little Prairie by a boat attached to a cable. Upon their return they were thrown into the river when their boat was caught in the river current. One girl Gloria, was able to hold onto the boat and her life was saved. The father and other daughter, Gayle, were swept down the river and were drowned.

Site 18. The original buildings on the Brooks Ranch up Big French Creek were built entirely of materials obtained on the property.

Site 17. Dahlstrom Ranch (Allan Place)

This little ranch is situated on the east side of Big French Creek and sits on a 40 acre bench on the side of the mountain. It is reached by a trail leading from the French Creek Road. Another old trail joins with the trail that connects the Lower and Upper Waldorff Ranches, coming in at about half way between the two places.

Robert C. Dahlstrom homesteaded and received a patent to the property in 1928. He had lived there since 1919. Mr. Dahlstrom lived alone, kept a horse and some cattle, raised hay and had a fine vegetable garden. Linda, Michael, and Lory Allan are the present owners of this remote ranch.

Site 18. Williams Ranch (Bunch Ranch) (Brooks Ranch)

This piece of patented land consists of 75 acres on the mountain side above Big French Creek and is the major clearing in the area. Jack Rupp lived there first. He was followed by a German who started proceedings to acquire a patent to the land but was unable to carry them out when he became confined to a Concentration Camp during World War I. Ray Howard then lived there for a time, eventually selling it to Charlie Williams for $50. Williams made this his home for many years. He raised a nice garden and was able to harvest enough alfalfa hay each year to feed his horses and cattle. He cut all of the alfalfa with a hand scythe. In order to provide a cash income he worked as a packer for the Forest Service.

The ranch was purchased by Jess and Ruby Bunch in 1941. Jess was a tractor mechanic who had come to Trinity County from Los Angeles during the depression years of the 1930's to work for a mining company operating near the French Creek Tunnel. Mr. and Mrs. Bunch continued to spend their vacations here and built a cabin one and one-half miles up French Creek. The cabin was reached only by trail. In the meantime a narrow road had been built to the

238

Williams Ranch by the Civilian Conservation Corps and a telephone soon followed. Mr. and Mrs. Bunch were pleased when the opportunity to acquire this more accessible ranch occurred. It became their home full time following World War II. Ruby Bunch described the one room cabin and barn as being made entirely of materials obtained on the property. The doors and window casements were made by hand and the shakes for the roof had been hand split. A big, crystal clear spring provided water for the home and meadow. Rich soil made a fine garden possible. A neat hand split picket fence enclosed the garden and barn yard.

Delmar and Geneva Brooks are owners of the property at the present time.

Site 19. Lower Waldorff Ranch

The Lower Waldorff Ranch is one of two ranches situated along Little French Creek that were once owned by the Waldorff family. The lower ranch was first settled by Alex Tinsley sometime prior to 1875. Soon after 1890 he sold the property to Jacob Theodore Waldorff, Sr., a German who had come to America about 1846. Upon arriving in Trinity County in the early 1850's, Waldorff first settled in Lewiston where he built and operated the Trinity House, a well known stopping place on the Weaverville and Shasta toll road. He and his family next lived for a time at Chaunceyville on the outskirts of Weaverville. In 1875 the family moved to Hyampom. It was here that his wife and daughter drowned while crossing the South Fork of the Trinity River on horseback. After this drowning the father and sons, Earnest and Jacob, Jr., moved to Little French Creek where they purchased what has become known as the Lower Waldorff Ranch. They also acquired an upper ranch situated three miles beyond. By 1899 the three men were successfully farming both places. Jacob Waldorff, Sr. died in 1902. His sons continued on at the ranch. After them, Earnest's daughter, Elsie (Waldorff) Tye, and her husband, Fred Tye, farmed the place. They sold it in 1961 to Robert J. Morris. Tragedies, other than the drownings of Mr. Waldorff's wife and daughter, were to befall the family. Earnest Waldorff had married Josephine Pattison of Big Bar in 1889. Josephine died following the birth of their only child, Elsie Waldorff (Tye). Then Earnest, like his mother and sister, died of drowning while fording a river on horseback. His drowning occurred in 1920 as he was attempting to cross the Trinity River at the mouth of Prairie Creek.

The ranch house at the Lower Waldorff was constructed in 1902-03 by Joe Picotte, a French Canadian. He employed an architectural style that he brought with him from eastern Canada. The house is 18' x 26' and is constructed of hand-hewn twelve inch logs. The corners are full dovetailed and the craftmanship is meticulous. The upper story is of pole construction with vertical weathered boards at the gable ends. The roof is of hand split shakes. An open porch borders the four sides of the cabin. Four downstairs six over six windows contain many panes of the original glass. The floor is of original planks. In 1962 the cabin was rechinked with cement. This house is one of the best preserved examples of pioneer log construction in Trinity County.

An orchard containing old fruit trees is above the house. Below the house is a small barn of pole construction covered with natural weathered boards. A larger barn collapsed under the weight of heavy snow in the 1920's. The hillside meadow surrounding the house, yard and barn is bordered with virgin evergreen forest. This remote ranch, in its early days, was reached by seventeen miles of trail from Helena. After the Trinity River Highway was built, the ranch still was three miles by trail from a road. Today, a narrow private road gives access to the property. This ranch with its surroundings is an excellent

Site 19. This barn is located on the Lower Waldorff Ranch. The ranch, first settled prior to 1875, was purchased by Jacob Waldorff, Sr., in the 1890's.

Site 19. This is how the Lower Waldorff Ranch appeared in 1910. A well preserved house of hand hewn logs still stands.

Site 19. This closeup of the log house at the Lower Waldorff Ranch is an example of dovetail construction. The second story is constructed of poles and the roof is covered with hand split shakes. This house was built in 1902-03.

example of the living style that existed at the turn of the century in remote areas of Trinity County. It still has a wilderness character that is much the same as it was when Alex Tinsley settled here and when it was earlier occupied by native Indians. There are no sights or sounds of modern civilization. Deer browse freely in the meadow; bear come to the orchard to eat apples; and birds and other wild creatures are numerous.

Site 20. Upper Waldorff Ranch

The Upper Waldorff Ranch on Little French Creek was acquired by the Waldorff family around 1900. Jacob Waldorff, Sr., and his two sons, Earnest and Jacob, Jr., also owned the Lower Waldorff Ranch located about three miles away by trail. Another trail connects it with the North Fork. Father and sons farmed both places and made a good living for themselves. At its peak (about 1910) enough hay was raised on the two parcels to feed 100 head of cattle. The cattle were wintered at the lower ranch which was usually free of heavy snows. Communication between the two ranches was difficult. As there were no telephones, a code system was worked out using gongs which could be heard up and down the canyon.

The original homestead cabin is no longer standing. A one and one-half story cabin built in the 1930's sits on the hillside meadow and is suffering from neglect. There is an old orchard near the house. All of the buildings on this ranch were constructed of logs or peeled poles and the roofs were hand split shakes. A fence of hand split pickets enclosed the fields and pastureland. A heavy stand of virgin forest surrounds the property.

The ranch remained in the Waldorff family until 1959. Jacob Waldorff, Sr.'s granddaughter, Elsie (Waldorff) Tye and her husband, Fred Tye, were the last owners. This ranch is perhaps the largest ranch in Trinity County that is still accessible only by trail.

Site 21. French Creek Tunnel

At a point east of Del Loma near the mouth of French Creek, the Trinity River makes a sharp hairpin turn. In 1877 William Fowler made plans to dig a tunnel across this narrow river turn and to divert the river through it thus exposing the river bed for mining. This was to be a joint venture with the Taylor Flat Hydraulic Mine. Thirty men were employed in this joint venture. William S. Lowden did the surveying of the site. The tunnel was completed in 1888 and was 400 ft. long, 16 ft. wide and 6 ft. high. The project was not successful as the river seldom became low enough for all of the water to pass through the tunnel.

At the time of construction there was no road along the Trinity River. Over half a ton of tools and materials were packed to the site by pack trains. O.H. Powers, the superintendent of the project, greatly improved the trail by doing considerable blasting and by building a bridge over French Creek. This was greatly appreciated by travelers along the trail. George Costa, who was born near Rush Creek and has mined extensively in Alaska, is the present owner of the mine and equipment that is near the tunnel.

Site 22. Taylor's Flat (Del Loma)

Taylor's Flat is now known as Del Loma. It was settled in 1853 by a Mr. Taylor. Little is known of this man for he did not remain in the area long. It was the Washington Fluming Company which, soon after, brought life and activity to the flat. This company constructed a water race from French Creek

Site 20. This cabin was built in the 1930's and is located on the Upper Waldorff Ranch near an old orchard.

Waldorff's - a mountain ranch in Trinity County, California

Site 20. This overview of the Upper Waldorff Ranch, taken in the early 1900's, shows this prosperous ranch surrounded by heavy forest. It is accessible only by trail from the Lower Waldorff Ranch.

with (according to Cox) "much labor and at a great expense of $60,000." This flume was three miles in length and capable of transporting 80 sluice heads of water. The great cost caused some stockholders to go broke. But, according to The Humboldt Times of 1855, the project cost between $20,000 and $25,000 and not the $60,000 stated by Cox. And, according to The Times, this project assured Taylor's Flat of water from then on. Two sawmills were set up on French Creek to make the flume lumber. The logging was done with oxen. When a Mr. Hazeltine became president of the Washington Fluming Company the project was pushed to completion. Many old mining tunnels are still found in the area.

About 1926 Mr. and Mrs. James King moved to Taylor's Flat from the Moliter Mine on Grizzly Creek. Not liking the name Taylor's Flat, Mrs. King changed it to Del Loma. Much of the one hundred acres that was farmed earlier is now idle. Old fruit trees still survive in the meadow below the Del Loma Lodge. The present lodge and restaurant have had an "on again-off again" existence. Cabins and trailer spaces are provided for people fishing the Trinity River.

High on the hillside above the cabins at Del Loma are limestone caves believed to have been discovered by Henry Curtis in 1855, although the Indians of the area were, no doubt, already familiar with them. Cox wrote glowingly of the caves, describing a great labyrinth, an underground lake and a passage to the other side of the mountain. According to Cox "petrified human and animal remains were spread all over the floor." At present the once well established trail to the cave shows very little use.

Site 23. Canadian Bar

Canadian Bar is on the south side of the Trinity River across from Taylor's Flat (Del Loma). Issac Cox in his Annals of Trinity County takes note of this place by making the following statement: "Canadian Bar has only a few white miners but is crowded with Chinamen who make good wages. A flume of small capacity waters the diggin's."

Site 24. Hayden Flat

Hayden Flat is about one half mile downstream from Del Loma and is the site of the former Joe Hayden home. The U.S. Forest Service has built the Hayden Flat Campground at this spot. Construction of this campground was carried out by the Civilian Conservation Corps in the 1930's.

Site 25. Don Juan Bridge

The Don Juan Mule Bridge was originally built in 1895 under the direction of James McDonald. It crosses the Trinity River one and one-half miles above Cedar Flat. This suspended cable swinging bridge is approximately 200 feet long and 50 feet above the river. It has been rebuilt twice in the past 40 years. The present structure is metal with wood decking.

Bridges have always been significant in Trinity County where topography forces trails to continually cross over potentially dangerous water. This important bridge on the trail between the Big Bar and Burnt Ranch areas was used by every wayfarer and packer, even by cattle and pig drovers following the trail between Arcata and the Big Bar mines. At present it is used as a foot bridge providing access to the Willie Jack Trail.

James McDonald, the man who directed the building of this bridge, was the road overseer; he also had the Junction City/Burnt Ranch mail contract for over 30 years. He was related by marriage to the pioneer McWhorter family.

Site 21. The French Creek Tunnel was constructed in 1888, near the mouth of French Creek, to divert the Trinity River so the river bed could be mined. The venture was not successful as the volume of water was always too great. The other end of the tunnel can be seen around the bend of the river.

Site 22. Taylor's Flat, now known as Del Loma, was first settled in 1853. Apple trees seen in the distance mark the site of the early settlement.

Site 25. This view of the Don Juan Bridge was taken in the early 1900's. It was originally constructed in 1895 and crosses the Trinity River at the mouth of Stetson Creek.

Site 26. Don Juan Point—Hailstone Ranch

Don Juan Point, a rough semi-circular piece of land bordered by the Trinity River on the south and Highway 299 on the north, one mile east of Burnt Ranch, is a piece of the Hailstone Ranch. There is evidence of mining activity including mined-off ground now overgrown with brush and a water ditch dug between Don Juan and Halsey Gulch. Don Juan's reservoir, dating from the 1850's, has been filled in. Near the river is the Jay Hailstone residence built in the 1950's. It stands on the site of the Don Juan trading post and school.

Don Juan was settled in the early 1850's by Don Juan Tiseran, a Spaniard. He mined and kept a trading post. In 1857 he started a water ditch from Don Juan Creek for "hydraulicking." His store was once the scene of a coroner's inquest into the death of a young miner. The victim, Thomas Thomson, fell from the steep, perpendicular cliff which made the trail along Don Juan the most hazardous part of early day travel on the river. Tiseran eventually left in search of new strikes and later the George W. Huestis family lived on the site, digging a tunnel through the place while searching for a ledge of gold. The ranch was homesteaded in 1918 by the Zachariah (Mike) Hailstone family. They farmed, placer mined and raised stock, ranging cattle as far north as Hailstone Camp or Green Mountain.

The Hailstones were early Trinity River pioneers. Mike was born at Hawkins Bar in 1878. In 1881 the family moved to Hayfork, purchasing one of the most prominent ranches in the valley, the Big Creek Ranch. They later opened and ran the Hayfork Hotel. Ethel Hailstone was a McDonald from Burnt Ranch and was related by marriage to the McWhorters. Both families were pioneers in the lower Trinity area. Ethel taught school at Willow Creek, Hawkins Bar, Big Bar and Hayfork before her marriage. Mrs. Hailstone (now Ethel Chandler) started a private school to teach her nine children. This school was mentioned in Ripley's Believe It or Not because the school was built by the Hailstone family, on Hailstone property, taught by Mrs. Hailstone, and all but one of the pupils were Hailstones. The school later became a public school.

This ranch and family name remain significant in the lower Trinity area. The ranch is owned and occupied by members of the family who still possess the original Hailstone cattle brand so symbolic of a Trinity way of life in earlier times.

Site 27. Cedar Flat

Cedar Flat, located twenty miles below Big Bar, at the west end of Cedar Flat Bridge on Highway 299, was described by Cox in 1858 as being a "beautiful flat, one mile in circumference, one hundred feet above the river and covered with a beautiful grove of cedars." By that time a thriving village had sprung up. A store as well as a hotel and cabins had been erected on the rocky point at the west end of the flat. Two men by the name of Huestis and Moody were the first to hold title to the mining claim on this flat. Later the property was sold for taxes to Hiram Flowers who homesteaded it and added another twenty acres to his holdings by a quit-claim from Oscar Hayward. C. C. Kise followed Flowers as the next owner of these properties. He, in turn, sold to Katherine and D. J. Phelps in 1927. The present owners are Katherine and Joseph J. McGowan. The McGowans built a home and erected cabins on the lower flat which they rented to vacationers. In 1963 the McGowans sold the cabins to the present owners but retained the upper 20 acres (the old Hayward parcel) for their home.

The old down-river trail went through the portion of land now occupied by the McGowans. An old woven picket fence follows along the road near their house. In the mid-1920's state convict crews were being used for the construction of Highway 299. When the Cedar Flat bridge was being built their construction camp occupied ground at both ends of the bridge.

Site 28. China Slide

China Slide is located approximately 45 miles west of Weaverville on the Trinity River and Highway 299. The highway crosses the slide area and at one point makes an abrupt turn where it is possible to look 500 feet down to the river or 500 feet straight up the mountain. At one time the area which the highway traverses was a high ridge which sloped to the river.

The bar at river level directly below the slide area was known as Dixon's Bar and was once rich in gold bearing gravels. In 1881, a portion of the mountain slid down, burying a number of miners and damming the Trinity River for an hour. After this, white miners refused to work the bar and it was leased to a Chinese mining company and was successfully mined until the winter of 1889-90. That winter brought the heaviest rainfall and snowpack in county history. About 9 A.M. on January 3, 1890, the whole mountain slid into the river, damming it for seven hours and backing water up for 12 miles. The slide was 400 yards wide and extended one mile up the side of the mountain. Two Chinese miners were killed and a number of cabins were destroyed.

China Slide today, from the river to its summit at the top of the mountain, still appears as a rocky area swept clean of all vegetation by the slide. The old scars and gravel deposited by the slide along the river also are still there.

Site 29. Dixon's Bar

Dixon's Bar is located on the Trinity River at China Slide. This is about half way between Cedar Flat and Burnt Ranch or about 45 miles from Weaverville on Highway 299. (See Site 28.)

Dixon's Bar was named for "Old Joe" Dixon, a Texan who had an inordinately strong hatred for Mexicans and who, by 1858, is purported "to have killed more Mexicans than any other living person". Cox reports that the area was paying extremely well when water was sufficient. Cox implies that the white miners at this place were not an enterprising lot as "no artificial appliances" (flumes, etc.) had been constructed and the place was neglected. In fact, it appears that the Chinese were dominating the bar when Cox made his report in 1858.

Site 30. McDonald-McWhorter Ranch Site (Timothy Brainard Place) (Burnt Ranch)

The McDonald-McWhorter ranch was where Burnt Ranch Estates now are. This ranch was at one time a productive hillside ranch of over 600 acres, with alfalfa grown in the meadows and cattle grazed on its range. It ceased to be a working ranch in the 1920's and has since been subdivided for homesites. The upper field contains an airport and the barn built by James McDonald. This impressive all-shake structure is the only original building left. The lower field, known as the Big Meadow and used for farming, is now a lumber mill. It was also the location of the State Prison Road Camp and Free Camp which furnished the labor to construct the highway through the lower part of the place in 1923. Between the upper and lower fields is the site of the original ranch house, overgrown but surrounded by old fruit trees. Nearby are portions of old hand dug ditches and the ruins of fencing and a small barn.

Previous to the white settlers, Indians had a rancheria just above the location of the present mill. The ranch was first owned by J. R. Fish; it was acquired by Timothy Brainard in September 1855 and became known as the Timothy Brainard place. During the early 1850's troublesome Indians burned the ranch causing it to be named "The Ranch known as Burnt Ranch." Brainard refers to "What is known as Burnt Ranch Creek" on his land claim. Because of later Indian troubles Brainard had to abandon the ranch when all of the buildings burned in 1863. His house sat near the little cemetery. Brainard Creek on the ranch bears his name.

The next owners were P. F. Bussell and William A. Pattison. Bussell came from Maine, arriving in the area in 1852. He received 160 acres of the ranch in 1868 as a land bounty warrant for his services in the Humboldt-Klamath Indian War. He mined, ranched, ran a sawmill and was active in civic matters. William A. Pattison went to Big Bar in 1871 and mined, farmed, and ran a pack train there after selling out at Burnt Ranch.

Adam L. McWhorter and James Mullane bought the property from Bussell and Pattison in 1870. James Mullane is best known as the supplier of beef to the miners in the New River country. He raised cattle at Corral Bottom near Big Bar and drove them up to Mullane Corral near Old Denny for slaughter. He had the butcher shop in that town and also ran the hotel. A. L. McWhorter had come to Trinity in 1850 from New York and was a member of the Trinity County Pioneer Association (an association of residents who were in the county during the first year of settlement, 1850-51). He first lived at North Fork where he raised and sold cattle in partnership with Mullane. He was also constable, road overseer and tax collector. In 1872, McWhorter bought Mullane out and

Site 27. The Trinity River at Cedar Flat.

Site 30. The McDonald-McWhorter barn was built by James McDonald in the early 1900's. It is the only ranch building still standing to mark the site of this once prosperous ranch.

used the 'Burnt Ranch' for farming and as a stopping place for travellers. He mined and was postmaster from 1886-1897 when the post office was at the ranch. He was a long time member of the Democratic Central Committee. McWhorter died in 1900 and is buried on the ranch. His son-in-law, James McDonald, managed the ranch until his death in 1923, during which time it flourished and became debt-free. Many of the local young men were employed on the ranch. The McDonald family lost the ranch during the depression. It was acquired by the McKnight family. It has since been subdivided. Descendants of some of the early day owners still reside in the area.

This ranch is one of the original Trinity County ranches. Located on good agricultural land, it was taken up during the first ten years of the settlement of the county. It experienced the turmoil of the 1860's Indian wars which resulted in its abandonment by Mr. Brainard. These wars were responsible for the formation of a Trinity County militia and the presence of the U.S. Army in the area. It was not occupied again until it was issued as a land bounty for service against the Indians. The ranch has always been at the center of life on the lower Trinity River. Its fragmentation today is representative of the fate of many old time ranches.

Site 31. Hennessey Road

The Hennessey Road begins near Burnt Ranch and is newly paved up to the Hennessey Ranch. From that point it ascends over mountains into the South Fork drainage, passing south of Hennessey Ridge at approximately the 3,000 foot elevation and joining an old South Fork logging road just below the midway point between Sections 25 and 26 T6N R5E.

The P.O.M. Hennessey family were early residents of the lower Trinity River area, living first at Big Flat. In 1870 they moved to Burnt Ranch, acquiring a large water right from Brooks Creek which is presently known as Hennessey Creek. John Hennessey, a son, was born on the ranch but moved to Nevada where he struck it rich in lode mining. In 1913 he decided to fulfill his parents' dream of a road linking their ranch to the Humboldt County road which then ran from the coast as far as Willow Creek. At that time there was no road through to the ranch. John hired a number of people to work on the road, several of whom later became prominent people in Trinity County. He started from both ends and work progressed well until funds ran out with only two miles left. The road lay unfinished until 1937-38 when it was completed by the Civilian Conservation Corps. By this time a state road from Burnt Ranch to Willow Creek along the Trinity River had also been completed and the Hennessey road was used mainly for traffic diversion. Nonetheless, members of the Hennessey family did finally use the road and it remains a local landmark.

Site 32. Burnt Ranch Store

The Burnt Ranch Store is located on Highway 299. It is the center of the Burnt Ranch community. The present structure is the third at this site. It is a one-story, medium gable roof structure with a false front that rises higher in the center section to cover the peak of the gable. A stoop entry porch is attached to the front. The exterior wall siding is board and batten and the structure has a composition shingle roof.

In 1918 Bud and Belle Carpenter moved to Burnt Ranch from Willow Creek. Both were from old time Trinity families. The Carpenters came from up the South Fork River and the Irvings (Belle's family) were from New River and Hawkins Bar (where the Irving Ranch is today). They built a small store which burned. They rebuilt, adding cabins. In 1928 Bud, a deputy sheriff, was killed in front of the store while trying to apprehend a bank robber. Bell stayed on, opening a boarding house. In 1932 she enlarged the general store which was again destroyed by fire in 1944. The present store was built on the same site. Mary and Jim Carpenter assumed management of the store in 1950.

Site 33. Gray Ranch Site

Gray Ranch is located on the north side of Highway 299 between Burnt Ranch and Hawkins Bar. This ranch was taken up by brothers William and David Gray in the early 1900's. Both men were bachelors. William was a school teacher and later carried the mail between Burnt Ranch and Junction City. He also served as a deputy sheriff in 1918 and as deputy county clerk. The Grays both farmed but were principally involved in mining. William had an interest in five area mines, namely Pony Bar Placer, Pony Bar Extension, Little Flat, the I.X. and the Ridge. David had five placer mines in the county: Cape Horn, Davis Point, Junction Bar, New River Bar and Pony Bar.

The Gray Ranch area was undoubtedly mined in the 1850's, as was much of the area. An 1882 General Land Office survey map shows a well established trail passing through the ranch. Evidence of a water ditch was discovered by Cal-Trans archeologists 0.8 mile east of Gray Creek. The report notes that the ditch has a very gentle downhill grade, suggesting that it was used to bring water from Gray Creek to placer operations at Gray's Flat. At present there is a subdivision located on this site.

Site 34. Bill Jackson Bridge

The Bill Jackson Bridge spans the Trinity River linking Hawkins Bar with the Denny Road. This point of crossing has seen several bridges destroyed by fire and the elements. The immediate predecessor to the Jackson bridge was a Bailey bridge borrowed from the U.S. Army after the then existing bridge washed out in the 1955 flood. The present structure is an all-metal suspension bridge approximately 200 yards long and 75 feet above the river. The suspension towers are about 20 feet high and are fastened to the bank by cement columns. The bottom is constructed of spaced metal grating to allow for snow melt. The bridge has only one lane. It was finished and painted in 1958 and stood nameless until 1972 when it was named in memory of Bill Jackson, a lifelong Trinity County resident and deputy sheriff who was killed in performance of his duties. A memorial plaque is found on the Hawkins Bar side of the bridge.

Site 35. Salyer Community Wayside Chapel

The Salyer Wayside Chapel is located on Forest Service land on the south side of Highway 299, west of the Ranger Station. The front yard has a lawn and oak trees and a thick forest is in the back. The chapel building was originally constructed in 1923 as a cafe. Sometime before 1933 it became the property of the Assembly of God Church. In 1947 it was sold to Mrs. M. A. Ferguson who then sold it to Reverend Norman McCutcheon. It was sold again in 1949 to the Salyer Community Church and is presently known as Salyer Community Wayside Chapel.

This chapel is a medium cross gable building with a one and one-half story hip roof steeple and a gable porch over the entry into the steeple. The short steeple is without a belfry but has two casement windows with a triangular structural opening. The adjacent Parish Hall is a single gable structure. The church is sided with new, smooth board and battens and is roofed with tin. It sits on a stone foundation.

Although it has been remodeled, the church is still one of the older buildings in Salyer, a small community in lower Trinity which was organized about 1920. It occupies a prominent position above the highway in the central part of Salyer.

Site 36. Campbell Ranch (Fountain Ranch)

The Campbell place is a beautiful 205 acre ranch situated across the Trinity River to the north from Salyer. It includes the original Campbell house built in 1884 and a newer barn, together with a large woodshed and several outbuildings. Across the road from the house is a large open field backing up against a hillside grown up to brush and timber. The house was originally a white clapboard Greek Revival with a dominant "T" cross gable plan. Around 1912-13 alterations were made to the siding. A shingle style hip roof veranda was added over the front and side, giving the house a low horizontal profile in contrast to the surrounding locust trees which are as old as the house. Metal chimneys rise from both kitchen and bedroom areas and a rock chimney extends from the unused original living room fireplace. An original hip roof porch covers the entrance to the kitchen in the rear and is supported by handsome square columns. The ranch house successfully combines two very different early architectural styles, the 1884 Greek Revival and the 1900's shingle. These reflect the backgrounds of its two owners, the first a southerner and the second an Arcata dentist who spent considerable time in the Bay area.

The Campbell Ranch was settled in the 1860's by Thomas Campbell, originally from a Bowling Green, Kentucky family which had raised thoroughbred horses. Campbell married a full-blooded Indian woman from nearby Hoopa. He raised stock, farmed, ran a sawmill and kept a combination store and stopping place in a large building across the road from the ranchhouse. He also had two 30-mule pack trains, transporting goods to the New River mines. The Trinity Journal dated March 18, 1893 states "The Campbell Ranch is furtherest advanced in cultivation on the Lower Trinity and is a favorite stopping place for travellers." Campbell gave his name to Campbell Ridge and nearby Madden Creek was formerly Campbell Creek. Campbell is an excellent example of an early Trinity resident who saw opportunity in supplying the miners rather than mining himself. In 1911, the ranch was purchased from the Campbell estate by a prominent Arcata dentist, Matthew Fountain. Some remodeling was done to the house and walnut trees were planted on part of the ranch. In 1917-18, he built the bridge from Salyer proper to the ranch side of the river, hiring Jim and John Larson who had built the bridge at the mouth of the New River to do the engineering. This bridge was later given to the county and was used for all transportation until 1936 when it was replaced by the Forest Service with the present bridge. This is a working cattle ranch with irrigated hay fields and is presently operated by Dr. Fountain's son, Everett, and his wife Delphine.

Site 37. Irving-Wallen Ranch Barn

The Irving ranch is situated on the Denny Road at Hawkins Creek. The all shake, moss-covered calving barn is the only building remaining from the heyday of this ranch. It sits on a flat area in the upper part of the large field directly behind the site of a big hay barn. It is beautifully constructed of poles and long sugar pine shakes.

George Irving, born in Nova Scotia, Canada, was one of three prospectors to escape an Indian massacre in the Black Hills of the Dakotas. He was subse-

Site 37. This is an overview of the Irving-Wallen Ranch. Settled in the late 1800's, it was a popular stopping place for travellers to and from the New River mines.

Site 38. Five Waters Ranch is located on the site of the Indian village of Itcxapostu. It is one of four spots in the rugged New River area where there is enough level, open land for farming.

quently hired by a titled Englishman to take a load of mules to his estate in Ireland. There Irving met and married the caretaker's daughter, Kathleen. He returned to the United States, spending time in Philadelphia and then moved west to Arizona where he heard of the rich gold strikes being made on the upper New River. He arrived there in 1888, locating the Hidden Treasure mine on Plummer Creek. After his cabin burned, he moved to old Denny. Eventually the family left the New River area and took up a homestead on Hawkins Creek, the location of the present ranch. A large two story log house and barns were built and the land was cleared for farming. They raised hogs and cattle, carried the mail from Hoopa to Burnt Ranch, and ran large mule trains with supplies for Burnt Ranch and Quimby. (At Quimby the supplies were reloaded on the Ladd mule trains for the upper New River mines.) The Irving ranch was a popular stopover for miners going either direction. It is still owned by the Irving family.

Site 38. Five Waters Ranch

The Five Waters Ranch, also known as the Dyer-Ziegler Ranch, is located on New River just above the mouth of Dyer Creek. The site is a large flat containing old fruit trees, an old cabin and newer buildings associated with the present operation of the ranch. A two story house which once sat under a group of cedar trees nearby has burned.

This ranch was originally the site of the Indian village of Itcxapostu. It was later settled by a pioneer family named Dyer whose children, George and Martha Dyer, homesteaded it in 1906. George was an early day packer and stockman. At first this remote ranch was off the beaten path. It became more accessible in 1918 when a trail was constructed from the Trinity River up the New River canyon. George Dyer was the foreman of this construction project. Martha married Charles "Bemay" Ziegler who raised stock and ran pack trains to the mines. Charles Ziegler and his brother Hiram were members of an early day family in the lower Trinity area.

The ranch is one of four places in the New River drainage where there is a large piece of open land suitable for agriculture. The present owners hope to use it as a summer camp.

Site 39. Hoboken Site

Hoboken is a large flat or meadow along New River about seven miles upstream from the mouth. It is three-quarters of a mile long and one-eighth of a mile wide, on two river terraces. It is one of the few places in the drainage where sheer walls widen to permit existence of a meadow. Hoboken is watered by a deep spring. No signs of the original mining community are apparent but circles of stones remain at the south end of the flat. On the east side of the river parts of large logs cut for the Hoboken mill are still visible. The old ditch from Bell Creek, serving the Dailey ranch and ending at Hoboken Flat, though eroded, is still visible.

Hoboken was an important mining community as early as 1858 when it was described by Cox as being "The principal mining and trading place" on New River. It contained a store, a butcher shop and a blacksmith shop and later reports describe hotels, saloons and whipsawmills as well. Main Street ran north and south along the upper river terrace near the ranch house. This community was a convenient stopping place for packers going into the upper New River area and remained the center of population until the 1890's. Hoboken remained the name of the voting precinct until much later. In 1880 the New River Hydraulic Mining Company built a 275' long dam, backing the river up one mile in order to float the logs from the east side over to where the steam sawmill was running. Chief Engineer Robert Palmer reported the mill and boiler were among the best in the state. Unfortunately, all was wiped out by a disastrous flood in January, 1881. After 1881, the flat served as a camp for mule pack trains.

The trail up river passes within 20 feet of the meadow on the uphill slope. Hoboken was later patented by two brothers from Sweden, John and Jim Larsen, who had the contract to build the bridge at the mouth of New River. The property was purchased in 1928 by New River pioneer, Charlie Schwedler. It changed hands again in 1953 when it was purchased by Mr. Christiansen. It is presently a private ranch with a large house, swimming pools and several outbuildings.

Site 40. This house, built partially of whipsawed sugar pine in 1868 and later completed by the Dailey family still stands on the Dailey Ranch near Denny.

Site 40. Dailey Ranch

The Dailey ranch is situated on a cleared glade on land bisected by the road to Denny. The road drops abruptly into the ranch after passing under a wooden flume which is part of the ditch system that carries irrigation water to the ranch. On the left is a small wooden house and a collection of outbuildings. On the right is the old house, built in 1868, but which is no longer in use and is heavily overgrown with vegetation. Also standing on the right, below the road in a field, is a large barn built in 1906. The ranch contains many acres of walnut trees.

This ranch was owned from 1852-1903 by Moses Patterson who homesteaded it and established an overnight stop for the various pack trains supplying New River miners. A few cleared acres were planted in hay and apple trees and a cabin was built. In 1868 a three bedroom house was partially built of whipsawed sugar pine. It is one of the very few original houses in the county still standing today. The house was later completed by the Dailey family using split lumber. Patterson built a number of small outbuildings and a large barn which collapsed under heavy snow in 1964. Still standing is a large barn with sheds for protecting livestock and hay, built by John Dailey in 1906-7. The Daileys sold dairy products and hay to the miners. In 1920 a 60 acre walnut orchard was planted, producing nuts that won gold medals at the California State Fair. The ranch represents one of the few choice agricultural spots on New River. The lower part of the Dailey Ranch comprises the historic Noble Ranch patented by Stephen and Sally Noble and was purchased by the Daileys in the 1920's. Sally was a Chimariko Indian. Stephen Noble had bought and sold mines along New River and prospected with sons Frank and George while son Bill Noble was trail foreman for the U.S. Forest Service. Stephen Noble was one of the County's earliest settlers, having settled here in 1851. The Nobles built a one and one-half mile ditch and acquired a water right from Panther Creek.

The Dailey Ranch has been divided by the Dailey heirs. Some family members still live there.

Site 41. Denny Historic District

Denny, sometimes called New Denny, is accessible by a winding mountain road approximately 17 miles from Highway 299. The town was established in 1920 by the Frank J. Ladd family in the vicinity of an early mining settlement formerly called Quimby. Ladd, who had worked in Humboldt County as a logger, discovered rich gold lode mines in Trinity County in the 1880's which initiated a rush into the upper New River country. This resulted in the establishment of New River City, later named Denny for A.H. Denny who originally ran the store there. Most of the claims were worked out after 1900. In 1920 the Ladds stopped working their Boomer Mine in the upper New River area and started building a new town of Denny. They obtained a series of mining claims from the New River Mining Company, cleared fields, constructed buildings and eventually homesteaded a 160 acre ranch. They moved the old store and post office from New River City to this location. Sons, Grover and Willard, helped with the store, ranched, ran a pack train (there was no road into this area until 1933) and worked in various local mines. The Ladd store, hotel and bunkhouse were all built in approximately 1932 after fire destroyed the original combination store and residence. They were all built by Andrew Z. Allen who was a packer for Ladd. Although these buildings are not especially old they represent the most visible part of the district and form the historical base for the community. Denny is a small, quiet place with a very strong sense of its identity and of its unique history.

Site 42. Francis Townsite

The townsite of Francis is located on a flat opposite the mouth of the East Fork of New River. A branch of the New River trail descends to the townsite at the forks. A combination general store and post office which served the miners in this particular part of the mining district comprised the town. The post office was established in February, 1881 and discontinued November, 1897. The store was supplied by the Alexander Brizard Company of Arcata.

There are no visible remains of the townsite except for the grave of an unknown girl. The trail through this small area is still evident.

Site 43. The Miller cabin was constructed by a Mr. Bailey in the mid-1800's. It is one of the finest examples of log cabin construction still standing in Trinity Co.

Site 43. This closeup of the Miller cabin shows the hand hewn logs and dovetail corners. The cabin is believed to be well over 100 years old.

Site 43. Miller Ranch and Cabin

The Miller Ranch is located above Caraway Creek on the New River Trail. This land was occupied first by a Mr. Bailey who constructed the cabin of hand-hewn logs with dovetail corners. Grover Ladd indicated it was an old structure when his father came into the New River area in 1883 and it still stands today. It is one of the finest examples of craftmanship and log cabin construction in the county. Mr. Miller homesteaded the property in 1915 and sold garden produce and hay to people as far up the river as Old Denny. Recently, the shallow pond on the ranch was a source of water for Forest Service helicopters while fighting a large fire.

The Miller Ranch is today an abandoned homestead used occasionally by transients. It is owned by a company in Palos Verdes. Though accessible by four-wheel drive vehicle, it is essentially back in the mountainous New River country. The 24' x 36' log cabin is an example of extraordinarily fine broad axe work. Until recently, there was a small addition on the north side and a good shake roof but they have been removed. The ranch is in a fairly wide, sloping swale that drops to a large but shallow pond built in recent years. In another small clearing there is a pole frame and shake roof building without siding. This is a beautiful setting where one can hear the rushing New River below.

Site 44. Jake's Hunting Ground

Jake's Hunting Ground is located on the Jim Jam Ridge above the East Fork of New River not far from Pony Mountain. The area was named for Jake Hershberger, a resident of the area in the 1860's. An expert shot, he killed deer during their winter migration to lower elevations, supplying winter meat for the miners along East Fork, Pony Creek and at Lake City. He employed several Indians to dress out the venison and backpack it to the miners. The meat was stored in snow lockers at Lake City and in snow banks at the miners' cabins. The miners paid for the meat in gold. In turn Jake paid his Indian helpers in gold dust and small nuggets, keeping the larger nuggets for himself. Because he carried this gold with him, when he disappeared in July 1900 without a trace it was believed at the time he may have been murdered for his gold. He was a large, strong man, "well regarded by those who knew him."

A fairly large A-frame, shake cabin with a large fireplace at one end was built by Jake and still stands. There is a Forest Service marker at this old camp.

Site 45. Lake City Site

Lake City was located near the mouth of Pony Creek. It was one of the first mining camps in the New River Country. An historical sign which marks the site indicates that about 1,500 miners were living there during the period from 1861 to 1864. The story is told that the gravels from Pony Creek were extremely rich, paying a million dollars to the mile in nugget gold. However, in 1863 Indians moved in and ran the miners out, ate their food, and then burned the town. Although most of the miners went over into Siskiyou County, some returned to Trinity County on the day of the presidential election in September, 1863, and voted at Election Camp. Lake City was never rebuilt.

The Lake City site is in the wilderness area with brush and timber reclaiming it. A Forest Service sign marks the site.

Site 46. Mullane Corral Site

Mullane Corral site is located near Old Denny. Going southeast from Old Denny toward Pony Buttes for about two miles the site would be near the common corner of Sections 20, 28 and 29.

James Mullane, who used the corrals and supplied beef to the miners, was an important figure in the New River country. In the 1870's Mullane, together with his partner A.J. McWhorter, ran a slaughter house and butcher shop in North Fork. After the partnership dissolved Mullane homesteaded several pieces of ground, including part of the Corral Bottom area southwest of Big Bar. Cattle were raised there and driven to the Mullane Corrals where they were pastured and slaughtered. In the 80's and 90's Mullane had a butcher shop in Old Denny and operated the Eureka Hotel there. He also ran a 10-mule pack train which he used to pack supplies to the smaller mines as well as to pack ore for them.

The Mullane Corral site is an open meadow located within the Salmon-Trinity wilderness area. There is a small lean-to log cabin on the site which is now used by hunters. The meadow contains good feed for stock. There are piles of bones lying on the ground which presumably date back to the butchering which was once done there. Evidence of the corrals is minimal. A good Forest Service sign marks the site.

Site 47. Election Camp Site

Election Camp is on the Trinity-Siskiyou Divide above Old Denny. It can also be reached by trail from the end of the road up the North Fork of the Trinity River.

The Election Proclamation for the 1864 presidential election published in the Trinity Journal indicates that the voting for the Lake City precinct was to be held at the John Flowers house. However, prior to the election, Indians ran the miners off and burned the town. Many of the miners fled into Siskiyou County. It is said that the election board spread the word throughout the mountains that the voting would be done just below the gap in the ridge which divided the two counties, near a point where five trails converged. It is said that a large, somewhat hollow incense cedar tree served as a ballot box. There was a good deal of interest among the miners in having President Lincoln re-elected. On election day, in a notable display of civic responsibility, 300 miners voted at Election Camp.

All that appears at the Election Camp site now is an enameled metal Forest Service sign stating "Election Camp, the presidential election of 1864 was held here by 300 miners of New River following the destruction of Lake City by Indians." The sign is attached to a cedar tree on the divide.

The above, however, does not agree with the Trinity Journal. The issue of September 12, 1863 gives the following account:

"ELECTION CAMP AT NEW RIVER

The 'Abolitionists' are accused of closing the polls 'long before the hour prescribed by law' on New River, 'thus necessarily excluding' Democratic votes that might come in. That's where the laugh comes in.

One month ago there were 35 votes on New River and of that number only two were Democratic. They were driven from their homes by the Indians, most of them going to Klamath county, at which time the Copperheads rejoiced, because if they remained there it was a clear gain of 30 votes to the Copperhead ticket.

But Billy Kirkham determined that it should not be so and accordingly, five days before election, started from here for Klamath and gathering about half the original number came across the line on election day and opened the polls on the highest point of land that voting was ever done, probably. The requirements of the law were filled as nearly as could be. Every man within 25 miles of the spot voted, including three 'Democrats,' two of whom had gone there from this end of the county.

Without a shadow of truth it is asserted that any single vote was excluded."

Site 48. Old Denny-Mary Blaine Mountain Mining District

The Old Denny-Mary Blaine Mountain area is reached by a 10-12 mile trail which begins six miles above the town of Denny. This area represents one of the greatest concentrations of mines and mining activity in Trinity County history. Although upper New River had been prospected as early as the 1850's, a whole series of gold deposits was discovered between 1882 and 1884. The initial and single most important claim, the Mountain Boomer, was discovered by Oliver Clements and Frank J. Ladd. The district was active until about 1920, and mined sporadically during the 1930's. The district produced approximately 4,000 ounces of gold and 1,500 ounces of silver valued at about $500,000. There was also some quicksilver recovered.

The new discoveries in this area in the 1880's resulted in a significant increase in population. Ten people were listed in the New River precinct in 1876 but soon an estimated 500 people lived in the area. This led to the establishment of three separate towns as business and trading centers: New River City, Marysville and White Rock City. New River miners' demands for goods had a significant impact not only on Trinity but on parts of Humboldt and Siskiyou counties as well. Ranchers in all three counties raised hay, grain, beef and pork to sell to the New River miners. Food and equipment were carried by pack trains from as far away as Arcata in Humboldt County and Cecilville and the Scott Valley in Siskiyou County. Perhaps the most notable pack train was operated by Alexander Brizard of Arcata. He also owned several stores in the New River area. Business was so lucrative that an early issue of the Trinity Journal reported considerable competition between Humboldt and Trinity counties to establish good trails to this area. Remote as the area seems today,

258

Frank Ladd related that at the height of the boom there were as many as 300 people a day passing through on the trails.

The district consists principally of the following lode mines, which are named, located and briefly described:

Boomer: This mine was located one-half mile SE of the town of Old Denny, Sec. 19 T37N, R12W. By far the most successful mine in the district, it was said to have produced gold valued at $350,000 between 1888-1901. An arrastra was used first. Later a three-stamp mill was built on the north side of Slide Creek to crush the ore from the Boomer as well as from some other small mines in the district. The mine was run by Frank J. Ladd who had originally come to Humboldt County from Maine to work as a logger. In 1920 Ladd abandoned the mine and the area and established himself at Quimby, renaming it New Denny. There he ran a store as he had in Old Denny. By virtue of the Boomer mine, the Ladd name, carried on by sons, Grover and Williard, is synonymous with New River history.

Hunter: This occupied approximately 100 acres about one-half mile north of Old Denny, or approximately 1,200' SW of the site of White Rock City. It was located by Ladd and Clements at the same time as the Boomer. Recorded production between 1892 and 1905 was 198 ounces of gold and 15 ounces of silver.

Toughnut: This patented claim was just north of Boomer property. It was found by Frank Ladd and later owned by his sons, Grover and Willard. Reported production was nearly 600 ounces of gold.

Hardtack: This was located approximately 900' S of the site of Marysville, and was found by Frank Ladd. Reported production between 1888 and 1897 was 873 ounces of gold.

Location of the Boomer, Hunter, Toughnut and Hardtack in 1883 started a mining boom and prospectors came into the district from every direction. Other mines of note are briefly described:

Sherwood: This was located approximately one-half mile west of the site of White Rock City. It was a very well known mine and a good producer. Operation began in 1889 and in the early years it had a two-stamp mill. Later ore was transported to the Ridgeway mill. Between 1889 and 1901 an estimated 3,652 ounces of gold and 159 ounces of silver were produced. The mine was at one time owned by James Barlett, Superior Judge for many years and annotator of Issac Cox's Annals of Trinity County.

Uncle Sam: This mine was located northwest of the Sherwood property, or approximately one mile west of Mary Blaine Mountain. Along with the Sherwood, the Uncle Sam provided employment for residents of White Rock City area.

Lucky Strike: The location of this mine was on a tributary of Battle Creek, approximately 5,000' W of Dees Peak.

Ridgeway: Located approximately 900' SW of the site of Marysville, the Ridgeway had a ten-stamp mill which did "custom crushing" for a number of mines in the district as well as processing the ore from the Ridgeway property. Supporting evidence includes a "road suitable for light trucks" (USGS) from the Sherwood to the Hunter to the Ridgeway mill site, built by Johnny Hennessey. Machinery for the Ridgeway mill was packed from Etna in Siskiyou County by a 50 mule pack train. Included were two batteries weighing 2,100 and 2,200 pounds.

Mary Blaine: This mine was approximately one and one-half miles NE of Old Denny or 1,500' S 75° W of the summit, elevation 6,500'. Recorded production between 1895 and 1897 was over 435 ounces of gold. There was a five-stamp mill and a small sawmill. The stamp mill was later moved down to the Uncle

Site 48. This is a view of the Boomer Mine located near Old Denny (New River City). It was considered to be one of the most successful mines in the area, operating from 1888 to 1901 and producing gold valued at $350,000.

Site 48. This arrastra was used to crush ore at the Gun Barrel mine located on Battle Creek approximately 2½ miles from Old Denny (New River City).

Sam. The Mary Blaine Mine and a nearby meadow were both named for a madam who was extremely popular and well-respected among the miners of the district. The Mary Blaine was discovered June 16, 1884, and incorporated in January, 1885, with capital stock of one million dollars.

Cinnabar: (Esther or Blue Jay Mine) The location of this mine was on the south side of Mary Blaine Mountain, approximately one mile northeast of Old Denny on the trail from Mary Blaine Meadow to Old Denny. It was found by Pete Larsen, also known as Peter Larcine, founder of Marysville. He worked it until the 1930's when it was sold to a Chinese family named Hong who came from the Altoona quicksilver mine. USGS reports "the mine has potential as a small-scale mercury producer."

Gun Barrel: This mine was located at the head of Battle Creek about two and one-half miles northwest of Old Denny. Frank Ladd built a trail from Old Denny to Gun Barrel in 1906, later extending it down Plummer Creek into Siskiyou County.

There were many more mining claims made during the heyday of the district which are not listed here but may be found by consulting the official district records. However, the only recorded placer production in the Mary Blaine Mountain area is from the Boyd claim near the mouth of Emigrant Creek and Emmons' cabin. It yielded 200 ounces of gold between 1904 and 1907.

The entire mining district is now part of the Salmon-Trinity Alps primitive area and is being reclaimed by vegetation. Heavy stands of coniferous trees grow at the lower elevations, thinning as higher elevations are reached and becoming interspersed with dense brush. Evidence of mining activity, however, is easily found. There are pieces of metal, pottery and machinery scattered about; the outline of mine drifts and dumps, as well as timbers from the mine buildings are to be seen. Well established trails still exist connecting the mines.

Site 49. Old Denny or New River City Site

The Old Denny or New River City site is located up the New River trail from Denny via the Slide Creek branch of the trail. The distance is about 12 miles from the end of the road. It was the earliest of three rival townsites established after new discoveries in 1883-84 resulted in a gold rush to the New River area. New River City, White Rock City and Marysville all became thriving mining communities. New River City contained a store, hotel, butcher and blacksmith shops, three or four saloons and several whipsaw sawmills. The store was originally managed by John W. Shuford, a member of an early mining family in Trinity County, and the hotel was run by Hannibal Soule. Both of these buildings were owned by John Thomson of Eureka. Later, the hotel and butcher shop were run by Jim Mullane, an important figure in Trinity history. Stables and barns were built here to shelter and feed the local riding and pack stock as well as the many animals used by travelers into the area. All hay and grain were packed in from Scott Valley in Siskiyou County.

A feature article on this mining district, appearing in the January 2, 1885 edition of the San Francisco Evening Post, states: "New River City, being in the vicinity of leading mines and situated at the gate of the new El Dorado will probably become the metropolis of the district." The appearance of this article suggests the widespread fame and drawing power the area attained. Reference is also made to the relationship of New River City to the Boomer Mine which was the most successful mine in the district and which was located approximately one-half mile SE of town.

In 1888 the store was taken over by the Denny Bar Co. of Siskiyou County. Mr. A. H. Denny was extremely prominent in his own county, having estab-

Site 49. This overview shows how Old Denny appeared in 1889. As the mines were worked out, the population dwindled and finally in 1920 the town was abandoned.

Site 49. The store at Old Denny (New River City) served the miners of the area from the mid-1800's until 1920 when it was closed by Frank Ladd, the owner, who opened a new store 20 miles down-river at what is now known as Denny.

Site 50. The Ridgeway Mill, located near Marysville, crushed ore from the Ridgeway Mine and from a number of nearby mines. It was a steam powered 10-stamp mill. The mortar beds, weighing 2100-2200 pounds each were hauled in by horses from North Fork. The trip took six weeks. Other machinery was brought in by 50-mule pack train from Siskiyou County.

lished the first bank in Etna. In 1890 New River City was renamed Denny in his honor by the miners, and Denny was also chosen as the name for the post office although both names, Denny and New River City, were used after that date. A State Mining Bureau Register for 1898 lists both names as trading centers for mines in the region. By that time, however, the mines were being worked out and the population was dwindling. In 1920 Frank Ladd ceased to operate the Boomer and abandoned his New River City store and hotel. He purchased property 20 miles down the river at a settlement formerly known as Quimby. He established a store and hotel there, renaming the town, Denny.

As the New River City site is now part of the wilderness area, vegetation is reclaiming it. However, there is considerable evidence of former activity, including pieces of metal, wood stoves, timbers, nails, foundation rocks, parts of a wagon (used on the road which connected Old Denny with Marysville and White Rock City) and a cabin which was built in the 1930's. There is also a Forest Service sign marking the site.

Site 50. Marysville Site

The Marysville site is located one-quarter mile north of U. S. Mineral Monument 42 on the trail to the Sherwood mine. It represents one of three rival townsites established in the New River-Old Denny mining district to meet the miners' needs for food, drink, supplies, lodging and a general gathering place. It was started about 1883-1884 by a Frenchman from Humboldt County, Peter Larcine, who had been a cook for several Eureka hotels. Larcine decided to build a hotel above New River City, starting with a log cabin and adding to it. He and his wife had one daughter, Mary, who died there at the age of 18. The town was named for her. A feature article on the New River district in the January 2, 1885 edition of the San Francisco Evening Post stated "mine host Peter Larcine dispenses good food, lodging and 'mountain dew' to man, provender and shelter for his four-footed beast and with a country store where the miner can obtain the necessary supplies for his camp." The appearance of the article, subtitled, "The Modern El Dorado," suggests the wide fame and drawing power of the area. Mrs. Larcine's niece, Alice Jacobs, resided in Marysville until 1914 when it was abandoned because the mines had been worked out.

The Marysville townsite is being reclaimed by vegetation although evidence of former activity remains, including scattered boards and nails, bits of pottery and a few heavy timbers standing in the brush where the hotel was located. There is a wagon road connecting this site with two others in the district, and Marysville is marked by a USFS sign.

Site 51. White Rock City or Couer Site

The White Rock City site is 1200' northeast of the Hunter Mine and approximately one-half mile north of the site of the old settlement of Marysville. It represents one of three rival townsites established in the New River-Old Denny mining district to meet the miners' demands for supplies and entertainment. It was settled mostly by people from Humboldt County. The main sources of employment were the Sherwood and Uncle Sam mines and the Ridgeway mill. White Rock City was the location of a branch store belonging to Alexander Brizard of Arcata. His mercantile interests stretched over three counties. The Brizard pack train brought in supplies on the Happy Camp Mountain trail, taking about eight to ten days to make the trip from Arcata. The store and post office were first operated by Alexander Couer. The post office, which was named for Mr. Couer, was established January 26, 1885, and operated until October 20, 1896. The store continued in operation until 1904 when White Rock City was finally abandoned. In its heyday, White Rock City actually had more people than Old Denny. Its population included many Chinese.

The townsite is now part of the wilderness area and vegetation is reclaiming it. Considerable evidence of former activity remains, including parts of wood stoves, building timbers, nails, foundation rocks, as well as a wagon road connecting the three townsites in the district. There is also a cemetery to the south of the site. A Forest Service sign marks the site.

Site 52. Mary Blaine Meadows

The lush green of the Mary Blaine Meadows can be seen from miles around. They are located on the southwest side of the odd shaped, granite Mary Blaine Mountain. The meadows are surrounded with evergreen forest and covered with beautiful wild flowers. There is a spring at the top of the meadow and a small fenced enclosure for stock is in the middle.

During the final twenty years of the 19th century when new gold discoveries resulted in the establishment of three mining communities in the upper New River area, Mary Blaine Meadows provided summer pasture for the many saddle and pack animals used by the inhabitants of the area. The meadows were at the junction of two branches of the trail into the New River area from Cecilville. One branch went to Old Denny and the other extended into the North Fork drainage. Mary Blaine operated a saloon and stopping place about 100 yards below the meadow. She was a prostitute who was well regarded and respected by the miners for her kindness and open ear, for she often grubstaked miners whose luck was bad. It is not known where she came from or where she went, but she remains a legend in Trinity history. The meadows which bear her name are an important pasture spot in the wilderness.

This photo of the Ladd pack train was taken about 1914. Pack animals provided the main source of transportation into the New River area using three major trails. A wooden flume can be seen in the foreground.

New River Trails

There were three major trails into the New River area providing the only access into this rugged back country.

One trail came from Siskiyou County. It started at Callahan in Scott Valley, came up the South Fork of the Salmon River to the New River divide a little north of Mullane Corrals, and then descended into New River City (or Old Denny as the site is now called).

Another trail went from New River City down New River following the creek grade to Panther Creek. It then went up to Bell Creek, crossed and continued to climb to a ridge near the Hackerman cabin. From that point the trail turned south to Happy Camp Mountain and thence west along the ridge to Willow Creek.

The third major trail ran from New River City down Slide Creek, up Emigrant Creek, and across the ridge to Pony Creek. From there it went up the East Fork of New River by way of Blue Ridge to Rattlesnake Lake and then down the North Fork of the Trinity River to Helena.

These important trails were used by pack trains to transport supplies to the New River area until 1933 when a road was completed as far as the present community of Denny. Substantial parts of these trails remain in use. They all pass through rugged mountain wilderness.

The Clement Ranch on Reading's Creek in the vicinity of Douglas City was one of Trinity County's early productive ranches. Its original buildings still stand (see page 301).

DOUGLAS CITY - LEWISTON

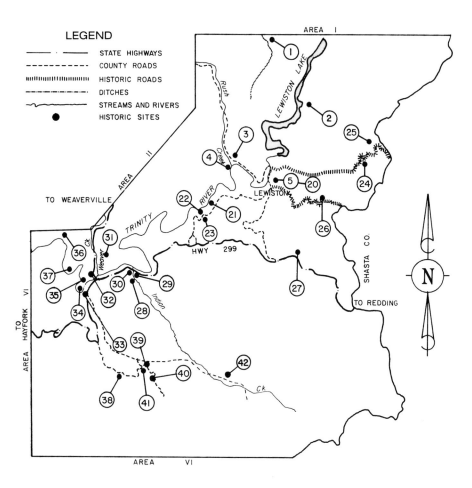

LEGEND

— · — STATE HIGHWAYS
---------- COUNTY ROADS
IIIIIIIIIIIIIIIIIIIIIII HISTORIC ROADS
—·—·—·—·—· DITCHES
〰〰〰 STREAMS AND RIVERS
● HISTORIC SITES

KEY TO HISTORIC SITES

1. Buckeye Ditch
2. Sites covered by Lewiston Lake
3. Domenici House
4. Paulsen Ranch Site
5-20. Lewiston Sites
21. Lunden Ranch Site
22. Lowden Ranch Site
23. Thomas House
24. Deadwood
25. Deadwood Road
26. Lewiston Turnpike
27. Buckhorn Station
28. Rais Ranch
29. Vitzthum House

30. Vitzthum Barn
31. Union Hill Mine
32. Douglas City Water Tower
33. Marshall Ranch
34. Readings Bar
35. Graveyard Point
36. Steiner Flat
37. Trinity River Mining Bars
38. Bigelow Ranch
39. Clement Ranch
40. Edgerton Place
41. Fossil Beds
42. Indian Creek Townsite

268

AREA V

DOUGLAS CITY-LEWISTON

Douglas City
Historical Overview

Douglas City is the site of one of the first white settlements in Trinity County. Major Pierson B. Reading, whose ranch was in the northern Sacramento River Valley, made a trapping expedition into the county in 1845 and gained some knowledge of the terrain. In 1848 he visited the gold discovery site at Coloma and noted that the characteristics of the gold bearing gravel there were similar to those on and near his ranch. He did some prospecting in Shasta County and in July, 1848, came into Trinity County prospecting Reading's Creek to its mouth near the present day Douglas City. Here he discovered enough gold to warrant returning to his ranch for additional men and equipment. He returned in ten days with 64 Indians, three whites and a large herd of cattle. Major Reading and his crew had been at work for only about six weeks when a group of Oregonians appeared and apparently objected to the use of Indian labor. Rather than risk a fight with the newcomers, Major Reading and his crew packed up and left, returning to Shasta County with approximately $80,000 in gold. The news of his discovery triggered the big rush to Trinity County in 1848-50.

The original town in the Douglas City area was named Kanaka Bar by the Oregonians who chased out Major Reading. The location was down on the flat where the mobile home park is located today. In 1859 it was moved up the hill about a quarter of a mile west of the present town. The old locust trees which line the road to Steiner's Flat near its junction with the schoolhouse road mark this spot and are all that remain of the town from that period.

It was at the time of this move that the residents decided to rename the town after either Lincoln or Douglas who were having their famous debates that year. A vote was taken and Douglas won by one ballot. In the late 19th century Douglas City boasted a large store, hotel and stage stop, billiard saloon, barbershop, warehouse, post office and a number of other buildings. The town also had its own militia and newspaper. The present day Douglas City site was not occupied until well after 1900. In earlier times this was the location of the Chinatown settlement.

Freight team fording Trinity River near hotel in Lewiston when bridge was temporarily out.

Lewiston
Historical Overview

Lewiston, the third largest community in Trinity County, was built on the old main trail from Shasta to Weaverville. It was here that Frank B. Lewis first erected a trading post and started a ferry. The community that developed bore his name and was originally called Lewis Town. After the discovery of gold in the 1850's it became a sizeable mining community. The first post office was established in 1853. The forerunner of the present hotel was built in 1862. A Chinatown large enough to support a small Joss House sprang up on the flat south of the present steel bridge. Most of the Chinatown was destroyed by fire in 1882 and the Chinese gradually left the area. None remain today. The Joss House and a few of their cabins were still standing as late as 1918.

The first bridge across the Trinity River at this spot was erected in 1851. It was washed away a few years later. Subsequent bridges met the same fate until the present steel bridge was constructed in 1900.

During the last part of the last century most of the gold taken around Lewiston was obtained by placer mining with the result that much valuable topsoil was washed down the river. About 1889 the first dredge was built on the river but it was soon broken up by a flood. Other dredges were later in operation both above and below Lewiston. They continued to devour the earth and leave mounds of tailings in their wake until World War II caused them to shut down.

The years 1956 through 1962 saw major changes in Lewiston. It was at this time that the construction of the Trinity and Lewiston Dams was underway. There was a great influx of workers. The U.S. Bureau of Reclamation constructed headquarters and a housing project; the project contractors built a shopping center; the new school was built. A small city quickly grew but it as quickly declined when the job was completed. Today, many of the residents of Lewiston are retired people and tourism brings others to the area. A number of historic buildings of the town remain in use and are described in this section.

Douglas City Hotel and Stephen Thayer family about 1880.

Site 1. Buckeye Ditch

The Buckeye Ditch is considered to be one of the longest mining ditches ever constructed. It took water out of the Stuart Fork at a point just below Salt Creek and carried it to a point southwest of the present Trinity Dam. The first portion of the ditch parallels Stuart Fork on its east side as far as Cherry Flat. A small section of the present Stuart Fork trail is along this part of the ditch grade. At Cherry Flat it was siphoned across the creek to the west side and then contoured around the mountain, finally reaching a point in the Slate Creek drainage just below the present Kinney Camp. From there it progressed down Buckeye Ridge in the direction of Pettijohn Mt. It ended in a mining area then known as Bolt's Hill on the west side of the Trinity River between Baker and Posey Gulches, a length of about 40 miles.

Bolt's Hill was an area of unusually rich gold bearing gravels five to fifteen feet deep but there was very little water available for its extraction. It was such a rich area, in fact, that at first the miners would even carry the dirt a considerable distance to the Trinity River to wash it. In 1873 the Buckeye Water and Hydraulic Company located the land and started developing a plan for bringing Stuart Fork water to the mining area. Construction of the ditch started in the spring of 1874 and it was completed with water running through it by February of 1876. The ditch was built by Atkins and Lowden with the help of Chinese labor. The project was not considered to be a highly successful one for records show that by 1895 the ditch had long since reached a state of disrepair and no longer carried water.

Site 2. Sites covered by Lewiston Lake

The following are some of the places that figured significantly in the early history of this area and which now lie buried by the waters of Lewiston Lake:

CUNNINGHAM FLAT. This was the site of a small ranch. There were a number of very old fruit trees at this place before the filling of Lewiston Lake.

CLAYTON RANCH (WILLIAMS RANCH) (MARY SMITH CAMP-GROUND). Cox wrote that the first of the big (30-40 foot) water wheels were operated along this stretch of the river above Lewiston. The George Clayton family first lived here and farmed. They sold the ranch in 1898 to Samuel and Annie (Caton) Williams. Their son, Melvin, was born here and the property later became his. A small portion of the field not covered by the lake became the U.S. Forest Service Mary Smith Campground. (Miss Smith was owner-manager of the Trinity Dredge — see Blakemore Ranch.)

JENNINGS GULCH. There was a fine piece of land at the mouth of this gulch. It sloped gently down toward the river. Blakemore used it for pasture in conjunction with his ranch on the opposite side of the river.

EASTMAN GULCH. In 1850 William Woodin first mined this area. In 1853 Charles Eastman acquired the land and mined part of it but retained a portion for agricultural purposes and planted a large orchard. Much later the property was mined by a company of Chinese. In 1881 the ranch was the scene of a double wedding when Goldie Blakemore married Eldridge Eastman and Anna Koelle married William Jasper Scott.

BLAKEMORE RANCH (TRINITY DREDGE CAMP). This ranch, four miles above Lewiston, was a productive ranch before it was purchased by the Trinity Dredge Company from Jeff and Ursula Blakemore. The Blakemores had provided fresh produce to many people in the surrounding area. (Mrs. Blakemore and Anna (Koelle) Scott were sisters.) The Dredge Company built a bunkhouse, cookhouse and the superintendent's quarters on the old home site. They continued to use the barns and a portion of the garden spot. Several homes

LEWISTON

KEY TO HISTORIC SITES

5. Old Lewiston Bridge
6. Phillips House
7. Paulsen House
8. Lewiston Hotel
9. Paulsen Store
10. Goetze Butcher Shop
11. Siligo House
12. Conner House
13. Kise House
14. Old Lewiston School
15. Van Matre House
16. Congregational Church
17. Van Cleave House
18. Lewis-Scott House
19. Wilson House
20. Wilson Granary

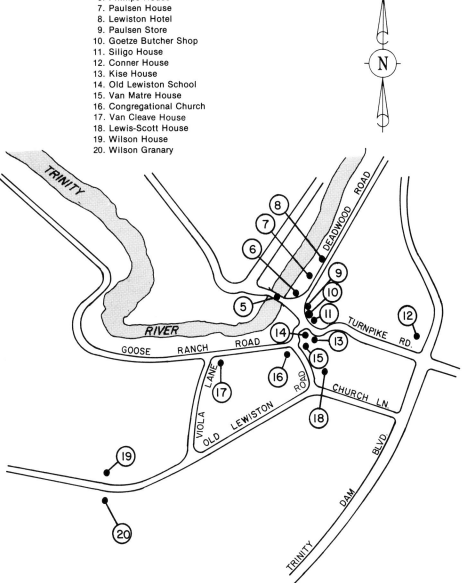

Site 6. July 4, 1897 at Lewiston. View is of Deadwood Road looking toward the old bridge,

were built a short distance north of the ranch to accommodate the families of the workers. The dredge set up by this company worked the upper portion of the Blakemore Ranch and continued to work up the river channel for a distance of three and one-half miles. Unlike other dredges, this boat left no high tailing piles. It used a flume in the rear to release the worked gravel and rock. This was the most successful of any of the large bucket line dredges. The Trinity Dredge worked from 1912 until 1940. Ed L. Smith managed the company until his death in 1924. His son, Ed L. Smith Jr., carried on but did not have a liking for the work. Mary E. Smith bought out her brother's stock and managed the Trinity Dredge Company until 1938 when she leased it to two brothers, T. D. and C. R. Harris who operated it until 1940. Miss Smith was the only woman to have had the distinction of managing a gold dredging operation.

MOONEY GULCH — FERRY GULCH. This was the site of a ferry crossing on an old trail which connected Clear Creek in Shasta County with Weaverville. This trail crossed Trinity Mountain above the Brown Bear Mine, passing through Keno. At Keno there was a pasture for livestock and a stopping place for travelers. From here the trail continued its way down Mooney Gulch to the river where Mr. Mooney operated the ferry. The trail then followed along Buckeye Ridge, crossed Rush Creek near the Junkans-Costa Ranch and continued to Weaverville. Cox wrote of Mr. Mooney as "having a ranch on the west side of the river."

In 1854 a bridge crossing the Trinity River was built two miles upstream above Mooney's Ferry. This was on a trail catering to packers going north to Salmon River and Yreka.

Site 2. Gold Mining Dredge which operated on the Trinity River near Lewiston prior to 1940.

Site 3. Domenici House

This house was built by Domingo Domenici in 1872 on Rush Creek Road where Rush Creek merges with the Trinity River and although it has undergone considerable renovation and a 25-yard move in 1940, the older section remains in fine condition due to excellent care. The original portion of the house is a single gable, one and one-half story clapboard structure with 6/6 windows and a wide lean-to veranda across the south side. The veranda faces the Trinity River and the house is surrounded by a large lawn.

The Domenici family were Swiss-Italians who farmed along Rush Creek rais-

Site 3. Domenici House at junction of Rush Creek and the Trinity River. This house, built in 1872, had been extensively remodeled.

ing hay, potatoes and other garden produce. They were related to the Anderline family who were their neighbors and were also related to the Siligo family of Lewiston. George Domenici, son of Domingo, was a teamster and drove the last Concord stage in Trinity County. He also drove some of the first auto stages.

Site 4. Paulsen Ranch Site

The Paulsen Ranch was located on both sides of the Trinity River just above its junction with Rush Creek. Little that once was on the original site of this ranch remains. Several small homes and trailer spaces cover the area of the ranch house, barns, gardens and hotel. Much of the ranch land on either side of the river has been reduced to mine and dredge tailings. New homes are being built on the Grass Valley side of the river.

The first ranch at this location was established in 1850 and was known as the Chamberlain Ranch. It was purchased in 1874 by Jacob and Louisa (Goetze) Paulsen. They and their five children, Edwin, Charles, Henry, Fred and Bertha, built this into a productive farm, freight stop and hotel. The Paulsens had a store at the ranch and later purchased an interest in the store in Lewiston, one and one-half miles away. Mining land was added to the ranch and son Fred was active in this part of the family enterprise. Much of the land on the Lewiston side was mined by hydraulic methods. The Grass Valley Creek side of the ranch was mined by the Gardella Dredge; later, about 1930, the Gold Bar Dredge operated here for a short time. (Fred Paulsen is remembered for his service in World War I, as an owner for a time of the 2-Mule Borax Mine in Death Valley, and as a former Trinity County Supervisor.) After Jacob Paulsen died the ranch and hotel were run by Henry Paulsen and his mother. The ranch and hotel were eventually sold by the Paulsen family and shortly thereafter the beautiful hotel and outbuildings were destroyed by fire.

276

The ranch, store and mine contributed greatly to the economic stability of Lewiston in the early days of this century. The big hotel provided a place for many social gatherings and the passing of the Paulsen family was a permanent loss to Lewiston and the county. (The five children of Jacob and Louisa Paulsen left no heirs.) That Herbert Hoover spent some time at this ranch in 1920 is an historic footnote to the history of the Paulsen Ranch.

Site 5. Old Lewiston Bridge

The Lewiston bridge spanning the Trinity River in the center of old Lewiston is a steel one-way "truss" span resting on two concrete abutments. It is about 200 feet long and has three structural bays that join at the top over the road. This old bridge was designed and built by James "Cap" Phillips in 1900. Phillips was a member of the Olney Phillips family that had kept a toll bridge across the river at this location for many years. The present bridge, conveyed to the county by the Phillips family, replaced a covered bridge that was destroyed by floods. The bridge has survived for over three-quarters of a century and withstood the last great flood in December, 1955, when the approaches to both ends were washed out.

Site 6. Phillips House

The Phillips House is the first house on the left on Deadwood Road near the east end of old Lewiston Bridge. This house is a one and one-half story cross gable structure with a veranda running the length of the front and two roof dormers with casement windows looking into the street from the attic. A narrow front yard is enclosed by a decorative wire fence with wooden posts. The yard contains locust and fruit trees, grape and rose vines and lilac bushes, all of early vintage.

Morehead and Palmer, among the first permanent settlers in Lewiston, built a small house and public place at this spot in 1851 together with a toll bridge across the river. By 1854 Olney Phillips had become the proprietor of this bridge on the main Shasta to Weaverville trail. The original bridge was destroyed by flood and Phillips built a new bridge in 1855; he also began to improve the house and surroundings. The present house was built by Phillips in 1864. The existing old Lewiston bridge was erected by Olney Phillips's son, James W. "Cap" Phillips, in 1900. For many years Cap Phillips was the County Surveyor.

Although her home stood but a few yards from the Lewiston school Mrs. Cap Phillips chose to teach her eight children at home. In addition to teaching her children, (Wendell, Roy, Lawrence, Marjorie, Russell, Floyd, Dorothy, Llewellyn, and Lloyd) she managed to maintain a yard full of beautiful plants and flowers. This corner property, sixty years ago, was the pride of Lewiston.

Site 7. Paulsen House

Located second along Deadwood Road, the Paulsen House is named for the old time Lewiston family who were involved in business and ranching. The house was built in 1875 and has undergone considerable alterations by the several owners over the years. Some of the additions to the original metal roof structure include a low wing to the rear of the house, a one and one-half story gable addition and a by window on the right front of the house.

During its early years the home was the residence of the Baker and Dickey families. In the 1890's Lucy Phillips and her mother lived here. The house was sold to Charles and Deda (Joseph) Paulsen. Later Henry Paulsen lived here and much later it was the home of Fred Paulsen's widow, Mildred.

Site 4. The Paulsen Ranch at the Trinity River and Rush Creek; home of prominent pioneer family of miners, farmers and merchants.

Site 8. Lewiston Hotel on Deadwood Road.

Site 8. Lewiston Hotel

The Lewiston Hotel, also on Deadwood Road, is presently the only commercial building still operating in the old town center. It is a large two and one-half story, hip roof building with a wide one story shed roof veranda running the length of the street side and across the north end.

The original hotel was built by Howe and Boger in 1862-3 on the flat behind the present structure. It was purchased by Mart Van Matre of the pioneer Van Matre family in 1890. John Koll bought the building in 1897. In 1898 the hotel was destroyed by fire and the present structure was erected in the following year. John Koll and his wife, Louise (Joseph) Koll, ran the hotel for years. They also made the building their home along with their four children, John, Winnie, Burton and Audrey. Daughter Winnie taught at Lewiston and Weaverville schools.

Declining business caused the hotel to close in 1939 but it was reopened in its present shape in 1956 by Mr. and Mrs. Mason Gray. It is now principally a restaurant. A recent addition is a one story gable on the west side which serves as extra dining space. The outside of the hotel is decorated with paraphernalia of older days: moose and buck horns, spurs, plows, traps, chains, spades, etc. Trumpet vines and honeysuckle protect the building from the sun and in the rear where the old hotel garden was located wild grapes cover the fences and cottonwood trees. The present owner is Jeff Talbot.

Site 9. Matlock's Store (Paulsen's Store and Post Office)

This store building which stands at the junction of the Old Lewiston and Deadwood Roads in old Lewiston has had several owners and operated under several names over the years. It was built and first run by L.B. Matlock in 1860. It was sold to Hi Hays in 1870 and later to Tom Baker in 1885. Baker was popular in the community and his business prospered. When he died his business passed to his sons, Walter and Willis. Willis's half interest was eventually sold to Jacob Paulsen. At this time the store became known as the Baker and Paulsen Store. Paulsen later assumed complete ownership. Upon his death, his wife, Louisa S. Paulsen, continued to run the store under the name of the L. S. Paulsen Co. Her sons, Charlie and Henry, eventually ran it, using the name Paulsen Brother's Store.

The building was a general merchandise store selling everything from groceries and clothing to tools and dynamite. It also served as a post office with the post office situated in the store at the left end. Beer, wine and whiskey were sold in the basement and upstairs there were living quarters for a caretaker. This one and one-half story gable structure has a porch facing the street and in the back there is an enclosed storage lean-to. It has undergone little alteration during its 120 year history. In front of the building are four locust trees growing from stumps of very old trees which were nearly as old as the building before they were cut down by highway maintenance crews. Adjacent to the building on the right side is the old Goetze-Siligo butcher shop.

Charlie and Henry Paulsen were pleasant, kind and respected men. The store for many years was a social gathering place and community center. Townspeople would gather here while waiting for the mail or for an order of merchandise to be "put up." In summer a long row of captains' chairs lined the front porch. In winter the chairs surrounded the big wood stove in the center of the establishment.

Paulsen is an old and prominent Trinity County name. Jacob Paulsen had come to Trinity County in 1851. In 1855 he was mining at Turners Bar with

Site 9. Old timers visit on porch of Paulsen's Store, circ. 1900.

Site 10. Goetze Butcher Shop, Lewiston, about 1894. H. W. Goetze stands behind the box in the center.

Site 12. The Conner House was built in 1910 and located at Turnpike Road and Trinity Dam Boulevard.

his two brothers, Peter and Charles. He continued to mine in the Douglas City area near Steiner's Flat until 1870. In 1874 he purchased a large and beautiful ranch and stopping place in Lewiston at the mouth of Rush Creek.

Site 10. Goetze-Junkans-Siligo Butcher Shop

This building is located between the Paulsen Store and the Siligo House at Old Lewiston and Deadwood Roads. It was built in 1859 and is a simple, high gable building with a rusty metal roof and a lean-to veranda along the street side and west end. Second growth locust trees are growing from the surviving stumps along the street. During its early years the upstairs of this building was used as a bunk house for the drivers of freight teams and stage drivers staying overnight in Lewiston. The stage barns were just across the street from the store, post office and butcher shop. There also was a blacksmith shop next to the bridge.

J. W. Ransom was probably the first owner of the butcher shop. Ownership changed frequently. Loomis, Watson and Brown, Hays, and, later, Goetze had a butcher shop here. Mr. Goetze also raised cattle on their Trinity Alps Ranch as part of his cattle business. The butcher shop was later bought by the Junkans family who also ran cattle and owned what is now known at the Costa Ranch on Rush Creek. The building was next sold to Louis Siligo who built the barns across the street. These barns were destroyed by the 1955 flood. During the building of the Trinity Dam, the old butcher shop served as a card saloon.

Site 11. Siligo House

Located on Old Turnpike Road near Old Lewiston Bridge, the Siligo house was built in the 1880's and its early residents were Chamberlain, Goetze, Junkans and then Siligo. Louis Siligo ran the butcher shop next door to the residence. Originally the house was a rectangular building with a front yard beyond a picket fence. A wing was added to the north side about 1900 making it an "L" plan and the widening of the road caused the removal of the fence. A covered area between the house and butcher shop was the location of a fine well of unusually cold water which was enjoyed by townspeople and travelers alike. In recent years the house has been rented by a number of residents and is showing signs of wear.

Site 12. Conner House

The Conner House is set back from the road at the intersection of Old Turnpike Road and Trinity Dam Boulevard in Lewiston. This house was built in 1910 for John and Henrietta (Denison) Conner by George Shreaves, a family friend. Some part of the Conner family consisting of parents and seven children, George, Roy, Ora, Harold, Helen, Elmer and Ruth, has always lived in this house. The late Roy Conner worked his entire adult life in Paulsen's store and post office. George Conner built and operated the first wireless in the county. The house is reached by walking along a path through a small field. It is a one and one-half story structure with a one-story cross gable. A veranda covers the front and one side and serves as a grape arbor.

Site 13. Kise House

This house stands on a narrow strip of land, off Old Lewiston Road, between Hoadley Gulch and the hill where the school is located. The Kise or "Lish" Kise house is of Greek Revival construction with a big veranda that covers the

Site 14. The Old Lewiston School, in 1897 with the teacher, Winifred Blakemore, and entire student body.

Site 16. Congregational Church, Lewiston, built in 1896 at a cost of $750.00.

Site 18. The first home in Lewiston. Residence of the Lewis, Scott, Richards and Cox families.

front and side. A woodshed made of log and pole construction is built against the hill on the north side. The house is historically known as the Lish and Lizzie (Rule) Kise home. Both Kise and Rule were important old-time families in this area. Lizzie Kise was a fine seamstress and continued sewing professionally for many years after she, Lish, and son Earl moved to Redding. Elijah "Lish" Kise was an expert wagon maker and blacksmith. His shop was between Phillip's house and the east end of the steel bridge. It was destroyed in the 1955-56 flood.

Site 14. Old Lewiston School

Located on Old Lewiston Road near the junction with old Turnpike Road, the old Lewiston School is a classic one room schoolhouse with a gable entry porch matching the gable roof and topped with a belfry. The entry porch was added in the 1940's. The schoolhouse was built in 1862 by the Good Templars Lodge as a temperance hall. The lodge surrendered its charter in 1865 and the building became a school at that time. For many years the school had no plumbing or running water. It was the chore of the children to take turns keeping the water pails filled from the good well at the Kise house. One pail was in the girls' ante room and the other in the boys'. All children drank from a common dipper in each bucket. In recent years a new Lewiston school was built to accommodate the increase in population caused by the building of the dams. The old schoolhouse which is in good condition is presently used for public meetings and storage.

Site 15. Van Matre House (Steffens House)

This house is a high gable building with a veranda on the front and side, located on Old Lewiston Road across from the old cemetery. George Washington Leas built the house in 1897 for Mart Van Matre and his wife, Mary (Leavitt) Van Matre. The Van Matres, with son Clarence, occupied the home for many years. Mart ran the Lewiston Hotel for a time. He also had an interest in the Frick and Davis Ranch and in the Poker Bar Dredge. The house has remained in the family throughout its existence. The latest owner is the Van Matre's granddaughter, Marjorie Steffens.

Site 16. Congregational Church of Lewiston

The Lewiston Congregational Church is a one story, high gable structure with an extremely high peaked roofed steeple on the north corner. This old church is situated on a knoll overlooking the old section of Lewiston and the Trinity River. Across the street from it is the old cemetery surrounded by a picket fence.

The church was organized in Lewiston in October, 1889, and incorporated in 1896 when the church building was erected at a cost of $750.00. The contractor was Mr. Canfield for whom the Canfield Road was named. Upon completion, the Trinity Journal described it as being on "a most commanding site in the center of town, making it visible for miles around, a tasteful, commodius structure, with graceful tower and spire." During its early years ministers came from Weaverville to conduct services.

The beauty of the church inspired the town to repair and improve its 1862 schoolhouse, which still stands nearby, giving to the town an impressive set of public buildings. The church building eventually fell into disuse and it was purchased by Mr. and Mrs. Carl Steffans and presented to the Lewiston Community Services District for preservation as an historic building. During the

Site 19. The Wilson House on Old Lewiston Road, built in 1850 and at one time the center of 660 acres of farm land.

Site 19. Wilson Ranch, formerly Frick and Davis, at Lewiston. Site of Bureau of Reclamation camp in the 1950's.

construction of Trinity Dam, and before the present school was built, the church was used as a classroom.

Site 17. Van Cleave-Ralph House

This house sits on a knoll overlooking the Trinity River, at the junction of Viola Lane and Goose Ranch Road. It was built before 1900 and is on e of the few pyramid hip roof cottages in the county. The building is structurally sound and has recently been remodeled. It is surrounded by neglected fruit trees and overgrown grass.

Site 18. Lewis House (Scott House) (Cox House)

Located on Old Lewiston Road near the junction of Church Lane, this house is a very small two story, high gable building with an enclosed lean-to on the north. A flat roofed veranda covers the front side and serves as a balcony porch for the second floor. The original house was a one story, four room building. The two story addition was made in 1896 with further remodeling taking place over the years.

This 1850's house, overlooking the town and river, was built for Frank B. Lewis, after whom the town of Lewiston was named. It occupied a 14 acre parcel of land. The property was purchased by William J. Scott had his wife Anna (Koelle) Scott in 1891. Family members occupied the house for the next sixty years. Their six children all continued to live in the area throughout their lives, occupying important places in the county's history. They were Clara May, Nellie J., William Irvin, Leland Stanford, Edwin W. and Lynton Howard Scott. May married William Richards of Deadwood; Nellie married packer William Pattison of Big Bar; Irvin married Nova Owings of Trinity Center. Stanford founded McDonald and Scott, a funeral parlor serving Shasta and Trinity Counties for many years. Lynton was one of four Trinity County boys who died while serving in World War I. Irvin, Stanford and Edwin purchased the pioneer Owings Ranch at Trinity Center when they were young men. The Scott family is still prominent in Trinity County. Part of the old Scott ranch became the new site for Trinity Center at the time the Trinity Dam was built in 1959.

Site 19. Wilson House

The Wilson House, on Old Lewiston Road, was originally surrounded by ranch fields, but today the elementary school and some houses have been built on what used to be ranch land. The house is located behind a high hedge and only the upstairs can be seen from the road. This house was the center of one of the oldest, finest and most valuable ranches of Trinity County. It was originally known as Mud Ranch because of its rich, black, alluvial soil. It was first settled by George W. Davis and later by Christian Frick who made considerable money in the quartz mines at Deadwood. By 1858 there were 300 acres under cultivation and by 1883 it contained 660 acres.

The ranch was purchased in 1914 by James Wilson who ran it with his sons. Wilson was foreman at the Deadwood mines for a number of years. The Wilsons expanded the acreage by buying a number of smaller, nearby ranches including the Wheatfield and Valentine places. James and Hattie Wilson raised seven children on the ranch. Daughter Harriet married Robert Cummings of Cedar Stock Farm near Minersville and daughter Elizabeth married Fred Lowden of Lowden Ranch. One son, Harold Wilson, served four terms as Trinity County Sheriff. The ranch is still owned by the Wilson family although the acreage was much reduced after condemnation in 1956 by the Bureau of Reclamation during the building of Trinity Dam.

The Wilson House is a T-gable construction with a one story cross gable in the rear. The house and yard are shaded by large walnut trees. Two outbuildings accompany the house. One of the outbuildings is a woodshed, the second is a pantry on the east side. The pantry is reached by a little bridge over the spring that feeds the house.

Site 20. Wilson Ranch Granary

The Wilson Granary, across from the old Wilson House, also known as the Frick and Davis Granary, is one of the oldest buildings in Trinity County. The granary was part of the Frick and Davis Ranch and was primarily used for grain storage. It is said that Mr. Frick lived upstairs in the granary for a time. In 1914 the ranch was purchased by James Wilson. The granary is still owned by the Wilson family. The building is a two story board and batten structure with a high gable roof and a one story lean-to on the west gable end.

Site 21. Lunden House and Barn

Located three miles south of Lewiston on the Old Lewiston Road, the Lunden House was built for Louis Siligo, a member of the Swiss-Italian family who owned the butcher shop in Lewiston. Siligo raised wheat and cattle on the land. The property was purchased by Arthur and Edith (Adrian) Lunden in 1930. Edith Lunden was a member of the Adrian family who were the owners of the adjacent and historic Lowden Ranch property. The house is a one story rectangular structure with a metal, medium pitched gable roof. It is a tiny and extremely simple home compared with houses serving ranches of similar status. In the 1920's a board and batten addition was built on the east side.

Site 21. The Lunden Barn, 25-30 feet high, built in the 1920's.

Site 22. The Lowden Ranch Hotel burned to the ground in 1925.

Site 22. Bridge built by William S. Lowden at his ranch on Trinity River four miles west of Lewiston.

The Lunden barn is one of two barns which are still standing on the property. It is a high gable structure, 25' to 30' tall, which is visible across the pasture from the Lewiston road. It stands as a visible reminder of the days when this was an active ranch and important in the life of the area.

Site 22. Lowden Ranch (Adrian Ranch)

Little remains of the original Lowden Ranch on Lewiston Road west of Lewiston, but it is noted here because of its significance in the early development of Trinity County.

In 1852 William S. Lowden purchased 160 acres along the Trinity River at this site. He became the most prominent early settler in the county. Not only was he a farmer but he was also an express rider, surveyor, land attorney and road builder. In 1855 he built a toll bridge across the river to connect existing pack trails. An abutment to this bridge can still be seen. In 1858 he built the first wagon road into the county. Known as the Grass Valley or Buckhorn Road, it brought travelers from Shasta County to the ranch, over the toll bridge, and on to Weaverville. After Lowden's parents and brothers and sister moved to the area the Lowden holdings increased to 640 acres and the property was developed into a fine hotel and stage stop. It also became a productive ranch as records for 1858 list 3,555 fruit trees, a yield of 300,000 potatoes and acres of vegetables. The family also pursued mining and logging activities. In 1866 his brother, Owen Eugene Lowden, became the proprietor and continued to operate the ranch for nearly 40 years. Following his death in 1904 the 640 acres were divided among the family members and the various parcels have had several owners since that time.

In 1919 James Adrian purchased the property and moved his wife and most of their 14 children from Oregon to live in the home. On November 1, 1925 the big Lowden home burned to the ground. In 1929 the Adrians constructed a new log cabin and in 1940 this also was destroyed by fire. There is still standing on the property a milk barn built by the Adrians in the late 1930's.

Site 23. J. B. "Brig" Thomas House

Located across the road from the old Lowden Ranch, this house is situated well back from the road on the north side of a forested hill. It is a rather secluded site, separated from the road by thick berry vines and trees which line the historic Lower Grass Valley Creek Ditch at its southwest corner. The house was built in 1914 by Wiley Lowden of the pioneer Lowden family. In 1919 it was purchased, rebuilt and remodeled by J.B. "Brig" Thomas who lived in it until his death in 1977. The Thomas house is the only structure in Trinity County with a combination hip and gable roof. The lot is also unusual being bounded on three sides by running water.

Site 24. Brown Bear Mine and Deadwood

The Deadwood mining district comprises numerous claims in an area of rich gold bearing ores along Deadwood Road. The first major strike was made in 1872 by a Mr. Kline. Successive discoveries were made by Kline and others over the next several years. The most famous of these quartz mines was the Brown Bear Mine that was discovered by Sebastian and Balleau in 1875. Many millions of dollars have been taken from this mine which has been operated intermittently through the years. Its greatest period of activity ended in 1912, but it was worked again briefly in 1939 and again following World War II from 1946 to 1950. In recent years the rising price of gold has again brought activity to the Deadwood area mines.

Site 24. The Deadwood Mining area in 1902.

The mine buildings at the Brown Bear have been almost entirely dismantled, but there is still evidence of the considerable activity that took place here around the turn of the century. Gold was obtained at two locations: the upper and lower workings. The upper, or older, workings are now reduced to rock formations where old houses clung to the hillsides, and to the large dump from the old mill. The lower mine area includes the mill with caved-in roof and huge timbers rotting away and machinery scattered about. Doors and windows have been removed from the boarding house, and the superintendent's house has been dismantled for salvage material.

Bustling communities arose at both of the mine locations. At the peak of the mining activity, between four and five hundred people lived in the vicinity. In 1896 there were 92 men registered to vote in Upper Deadwood alone. When the mines appeared to be running out of ore, people began moving away. By 1915 the post office at Deadwood was abandoned. When the mines shut down, the economy of the County was seriously affected.

Site 25. Deadwood Road or Tom Green Road

This road extends up Deadwood Creek from Lewiston to the top of Trinity Mountain and then down to French Gulch in Shasta County. It is dirt most of its length but still usable, although narrow and steep. This road, one of three major roads leading into Lewiston from Shasta County, was constructed in the late 1800's during the height of the quartz mining activity in the Deadwood district which lasted from 1880 to 1905. The creek had been mined in the early 1850's and later by Portuguese and Chinese miners, but it was the chance discovery of a quartz ledge in 1880 that led to a large influx of people and capital. A good wagon road was needed to bring in supplies. The Deadwood Road is also known as the Tom Green Road because of the Tom Green mine on the Shasta side of the mountain. Tom Green was the owner of the mine and builder of the road.

Site 25. Wreck of the Weaverville Stage in Deadwood Creek. The stagecoach went off Deadwood Road in 1909.

Site 26. Lewiston Turnpike or Hoadley Road

The Lewiston Turnpike extends from a point a mile west of the Tower House in Shasta County, westerly about nine miles to Trinity Mountain and then down Hoadley Gulch about five miles to the center of old Lewiston. It is a dirt road with a very easy grade that attests to the ability of the pioneer road surveyors. There were two watering spots along the road used for the horses. The road was one of the three major roads into Lewiston and, to date, has survived for 114 years. It was built in 1865-6 by Lewiston Turnpike Co..pany and completed October 1, 1866. The road was constructed because the Lowden road had a number of bridges across Grass Valley Creek that kept washing out. The Lewiston Turnpike, using an alternate route, faced the challenge of heavy grading through slate and granite formations. The turnpike was also known as Hoadley Road, after J. F. Hoadley who came to Lewiston in 1853. He established a trading post which he closed in 1858 so he could open a sawmill and build a toll road. Hoadley was active in community affairs, serving as a justice of the peace and postmaster. The Hoadley Toll Road was incorporated into and became part of the turnpike.

Site 27. Buckhorn Station

Buckhorn Station is on Highway 299 four miles west of the Shasta-Trinity County line.

The cafe building at the Buckhorn Station is a low gable structure with few windows and a shed roof which covers the entry and gas pumps. Mobile homes look down on the site from the surrounding hills. There is an open field between the present highway and the old road which runs close to the cafe. Along the old road are walnut trees and in the field are scattered fruit trees, always an indication of earlier day activities.

Site 27. Buckhorn Station as it appeared prior to 1900. The building at the left is the hotel.

The Buckhorn Station was, in early days, a stopping place located on the Shasta-Weaverville wagon road about six and one-half miles from Lowden's Ranch. Ownership and building dates in the early days have proven elusive but some evidence indicates that George Washington Leas, a Lewiston pioneer, purchased it from John Arn and expanded a small stage stop into a major 16-room hotel in the 1870's and 1880's. The inn served as an overnight stop for stagecoaches and freight teamsters and there were large barns, a farm and sheds on the site. The name Buckhorn was given because of the proximity to Buckhorn Mountain, the major summit on the road from Redding to Weaverville. In keeping with the name, deer antlers were placed on all the walls of the buildings. None of the original Buckhorn Station buildings exists today. The present structures on the site were built in the 1930's.

Site 28. Rais Ranch (Letton Place)

The Rais Ranch is located on Indian Creek about one-half mile upstream from Highway 299. The present house was built in 1919 by Manual Rais (originally spelled Reis). The ranch was a productive cattle ranch. The herd numbered as many as 400 head of cattle but during the winter months was reduced to as few as thirty head. The barn was built in 1923. John and Sara Letton purchased the property in 1977 and are the present owners.

Site 29. Bill Vitzthum House

Located on the south side of Highway 299, between Indian Creek and Douglas City, the Vitzthum House is a one and one-half story gable structure with a hip roof and two-story porch that extends almost the full length of the east and west sides. This home was built from lumber taken from buildings at the LaGrange Mine four miles west of Weaverville. The original house was constructed during the period of greatest activity at the LaGrange Mine (1893-96). The building was purchased by the Vitzthum brothers, torn down and hauled by wagons to its present site where it was reconstructed. The Vitzthums were a well-known ranching family and Bill Vitzthum made his home at this place.

Site 30. Bill Vitzthum Barn

This barn was built about 1914 and was originally located closer to the river and was twice its present size. When the state highway established its right of way through the area, the barn was cut in two and the two sections were moved to the south side of the highway just west of the Vitzthum House. One of the barns was later sold and moved. The remaining barn was recently converted to a house by Mr. & Mrs. Roger Hardison. The barn, or house, is 30 feet high, with metal windows which have been installed and with a hip roof porch which has been attached to the rear. The yard used to be a ranch corral and is defined by a post and rail fence.

The area where this property is located was originally known as Texas Bar and was one of the earliest mining sites in Trinity County. The original Vitzthum family home and barns were located about three-fourths of a mile up river from the mouth of Indian Creek at the lower end of the field that extended from that point to McIntyre or Last Change Gulch. The family also farmed the field immediately upstream from the mouth of Indian Creek.

Site 31. Union Hill Mine

Union Hill Mine is on Union Hill in the angle formed by the Trinity River and Weaver Creek. It is reached by the road that goes east from Highway

Site 29. Bill Vitzthum House near Douglas City. Originally built at LaGrange mine it was taken down and reconstructed at this site.

Site 31. Union Hill Mine Bridge (Steel Bridge) with 30 inch siphon for bringing water to the mine.

299 near the bridge across Weaver Creek.

The discovery of gold in Union Gulch led to the development of this mine which, at its peak in the early 1900's, was one of the largest hydraulic mines in the country. Almost nothing remains of any construction at this extensive hydraulic mining operation which began in 1862 and was abandoned in 1928. For its first forty years the Union Hill mines were worked with water taken from Little Brown's Creek, Weaver Creek and from the Davidson Ditch which brought water from the lower end of Weaver Basin to the mine site.

In 1900, P.M. Paulsen acquired control of enough claims on Union Hill to put together a large scale venture. The main source of water during this period was Grass Valley Creek. A large ditch, about 15 miles long, beginning at a point about one mile above the present Oddfellows' Camp was constructed. The ditch also picked up water from Sawmill and Tom Lang Gulches. It then ran out the ridge between the Poker Bar development and what is now known as McIntyre or Last Chance Gulch. It dropped off this ridge to cross the Trinity River by means of an inverted siphon supported by a steel bridge. The siphon then carried the water up the hill on the west side of the river and through a 6½ x 4½ foot tunnel, 570 feet long, to the reservoir above the mine.

The steel bridge (from which Steel Bridge Road derives its name) was a 165 foot steel span set on two concrete piers. It was wide enough to accommodate the 30-inch pipe as well as a wagon. The siphon itself was 5000 feet long and dropped 300 feet in elevation. (This steel bridge remained standing until World War II when it was dismantled for scrap.)

When increased mining activity plugged up Union Hill Gulch with tailings, a drainage tunnel was bored through the ridge to the south in order that the tailings could be dumped into the Trinity River to be carried away by high water. The tunnel outlet is now barely visible from Highway 299 about .3 miles east of Douglas City. It was the later collapse of this tailings tunnel after the mining operations had ceased that caused Union Hill Lake to form.

The mine was continually operated until 1911 when it was taken over by Trinity Consolidated Mining Co.; however, little mining activity was undertaken by them. In 1921 T.R. Arbuckle leased the Union Hill Mine and operated it until 1928. At that time operations were forced to close as the deep and fluid overburden kept caving in and covering the pipe and giants and creating hazardous working conditions. Declining profits did not allow for further maintenance under such difficult conditions.

Site 32. Douglas City Water Tower

Located just off Highway 299 at the westerly end of the Douglas City Bridge, this 35-40 foot water tower is larger at the bottom than at the top since part of the siding slants inward to the two-thirds point and then rises straight up to the pyramid hip roof. The state purchased this land known as the "Dad Hinckley Placer Mine" from Irving Jordan for $100.00 in 1925. It built a house and water tower to be used as a maintenance and supply station for highway workers. The water came from a spring on the nearby hillside and was stored in the 5,000 gallon redwood tank. The station was abandoned in 1960 and the house was sold. The water tower is now used by the Douglas City Volunteer Fire Department.

Site 33. Marshall Ranch (Albiez Place)

The Amos H. Marshall Ranch was located across the Trinity River from old Douglas City at the confluence of Reading's Creek and the river. Amos Marshall came to Trinity County from Selma, Ohio during the 1849 gold rush. Upon arriving in San Francisco by ship he walked to Trinity County. For the next five years he mined in northern California and then returned to his home in Ohio. About 1860 he returned to Trinity County and bought the ranch property. Mr. Marshall became a partner with Jack Mason in the nearby Douglas City store and hotel. Later, in the 1880's, he served as County Assessor. The ranch remained his home until 1919. He died there at the age of 91.

Amos' son, Robert C. Marshall, acquired the property and later sold all but about two acres of it to the Viking Dredging Company which dredged the stream channels in the 1940's. Amos' grandchildren, Robert L. Marshall, Verna Reynolds and Mary Flournoy, still own a portion of the small parcel which the family had retained. The Viking Dredging Company has since sold their portion. The original ranch house is situated upon that part which is now owned by Mr. and Mrs. George Albiez.

The old walnut trees that still stand on the property grew from nuts which Amos Marshall had brought with him from Ohio. It was on this property that Major Pierson B. Reading made the first discovery of gold in Trinity County.

Site 34. Reading's Bar Marker

Located at the bend in the Trinity River adjacent to the Douglas City Campground, this 4 x 6 foot redwood slab plaque commemorates the first documented gold mining site in Trinity County. It marks the vicinity where Major Pierson B. Reading discovered gold while prospecting on the river in the fall of 1848. It was his report that triggered the big rush to the Trinity mines in 1849-50, and hence, the settlement of the county. The exact location of the area worked by Reading is debatable. There were flats or bars on both sides of the river at the mouth of Reading's Creek. Some old timers believed the original workings were on the inside of the big bend of the Trinity River; however, there is easily accessible bed rock on the south side of the river at the mouth of Reading's Creek.

Site 35. Graveyard Point

Graveyard Point is one-quarter mile west of Douglas City southwest of the junction of the Steiner's Flat and Campground Roads. It is the site of one of the first, if not the first, documented cemeteries in Trinity County. The first burial here took place in 1850 when a man named Hayes from Texas Bar was interred. The only other person known to be buried here is a Mrs. Emma Trask who died of smallpox around the 1870's. This cemetery was abandoned about 1880. In recent years the site has almost been destroyed by one of the local utilities which has used the ridgetop as a service road to a telephone line equipment shelter.

Site 36. Steiner's Flat

Steiner's Flat, on the north side of the Trinity River four miles below Douglas City, was settled in September 1850 when Benjamin Steiner established a ranch on this fertile bench. The area extends along the north side of the river from the lower edge of Red Bar to the mouth of Dutton's Creek. Steiner's Ranch comprised 160 acres of excellent soil on which he produced vegetables and fruits for the mining community. The area was sufficiently populated that an election precinct was set up here with about 90 votes being cast in 1856. It is estimated, however, that there were as many as 280 people residing in the vicinity, only nine of which were women.

Henry Lorenz acquired the flat in the 1860's and collaborated with Peter Paulsen, who had been mining at the nearby Turner's Bar, to develop a large mining operation in the area. Their mining association continued over a period of many years and was known as the Dutton's Creek Mine. One of the objectives of the Trinity Canal had been to bring water to this mine. In later years it was also hoped that the Union Hill ditch could be extended so as to bring Grass Valley Creek water to the Steiner's Flat area mines. Both propositions failed. In 1911 a grandiose scheme was proposed that would have combined the large mining properties around Douglas City, Steiner's Flat and the Weaver Basin. This scheme would have used a system of ditches and immense reservoirs to collect and distribute the waters of Grass Valley Creek, Indian Creek, Weaver Creek and Dutton's Creek to the various mines. This also failed.

Site 37. Mining Bars along the Trinity River between Poker Bar & Steiner's Flat

Following the discovery of gold near Reading's Creek in 1848, nearly every flat and bar up and down the Trinity River quickly became the scene of considerable mining activity. This was especially true along the Trinity River in the vicinity of Douglas City because of its proximity to the original gold discovery site. In general, the size of the mining claims that were established along the river in this area were 30 feet wide and extended back from the bar and river to the base of the adjacent hill or steeper ground. Later, "hill claims" developed. The width was increased to 60 feet. If bedrock rims were present making the cutting of drainage ditches more difficult the size of claims became 125 feet wide.

The accompanying map depicts the relative position of the numerous bars along this section of the river and the following statements pertaining to them are based largely upon Isaac Cox's observations made in 1858.

Mining at POLKA BAR, (now called Poker Bar) began in 1852 but Cox states in his Annals that by 1858 the bar had been abandoned except for a group of Germans who had assured themselves of enough water for their mining activity by constructing a water-race out of Grass Valley Creek. This was known as the "German Ditch" and was "six miles long and had a capacity of 20 sluice heads." This investment assured them of a good profit for it was rich mining ground. It was here at Polka Bar that later, about 1895, the first bucket-line dredge for recovering gold from the river gravels in Trinity County was built. Downstream from Polka Bar is POINT BAR. It also had been worked since 1852, but much of the gold still remained in the ground at the time of Cox's visit for he found miners few in number at this place.

A mile and a half farther downstream is an area of fertile land of about 50 acres in size which was settled by a Mr. Lathrop in 1853. He cultivated the land and also constructed a sawmill at this place. This enterprising man built a low dam upstream to permit the development of water power for the mill and used the excess water for mining activity downstream. The next year the property was acquired by Mr. P. W. Reas who was equally as enterprising. In 1857 new owners, Messrs. Curtis, Garland and Kelly, purchased the property for $8000. These men formed a company which elevated the dam and started construction of a water-race or "canal," named the "Trinity Canal" with which they proposed to carry water as far as Steiner's Flat and the intervening gold fields on the right bank of the river.

Next along the river is UNION BAR which was unoccupied at the time of Cox's writing although Cox speculated that 100 miners could make a livelihood there for 20 years to come.

At FERRY BAR (which is upstream from Indian Creek near where Highway

TRINITY RIVER MINING BARS
Douglas City Area

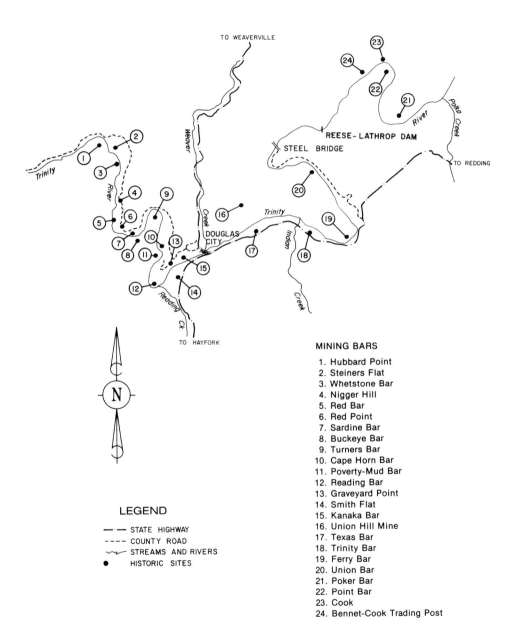

MINING BARS

1. Hubbard Point
2. Steiners Flat
3. Whetstone Bar
4. Nigger Hill
5. Red Bar
6. Red Point
7. Sardine Bar
8. Buckeye Bar
9. Turners Bar
10. Cape Horn Bar
11. Poverty-Mud Bar
12. Reading Bar
13. Graveyard Point
14. Smith Flat
15. Kanaka Bar
16. Union Hill Mine
17. Texas Bar
18. Trinity Bar
19. Ferry Bar
20. Union Bar
21. Poker Bar
22. Point Bar
23. Cook
24. Bennet-Cook Trading Post

LEGEND

—·— STATE HIGHWAY
---- COUNTY ROAD
~~~ STREAMS AND RIVERS
● HISTORIC SITES

299 leaves the Trinity River) was Shrader's Ferry. A ferry crossing here connected the trail from Shasta and Lewiston to one extending on to Weaverville. George Vitzthum (Sr.) succeeded Schrader at this place which also embraced 70 acres of productive land. Mr. Vitzthum created a very fine ranch here that was later taken over by four bachelor sons: George, Charlie, Henry and Frank. The Vitzthum Ranch extended downstream to the area of TRINITY BAR. In 1858 Cox found no mining activity here although several claims had been registered.

Between Indian Creek and Douglas City is TEXAS BAR, a fairly large bar of about 50 acres. A ditch out of Indian Creek supplied water to this bar but it was insufficient to meet mining needs. At Cox's writing the miners were anticipating the completion of the Trinity Canal to bring them the water so sorely needed. The land, however, was producing a garden "of good promise." It belonged then to a Mr. Soule, but it later became the Bill Vitzthum Ranch. Bill was the only one of George Vitzthum's five sons who married and established his own place. (Also see Site 29.)

Near the mouth of Weaver Creek were 300 acres of rich land, 150 acres of which were under cultivation when Cox wrote his Annals in 1858. This place was known as Trinity Ranch and had been purchased by Morse and Mabie in 1855 from Mr. Lathrop who had settled it in 1851. Being at the confluence of Weaver Creek and the Trinity River the land was subject to destructive flooding. The present day community of Douglas City occupies portions of this old ranch.

KANAKA BAR is the low land along the river in the vicinity of Douglas City. (See introductory description of Douglas City.)

SMITH FLAT, located on the left bank of the river across from Kanaka Bar, was originally a ranch encompassing 100 acres of cultivated land established in the early 1850's by John and Nat Smith. A toll bridge across the river at this place accommodated travelers to Hay Fork. Eventually this flat was mined using water from Reading's Creek. In the 1940's to 1960's period a medium sized sawmill occupied this site, but the operation was forced to cease when the mill burned in 1966 and was not rebuilt.

Beyond Smith Flat are Reading's Creek and READING'S BAR. (For the account of this significant spot see Site 34.)

Across from the Douglas City Campground and downstream from Reading's Bar is POVERTY BAR (sometimes called MUD BAR). This bar, as with all the other bars, had been mined shortly after P. B. Reading's discovery of gold started the rush to the northern mines, but by 1854 it had been abandoned. It was subsequently reopened by Chinese miners with some degree of success although, probably, its greatest period of productivity was in the late 1930's when the low land was dredged.

On the high bench which comprised Douglas City Campground is an area known as FILIBUSTER FLAT. It contained a large Chinese camp and was mined in the 1860's with water via a high ditch from Weaver Creek.

Below it on the river is CAPE HORN BAR. A water race from Weaver Creek was used here by a company of four Germans. When Cox visited the camp in 1858, he was surprised to find a camp with a home-like neatness that bespoke an interest in the finer and more intellectual aspects of life — a marked contrast to the nature of most miners. These intellectual Germans were each making $12.00 to $16.00 per day in their gold mining pursuits and there appeared to be enough gold bearing gravels to last them for twenty years.

The next bar on the river, the TURNER BAR, was a successful operation. Rich gravels here were first mined with aid of a small water wheel. In 1857 a wheel 54 feet in diameter was erected and a water race was built to bring water

Site 37. The George Vitzthum (Sr.) Ranch embraced 70 acres of productive land at Ferry Bar near the point where Highway 299 leaves the Trinity River.

from Reading's Creek. The Paulsen brothers, Peter, Jacob and Frederick, mined at Turner's Bar over a period of ten years. Enough gold was taken out by them to enable Peter to buy the Union Hotel in Weaverville and Jacob to eventually buy a large ranch in Lewiston. (Frederick was drowned in a fall from a water wheel in the spring of 1858.)

BUCKEYE BAR, one-half mile below Turner's Bar, also paid well. Here, also, a water wheel was erected, this one being 42 feet in diameter.

SARDINE BAR was not an outstanding producer. It was prospected in 1852 and like so many others, soon abandoned. There seemed to be sufficient gold, however, to warrant resumption in 1855.

Below Sardine Bar is RED BAR, named for the very red soil that is found here. It was first mined in 1851, with a succession of parties working the bar over the next several years. Here, also, waterwheels were utilized in their operations. Although no big strikes were found, the ground paid well.

The last bar to be considered in the Douglas City section of the river is WHETSTONE BAR. This is a large one that was first worked in 1850. Water for the claims on this bar came through a ditch from Dutton Creek which was brought across the river by flume. A 47 foot wheel also was being utilized at the time Cox wrote his account.

The above observations were largely made in 1858. Mining continued off and on over the years. The most significant mining in this area occurred in the late 1930's and early 1940's when practically all of the creek and river bottomland, including much worked over ground, was turned upside down by dragline-floating washing plant operations.

300

Site 38. Bigelow Ranch and Barn

Located approximately two miles from Highway 3 on Brown's Creek Road, the Bigelow Ranch is the first place on the right along the Brown's Creek Road when traveling from Highway 3 toward Deer Lick Springs. The property had been purchased in 1889 by William Ralph Bigelow from the heirs of Archibald McIntyre. Bigelow was a New Englander who came to California when only 17 years old. He worked in the Union Consolidated Shipyards in San Francisco and became a partner in that business before coming to Trinity County in 1885 or 1886. He became sheriff of Trinity County in the early 1900's.

Mr. Bigelow also purchased what was known as the John Coumbs Ranch which was located upstream from the Brown's Creek bridge but which did not adjoin the McIntyre Ranch that he had already purchased. The two ranches combined to become known as the Bigelow Ranch. The Coumbs Ranch portion was the larger of the two. Both ranches were irrigated with water out of Brown's Creek which flows through each of them.

There are no buildings left on the Coumbs portion of the ranch. On the McIntyre portion there still stands the old barn built in 1908. It is a tall two story structure with a high gable dormer on the east side and a shed addition on the west. It is extremely long, almost 125 feet. Also standing is a ranch house which was built in 1923 to replace the original one that burned. The former owner of the McIntyre portion of the ranch, Archibald McIntyre, is buried on the small hill overlooking the property.

Site 39. Clement Ranch (RK Ranch)

Located approximately five miles up Reading's Creek Road at its junction with Indian Creek Road, the Clement Ranch is among a select group of early agricultural claims which still have their original buildings standing. This ranch sits on a large, cleared and relatively flat area; its ranch houses, barns, grassy fields, fenceline, flowers and vegetation combine to provide a beautiful scene.

This property was claimed by William Clement, a native of New Hampshire, in December of 1855 and has been ranched to this day. It was owned by the Clement family until 1941. They ran cattle and raised hay and produce, especially potatoes, which found a ready market with the miners of the area. The ranch was irrigated by a large ditch out of Reading's Creek. The old ranch house, built in the 1850's or 1860's, contains hand-hewn studs still visible inside. Despite several remodelings, including a major one about 1906, the house retains its original shape. The main barn was built in 1901. On a knoll south of the ranch house sits the "little house" which was built for William Clement's widow. Above the houses on a hill is a family cemetery surrounded by large oak trees and a split rail fence.

Site 40. Edgerton Place

The Edgerton Place is located up Reading's Creek Road on the west side of the road above Panwauket Gulch.

The Edgerton Place was formerly known as the John Henry Coumbs Ranch, the Wallace Ranch and The House That Jack Built. The central complex of the ranchhouse, yard, storage sheds and barn is situated on a small rise above the fields. The house is a one and one-half story, high gable, rectangular structure with a cross gable extending on the north side. There is a veranda porch on three sides. The house is painted white with green trim.

John Henry Coumbs bought the Panwauket mining claim and hired Joe Enos to build the house that stands today. John, his wife Mary (Wallace) Coumbs and their small son Thomas Wallace "Bub" Coumbs, moved into the new house in 1902. Both John and Mary were from old-time Trinity families. John's father, Thomas, came from Canada to Trinity County in 1876 and ranched on nearby Brown's Creek. Mary's grandparents, David and Elizabeth O'Connell, arrived from Ireland in the 1860's to mine, farm and raise cattle.

In 1903 Mary Coumbs died after the birth of her second child. The farm was sold to her brother, William O. Wallace. The house remained in the Wallace family until 1962 when it was bequeathed to the present owner. This small ranch with its old ranchhouse, barns, fenceline, ditches and fields is one of the most beautiful in the county.

Site 41. Blanchard Flat Fossil Beds

A bit of pre-human history has been found in the Blanchard Flat area south of State Highway 3. Fossils from the Cretaceous Period of geologic time have been unearthed near the site of the old Blanchard Flat School which was located one-half mile south of the old Clement Ranch on the road which connected the Reading's Creek and Brown's Creek areas. George Anderline, LeRoy Eisele and Robert Turnbull spent a period of seven years during the 1960's making extensive digs in the area.

Ammonites, an extinct form of mollusk and Belemnites, an extint kind of cuttlefish, are both found in abundance in the geologic formation of marine origin which surfaces here. Clam shells and turtle eggs have also been unearthed. This shale and mudstone formation extends for a considerable distance in the direction of Bully Choop Mt. Many of the fossil finds from the area are on display at the Trinity County Museum in Weaverville.

Site 42. Indian Creek Townsite

Located at a point just west of Freitas Gulch where the county road crosses Indian Creek is the old townsite of Indian Creek. (Freitas Gulch, in this instance, is the gulch so named on current Geologic Survey or Forest Service maps. Historically, Freitas Gulch was a gulch located about two and one half miles beyond at the site of the old Freitas Ranch.) Nothing remains of this community. Between 1850 and 1900 it was the center of a gold mining area which, until it played out, yielded an especially high grade of ore. The community included, at one time or another, a store, saloon, butcher shop, livery stable, corral and stagecoach stop. A stage road connected Indian Creek to Weaverville and to Red Bluff. This road skirted Bully Choop Mountain. For a time the community had a post office which was named Indeek, a contraction of the words Indian Creek. Many of the inhabitants of the community were Portugese immigrants, one of whom was Joseph Freitas for whom Freitas Gulch was named.

AREA VI
HAYFORK - HYAMPOM - WILDWOOD

Historical Overview

The first white men to enter the territory which became Trinity County crossed the divide into Hayfork Creek near the present site of Wildwood on April 17, 1828. It was a party of eighteen American fur trappers led by Jedediah S. Smith. On the 22nd of the month the party arrived at the juncture of Hayfork Creek and the South Fork of the Trinity River which Jedediah named "Smith's River". Maps and journals of the expedition were lost to historians for nearly one hundred years. As a result the Smith's River name did not endure but has been erroneously applied to a river in Del Norte County. The trails followed by Smith and his party through the Wildwood, Hayfork, and Hyampom areas had been used for generations by the Indians who inhabited these valleys. Later, farmers would move their herds and wagons to the Sacramento Valley over these same routes.

Miners came to Carrier Gulch on the east side of the area in 1850, but the main attraction was the agricultural potential of the valley of the Hay Fork of the Trinity as it was known in the early days. Settlers led by B. M. George came from Weaverville and Steiner's Flat in 1851 to farm and produce for the mining sections. Homesteaders went into the Hyampom Valley for the same reason in 1855. Hank Young and Pierce Trimble are credited with being pioneers in Hyampom. Trimble lived in Big Bar and wandered into Hyampom accidentally. He came back to settle 160 acres, and sent for his brother, John Wesley, to settle there also.

Historically, Wildwood has played a supportive role in its relation to Hayfork Valley. It lies on the route to Red Bluff, from early times the trade center for Hayfork farmers. The route up Salt Creek developed into a road (old Highway 36), in the late 1880's. It seems to have been the principal wagon road and stock trail to the Sacramento Valley. Movement up and down Hayfork Creek also passed through Wildwood. The California Gazeteer of 1890 first mentions Wildwood as having a recently established post office. Ed Landis is the only business man listed and he is listed as postmaster, saw mill and hotel operator, and blacksmith.

303

HAYFORK-HYAMPOM-WILDWOOD

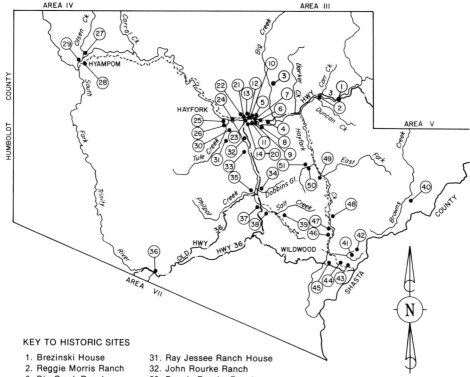

KEY TO HISTORIC SITES

1. Brezinski House
2. Reggie Morris Ranch
3. Big Creek Ranch
4. Glass House
5. Lyle Blick House
6. Root House
7. Community Church
8. Bayles Mill
9. Langberg House
10. Len Campbell House
11. Erna Laffranchini House
12. Dockery House
13. Ernie's Old Store
14. Hayfork Hotel
15. Irene's
16. Flagpole
17. Market
18. Theater
19. Laundromat
20. Dallaire House
21. Montgomery House
22. Thorne House
23. Blanchard Flat School
24. Albiez Barn
25. Pony Ranch
26. Japanese Balloon
27. Augustine Barn
28. Greenleaf House
29. Hyampom School
30. Laverne Laffranchini House

31. Ray Jessee Ranch House
32. John Rourke Ranch
33. Dennis Rourke Ranch
34. Cuff Barn
35. Patton Barn
36. Forest Glen
37. Duncan House
38. Schmidt House
39. New Pioneer Ranch
40. Deer Lick Springs
41. Hall City
42. Hall City Caves
43. Powers Mill
44. Knight Ranch
45. Riewerts Ranch
46. Roy Schiell Ranch
47. Gemmel Flat
48. Old Schiell Ranch
49. Leach Ranch
50. Natural Bridge
51. Bridge Gulch Massacre

LEGEND

————	COUNTY LINE
—·—·	STATE HIGHWAY
------	COUNTY ROADS
~~	STREAMS AND RIVERS
●	HISTORIC SITES

HAYFORK

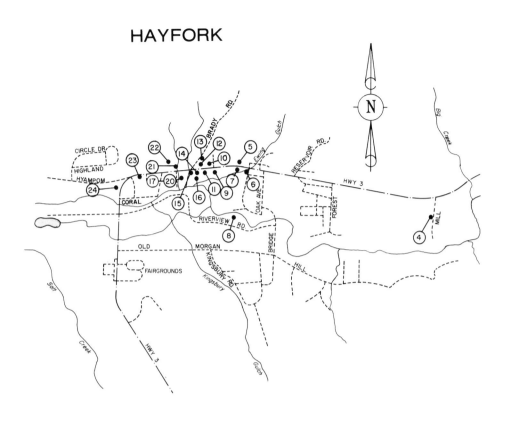

KEY TO HISTORIC SITES

4. Glass House
5. Lyle Blick House
6. Root House
7. Community Church
8. Bayles Mill
9. Langberg House
10. Len Campbell House
11. Erna Laffranchini House
12. Dockery House
13. Ernie's Old Store
14. Hayfork Hotel
15. Irene's
16. Flagpole
17. Market
18. Theater
19. Laundromat
20. Dallaire House
21. Montgomery House
22. Thorne House
23. Blanchard Flat School
24. Albiez Barn

LEGEND

——— · ——— STATE HIGHWAYS
- - - - - - - COUNTY ROADS
‿‿‿‿‿ STREAMS AND RIVERS
● HISTORIC SITES

Site 1. Morris Home (Brezinski House)

This home, which was the family home of the Reggie Morris family, is on Summit Creek Road off of Highway 3 east of Hayfork Valley.

It is now the home of the Brezinski family. This house is the second home of the Morris family, an old and prominent family of ranchers in the Hayfork Valley. The original house was situated on the other side of the creek opposite the present house. It was destroyed and the new one built on the cool side of the creek. This typical Trinity County ranch house has one and a half or two stories, shiplap, endboards, a veranda porch, and a lean-to on the back.

Site 2. Ruch Ranch (Reggie Morris Ranch)

Michael Ruch claimed this land on Coyote Flat in what is now called the Carr Creek drainage in April 1853. James Stanmore and R.B. Wells had already staked claims for land adjoining it. Ruch sold his Ranch which now contained the Stanmore and Wells parcels to John Carr in April 1858 for $2000. J.S. Hoyt bought the property from Carr in 1873 and in 1886 it was sold to Ed Newman who built the house and barn shortly thereafter. It remained in the family, passing on to his daughter and eventually to a nephew, Reggie Morris. For over half a century it has been known as the Reggie Morris Ranch.

The first school in Hayfork valley was called the Ruch School and was located about one mile down the valley near the old Hayfork road on the south side of Carr Creek.

Site 3. Big Creek Ranch House (Ewing's Ranch)

The ranch house at Big Creek, the most important building there, was totally destroyed by fire on April 1, 1981. This ranch house was located up Hayfork Bally Road from its intersection with Highway 3 in Hayfork Valley.

Big Creek Ranch was originally Ewing's Ranch, named after the founder of the ranch. Later both the name of the creek and ranch were changed to "Big Creek." After Ewing, the ranch, which had started in the 1850's, was purchased by Jacob Vodges and later by John Hailstone of the Burnt Ranch pioneer family. The house was originally a log house which had the shingle siding added over it as suggested by the thick walls. It had been shingled, however, for as long as anybody can remember, probably dating from about 1900 when the shingle style was popular in the county. The actual date of the house has been lost. Nevertheless, the house was in good condition and survived as one of the rare shingled structures in the county. The barns are all old, including one built with hand-hewn timbers, and are an integral and beautiful part of the ranch. The entire ranch was one of the earliest and finest agricultural land claims in the county.

Site 4. Glass House

The Walter Glass house is on Mill Ave. south off of Highway 3 in Hayfork. The house was built in 1921 by a community effort to aid Walter after his house burned. Walter was left with $5.00 cash after the fire. The house was built from lumber donated by the Big Creek Lumber Company and the labor of many willing friends. Two rooms were added in 1928. It stands as testimony to community cooperation.

Site 5. Coumbs House (Lyle Blick House)

This house is located on Highway 3 in Hayfork across from the Community Church. John Shock built a small two room house here in 1904-1905. It was purchased from the Shock estate by John Coumbs in 1914. That same year

Site 2. Farm buildings at the Reggie Morris Ranch on Carr Creek.

Site 3. Barns of various ages which function for Big Creek Ranch.

Coumbs hired a carpenter named Bill Hardy to remodel and enlarge the house which became the home of the Coumbs family, well known storekeepers.

Now it looks like a barren prairie house alone on the lot without any large trees or shrubs around to soften its image. It is one of a few truly two story houses in the county.

Site 6. Joe Layman Ranch House (Root House)

This house, now located at the corner of Manzanita Ave. and Highway 3 in Hayfork, was originally the Joe Layman Ranch House and was located on the Layman Ranch, west of the Sierra Pacific Mill in Hayfork at the western end of Hayfork Valley. In the 1930's Lon Layman moved the house to its present site. It was later owned by Charlie Crews. It is now owned by the Root family who have a small nursery. No alterations, save for a brick chimney, have been added to the original house which is in excellent condition.

The house is the only one in the county to use the unusual feature of extending beams and lath shutters. It makes an otherwise ordinary house rather special.

Site 7. Plymouth Congregational Church (Hayfork Community Church)

The church is located on Highway 3 in Hayfork. In 1920 Whitmore Hall in Weaverville was to be demolished after serving the community for many years as a community meeting and dance hall. At the same time, Protestants in Hayfork were without a church meeting hall and also without money. The Hayfork group offered to dismantle the old building if they could use the lumber to build themselves a church. An acre of land valued at $100 was donated by Mrs. May Ross. Boy Scouts cleared the land. Charley Moser donated the labor to split shakes for the roof. (He had recently spotted a "shake tree" that would be perfect for the job). During the school session that year his children delivered one load of shakes a day until enough were collected to roof the church. Daisy Coumbs, Tom Montgomery, John Coumbs, Will Shock, and H. R. Given donated the paperwork involved to establish a church. The transformation of Whitmore Hall was completed by 1921 and the Plymouth Congregational Church was officially dedicated in 1924.

The church, which also served as a Grange hall for short time, has survived two natural disasters. In 1928 a tree smashed in the roof, and in 1936 snow crashed through the center of the roof. Each time it was rebuilt by the community. It is still used for church services by the independent Hayfork Community Church which was formed when a merger between the Bible Church and the Hayfork Baptist Church was completed in 1971.

Site 8. Bayles Mills

The site of the Bayles sawmill and flour mill is on Hayfork Creek, off Riverview Road, about one-quarter mile below Bridge Road.

This historic site is certainly marginal as very little evidence remains of the flour mill and nothing of the sawmill. The flour mill was so important to Hayfork farmers and northern Trinity residents that it must be noted. The mill was a fine one capable of milling the 8,000 bushel wheat production of the area in only three to four months. The site retains the ditch known as the Mill or Howe Race that provided the water for the mills. The water dropped 14 feet through an 18 by 40 inch turbine to power the mill. The turbine is probably the old mill machinery in the field across the stream.

Adam Bayles came to Weaverville from New York in 1851 and moved to

Site 5. When the Coumbs moved in to Hayfork from Coumbs Springs, John Coumbs had this house built.

Site 7. Hayfork Community Church began as Whitmore Hall in Weaverville and served as the Grange Hall for a time in its Hayfork life.

Hayfork to build these mills in 1855. He brought his family in 1859. Bayles' only son died at the age of 21; his daughter married Frank Young of Weaverville.

Bayles also had a general merchandise store in Hayfork. John H. Vanderhoff, the husband of Bayles' granddaughter Stella Young Vanderhoff, was clerk, partner and eventually owner of the business. When Adam Bayles died in 1894 the property remained in the family going first to his daughter, Mary Eliza Bayles Young, then on to this granddaughter, Stella Young Vanderhoff.

Site 9. Langberg Residence (Hayfork Grammar School)

This converted building is located on Highway 3 near the Community Church. The main part of this building was originally three rooms of the old Hayfork Grammar School built sometime before 1915 by the community. Though it has been altered by the addition of decorative cement blocks, new windows, doors, etc., the building still retains its basic shape and much of the original building material.

Site 10. Lin (Lindsey) Campbell House (Charlie Crews rental)

This cottage is located on Highway 3 in downtown Hayfork. Historically, other than being over 50 years old, the Crews rental is not outstanding. Basically, it is a transplant from another county, having been moved from Harrison Gulch in Shasta County about 1918-1920. However, the building has had an incredible architectural presence and ability to blend into its site. It is the epitome of the humble cottage yet possesses an admirable dignity. The roof proportions established by the combination of the pyramid and veranda roofs are superb and serve to settle the house into the hill on which it rests. Furthermore, the porch railing increases the visual depth into the house and creates a cafe-like sense of security and stability. An ancient weeping willow to the west graces the yard. The exposed rafter ends lend a nice rhythmic counterpoint to the porch railing.

Site 11. Erna Laffranchini House (Clem Carter House)

The old Carter residence is on Highway 3 in downtown Hayfork. This house was built in 1900 by George Carter for his brother Clem, who lived in it with his wife Dora, a member of the Drinkwater family. The Carter brothers were sons of John Carter, related to the famous King Carter family of Virginia. They ran the prominent Carter House (hotel) on Main Street in the best southern tradition. Erna's house suffered undue humiliation when Highway 3 was widened and most of its front yard and trees were removed. However, the house is well maintained and presents a very serene, dignified appearance. It remains, along with the Dockery house, as a reminder of the rural character of Hayfork before the recent commercial buildup.

Site 12. Dockery House (Vanderhoff House)

This house is on Highway 3 in the center of Hayfork across from the post office and flagpole.

The property was patented in 1882 by John S. Hoyt and was conveyed in May of 1883 to John Henry Vanderhoff. Mr. Vanderhoff ran a general store across the street in a building which also bore his name. The house at one time had a large windmill and a yard over twice the present size. It was cut back when the state highway was widened. The house served as the post office for awhile. Vanderhoff later added the front section to the east and the small kitchen to the west. The property is now owned by the James Dockery family, an

Site 11. The Erna Laffranchini house with its well-kept garden is difficult to show to its best advantage.

Site 12. The Vanderhoff house was built by one of Hayfork's leading 19th century businessmen.

oldtime Hayfork family that formerly had the Dockery ranch east of town.

It is the only Greek Revival house in the Hayfork Valley and is the best preserved and most visible house in town. Together with the old trees and picket fence, it recalls Hayfork of another era and serves a crucial role in providing continuity with the past.

Site 13. Ben Murphy Store and Post Office (Ernie's Old Store)

This store has been moved from its original location along the old Hayfork road and is now behind Ernie Glass' Store in downtown Hayfork.

The old store building was built by the Carter family or by the Knights of Pythias in the 1920's. Frank Taylor ran the store there, and it also served as the post office for awhile in the 1920's. The Knights of Pythias used the upstairs as a meeting hall. Later Ben Murphy operated the store when he moved to Hayfork from Peanut. After World War II, Ernie Glass purchased the building, then vacant, and started a variety store. When the highway was widened in the late 1940's, Ernie moved this building up the hill and built his new store down below along the new road. The old store was covered with light green stucco in the early 1950's resulting in the unusual combination of a high gable structure with stucco.

Site 14. Hayfork Hotel (Hailstone House)

This important old building is located on the south side of Highway 3 next to the Post Office Square in Hayfork.

The original portion (east end) of this building was built by John Hailstone in 1903. Hailstone, a member of a pioneer family that had come to Trinity County in the 1850's, moved from the Burnt Ranch area in the 1880's and purchased and ran the famous Big Creek Ranch. After the turn of the century he moved to town and built the Hailstone House. It was purchased by the Norgaar family in 1918 and continued to be operated as a hotel by daughter Erna and her husband, Frank Taylor. In 1920 they added the large west section on the site of a small store that originally accompanied the hotel. In 1921, the year of the first county fair, the dance hall to the rear was added. Mrs. Irene Dockery recalls that at the time of the fair that year there was only a large open-air platform. Another addition was made on the west gable end in the early 50's. In 1958 the hotel was sold out of the family. At this time the front porch was removed and the new siding was placed on the front.

The hotel is significant because of its presence in the center of town for over 75 years. An important consideration regarding this building is the fact that the board and batten front could be easily removed and the front restored to its original appearance.

Site 15. Tom J. Montgomery Building (Irene's Cafe)

This building is located on Highway 3 in Hayfork across from the Montgomery House.

Irene's Cafe was originally known as the T. J. Montgomery building and was probably built about 1906. Montgomery, who was county surveyor, built it for a rental. It was used as Hayfork's first high school from 1919-1928 but since then has been used as a restaurant.

The building is unrecognizable as being an old structure. In fact, if a large locust tree did not shade most of it, it would lose its appeal.

Irene's is an institution in Hayfork. It opens at the crack of dawn to serve a host of loggers, farmers and businessmen who discuss business before work; it greets them again for lunch and afternoon coffee and dinner in the evening.

Site 16. Hayfork Flagpole and Bronze Finial

The flagpole is located just off Highway 3 in Hayfork's Post Office Square.

The finial was originally on top of the first flag pole at Mission San Jose. Paul Bradley's father lived near the mission and salvaged the bronze ball when the old flagpole was replaced. The Hayfork Flagpole with the mission's finial was put up by three members of Hayfork's American Legion Post: Andy Norgaar (commander), Lee Murdock and Paul Bradley. The flag was raised on July 4, 1933.

Site 17. Hayfork Market (Hayfork General Store)

The old store is located on Main Street and Highway 3 in Hayfork.

The market was built in 1919 by Andy and Helgaar Norgaar when they moved their business from the old store next to the Hailstone House. The studs and rafters are made from peeled fir poles. Sawn lumber came from a steam power mill that was pulled by horses. The Norgaars sold the market in the 1940's; successive owners were Rufus Knapp, Beck and Lowe, Hollinger and Cominsky.

The Hayfork Market, along with the theater and laundromat, represents a unique kind of commericial architecture for Trinity County. They are two-story frame buildings that are big and barny on large lots which have lots of space in between but little, if any, landscaping. This is very different from the row-brick businesses of Weaverville or the framed false-front one story markets usually found elsewhere. Being agricultural, Hayfork is built for wagons, teams and big rigs necessitating space and simple straightforward buildings.

Site 18. Hayfork Theater

This three-story building was built in 1949 and is on Highway 3 just west of the Hayfork Hotel and Laundromat in Hayfork.

Although not an historical building, the theater fits in with the two old buildings nearby. It adds to the feeling of Hayfork as a town with open space and big raw-boned buildings on bare lots.

Site 19. Coumbs Building (Hayfork Laundromat)

The Coumbs building is located on Main Street south of Highway 3 in Hayfork.

The laundromat building in Hayfork was originally built for commercial use. Although it has been used for many different things, it has always been used as a commercial building. It was built by John Coumbs in 1915 and 1916 for a store, but actually it was used only as a warehouse. In 1925 Coumbs quit the business and eventually lost the building to the bank during the depression. The bank then sold it to Tom and Stella Kelly. Over the years it has been used intermittently as a theater, restaurant, store, dance hall, apartments (upstairs only) and now as a laundromat.

Architecturally, it is different from most commercial buildings in Trinity County. In Hayfork, early commercial buildings were characteristically large and barn-like, wooden framed and usually two stories. Like the market across the street, the Coumbs Building has this type of architecture. It is simple and straightforward with no romantic frills and sits on a big roomy lot so typical in Trinity County's only real agricultural town.

Site 14. The Hayfork Hotel is the only one of Hayfork's old hotels surviving today.

Site 17. Hayfork Market illustrates the style of rural commercial building built in the early part of this century.

Site 18. Hayfork Theater is not very old but its frontier style fits in with the other commerical buildings of this section of Hayfork.

Site 20. Bill Hardy House (Tommy Dallaire House)

The house is located on Main Street on the east side of downtown Hayfork.

Bill Hardy built this house on the old main street probably in the early 1900's. Hardy ran the post office in this house which used to have a metal flag on the roof. The house passed to his niece who sold it to Walter Glass. It is still owned by Mrs. Walter Glass and rented by Tommy Dallaire. The house has a friendly charm about it, set as it is away from the street and under the locust trees. It was formerly located on the main entry road to Hayfork, now abandoned in favor of the state highway.

Site 21. Montgomery House

The Montgomery home is located in downtown Hayfork on Highway 3.

Kenneth Montgomery was a grandson of John Carter, owner of the famous Carter House Hotel which burned in 1906. The Montgomery house sits on the same 160 acre parcel held by the Carters. The large locust trees in front of the present house were planted at the time of the establishment of the Carter House. Kenneth's father, T. J. Montgomery, was a noted county surveyor whose brother Buck was the Wells Fargo shotgun rider who was killed in the Ruggles brothers' notorious stage robbery.

The Montgomery house, in its simplicity, is indicative of the financial condition of the Hayfork Valley in the 1920's. It is owner-built and simple in concept. Certain features have never been completed, such as the ceiling to the entrance porch which is still open to the attic. The presence of a residence, and especially one that maintains a sense of quiet dignity amidst the commercial bustle, lends both variety and stability to downtown Hayfork.

315

Site 22. The Kellogg Hotel burned about sixty years ago leaving only its carriage house now known as the Thorne house.

Site 22. Thorne House (Kellogg Hotel Carriage House)

The Thorne house is located on Highway 3 in downtown Hayfork. It is set back from the street behind the site of the old Kellogg Hotel.

The Thorne house and the surrounding old locust and fruit trees are the only visible evidence of the existence of the old Kellogg Hotel established in 1866 by Langdon Jack Kellogg, a leading citizen of Hayfork. The house was originally the carriage house for the hotel and is situated behind the site of the hotel which burned on June 27, 1921. The lean-to room was originally the section for the unharnessing of the buggies. The house has had very few alterations other than the enclosure of the lean-to which serves as the main entrance to the residence.

Site 23. Blanchard Flat School

The school building has been moved from Blanchard Flat on Readings Creek near Douglas City to the Hayfork Community Park in Hayfork.

The original Blanchard Flat School, instituted in 1901, was located on Blanchard Flat, six miles south of Douglas City. It was a one teacher school, handling ten and later eight grades simultaneously. Made of rough-cut lumber, it had desks made by local carpenters, wood heat, and a small wash basin in the corner. This school was replaced by the present log school built in the early 1930's as a Works Progress Administration project, and remained part of the Douglas City School District until purchased in 1974 by a group of Hayfork citizens. They arranged for the relocation of the school to its present site. Its exterior refurbishment was a community project. Turn of the century desks were placed inside. Future efforts will be directed towards completing the interior in keeping with the one teacher school so characteristic of early day education in Trinity County and elsewhere. The bell placed in the newly added belfry is from Hayfork's first school house in the early 1870's, according to Hayfork history buffs.

Site 24. Charles Albiez Barn (Wines Barn)

This old barn is down the first lane to the left off of Hyampom Road after it leaves Highway 3. It sits in declining condition surrounded by several houses and other small buildings.

According to Cox, the west end of Hayfork Valley in the 1850's was occupied by the ranches of B. M. George, George Williams, Jacob Hilliard and Caleb Duncan.

In 1878 Adam Bayles sold the James Howe Ranch to Nicholas C. Wines who probably built the barn. Nicholas and Christina Wines gave the Catholic Church a parcel for its purposes in 1909. They sold out to Margaret Miller and Elizabeth Williams in 1910 and moved to San Francisco.

Erhard Albiez had a ranch on Tule Creek before 1894. Karl, his brother, began acquiring land in the township in 1908 and continued to expand through the years. The Albiez holdings were broken up around 1960. In the meantime, Elizabeth Williams had gained control of family lands. She sold off parcels to Andy and Helgaar Norgaar in 1925 and to John Rourke and Crawford in 1936.

Site 25. Charles Laffranchini Ranch (Pony Ranch)

The ranch house is located on the Hyampom road out from Hayfork.

The Pony Ranch originally belonged to Henry Knowles who sold it to Judd Van Matre, member of a pioneer Trinity family. In 1910 Van Matre built all of the present ranch house except the upstairs, stopping because his wife, a member of the prominent Kellogg family, ran off with the blacksmith. Van Matre sold out, giving up the ranch to go into the cattle business and to run a butcher shop in Harrison Gulch with his son Warren. The new owner of the ranch and house, Charley Laffranchini, finished it in 1911. Laffranchini later sold to Waldo Jones who raised ponies giving it its present name.

The Pony Ranch house is the only Victorian in the entire Hayfork Valley and occupies a prominent place above the road which leaves the west end of the valley.

Site 26. Japanese Balloon Landing Site

A site marker is on the fairgrounds in Hayfork. The actual site is two and a half miles away to the northwest on the Charles Laffranchini Ranch.

Following the Doolittle raid of April 18, 1942, when 16 American bombers attacked Japan proper, the Japanese High Command decided to bring the Pacific War to the American people. In September, 1942, the aircraft-carrying Imperial submarine I-25 was off the California-Oregon border and launched its aircraft. The pilot dropped incendiary bombs which started a forest fire in Siskiyou County. The cost of sending submarines with but a single aircraft was too high, so Japanese scientists developed the first transoceanic missile — the free floating gas filled paper balloon under which dangled incendiary and high explosive bombs. The large balloons rode the jet stream and some crossed the ocean from Japan in as little as one and one-half days. Fugo ("wind-ship weapon") was a mysterious, subversive weapon. After the last bomb dropped, the entire mechanism and balloon self-destructed. Some balloons malfunctioned, however, and the Hayfork balloon caught in the top of an old snag on February 1, 1945. Suddenly, the gas bag exploded and all the ballast gear (including bombs) crashed to the ground without going off. The next day a United States Army balloon recovery team picked up the parts. The Hayfork incident is memorable. It was one of the first recoveries of an entire load of instruments and bombs. By the end of the war nearly 350 balloon incidents were documented in 26 states and provinces.

Site 25. Charles Laffranchini, the 1911 owner of the ranch, completed what is now the only Victorian house in Hayfork Valley.

Site 27. Griffith Barn (Boyce Barn) (Carr Barn) (Augustine Barn)

This very old barn sits on River Running Ranch above Hayfork Creek along the road from Hyampom to Big Bar and is a short distance from the village of Hyampom.

The barn is built of poles and hand-hewn timbers with vertical plank siding and shake roof. The ranch was homesteaded in 1894 by Frank Griffith; the barn was probably built within the first few years. The ranch belonged later to Goe, Boyce, Carr, and then Augustine c. 1938. The ranch has been split up with the barn being used now by the River Running Ranch School.

Site 28. Zachariah McKay House (Gene Greenleaf House)

This log house has had some additions, especially in the 1930's, but the main building is the oldest in Hyampom and one of the oldest in Trinity County. One may find it on the Hyampom to Hayfork road in the eastern part of Hyampom near the cemetery.

McKay came west as a wagonmaster and settled in Hyampom around 1857. He fought for the freedom of an Indian woman named Mary and married her. Together they built a new home to replace one lost in a flood. This second home burned, so the present McKay house built in the 1860's is the third to occupy this site. The house is built of hand-hewn logs, wooden pegs, and square nails. The large adobe fireplace is a rarity.

Zachariah McKay died in 1895 at the age of 73, and Mary McKay died in 1934 at the age of 95. Both are buried in the McKay cemetery on the ranch which has become the county cemetery.

Site 29. Hyampom Schoolhouse (Hyampom Community Church)

The schoolhouse is the second oldest building in Hyampom and is located in the western part of the village near the South Fork of the Trinity River.

The old schoolhouse was built in 1903 and used as a school until 1953. In 1957 the one room school became the Hyampom Community Church and has been used for church services, weddings and funerals since that time.

Site 30. LaVerne Laffranchini House (Vaughn House)

The Vaughn ranch house is on Tule Creek Road which intersects Highway 3 west of Hayfork.

William Overton Vaughn was an early settler in Trinity in the 1870's. Originally from Virginia, he came west in 1861 and later moved to Indian Valley, southwest of Hayfork, where he built a good house and barn. He then bought out Kellogg and acquired what is still known as the Vaughn ranch on Tule Creek where he raised cattle. This ranch was purchased by his son, Willis H. Vaughn, who continued to raise cattle and hay. He built the present house in 1891. It is now owned and resided in by his granddaughter. It is one of the few pre-1900 houses still standing in the valley.

Site 31. Jessee Ranch House

The ranch is reached from Highway 3 by way of Tule Creek Road to Jessee Road.

In 1908 two men, Joseph Bebeau and Frederick Holmes, were murdered in their own house located on what is now the Jessee Ranch. The murder was never solved and the ranch house burned to the ground a year later. Bob Crews bought the ranch at auction after the murders. In about 1920 he built a small house and later pulled a small wagon shed over and added it to the house. This

Site 28. Zachariah McKay built this house of logs in the 1860's. In the 1930's several additions were made.

Site 29. Hyampom Community Church was originally the school serving this function for fifty years.

house is now the main ranch house. Through the years Georgia Jessee and a hired man, Al Russell from Tennessee, fashioned wood carvings that decorate most of the interior. Georgia made the designs and Al did the carving. The house is famous for this interior woodwork. The house has a unique individuality on the outside as well. Its charm is derived mostly from the pattern of the pole construction of the veranda.

Site 31. The Jessee Ranch house is the result of combining buildings and making additions. The charm, especially of the interior, is the result of Georgia Jessee's inspiration.

Site 31. The barn on the Ray Jessee Ranch.

Site 32. John Rourke House

This location is the older of the Rourke homesites and is the first to be reached as one goes along Salt Creek driving south from Hayfork toward Peanut on Highway 3.

Part of the original Rourke Ranch was known as the Jacob Hilliard place. It was purchased by Dennis Rourke in 1876. Dennis, a native of Ireland, came to America in 1848 and to California in November, 1853. In 1854 he came to Trinity. He mined in the Douglas City area and later, in the 1860's, he moved to the Hayfork Valley. In 1876, anxious to begin farming, he purchased the Hilliard place. He began to increase the acreage of his ranch by purchasing two other homesteads and planting the majority of the land in grain. He and his wife, Mary Ann, lived in the Hilliard cabin (still standing) until the early 1880's when he built the large two and one-half story home for the family. This house was a center of social activity in the valley as well as the scene of many family gatherings. Unfortunately, it burned May 15, 1921. The present home was built as a replacement shortly thereafter and its simplicity reflects both the disappointment the family felt at losing their home and the hard times in the valley. The large barn, built in 1888, burned December 19, 1964.

After the death of Dennis in December, 1900, the ranch was run by Mary Ann with the help of the children, especially Denny and John Donald. Denny moved to his own adjoining ranch in 1917, and John stayed on the home place which Denny and John continued to farm together.

A 1928 Chamber of Commerce publication notes another ranch activity pursued by John Donald: "The racing stock of the John Donald Rourke Ranch is rapidly attaining fame for their owner and for the valley of Hayfork. Babe O'Rourke and Orphan Girl have been consistent winners throughout Northern California and Oregon the last two seasons. This ranch has also produced several winning relay teams and is raising pinto horses that are nearly thoroughbred; the latter are proving very popular for show and trick horses."

After the death of both Dennis and John, Dennis' youngest son, John David, took over the ranch. The Rourke Ranch has been in the Rourke family 103 years at the time of this writing. It is still run by Dennis' grandson, John David, and is truly a landmark in the county. The Rourke Ranch is a good example of an old time working ranch in the Hayfork Valley, Trinity's finest agricultural area.

The Rourke ranch house is a typical example of an early 1900's Trinity County board and batten house. It is a simple rectangle with a veranda covering one side and a gable roof. Its extremely simple features, such as exposed rafters and plain trim, are indicative of a functional architecture and frugal living of a Trinity farm family.

Site 33. Dennis Rourke House (Hayfork Creamery)

The Dennis Rourke house is south from Hayfork along Salt Creek and Highway 3.

This ranch was originally known as the Ben Stinchacum place and was purchased in 1917 by Denny and Sophia Rourke. Denny was the son of Dennis Rourke who had come to Trinity County in 1854 and, in 1876, had taken up a ranch neighboring this one to the north. When Denny decided to move off the family place and build a new home, he bought the old Hayfork Creamery building which was located near the mouth of Big Creek at the east end of the valley. He tore down the creamery and salvaged the lumber. He also milled

Site 33. The Dennis Rourke house started with lumber from the Hayfork Creamery building moved over from Big Creek.

Site 33. The barn on the Dennis Rourke Ranch, an imposing tall building, is now nearly 100 years old.

lumber for this house which he built on the site of the old log cabin. Denny and Sophia built up a fine ranch that was described by the Chamber of Commerce as follows: "The Dennis Rourke Ranch, while mostly given to the production of wheat, has also as profitable sidelines, a turkey flock, goat and dairy herds. Salt Creek furnishes water for alfalfa and garden. The Rourke sawmill on this ranch has furnished a great part of the lumber used in the Hayfork Valley."

The original date of the creamery building is not known but the company was incorporated in 1896. The house has remained unaltered since 1917. The site is shared by a barn of unusual vertical proportions, probably built by Ben Stinchacum, and that probably dates from the 1890's at least. The whole ranch is a well known place, particularly because of its association with the old-time Rourke family.

Site 34. Cuff Barn

The Cuff barn can be seen from Highway 3 and Highway 36 on the west side of Salt Creek. It is all that remains of Peanut.

The Cuff family was a well known ranching family in the Peanut area and at one time had the post office in their house. The site of the house, which no longer stands, is beneath some old trees. The fields around the barn were planted to alfalfa. The Cuffs kept these fields and those of the Grigsbys in Dobbins' Gulch in immaculate condition, averaging five cuttings of alfalfa annually. The big Cuff barn is not as old as it looks, having been built to replace the original barn which had burned in 1921. The barn stands out prominently on the approach to the area once known as Peanut and is all that remains of the small settlement whose name continues to intrigue many.

Site 35. Patton Barn

This barn is all that remains of the Patton ranch buildings. It is located on Post Mountain Road near Highway 3.

Sarah Patton, a widow with four boys, moved to Trinity from Fort Bragg in 1887. She purchased this ranch from Willis Vaughn who lived here before he acquired the original Vaughn ranch on Tule Creek from his father, William Overton Vaughn. Sarah's four sons were Bill, Sam, Rayce and Arthur. Bill, the only one to stay in Trinity, married Lottie Vaughn and took over the Patton Place. He raised cattle and ran them in the Indian Valley country, land held by the Vaughn family. Bill was also the first Forest Ranger in this part of the county and, by all accounts, was respected and able. Bill's son, Ralph, took up the Dillar place from Schennaman further down Salt Creek. The family still resides in Hayfork.

Site 36. Old State Highway 36

By a fluke of legislative oversight, Highway 36 was created running from Peanut to Mad River. It did not connect with a state highway at either end. One could reach Highway 99 at Red Bluff and Highway 101 at Fortuna by county roads. The State Highway crew maintained the gravel highway and it later was extended out Salt Creek to Wildwood, Platina and Red Bluff by the old pioneer route of the 1880's. The western end was connected out through Bridgeville and the Van Duzen River to Fortuna making Highway 36 a state highway from the coast to the Sacramento Valley.

In the last 25 years, Highway 36 has been rerouted drastically from Forest Glen by-passing Wildwood toward Red Bluff. In the process it has been paved. One passing through this way must watch for turn-offs to find the history of the area.

Site 36. The stop offered to occasional travellers at Auto Rest was a unique experience.

Site 36. Later the Arthur Jeans bought Auto Rest, built this log inn, and named it Forest Glen Inn.

The region around Forest Glen is a very attractive area for isolated recreation. Charles Brewer started Auto Rest near the Highway 36 crossing of South Fork. An open-sided log structure offering meals welcomed the occasional traveler in 1912. In 1912 Arthur Jeans acquired the resort which operated on National Forest land by special use permit.

During the time of the Jeans family's ownership, 1912 to 1918, the log hotel was built above the highway. Andy Damgaard and Carl (John) Sihlis bought the resort in 1918. The Jeans family moved to Mad River.

Damgaard and Sihlis changed the name to Forest Glen and expanded the resort by adding several cabins. Years later, Damgaard was stricken and Carl Sihlis died. The Carl Sihlis estate and Damgaard sold Forest Glen to the Ray Leiths and the Robert Robertsons in 1945. Harold and Carol Huggler bought the resort in 1947. The Inn burned in January 1950 during the heavy snow storms of that winter. Hugglers never rebuilt the hotel, but sold the remaining facilities to the William Clausens in 1963. After the business failed, the location was cleared of buildings except for the old Forest Service Guard Station which was built in 1916.

In the 40 years after 1912 Forest Glen and South Fork were a favorite vacation retreat for relatively few families who knew of its attractions and were willing to make the journey in from the modern highways. The resort had its regulars as did the Forest Service camp across the river, the summer cabins upstream, and Ostrat's up the South Fork trail.

The Forest Glen area was never much of a mineral producing region. George Bergin operated the Klondike Mine several miles downstream from Forest Glen for the Little Klondike Mining Company. A short time after the South Fork was diverted through a four mile flume for hydraulic mining, operations ceased and the mine was abandoned. It did not produce well enough to meet expenses.

Site 37. Duncan House

This house is on 13 Dips Road (old Hayfork-Wildwood Road) and is on the Duncan Ranch near the present ranch house.

The Duncans are an old family in the Hayfork Valley. The first to arrive in the county was named Caleb Duncan. Originally from Scotland, he made his way to California via Georgia and Arkansas arriving in Trinity County in the early 1860's. He was interested in ranching, not mining. The Bill Duncan Ranch was started by Bill, Caleb's grandson, on land bought from Jeremiah Damsel. Bill was the father of Morris Duncan, the present owner. Bill and his father, Alfred, built the house when Bill was married and desired to move from the family ranch on lower Salt Creek. The house, basically a very functional structure, is unoccupied at present.

Site 38. Latimer Homestead (Schmidt House)

This remnant of log construction is located on 13 Dips Road.

The only portion of the original structure that exists is the west wall at the back of the center of the building. It was constructed of logs, notched to fit flush. The logs are chinked with a special cedar bark which has discouraged mold and decay. One window is centered on the wall and is not original.

The log construction in the Latimer homestead cabin was typical of many homesteads built during this time. The wall of the Schmidt cabin is the only surviving example of log construction successfully chinked with bark. Latimer bought the land from Bob Crews but left after he was accused of a murder in Indian Valley. The ranch returned then to Crews' ownership. It is now the home of Willard Schmidt.

326

Site 39. The barn on the Drinkwater Ranch, now known as the New Pioneer Ranch.

Site 39. Drinkwater Ranch (Damsel House, Trask, Byard, New Pioneer Ranch)

The ranch house with its barn is on old Highway 36 on 13 Dips Road east of Peanut.

The New Pioneer Ranch originally belonged to Joe Drinkwater, member of an early ranching family in Hayfork. Early general land office maps show this ranch as having miles of fence in the valley. Joe was killed during difficulties with the Indians over on the Van Duzen River and was buried in Bridgeville, or on the hill above this house according to another story.

Jeremiah Damsel bought the property from the Drinkwaters in 1887. This was the year that old Highway 36 was finished from Red Bluff. Now commonly called 13 Dips Road, this road was largely built by the people. Since the days of Jerry Damsel, subsequent owners have been Trask, Byard, and Robert Hooper, the present owner.

The house, probably built by Damsel, is a good, unaltered example of an 1880's Trinity County ranch house. The barn which shares the house site is one of the three oldest barns in the Hayfork Valley. It is constructed with the mortise and tenon system and wooden pegs. Still standing strong, it is testament to the worth of this building method.

Site 40. Deer Lick Springs

Deer Lick Springs is a health spa compound spread over about 100 acres. The springs are located off Deer Lick Springs Road twenty miles south of Highway 3, or they can be reached from Highway 36 near Wildwood.

The property was homesteaded by John Coumbs in 1882 after he had visited the area on a hunting trip. In the fall of 1885, Coumbs, his brother Tom, and a nephew began work on a two story log cabin which they completed in 1887. In his homestead papers, Coumbs also testified to other improvements: another house, barn, outhouses, fencing, two irrigation ditches, orchard with nine acres cleared, and five acres under cultivation.

The property contains a number of natural mineral springs around which Coumbs built a resort business based on their medicinal benefits. The water from the springs was used for bathing and for drinking. The springs became a very popular resort; some families were annual visitors over many years. In 1900 there was a definite need for lodgings. Access to the resort was still by trail up Brown's Creek from the Dinkel Place or by trail from Harrison Gulch.

In 1909 Russell Joy, a mining man of Reno, Nevada, purchased Coumbs

Site 40. The mineral baths at Coumbs Springs (now Deer Lick Springs) are essentially the same today as they were 90 years ago although the buildings, tubs, and type of fuel used have each been changed.

Site 40. The large cabin at Deer Lick Springs is now nearly 100 years old.

Springs and formed the California Medicinal Springs Co. He also initiated the building of a wagon road to the main road to Weaverville and Tower House. The springs were first renamed Mystic Springs and then Deer Lick Springs.

The water was touted for its effects on blood diseases and in 1926 the company announced plans to ship 2000 bottles a day to New York. The Owl Drug Company was handling the sales and distribution with more volume planned if sales warranted expansion. By 1934 the company had ceased activity. The springs were later sold to George Williams. The present owners are Claude and Virsa Patton Douglas. It is still possible to take the healing baths, drink the waters, and vacation at the resort.

There are four important structure areas at Deer Lick Springs: the bathhouse area, the Coumbs cabin, the mineral water bottling structure, and the headquarters of the resort.

The bath site consists of three buildings on a narrow ledge just above Brown's Creek. The pungent smelling sulphur springs are warmed in the heating shed and transported by gravity through troughs to two small bath houses and then allowed to descend into Brown's Creek.

The Coumbs cabin consists of a large offset gable structure constructed of logs. Some of the largest timbers possible in such hand-built work were utilized in its construction. The logs are about one and a half feet thick and two and a half feet high. The foundation is a series of giant square-hewn logs which are so well preserved they are nearly petrified. The door jambs and window frames are all hand-planed.

The Bottle Company, as it is called, is a one room, one and a half story, log cabin. The logs are more round than square and fairly uniform in size. The cabin is set near the creek in a flat among the trees.

The fourth building area is the headquarters of the resort and is of a later construction than the historical buildings described above. It consists of a store, restaurant, and dance floor.

Deer Lick Springs is literally miles off the beaten track and is reached over dirt roads. It is a prime example of an old time mineral springs resort that seems untouched by time. It is set in a beautiful wooded area where the deer still come to enjoy the naturally salty seepage from the many springs.

Site 41. Hall City

Hall City Creek road leaves Wildwood on the east side of Hayfork Creek. Hall City is on a dead end spur to Hall City Caves. Decaying lumber from a collapsed building and mine dumps on each side of the end of the road mark the location.

Hall City was established in 1896 by W. R. Hall, former County Clerk of Tehama County and Edgar Landis of Wildwood. Since the location was about three miles from the Midas Mine and other mines in Harrison Gulch, it was thought to be on the same vein. The miners were hoping that they had another French Gulch and Deadwood Gulch grouping.

In 1897 there were thirty locations with six buildings constructed. J. E. McCabe operated the only store. Hall had purchased the Kendall Mine and a miner named Green was processing his own ore with an arrastre. The ore was said to be rich but in a narrow ledge which made recovery of the gold difficult. A shaft was sunk for several hundred feet in one of the locations but the area never really paid off. The settlement was finished by 1915.

Site 42. Hall City Caves

The caves are reached only by trail and are located up on the mountain on the left side of the creek above Hall City.

Hall City Caves were once associated with the Hall City mining project in that the miners thought that the crystal pool in the cave was an artesian spring; they hoped to be able to siphon the water out of the caves for use at the mine. An attempt was also made to tap this water supply by tunnelling into the mountain but the supply was too small to be practical.

The caves are an interesting and popular natural feature of Trinity County. There are legends having to do with lost treasures. According to one, two Indian fugitives hid in the caves after robbing and murdering a miner. After capture, they claimed to have hidden $40,000 (old value) in gold in the pool, but it has never been found.

Site 43. Powers Mill

The location of this mill on the hill above Wildwood going toward Red Bluff is marked by groups of apple trees and a small pond.

The Powers Mill was involved with production of timbers for the Midas Mine, a major customer. There were also several wood camps in the area producing firewood for the mine. Powers sold the mill to Hoxie. It burned and Hoxie built a new mill on Goods Creek.

Site 43. One of the major economic activities of the Wildwood area was to supply mine timbers and fuel to the mines along Harrison Gulch. Here Brice Trimble and Austin Peters are returning for another load.

Site 44. Knight Ranch

The ranch was located on both sides of the road to Red Bluff up the hill to the east of Wildwood. Several old fruit trees mark the spot today.

Around the turn of the century, Billy Knight's ranch was a stopping place for travellers. Accommodations were available for travellers and their teams. Knight also had a large waterwheel in the creek, hoping that he could generate power to run a sawmill. He hoped in vain.

Site 45. Riewerts Ranch

This ranch is located along Hayfork Creek about a mile upstream from Wildwood, and is readily seen from the new Highway 36 where it crosses the creek.

The homestead was that of Gossier, or Garcia, Mrs. Riewerts' father. Pete Riewerts was a competent farmer who raised cattle for many years. His son George ran the farm until recently, and it continues as an operating cattle ranch. There is an interesting long ranch house that grew like a train as additions were made to care for the growing family.

Site 46. Roy Shiell Ranch

The newer Roy Shiell ranch lies right along the County Road and Hayfork Creek about a mile downstream from Wildwood. The old ranch had been downstream from Wildwood about four miles. The Shiell family lived on Hayfork Creek for many years. Roy Shiell grew up there and in the 1920's bought the Elkins place up near Wildwood. Prior to that time, a Mr. Wilson apparently owned it for it was acquired by Elkins after a bank had foreclosed on Wilson. A nearby creek bears Wilson's name. From the late 1920's Roy Shiell and his parents lived on the ranch, since known as the Roy Shiell Ranch.

Site 47. Gemmell Flat (Gimball)

Gemmell Flat is located along Hayfork Creek several miles below Wildwood. Gemmell Flat Picnic Ground along the County Road and some apple trees make locating this spot possible.

Bob Gemmell had a little ranch and sawmill here before 1894. Lumber milled here was used in building up the area.

Site 48. Shiell or Shields Ranch

The old Shiell ranch, Francis R. Shiell's homestead, is across Hayfork Creek to the east after passing East Fork on the slope of Chanchelulla. The open meadow area is clearly seen from a point on the highway and the buildings are tucked into the hill to the south.

Site 49. McCampbell Ranch (Leach Ranch)

This ranch is located on the road up Hayfork Creek from Highway 3 at the junction of East Fork and Hayfork Creek. It lies on a large flat on the west side of East Fork which bore the name Murrison Flat. It was the McCampbell home in the 1890's. There is no house there but the barn remains in good condition.

This area was the location of a cluster of homes. Several miles up the East Fork was the Wells Ranch and several miles downstream around Carrier Gulch James A. "Doc" Stafford had his place.

Site 44. The Billy Knight Ranch was a stopping place for travellers between Hayfork and the Sacramento Valley.

Site 45. This view of the Riewerts Ranch buildings is from the new route of Highway 36. The ranch is located on the upper part of the Hayfork Creek drainage.

Site 48. This is an early view of the Francis R. Shiell Homestead.

Site 50. Natural Bridge

The Natural Bridge spans Bridge Gulch and is off the Wildwood road several miles from Highway 3.

"Ages ago a trickle of water in a fork of Hayfork Creek found its way through a crevice in a limestone dike across a wooded canyon. Slowly, the bed of the stream was widened and flow increased until a fair sized cavern was worn above the creek bed, leaving the overhanging limestone dike as a natural bridge." (Hamilton Hintz). The bridge has a span of approximately 150 feet and is approximately 30 to 35 feet high forming a perfect arch. Under the bridge is a spacious cave approximately 40 feet in diameter as well as a deep canyon, heavily wooded and somewhat dark. It is a place of incredible beauty.

"The Natural Bridge has long been regarded as one of the choice natural scenic objects in Trinity County." (Barlett). Not only is the limestone bridge an amazing work of nature, but it is also associated with an important Trinity County historical event, the Bridge Gulch Massacre.

The Natural Bridge is now maintained by the Forest Service as a tourist attraction. A number of old-time names can be seen carved in the bridge, some dating from as early as 1852.

Site 51. Bridge Gulch Massacre Site

The site is located near the Natural Bridge on Bridge Gulch. It may be reached from Highway 3 by the road to Wildwood which intersects Highway 3 several miles east of Hayfork.

For approximately fifteen years after the county was first settled, there was, as might be expected, conflict with the native Indians resulting in death and destruction for both sides. Among the most famous and infamous incidents was the massacre of 153 Indians at this spot in 1852 in retaliation for the killing of a prominent citizen, Colonel Anderson, ironically a butcher by trade. Responsible for the massacre were the members of the Bridge Gulch expedition, under Sheriff Dixon, who had followed the trail of the Indians from north of Weaverville over Hayfork Mountain and up Bridge Gulch. Sheriff Dixon and his men were the first white men to discover the wonders of the Natural Bridge. The expedition surprised the Indians who were camping on a small flat above the bridge. Only two (some accounts say three) Indians survived this raid including one infant who was renamed Ellen Clifford and who lived in Weaverville until her death in 1927. Six years after the incident, with Indian troubles still occurring, Cox wrote of the Indians: "The rascals had committed a glaring infraction into the peace and security of the county, and to chastise them was proper and laudable." Contemporary accounts thus furnish us with history by the victor and an excellent example of white man's perspective of its manifest destiny. But Cox's annotator, James Bartlett, wrote in 1926, "The massacre . . .was an event that has never been forgotten in Trinity County. No one in their far-removed days can have feelings other than those of regret at the killing of the Indian women and children. The incident shows what men stirred by passion will do when acting without law." Bartlett did not absolve the Indians of responsibility, pointing out the many depredations committed in the crossing of the plains, but did present a more balanced view of this key event.

Gracie McKibbin, the last full-blooded Indian of the Hayfork area tribe has another version of the massacre. She recounts the story as told to her by an uncle who survived the disaster as a ten year old. According to him the young warriors who were guilty of the murder of Colonel Anderson passed by Bridge Gulch fleeing on up Hayfork Creek in the night. The large band camped in the Gulch were mainly women and children and were apparently unaware of danger as the men were away hunting. The people were attacked at daybreak with a loss of life totalling nearly 300. This account of the massacre describes a much higher loss of life than does the first account. Apparently, the raiders who stole the cattle and killed Anderson escaped punishment, at least for the time being.

Site 51. In the small basin above the barrier of the Natural Bridge scores of Indians were killed at daybreak in 1852 by a sheriff's party.

Ranchers in southwestern Trinity thresh and sack grain on one of the many homesteads scattered throughout the rolling hills.

RUTH VALLEY

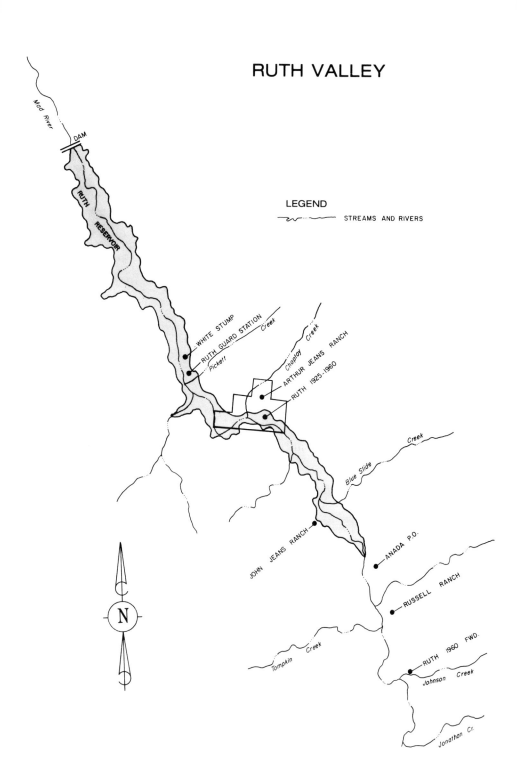

LEGEND

STREAMS AND RIVERS

Mad River

DAM

RUTH RESERVOIR

WHITE STUMP
RUTH GUARD STATION
Pickett
Creek

Choploy Creek

ARTHUR JEANS RANCH

RUTH 1925-1960

Blue Slide
Creek

JOHN JEANS RANCH

ANADA P.O.

RUSSELL RANCH

Tompkin Creek

RUTH 1960 FWD.

Johnson Creek

Jonathan Cr.

N

AREA VII
SOUTHERN TRINITY

Historical Overview

Beginning with the absence of Southern Trinity from the pages of Cox's "Annals", and continuing with the indifference or ignorance of many today, there has been a distinct failure on the part of the rest of Trinity County to appreciate the rich history of that portion lying south of South Fork Mountain.

One of the principal reasons for such a separation from an area that represents one-quarter of Trinity County is the imposing physical barrier, South Fork Mountain, known to be the longest continuous ridge in the United States. Cut off to the north by this mountain, and especially from the county seat at Weaverville, it was natural for the southern part of Trinity County to orient itself to Mendocino County to the south and Humboldt County to the west. Bridgeville, Alderpoint, Fortuna and Covelo were much more easily accessible as trading centers than were Weaverville, Hayfork, or other Trinity County settlements to the north. Not only did the absence of any natural passes over South Fork Mountain discourage settlement from the north, but neither was there the lure of gold to draw miners to the area. The most recent mineral resources map of Trinity County published by the State Division of Mines and Geology shows only nineteen mines in the area south of the mountain, as compared with hundreds in the area to the north. Instead, the wealth of Southern Trinity lay in what James Bartlett called "the splendid grazing lands" with its plentiful feed so ideal for sheep and cattle. It is not surprising then that many of the earlier settlers were ranchers from Humboldt and Mendocino Counties.

With the possible exception of explorers from the Hudson's Bay Company who may have been in the area as early as 1833, the first white men to reach this part of the county were those of the Asbill-Kelsey party in 1854. Brothers Frank and Pierce Asbill were explorers and hunters who were leading a party north through the Russian River Valley when they met and joined the Kelsey party. Samuel Kelsey had been hired by a group of enterprising Petaluma merchants to locate a trail from Petaluma to Weaverville. Kelsey was also

South of SOUTH FORK MOUNTAIN

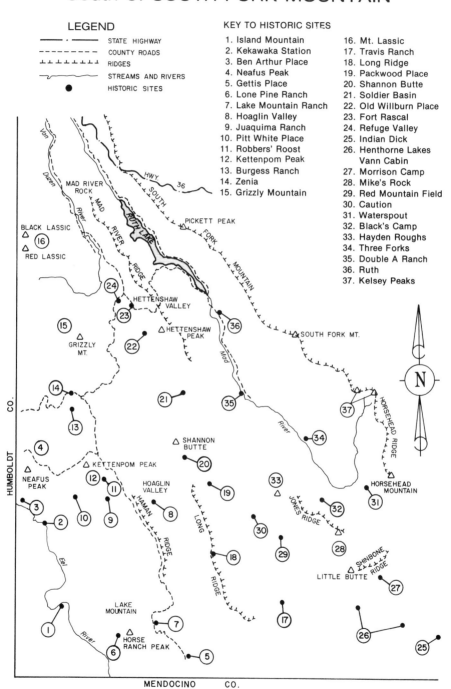

LEGEND

— · — STATE HIGHWAY
– – – – – – COUNTY ROADS
⊥⊥⊥⊥⊥⊥ RIDGES
∿∿ STREAMS AND RIVERS
● HISTORIC SITES

KEY TO HISTORIC SITES

1. Island Mountain
2. Kekawaka Station
3. Ben Arthur Place
4. Neafus Peak
5. Gettis Place
6. Lone Pine Ranch
7. Lake Mountain Ranch
8. Hoaglin Valley
9. Juaquima Ranch
10. Pitt White Place
11. Robbers' Roost
12. Kettenpom Peak
13. Burgess Ranch
14. Zenia
15. Grizzly Mountain
16. Mt. Lassic
17. Travis Ranch
18. Long Ridge
19. Packwood Place
20. Shannon Butte
21. Soldier Basin
22. Old Willburn Place
23. Fort Rascal
24. Refuge Valley
25. Indian Dick
26. Henthorne Lakes Vann Cabin
27. Morrison Camp
28. Mike's Rock
29. Red Mountain Field
30. Caution
31. Waterspout
32. Black's Camp
33. Hayden Roughs
34. Three Forks
35. Double A Ranch
36. Ruth
37. Kelsey Peaks

North of SOUTH FORK MOUNTAIN

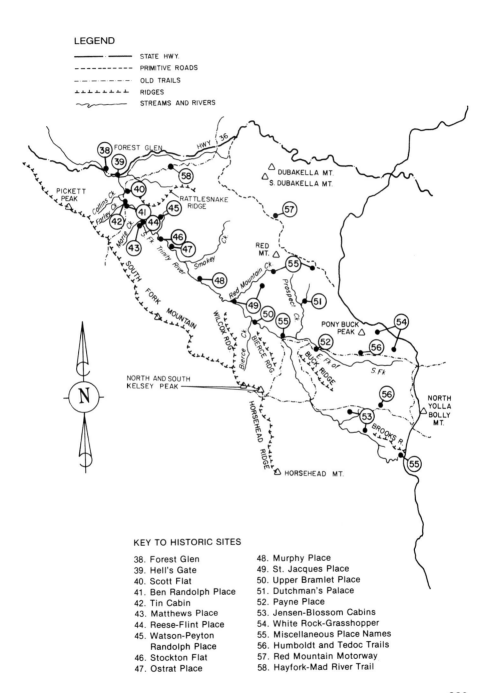

LEGEND

——— · ———	STATE HWY.
— — — — —	PRIMITIVE ROADS
— · — · — · —	OLD TRAILS
⊥⊥⊥⊥⊥⊥⊥	RIDGES
～～～	STREAMS AND RIVERS

KEY TO HISTORIC SITES

38. Forest Glen
39. Hell's Gate
40. Scott Flat
41. Ben Randolph Place
42. Tin Cabin
43. Matthews Place
44. Reese-Flint Place
45. Watson-Peyton
    Randolph Place
46. Stockton Flat
47. Ostrat Place

48. Murphy Place
49. St. Jacques Place
50. Upper Bramlet Place
51. Dutchman's Palace
52. Payne Place
53. Jensen-Blossom Cabins
54. White Rock-Grasshopper
55. Miscellaneous Place Names
56. Humboldt and Tedoc Trails
57. Red Mountain Motorway
58. Hayfork-Mad River Trail

thinking about a better route from the Sacramento Valley to the coast than one that had been established by a Josiah Gregg. Upon reaching the Hettenshaw Valley area of southern Trinity County, the Asbills decided to part from Kelsey and his men and to winter in the valley for the purpose of hunting deer for their hides. Although the Asbills moved out of Hettenshaw in 1855, others began to arrive and by 1858 there were several settlers in the area.

The Indians of the area posed a threat to the settlers here as they did in other parts of the county. At the same time the Indians rebelled at the encroachment on their lands by the whites. The Indian Wars of the 1850's and 1860's were the result. Although Trinity County was never the site of a permanent U. S. Army Post, there were at least six posts not far from county boundaries, and military expeditions into the county did result in the establishment of a number of outposts or camps. It was not until the mid-1860's that the roundup of the Indians and their transfer to reservations was complete enough for settlers and ranchers to move into the area in earnest. The Indians, however, continued to have a place in the history of the area. Some ran away from the reservations and returned to their southern Trinity home and others, of course, successfully eluded the military. Most importantly, many early settlers took Indian women as wives. Indian blood runs deep in Southern Trinity to this day.

Because of the rough nature of the terrain, most of the ranches and settlements were located in pockets on the hillsides, in small valleys, or along the waterways. The heavily forested or brush covered nature of this terrain precluded settlement elsewhere. The terrain contributed to the development of a rough, tough, half-outlaw style of living in much of the area. There were, of course, many respectable ranching families who settled in southern Trinity. Disputes, however, did arise over grazing rights, water rights and lands. This led to some violence and several killings which, in the period from 1870 to the early 90's, gave the area a poor image in the rest of the county.

Ranching still characterizes southern Trinity and is its major industry. The original network of trails still survives for the most part and is used by descendants of the early ranchers and homesteaders.

The area north of South Fork Mountain developed differently. It is a long, heavily forested drainage with steep slopes and a number of small pieces of open ground that are interspersed along the length of the South Fork River which drains this watershed. For the purpose of this chapter we are confining our coverage to that portion of the drainage above Forest Glen. (For the area below Forest Glen see Chapter VI.) Settlement of this part of the county did not really begin until after the turn of the century, much later than it did south of the mountain. Occupation of the land was largely confined to a limited number of pieces of desirable ground scattered along the river. The river was the predominant geographical feature which drew these early settlers to the area. Beyond the river scattered grasslands made ideal pastures which were used as summer range for cattle and sheep. Old Indian trails became driveways for stock driven into the high country from the Sacramento Valley. These trails, in turn, gave homesteaders access to the country.

With the establishment of the Trinity National Forest in 1905 changes began to occur. Since much of the area lay within the newly established national forest the Forest Service role in the area became an important one. A number of abandoned cabin sites were utilized as ranger stations and a grazing permit system was initiated. This controlled the number of animals permitted on the range and prevented the overgrazing that had threatened for a time. What at first had been primarily sheep range gradually became range for cattle.

Sheep and cattle raising brought many early ranchers to extreme southwest Trinity. The Kindergan place is one such early ranch.

This log cabin on the Chappell ranch near Island Mountain is typical of log cabins built by the early homesteaders throughout the county.

Today, forest use is no longer confined to grazing. In the 1930's road construction began to provide access for logging and recreation. Construction of these logging roads and more modern logging equipment have combined to give timber harvesting greater importance. The area, however, is still sparsely populated and habitation is still largely confined to land along the river.

Site 1. Island Mountain

Island Mountain is located in the extreme southwest corner of Trinity County. The only access to it is from Humboldt County over the narrow, winding Island Mountain Road. The Eel River which cuts across this corner of the county isolates this community from the rest of Trinity County. Agriculture, mining activity, and the construction of a main-line railroad through the area are responsible for the existence of this small community.

Sheep and cattle raising were once associated with such well-known early Trinity County names as Ramsay, Robinson, Charlton, Devoy, Drewry and Kindergan. The Robinson Ranch was the location of the first post office in the area, then known as Irma. The name was changed to Island Mountain when, in August, 1915, the post office was moved down the mountain to the railroad depot which had been constructed at the river.

Copper mining became an important industry at Island Mountain at about the turn of the century. The presence of copper in the area was noticed sometime prior to 1897 when a spring with a high copper content was found and given the name of Poison Spring. Many medicinal properties were attributed to this water. About 1897 Sam H. Price, while surveying the county boundary, noted the presence of some copper ore. He aroused the interest of F. A. Leach who later became one of the founders of the Island Mountain Consolidated Copper Co. In 1899 the London Exploration Company took an option on the property, but their 490' test tunnel did not reveal the wide vein of ore that had been expected. The U. S. Smelting and Refining Company of Devereau, Felton, and Associates also took out options but did no mining. It was not until 1914, when the Northwestern Pacific Railroad line was completed through Island Mountain, that mining began in earnest. The Island Mountain Consolidated Copper Company was formed and mined the area continuously from 1915 to October 31, 1930, except for a period of time between 1919 and 1922 when copper prices had dropped.

At first the ore was pushed in cars across a suspension bridge that had been used in the construction of the Island Mountain railroad tunnel. Later, ore was conveyed via an aerial tramway which extended 1500' from an ore bin at the mine to a large storage bin located on a railroad siding near the south end of the railroad trestle. W. W. Duncan, who was stationmaster for many years, recalled in a letter he wrote in 1951 that the mine produced 1400 cars of high grade ore which was shipped to a smelter in Tacoma, Washington, for processing. Total production of the mine from 1915 until 1930 was approximately 132,000 tons of ore which averaged 32.9% copper. From this ore approximately nine million pounds of copper were recovered as well as a considerable amount of gold. One old-timer, Fred Chappell, recalls that there was one shipment of seventeen express boxes of pure gold which was sent to the San Francisco Mint. According to Chappell, the saying went that "The gold paid the expenses and the copper was for free."

A huge landslide in 1937 completely buried the mine tunnels and shafts. All of the original mine buildings are gone. Streaks of copper color can still be seen coloring the hillside from the mine site to the river. Today, an attempt is being made to mine the area again.

Site 1. This picture was taken in the early 1940's when the Eel River, the railroad, and the store dominated the community of Island Mountain.

Site 1. Ten miles of railroad track traverse the extreme southwestern corner of Trinity County.

The completion of the railroad through Iron Mountain in 1914 is another significant part of Island Mountain's history. This section of line completed the railroad which connected San Francisco and Eureka. The Golden Spike was driven on Oct. 23, 1914, at Cain Rock. The first train from San Francisco arrived December 1, 1914. Regularly scheduled runs began in 1915 with the northbound train arriving each morning at 10:57 A.M. and the southbound train stopping at Island Mountain each afternoon at 3:46 P.M.. The depot at Island Mountain is Trinity County's only railroad station and the 10 miles of line which traverses Trinity County is the only railroad track in the county. Records show, however, that at one time there was a small station at Kekawaka as well as spur stations at Two Rocks and Quarry Spur. The Island Mountain station

343

Site 1. The construction of the Island Mountain tunnel, 4313 feet long, was a remarkable feat of early day engineering.

Site 1. This swinging bridge across the Eel River to the Island Mountain Copper Mine was destroyed by flood in 1937.

operated only intermittently; for nine of the years prior to 1934 it was closed. Since that date it has not had a regular schedule of operation except for the year 1937 when it was open full time. The large slide which occurred in the area in 1937 had brought an influx of railroad workers to Island Mountain. At that time employees numbered 484. Usually there were about 100 employees — 12 to 20 on the bridge gang and 60 to 80 on the extra gang.

Across from Island Mountain the Eel River makes a sharp horseshoe turn. Through the finger of land formed by this horseshoe there was constructed one of the largest railroad tunnels in the state. The Island Mountain tunnel, officially known as Tunnel #27, was built by the Utah Construction Company and is 4313.3' long. The construction of this tunnel took five years and was a remarkable feat of early day engineering. It was the completion of this tunnel which finally linked San Francisco and Eureka. The tunnel was damaged by fire of mysterious origin on September 6, 1978. Shoring timbers were burned and cave-ins occurred shutting down the tunnel until repairs were made.

The railroad, historically known as the Northwestern Pacific Railroad, was for many years the only access to the southwestern corner of Trinity County and was used for travel, mail delivery, supplies, and for the shipment of stock. In 1984 the line was sold to Bryan R. R. Whipple, a northern California financier, and the name changed to the Eureka Southern Railroad. Plagued by mudslides and washouts the new company filed for bankruptcy December 1, 1986. At the time of this writing the line continues in operation awaiting the outcome of the bankruptcy proceedings.

Site 2. Kekawaka Railroad Station

Located just north of Kekawaka Creek and the Eel River is the site of the Kekawaka Railroad Station. It was one of only two railroad stations in Trinity County. This stop along the Northwestern Pacific Railroad was used primarily

344

as a shipping point for cattle. Sheldon Potter, early owner of the Lone Pine Ranch, had a pasture here. There are still numerous corrals in a shaded area above the station site but the station itself no longer exists and all remains of the station building have disappeared. Kekawaka was also a freight and mail station. It appeared as a regularly scheduled stop in the published timetables of the Northwestern Pacific Railroad. Although the Island Mountain Station to the south of it was larger, Kekawaka was more important as a shipping point for cattle as it was located on the east side of the Eel River and cattle from the many ranches along Haman Ridge did not have to cross water to reach it.

Site 3. Ben Arthur Ranch (White Ranch)

The old Ben Arthur Ranch is located on the east side of the Eel River about five or six miles upstream from the town of Alderpoint. The property straddles the Humboldt-Trinity County line. Family history supplied by John Thomas, great-grandson of Ben Arthur, reveals that Ben Arthur had come to California from Ohio in 1843, going first to Los Angeles and then mining for gold along the Feather River, arriving finally in Round Valley in 1856. It was upon his marriage in 1870 to Elizabeth Murphy, the sister of his partner Dick Murphy, that Ben Arthur moved to the site of the Ben Arthur Ranch above Alderpoint. The property had previously belonged to Thomas Duncan from whom Ben purchased it.

The Arthur Ranch was a working sheep ranch. Many thousands of head of sheep were wintered on the ranch, and in the summer months the sheep were all driven to the Ruth Valley on what has become known as the Ben Arthur Trail. The trail followed a route from the ranch, through Soldier Basin, and came out in the Ruth Valley near the location of the present Ranger Station. By the 1880's, Ben had built up the sheep ranch to include well over 3000 acres.

In 1884 Ben had a run-in with a man named George Erickson who had been stealing his sheep. Erickson was taken to Weaverville and tried for sheep stealing. Although he was set free and warned not to return to southern Trinity County, Erickson did not heed the warning and was found dead near the Mad River Bridge on September 7, 1886. A man by the name of George Kunz was tried for this murder, and Ben Arthur, along with several other ranchers, was tried for conspiracy in the murder. As a result of Ben's efforts to defend himself, the ranch was mortgaged. In 1897 when Ben could not pay off the mortgage, the ranch was taken over by the German Savings and Loan Society (now the Bank of Hibernia). The Pitt White family acquired the ranch from the bank, and Floyd White, Pitt's youngest son, took over the ranch about 1938-39 as his share of the White estate. Floyd sold the ranch in later years to the Dean Witter family who are the present owners.

All that is left of the original ranch house are the foundation and stone fireplace. The old sheep shearing barn is still standing and is intact although it is leaning slightly. It is made of hand hewn lumber that is mortised and pegged and joined with square nails. The old apple orchard is still present, and the old carp ponds (Ben used to raise carp) can still be seen although they are now dry. Just down from the ponds, on an oak shaded knoll, is the grave of Susan Foster. Susan was Elizabeth (Murphy) Arthur's daughter by a previous marriage. She died from a rattlesnake bite on July 8, 1876, at the age of ten. The spot was a favorite of Elizabeth's and is marked by a marble headstone. When foreclosure of the mortgage required them to leave the ranch, Elizabeth would not go until Ben went to Eureka to get this headstone for her daughter's grave.

Site 4. Neafus Peak

Located just east of the county line in Sec. 5 of T26N, R6E, this peak was named after Jim Neafus, who was a member of the Asbill-Kelsey party and the first white man to discover many sites in southeastern Trinity County. (The Asbill party was the first to discover Round Valley, in May, 1854, and possibly the first in southern Trinity County, having watered their stock in Hettenshaw Valley in 1854-5.) Estle Beard relates that Neafus, after an unsuccessful chase after some Indians around Island Mountain, went hunting on the peak and after emerging a dusty red color from the chert declared, "It is such a useless piece of country that I'll name it after myself." Another story is that Neafus got in trouble with the law over horses and hid on the peak.

Site 5. Gettis Place (None of the Above)

The last house in Trinity County on the road to Covelo from Lake Mountain has historically been known as the Gettis Place. Today, however, the present owners, one of whom is a member of the Mellon family, call it "None of the Above". The property dates back to at least the 1890's. There have been various owners over the years. The ownership list is believed to go like this: Johnny White was the first owner, followed by a Moore, and then by Sam Gettis. It was during Gettis' ownership that the house burned. After Gettis came Dr. Frank Gilbraith who lived here two or three years. He started to build the present log house but he did not finish it. More recent owners have been Sam Brown, a Mr. Howard, and Smith.

Site 6. Lone Pine Ranch (Horse Ranch)

How does one describe 40,000 acres? Whereas most ranches in southern Trinity were settled along a ridgetop, the Lone Pine spans many whole ridgetops and the drainages that lie between. The Lone Pine was put together from a number of older ranches and now embraces more than 40,000 acres. It is the largest ranch in the county and has some of the finest cattle range in the state. Historically, the ranch includes old-time homesteads and ranches belonging to Hollingsworth, Lampley, Merritt, Armstrong, Arthur and Hill—names that jog memories of the past in this part of the county. Perhaps the most important of these were the Horse Ranch and the original Lone Pine Ranch. The Horse Ranch derived its name from one of the Asbill brothers (see Overview) who homesteaded it and raised thoroughbred horses there. Asbill left after an ownership dispute over some of the land and around 1872 the property was acquired by Charlie Fenton. (Pilot Peak was once named for this man and known as Fenton Peak.) Later the ranch was purchased by Dr. H. P. Merritt of Woodland, Yolo County. According to the Trinity Journal, Dr. Merritt was respected and esteemed and "one of the heaviest taxpayers" as he had vast stock and farming interests throughout the state. Dr. Merritt held on to the ranch until the 1890's. While under his ownership there was a successful sawmill operating on the property.

The Lone Pine Ranch derived its name from a lone pine which, although now a snag, still stands. It was Charlie Fenton who built a two-story house on the land. Lumber for his house had to be packed in as did the brick used to construct a nice fireplace. Fenton, at one time, had over 30,000 sheep on his ranch and his own pack train of 35-40 mules.

Land adjacent to the Lone Pine was proved up by the Hollingsworth brothers. This, together with Horse Ranch and Lone Pine Ranch, comprises the base from which the present ranch evolved. The consolidation process went about as

Site 9. This unpainted shiplap and clapboard structure is the original Frank Lampley Ranch, one of serveral Lampley family holdings.

follows: Merritt bought out Fenton, then Armstrong, then Sam Hill. (George Lampley recalls Merritt staying at the Armstrong Place sometime before his death in 1893.) Merritt then sold his holdings to A. Myerstein, a prizefighter. Myerstein, in turn, sold to Sheldon Potter, whose wife was an heir to the Miller and Lux cattle empire. (Estle Beard recalls his dad buying bulls from Potter in the early 1920's.) In 1942 Potter sold to the well-known businessman, Dean Witter, and the ranch has remained in the Witter family since that date.

There is considerable evidence of buildings, fencelines, and corrals, once belonging to these old ranches. Buildings of the Horse Ranch, Arthur Ranch, and Armstrong place still stand and there is also most of a homesteader's old shake cabin and some fruit trees at the site of the Sam Hill place. But prominent on the property is the large lodge built by Dean Witter. The building extends out over the hillside, commanding a breathtaking view of the grassy and rolling hills. The house with its book-lined interior filled with maps and pictures of the ranch has a big kitchen and numerous guest rooms. The county's only railroad track winds along the Eel River far below, passing by the Kekawaka Station which was the departure point for people, mail and cattle in days before there was road access to the outside world.

Site 7. Lake Mountain Ranch (Miller Ranch)

The Lake Mountain Ranch consists of approximately 600 acres of predominantly forest land with a 40 acre swale of open meadow pasture at the southern end of Haman Ridge. On a knoll in the meadow are clustered the ranch buildings, approached by a narrow road that passes by one of the shallow seasonal lakes that gives this ranch its name. All of the buildings were built by the Miller family, who started and still operate this ranch. The main house, dating from the late 1920's, is known for its custom oak interior milled from Lake Mountain trees.

Site 7. The original Miller cabin on the Lake Mountain Ranch was built of shake and pole construction. It is located across the road and south of the present ranch.

Site 7. For over 60 years the Miller Ranch has been a center of community life in the Lake Mountain area.

In southern Trinity, single ranches often carry the responsibility and identity for a whole area, either because of the character of the people or the location of the ranch or both. They are, or were, centers of activity and community affairs. Such is the case with Lake Mountain. It has had a school and a post office, and Leona Miller served as Deputy County Clerk for many years. The schoolhouse still stands on a part of the ranch; teachers used to board at the house.

The ranch is a fine example of the homestead era in southern Trinity. Leonard and Leona Miller, in response to an ad and with the help of a locator, packed up all their belongings and left the San Francisco Bay Area, arriving in Trinity County in 1919. Their original cabin of shake and pole construction, and known as "The Sunshine Shanty", still partially stands on the ranch. The Millers were not cattlemen; the ranch has been used instead for timber and wood-related production. Leonard Miller ran a sawmill near the schoolhouse and did carpentry and shop work for other ranchers in the area. The first sawmill was destroyed by fire but was rebuilt in 1945. Generally speaking, most homesteaders were primarily concerned with being self-sufficient. This is still true at Lake Mountain where the orchard, garden, and income from the trees are the means of survival. A pelton wheel on a drainage from one of the lakes provides electricity, and wood is still the only source of heat. Lake Mountain is an inspiration to all who know it, not only for its strikingly beautiful location and immaculate upkeep, but because it is an authentic example of the self-sufficient American homesteader and of what, with a family's hard work, can be accomplished.

Site 8. The Hoaglin Valley cemetery contains the graves of early settlers to the area.

Site 8. This historic barn built in Hoaglin Valley by Henry Holtorf about 1888 is a dominant feature in Hoaglin Valley.

Site 6. House on the Armstrong Place - now part of the Lone Pine Ranch.

Site 8. Hoaglin Valley

The early 1870's brought settlers to the Hoaglin Valley. Louis Meyers was one of the first, followed by D. Osborne (an early postmaster) and Henry Holtorf in 1888. Other early families were the Davises, the Grays and the Shannons. Holtorf and other early settlers are buried in the Hoaglin cemetery—a cemetery located on a peaceful knoll in the valley.

Holtorf's ranch was located on the Kettenpom Valley road. A large one and one-half story gable barn still stands. The barn has a central hayloft with aisles on each side; its siding is of vertical planks. The site of the original log house built by Holtorf in 1899 is east of the barn and orchard. Holtorf was an excellent farmer and he owned a thresher; he ran the post office from time to time. Henry Holtorf also had the first mail contract between Hoaglin and Alderpoint. The trees in the old orchard just east of the barn were transplanted by Holtorf from the Brooks place located on the Covelo road. Brooks had homesteaded, and planted trees, but then soon left the place. Holtorf, being a thrifty German, went over, dug them up, and transplanted them to his place.

The ranch was sold to Ward Paullus in 1933 and Merlin Goodwin became a later owner. Goodwin has sold most of the ranch acreage to the Louisiana-Pacific Company but he has retained the present ranch house, which had been built on the other side of the barn from the original house, as well as a small piece of ground that includes the other ranch buildings.

Sitting in the middle of a large overgrazed field is the old one-room Hoaglin schoolhouse. It looks like a classic example of an abandoned prairie schoolhouse. It was built in 1915 after an earlier school had burned. The use of this building as a school was not regular, for the doors were sometimes closed for lack of students.

The original part of the school is a one-story medium gable structure. A cross-gable has been added to the rear and the entire building rests on wooden blocks. The roof's original shingles are exposed in large patches where newer tin has been torn off. A hip roof entry porch and the use of a dental molding are exceptional features of this building which is located in a very rural, functionally oriented area.

Site 9. Haman Ranch (Juaquima Ranch) (Algy Lampley Ranch)

This ranch, now known as the Algy Lampley Ranch, is located on the west slope of Haman Ridge about eight miles south of Kettenpom Peak. Above the ranch is the Zenia-Covelo road; below it runs Kekawaka Creek. The buildings are unpainted shiplap and clapboard structures and consist of a house, barn, guesthouse and greenhouse. Only the house, which has been extensively remodeled, is original. An irrigation pond, striking in appearance, was added in the mid-1970's.

Historically, this has been known as the Haman Ranch, as it first belonged to the Haman family who were early settlers in the area and whose name also was given to the ridge along which the ranch is located. The ranch was later homesteaded by the Lampley family. Algy Lampley's father, Munroe, came here from Lake County in 1887. A year later Munroe's brother, Frank, also arrived. Patent records reveal that both Lampley families took up numerous homesteads in the area. Frank's ranch was located three miles south of Kettenpom Peak and is the present day George Lampley Ranch.

Site 10. The main ranch house on the Pitt White Ranch. Dating from the 1870's, it was originally two smaller cabins.

The open and rolling hills of this ranch typify the rangeland of southern Trinity.

Site 10. Pitt White Ranch (Jameson Ranch) (Stewart Ranch)

The original Pitt White Ranch, dating back to about 1875, is one of the earliest and largest ranches in the county. It was taken up by William Pitt White who had come to Covelo from Lewis County, West Virginia, in 1870, where he joined his brother, George White, as a partner in stock raising. (George was a powerful force in Southern Trinity and the adjacent areas of Mendocino and Humboldt Counties. He was a very rich rancher who owned thousands of acres of prime range land and controlled the transportation routes, hotels, and saloons of the area.) Pitt soon returned to West Virginia to marry, then came back to California and settled on this ranch in 1875.

The main house on the ranch is original and dates from the 1870's. It is made of two smaller white clapboard cabins that have been joined together, making it into a one and one-half story offset gable with a big veranda porch across one side. Another old house dates from 1910. It is a board and batten, cross gable building which sits across the creek from the main house. Both of these houses were built by or for the family. Other ranch buildings are of more recent origin.

The Kekawaka railroad station on the Northwestern Pacific line is located on the Eel River below the ranch. It was an important shipping point for cattle and part of the holding corrals are still visible.

There are three graves on the ranch: those of Newt Irwin, Harry Hise, and a young girl with the name of Simmons, who died in 1916.

For a time the property was owned by the Jameson family, and in 1975 this 11,000 acre ranch was purchased by Cal and Wendy Stewart.

Site 11. Robbers Roost

Located two miles (as the crow flies) southeast of the Kettenpom store, this place has a name which implies a history more illustrious than is the case. Robbers Roost was established by W. J. Robbers who lived there from 1915-19. It was later used as a summer camp, hunting headquarters, and general recreation area. Buildings were still standing as late as 1951. Traditionally the area has been known as Alexander Flat as a man named Alexander used it as a sheep camp for the Armstrong Ranch.

Site 12. Kettenpom Peak

Kettenpom Peak (4084') is one of the highest points in extreme southwestern Trinity County. About a mile to the north is the Kettenpom Store which is of significance because it serves as a central gathering spot in the area. This is especially so for it is equipped with one of the few telephones in this part of the county. The location of the Kettenpom Store at a road junction also lends importance to it. Here, one branch, the so-called "Peak Road", heads west to Alderpoint, while the other branch, the "Bluff Road", goes north to Zenia before turning west.

Kettenpom is a word of Indian origin meaning "little Indian potato land". Reference is undoubtedly to the Ketten lily which grows in the area. The bulb of this plant was very important in the diet of the native Indians.

Site 13. Burgess Ranch (Bennett Place) (McKnight Place)

The Burgess Ranch was originally patented in 1884 by Marcus Bennett; next it became the property of the McKnight family who left here about 1890 to settle in the nearby Ruth Valley (see Site 36.). The McKnights sold the land to Edward F. Burgess who had arrived in Zenia in 1882 and who was the brother of George Burgess, a founder of the settlement. When Edward's son, George Ralph, was married in 1908, a portion of the ranch property was given to him as a wedding present. His widow, May, was still living on the ranch in 1981 at the age of 90. Upon the death of his father, George Ralph acquired the remainder of the ranch and sold that portion to his brother, Edward Francis Burgess, Jr.

Members of the Burgess family have been prominent citizens of Zenia from its beginning. The continued association of this 400 acre ranch with the Burgess family is its overriding significance.

The ranch house was built in 1921 to replace an original building. It is a one and one-half story, hip roof, board and batten structure; nearby is a newer residence used by the family today. Of particular interest is the large kitchen in the older ranch house. It is 10'x25' in size and in it is a 4'x6' brick-lined stove which was used in earlier days to prepare food for a large family (Ralph and May raised ten children on the ranch) and for vacationers who rented cabins on the property.

Site 14. Zenia

Zenia is the only community in southern Trinity that was settled from the north. About 1860 a group of men that included George Burgess, James Howe, Green French, Commodore Peabody, and Abe Rodgers came over South Fork Mountain and established the town. They named it Poison Camp because of the larkspur growing there which had poisoned their cattle. (About 1905, postal regulations required that the name be changed.) Of this original group, George Burgess was the first to build a cabin in Zenia. It was located on the Bluff Road to Alderpoint on what is known as the Allan place. Abe Rodgers also settled at this spot, and Green French had his place farther down the road near what is now the Beckley place. With the completion of a land survey in 1875 there was another influx of settlers to the area. Among these were Ed Burgess, the brother of George, and others with names of Records, Shields, Eastman, Martin, Pearce, Barley, Goarden, Crank, Clark, Counts, Harmons, Beans, Miller and Ledgerwood.

Zenia is a hillside community situated on a small bench overlooking the valley of the Eel River. It is the business and social center of an area devoted largely to ranching.

Several old buildings comprise the historic center of the community. The oldest of these is the Ledgerwood cabin which still stands in an orchard below the present store. It was built in 1895 by Samuel Ledgerwood, early farmer, storeowner, and county supervisor for two terms. It is a one-story, notched log building with a gable shake roof. The building is in need of repair and the porch has long since fallen down. A barn sits across the yard to the west.

In 1898 Ledgerwood built a log store; it burned in 1908 and was replaced in 1910 by the present store which is a high gable, clapboard structure with a lean-to attached to it and a veranda across the front. The store is famous for its hand hewn pine ceiling.

Across the street from the store is the community hall, constructed in 1909 by joint effort of the community. It is a high gable, unpainted clapboard building with the original shake roof.

Behind the town center is the Grange Hall which originally served as a school. Classes were first held in the school in the spring of 1917. It was built by Edward F. Burgess, George W. Counts and Thomas C. Records. It replaced an older Sugar Pine School that had been established in 1897 and which was located a short distance outside of town on the south side of the road to the

Site 14. The old Zenia school which now serves as the Grange Hall was built in 1916. A porch has been added in recent years and the building is now painted white.

Site 14. This cabin, built by Sam Ledgerwood about 1898, served as a store in Zenia. It burned in 1908 and was replaced by a store which still stands.

Zenia Guard Station. Edward Burgess, son of Edward F. Burgess, taught in this school for 32 years. Lillian White, daughter of William Pitt White, also taught here. This building served as a school until 1956 at which time school district consolidation eliminated that need. It has since served as a Grange Hall.

Site 15. Grizzly Mountain

This mountain was the scene of the famous encounter between "Grizzly" Jim Willburn and a grizzly bear. Jim Willburn, one of the earliest settlers in Hetten Valley (see Site 22.), had his encounter with the grizzly while hunting. Jim shot at the bear but the shot, though accurate, had little effect and the bear kept coming on. With no time to reload, Grizzly Jim grabbed his knife and stuck it in the bear's mouth, stabbing away until the bear dropped, then fell unconscious himself. Indians later found him but left him for dead. Upon telling a squaw in Hettenshaw about it, they were told to go back for the body. When they returned to the scene Grizzly Jim was no longer there but had managed to crawl to Refuge Valley! His alertness had saved his life but he lost the use of his left arm in the struggle. It is believed that this event occurred in October, 1857, and that Jim would have been 26 years old at the time.

Site 16. Mt. Lassic (Black Lassic, Black Lassic Creek, Red Lassic, Red Lassic Peak)

This mountain, presiding over the headwaters of the West Fork of the Van Duzen River and straddling the county line, "preserves the name of a people of the Athapascan Family, named after their lost chief, Lassik." This explanation, taken from Gudde's "California Place Names" is based on information found in the "Handbook of American Indians" by Goddard and Hodge. The present spelling with the "c" rather than the "k" is the responsibility of the United States Forest Service. The Lassics had their main village in the Dobbins Creek-Alderpoint area to the west, where the fishing was excellent. Often in the summertime they travelled to Hetten Valley, and in the fall when the bears were fat they would go to Soldier Basin where some of the tribe would winter.

As white settlers began moving into this area in the late 1850's and early 1860's, they fenced off the land for their stock and began clamoring for protection from the Indians whose way of life they were upsetting. The fate of Lassic's band now became inextricably entwined with the government's effort to round up all Indians and locate them on reservations. To this end, the U.S. Army had at least six permanent posts near county boundaries which were used as mid-way stations in transferring the Indians to the Nome Lackie Reservation in Red Bluff or the Nome Cult Reservation in Covelo. In 1862 Captain Ketcham from Fort Baker on the Van Duzen noted in his records that local Hettenshaw ranchers, Jim Willburn, Jim Graham and Steve Fleming, had assisted him as guides in bringing this tribe to captivity. The records show that Chief Lassic was brought in by Fleming, although it is said that Lassic, after continual harrassment, surrendered voluntarily. According to the Asbill manuscript (written by Frank Asbill between 1936-39), Lassic, after he was relocated to Fort Humboldt, ran off the first night, back to his own area. Later he was captured again by local ranchers and brought with a group of his tribe to Fort Seward where he was shot and burned. One of the few Indian sources on early history is Lucy Young, an Indian who married a white and whose mother was a distant cousin of Lassic. She recalls that all male prisoners were taken out and shot and that, following, there was a terrible odor which she could not identify. After this, Lassic disappears from the records.

356

Site 17. Travis Ranch

This is a beautiful ranch that sprawls over 13,000 acres in the rugged, wooded country of the North Fork of the Eel River. The rolling hills are alternately green or golden brown, and, as seen from the top of nearby Long Ridge, make a stirring sight. The Travis Ranch has long been one of the largest cattle ranches in northwestern California and is one of the largest tracts of private range land in Trinity County. It takes its name from John and Benjamin Travis, who were originally from Forrestville, Sonoma County. As the brothers, both bachelors and sheepshearers by trade, were coming back from Humboldt County on the trail that passed through the ranch, they learned that the Bank of Mendocino was going to foreclose on the property. They decided to purchase 1000 acres. This was in 1895. They then gradually bought up additional land, piece by piece, until the ranch reached the present size. When John later married, Frank moved to the lower barn and fixed up a small cabin. But John's wife did not like living on the ranch, and so John sold his one-half interest in the ranch to a third brother, Al. Until that time Al had been living with his mother on the family ranch in Forrestville.

The ranch actually had quite a history prior to 1895 when the Travis brothers acquired it. It had been owned by the Asbills who were the first explorers and settlers in the southern part of the county. An old house on the property dates back to the 1860's. The house is still in use but has been extensively remodeled. Part of the ranch was indirectly associated with the famous Jack Littlefield murder, the prosecution of which nearly brought bankruptcy to Trinity County. Tom Hayden was living here when he got mixed up in that affair. The ranch also includes Vinton Flat on which was located the home of John Vinton, who also was involved in the Littlefield murder. Vinton ran a sheep camp for George White, a man who at one time was one of the richest ranchers in northern California.

But it was the Travis brothers who developed the ranch. John and Frank brought 1,000 head of white-faced Hereford cattle from Ukiah when they started the ranch in 1895. These were the first such cattle in the county. After John left, Al and Frank continued ranching on the property until 1939, when Frank died at the age of 77. Al died the following year at the age of 88. The ranch was inherited by Mrs. Florence McCulloch, the daughter of John Travis. She and her husband, "Wild Bill" McCulloch as he was called, continued to ranch the property until 1956. They improved the herd and were the first to import polled Herefords into the county. In 1956, the McCullochs sold to an Oregon lumberman, but retained 550 acres and some cattle for themselves and their son Travis, thus perpetuating the family and ranch name.

Site 18. Long Ridge

Long Ridge runs nearly north and south (on a slightly northwest to southeast line) beginning just out of Hoaglin Valley and ending abruptly in the bluffs overlooking the Travis Ranch. This ridge figured prominently in early Southern Trinity history. The name Long Ridge became associated with an outlaw element that was to be found here and in much of the sparsely inhabited region to the east. Land disputes and cattle rustling led to violence and killings. Some of these killings came to be known as the "Long Ridge Killings". Outlaws brought to trial at the county seat in Weaverville focused attention on the area and provided the first exposure that much of the general populace had to this part of the county.

Long Ridge is one of two major ridges running north and south in the area. Both Haman Ridge and Long Ridge are roughly equal in length and height,

Ranchers and homesteaders settled the Southern part of Trinity County. Ranching still remains the principle industry. This barn is on the Lamb Ranch.

but there the similarities stop. Up until about the middle 1960's the Long Ridge country, by many people's estimation, was the wildest country anywhere on the north coast. There were very few settlers: the Hoaglins at the north end on the west side of Salt Creek, the Duncans to the east above the Eel River, and Church Willburn at the south end. Wildlife, which was plentiful, included mountain lions, bobcats, wild pigs and bears. Travel through the area was infrequent; the major travel routes were the Red Mountain trail to the east and the Zenia-Covelo road on Haman Ridge to the west. Because of its central location it was a well-known geographical reference point. By contrast, Haman Ridge was heavily travelled and had numerous ranches and homesteads on its slopes — especially the west slope extending down to the Eel River. Here the heavy forest cover gave way to grassy hills. Even today, the forest covered lands of Long Ridge are within the National Forest whereas much of Haman Ridge, especially on the west side, is private land.

Further testifying to its central location, Long Ridge is the location of an old school site. The site is at the junction of five old trails on a small bench on the west side of the ridge near its crest. It is among a grove of oak trees and nearby is a natural spring that is still flowing. This is such a wild and remote country that it is almost inconceivable that there ever could have been need for a school here. But many old-timers recall hearing the school bell ring out early in the morning and walking the three to five miles of trail to school. Hazel Willburn, formerly of Hettenshaw and former chairman of the Trinity County Board of Supervisors, had one of her first teaching assignments here.

Site 19. Packwood Place

This place, located on Packwood Flat along the west side of Rock Creek, a tributary of the North Fork of Eel River, still bears the remains of a cabin built around 1880. It is named for Packwood, a brother-in-law of Gus Russ who had a place at the head of Rock Creek. According to Bill Hoaglin (who was running the Shannon Ranch in the 1940's), as passed on by Ted Shannon (old-timer

358

Site 21. The army units that camped here during the roundup of the Indians for relocation on reservations gave the name of Soldier Basin to this spot.

from Hoaglin Valley), Jack Littlefield is buried along the Packwood trail just below the flat. There are other alleged burial sites but this one seems plausible since the Packwood trail is a portion of the only trail through the county from the Hoaglin area.

Site 20. Shannon Butte

This 3067' butte is named for William Frederick Shannon who took up a homestead near here in 1902. Before him the property belonged to a Mr. Shields who reportedly built a cabin and two barns on the place. In 1919 Mr. Shannon sold his place to Otto Holtorf and moved to Tulare County, but in 1952 his son Ted returned to farm the land and to live in Hoaglin Valley where he remained until his death in 1980. Four generations of Shannons have lived in the valley. Ted's father was one of the earlier settlers in the area.

Site 21. Soldier Basin

Soldier Basin is a long, grassy swale located on the North Fork of the Eel River. It is an isolated and wild spot, yet one that is heavily grazed by cattle. Oak trees from the surrounding forest are slowly encroaching upon the area.

Military records show that both state militia and U. S. Army units were in southern Trinity County rounding up Indians in the 1860's, and even as late as the 1880's. Soldier Basin is one of the well-known spots where soldiers camped during that time. (Note also Soldier Creek which drains the area to the north of the basin.) The name is specifically attributed to the activities of Capt. Henry Flynn out of Fort Baker, in the early spring of 1863; Capt. William Hull from Fort Bragg, in the spring of 1864; and Capt. John Simpson out of Camp Grant, in the summer and fall of 1864. Capt. Simpson, commanding Company S of the 1st California Battalion of Mountaineers, was charged with gathering the Indians in the area of the North Fork of the Eel River. In later years, a consignment of soldiers under the command of Capt. Davis wiped out a settlement of Indians who had avoided the earlier roundups. Only a few Indians escaped. One of these, the famous Yellowjacket, was found dazed and wandering and was taken in by the French family of Zenia. He later became known as Jack French and worked as a sheepshearer in the area. He told the story of his escape to a few people, one of whom is Jim Gilman, of the Gilman Ranch in Soldier Basin. The only Indian spared in that infamous raid was a 17 year old Indian girl whom Captain Davis married and then settled down with on southern Long Ridge.

The late Ted Shannon of Hoaglin Valley once found a McHenry rifle in the basin and recalled seeing barracks there which were 150' long and which were divided into 10-15 rooms. Scattered remains of structures are still evident today.

The historic Ben Arthur Trail, named for an early sheep rancher, passes through the basin and is still used. Soldier Basin originally belonged to Lassic's band (see Site 16.) and was later homesteaded by a certain Saul Cox.

Site 22. Old Willburn Place

The Old Willburn Place is located at the headwaters of two rivers: the Van Duzen and the East Fork of the North Fork of the Eel. The Willburn brothers, James St. Clair and Hiram David, were the first permanent settlers in Hettenshaw Valley. They came here about 1856 and their descendants are still in the valley. The Willburn name is among the most well-known in the county.

This ranch belonged to Hiram David Willburn. The original house was recently demolished but the orchard, garden and barn remain. The barn is a simple one and one-half story gable structure built of poles and covered with vertical planks. The orchard lies east of the old house site and old roses, lilacs and grapes grow in the garden area. Countless daffodils and other bulbs have become naturalized and grow plentifully over numerous acres of the ranch.

Site 23. Fort Rascal (Cross Ranch) (Stapp Ranch)

The Fort Rascal site is located in a cattle corral on the present day Hetten Valley ranch owned by Lee and Irene Stapp. Ironically, the fort was built on an Indian archeological site and there is more evidence today of the Indian site than there is of the soldier's fort. The site is on an east facing slope from which the entire Hetten Valley can be observed—an excellent defensive outpost location. The foundation for a stone fireplace is barely visible towards the bottom of the hill. No other physical evidence remains.

Records of the U. S. War Department (predecessor to the Department of Defense) show that the U. S. Army travelled extensively throughout Trinity County during the 1850's-60's in its efforts to round-up and relocate the Indians. Though the county was never the site of a permanent army post, these military expeditions did result in the establishment of a number of camps, the most intriguing of which was Fort Rascal, part of a chain of forts used as midway stations. This fort is intriguing because, as of the date of this publication, the author has been able to find only a couple of vague and veiled references to this site in the War Department's official records of "The War of the Rebellion". Investigation is continuing with a detailed examination of the monthly post returns for nearby forts. Local residents, however, are able to quickly point to the location of the officers' quarters; Ray Willburn, grandson of the first permanent settler in the valley, says that the fort was twelve feet high and was made of cedar logs.

Site 24. Refuge Valley

Refuge Valley is the first valley above Hettenshaw on the road to Zenia. According to Hazel Willburn, it received its name because, at the time of the roundup of the Indians by the militia in the 1860's, the soldiers took refuge here during the winter (see also Site 21.). The valley was also the scene of a tragedy, however. It was here that Ned Willburn (father of Grizzly Jim Will-

360

Site 23. A cattle corral on the Stapp Ranch in Hetten Valley was the location of a U. S. Army outpost during the roundup of the Indians in the 1860's.

burn), Hiram David (Grizzly Jim's brother), and Hiram David's wife burned to death when their cabin caught fire.

Site 25. Indian Dick Ranger Station

This area in the extreme southeast corner of the county was settled early by John Franklin Brown, a pioneer cattle rancher from Covelo. Brown built the first cabin on the land and, along with his partner Pope Lewis, kept his stock here. The property was later homesteaded by an Indian named Richard Bell who was known as Indian Dick. Because he was hard of hearing, he was also known as Deaf Dick. Dick lived and trapped here during the summer and fall, then spent his winters at Island Mountain. Frank Brown tells the unhappy story of how the patent to Indian Dick's land was issued and sent out from Washington, was received by the post office at Covelo, but because Dick died before he could pick up his mail, the patent was cancelled, reverting it to public land. The Forest Service made it a guard station which remains today.

Site 26. Henthorne Lakes—Vann Cabin—Lightning Camp

All three of these sites are located in the southeast corner of Trinity County and are practically unknown to most Trinity County residents. The Henthorne Lakes are three beautiful natural lakes sitting above and draining into the Middle Fork of the Eel River. They are part of a large, privately owned piece of property that is surrounded by Forest Service primitive holdings and graced by one of California's wild and scenic rivers. The Henthorne Tract, part of the Trinity Forest Reserve set aside in 1905, was traded to Dr. John Wilson, a famous Los Angeles surgeon, in the 1930's as part of a Forest Service effort to

Site 14. This cabin still stands in Zenia today. It was built by Sam Ledgerwood in 1895.

Site 26. The Vann cabin is a very remote cabin near Henthorne Lake. It was once the home of an employee of the Indian Service.

consolidate their holdings to the east. Dr. Wilson packed in by mule all the materials necessary to build an attractive lodge and several other buildings which are still used by Dr. Wilson's son, Richard, a rancher based in Covelo.

The Vann Cabin, located perhaps a mile and one-half to the northwest of the Henthorne Lakes is today part of the Wilson Ranch and is used during the grazing season. The first cabin was built by a sheepman named Updegraff, who summered his flock here. (Nearby Updegraff Ridge bears his name.) The cabin was later owned by Vann, an employee of the Indian Service, who bought up a number of 40-acre timber parcels under a state public lands law which, unlike the homestead law, required no improvements. In addition to the 40-acre parcel upon which the Vann Cabin is located, he also purchased a 40-acre timbered flat at Cove Camp, two miles south, which contained a fenced Indian burial ground. Sometime after World War I, Lloyd Brown acquired the property and homesteaded it. Lloyd, in partnership with his brother Frank, raised cattle in the area. It remained the property of Brown until the 1960's when it was sold.

Lightning Camp, located just north of the county line and southwest of the Henthorne Lakes, was a camping spot along the busy trail north to Weaverville. It received its name at the time Hank Hayes was bringing some sheep into camp and lightning struck, killing 400 sheep and knocking Hank and his horse silly. The camp was homesteaded by a Mr. Westerman and later purchased by Frank and Lloyd Brown, who built corrals here and used the area while branding calves in the spring. There is still a good watering trough here.

Site 27. Morrison Camp

Located three miles northeast of Big Butte, this place is named for a Covelo rancher who camped here with his tuberculosis-afflicted son. In keeping with the then accepted medical theory that high altitude was beneficial for tubercular patients, Mr. Morrison and his son camped here all summer.

Site 28. Mike's Rock and Shinbone Cabin

Located in Sec. 23, T26N, R12W, this rock was named for Mike Flournoy, eldest son of Bill Flournoy, a Tehama County Supervisor who ran sheep in this area. Mike loved to sit on this rock when he was young. According to Frank Brown of Covelo, more than 10,000 sheep and 1,000 cattle were summered in this country around the main fork of the upper Mad River. A cabin just east of Little Butte at the end of Shinbone Ridge is known as Shinbone Cabin. It was built by Bill Flourney for use as a sheep camp.

Site 29. Red Mountain Field

This field which stretches along the upper reaches of Red Mountain Creek, west of Red Mountain, was the location of the Red Mountain House, half-way station and roadhouse on the trail from Covelo to Weaverville. This house, the remains of which are still visible, played a significant role in many events which occurred along this trail in the early days. Of particular significance was the Jack Littlefield murder in 1895, for it is said that Littlefield's assassins departed from this point to do their deed. The property was owned for awhile by Frank Doolittle who testified in 1896 that this had been his home (he probably had lived here since 1888). Mrs. Doolittle is said to have drowned in the river near here. There are at least two graves on the property near a large rock above the house site.

Site 30. Caution

An old U. S. Forest Service map of 1912 (found in the Platina office of the Yolla Bolly Ranger District) shows that Caution was located in Sec. 21, T4S, R8E. This is the site of an old post office which has long been out of existence. It was established on August 31, 1901, and was discontinued on July 31, 1913. It had a second period of operation between January 8, 1915, and July 15, 1938, at which time it was moved to Lake Mountain. It is not unusual that a post office situated in a sparsely populated area such as this would be affected by changes in the population which occurred from time to time. Caution was situated north of Long Ridge just across the North Fork of the Eel River and was reached by a trail from Hoaglin. Mail arrived by a carrier on horseback who travelled between Caution and Hoaglin twice a week. The first carrier was Henry Reid and the first postmaster, Georgia Ann Willburn. William F. Shannon was the carrier between 1904 and 1912 and during that time he failed only once to get the mail through on schedule. On that occasion the water was so high in Salt Creek that his horse could not buck the current to reach the opposite shore. For his services he received $30.00 per month. The Caution Post Office was a community gathering place and mail delivery was an important event. Many of the stories contained in the Miller collection of letters (museum collection) refer to this tiny settlement.

Site 31. Waterspout

Located in the headwaters of the Mad River in Sec. 7, T26N, R11W, Waterspout was a well-known pasture spot and camp named because of a hewn pole that was used as a pipe or spout to gather water from a spring. There used to be a fenced-in horse pasture nearby, and the Travis brothers (see Site 17.) would camp here while gathering steers. They would stay one or two nights and then take the stock to Red Mountain which had a bigger pasture. Water-spout was also the place of capture for several outlaws (one, reportedly, was a cousin of Frank Doolittle, a well-known figure in this area) and the scene of at least one duel.

Site 32. Black's Camp

This was the location of a cabin built by an old-timer named Black. According to Frank Brown, Black's Camp Ridge used to be the main ridge all the way to Four Corners Rock. Its present day name is Jones Ridge.

Site 33. Hayden Roughs

This area gets its name from Tom Hayden, a well-known cattleman who was mixed up in the Littlefield murder. Hayden bought this place, in the foothills of what had come to be known as the Hayden Roughs, in March, 1910. In earlier days (1900) he had a ranch near Three Forks and at the time of the Littlefield murder he lived on the Travis Ranch which name was associated with that episode. Hayden died on June 10, 1913; his wife and son Frank continued the cattle business here.

Site 34. Three Forks

Three Forks is the name given the area above the Ruth Valley where the various forks of the Mad River come together. An old log cabin and a good sized graveyard are located here. Historically it has been a place where several trails split. In October, 1895, this was a stopover place for Mendocino outlaws.

Site 35. Double A Ranch

The Double A Ranch, named for Ann Anderson who acquired the old ranch around the turn of the century, is traditionally the only ranch of any size or importance in the Ruth Valley. It is situated prominently in the southeast end of the valley. The ranch was originally homesteaded by the Bushnell family, of whom Ben and Charlie are well-known names. It is said that their father once killed a rare white panther while building fence on the ranch. The odds of finding such an animal are said to be one in 1,000.

Helen Wills Moody, a U.S. women's tennis champion of the 1920's, was the niece of Ann Anderson. Much of her skill was acquired during her summers spent at the ranch.

Once a spreading cattle ranch, the Double A is now a dude ranch complete with airport and tennis courts. Old buildings that are left include three barns and two cabins. One of the barns, now used for hay, is a one and one-half story knotched and chinked log structure with a high, shake covered, gable roof. Massive logs form the foundation, which allowed it to be skidded to its present location near the lodge. One of the old residences is Ann Anderson's board and batten cabin that has been considerably remodeled. The other old building is an old log cabin that is about 15'x15' in size. The cattle brand of the Double A Ranch is also a double A (AA).

Site 36. Ruth (Anada) (White Stump)

The first settlement in this valley along the Mad River was called White Stump. It was so christened by two inebriated old-timers, Clyde Barnes and Tom Elkins, after lightning hit, split, and made a twenty-foot stump out of a large pine tree. When, however, the first post office was established on March

Site 35. Massive logs form the foundation of this old chinked log barn on the Double A Ranch.

Site 36. The site of the old Forest Service Guard Station at Ruth is now covered by waters of the Ruth Reservoir.

3, 1898, it was located about six miles upstream at the Lacy Gray place (see Ruth map on page 336). The Grays had settled on Mad River in the 1890's and Gray became the first postmaster. The name Anada was given to the post office by John Jeans whose place was about a mile downstream. The name is a combination of the names of two girlfriends, Ana and Ada, whom Jeans had known in Missouri.

John T. McKnight also settled in this isolated area in the 1890's. He homesteaded 160 acres and with the help of his wife, four sons, and two daughters established a home which became a stopping place for travellers. From this beginning a hotel, store, stable and barns were built. Gradually, through the work of Mr. McKnight and sons, Milton and Joseph, a small community developed. The post office was moved from Anada to McKnight's place on June 3, 1902. When news reached the McKnights that a baby girl had been born in Utah to another son, Frank, and his wife on June 8, 1902, the happy family decided to name their new post office after their new granddaughter and niece and gave it the name of "Ruth". After the death of the baby's mother following childbirth and the death of her father in a mill accident two and one-half years later, baby Ruth McKnight came to live with her grandparents and was raised in this small community bearing her name. Milton McKnight became the first postmaster.

The McKnights sold their store in 1915 to Joseph H. Hutchens who also took over the post office. The store and post office again changed hands in December, 1924, when the property was purchased by Arthur Jeans who, with his brother John Jeans, had been an early settler in the valley. The following spring Arthur moved the store upstream about a mile and one-half to his ranch located near the mouth of Chopentoy Creek (spelled Choptoy on many maps).

Aubert Jeans, Arthur's son, acquired the property in the early 1950's and decided to relocate the store at a more suitable location nearer the road. His new, modern store and post office, built in 1955, continued to be the center of this community until 1960 when the construction of the Ruth Dam forced the "town" to be moved again. The waters of the Ruth Reservoir now cover much of this valley which had been the center of much activity. The present location of the town of Ruth is upstream from all of its previous sites at the head of the new lake near the mouth of Johnson Creek. Besides the store and post office, a Forest Service Guard Station also had to be relocated from its former site near White Stump to a site south of the new lake.

Site 37. Kelsey Peaks

North and South Kelsey Peaks are situated on the south end of Wilcox Ridge and the north end of Horsehead Ridge at the eastern edge of the Six Rivers National Forest. They are named for Samuel Kelsey, an early explorer with a long documented history of leading pack parties. In 1854, newspaper sources show that Kelsey was hired by a group of enterprising merchants in Sonoma to locate a trail from Petaluma to Weaverville. It was while on this trip, just north of the Russian River Valley, that the Kelsey party met with the Asbill party and the two parties decided to join together. They are believed to have been the first white men to see Round Valley, which they reached on May 15, 1854. They then headed into southern Trinity County, following either the Trinity Trail along the east side of the Eel River or proceeding up Long Ridge. In so doing, they were the first whites to see much of this area. When the Asbills decided to winter in Hettenshaw in 1854-5, Kelsey pushed on and explored the North Fork of the Eel extensively, and in 1856 it was known as the Kelsey River. The military records of Camp Wright confirm that Kelsey was in Humboldt County and vicinity in 1856. Kelsey's other interests were mining and finding a better route from the coast to the Sacramento Valley.

Site 38. Taylor's Flat (Forest Glen)

Taylor's Flat is the early name for the flat where the Forest Glen Post Office is located today. In the past the name Forest Glen applied only to the resort that was located across the river.

In 1888 only one person was believed to have been living on Taylor's Flat. According to Clyde Lewis, retired Yolla Bolly District Ranger whose grandfather was in the area in 1888, this person was an ex-surveyor, but it is not known whether or not this is the same man for whom the flat is named. It is known, however, that a grave of W. H. Taylor who died in 1900 is on the hillside on the north side of the road a short distance from the Forest Glen Store. The grave of Harry Coles is also at this spot. Coles is said to have come to the flat about 1916 and homesteaded. He built a cabin here in 1919-1920 using lumber which he floated down the South Fork from the Matthews Mill located several miles upstream. Coles' daughter Elizabeth married Peyton Randolph who had come to the South Fork in 1912 and lived up the river about five miles (see Site 45.).

About the turn of the century Bill Pratti had a 160 acre placer mining claim across the river. In 1904 he sold it to Charles H. Brewer who, after a road was built into the area, started a stopover place for travelers. This he named Auto Rest which later became known as Forest Glen (see Area VI, Site 34.). Brewer sold out to Arthur Jeans in 1912 for $1500. When Brewer had acquired the deed to the claim in 1904 he had given Pratti his two burros, pack saddles and

Site 38. 1916 saw the construction of a bridge across the South Fork facilitating travel to the west. At the same time the Forest Service built this nearby Ranger Station at Forest Glen.

Site 41. The Ben Randolph cabin was of sturdy log construction, seen here being erected in 1916.

saddlebags, and his last $20.00 gold piece for it.

Although Forest Glen is now located on a good state highway, in earlier days it was necessary to ford the river at a point near the present location of the U. S. Forest Service Campground. Automobiles often had difficulty in making the crossing. Charlie Brewer tells of pulling cars out, one by one, with his rawhide lasso tied to his saddle horn. A bridge was built at this crossing in 1916.

It was in 1916 that the Forest Service built a ranger station at Forest Glen. The cost was $300 for a 12'x24' building with 12' walls and a 6'x24' porch! This station saw service for the next 60 years. In 1976 the Forest Service acquired a new site to support its increasing crew and storage needs.

Site 39. Hell's Gate

A mining claim near the mouth of Rattlesnake Creek is known as Hell's Gate. Joe Risk, a cobbler by trade, was apparently the first to have this claim. He had built a cabin here by 1919. After his death the claim was later taken up by Dr. John Lawrence, a pioneer in radiation medicine and younger brother of Nobel Prize winner, Dr. Ernest O. Lawrence, inventor of the cycletron and founder of the Lawrence Radiation Laboratory. Old-timers in the area speculate that important atomic research may have been carried on at this site during World War II.

The U. S. Forest Service Hell's Gate Campground is nearby.

Site 40. Lower Ford and Scott Flat

About two miles above Forest Glen is a bridge over the South Fork of the Trinity River known historically as the Lower Ford. For many years it was one of two places where the river could be crossed. The original suspension footbridge is no longer in existence but has been replaced by a newer one slightly upstream. The bridge has been an important crossing on the Hayfork-Mad River Trail.

On the east side of the South Fork, near the ford, is Scott Flat. Bill Pratti first received the patent to this grassy flat; he later sold it to Scott who, in turn, sold it to the U. S. Forest Service. A white picket fence at one time surrounded it. A two-room log cabin which once stood on this flat probably dated back to the 1850's. Hay was raised here for the packers who used the Hayfork-Mad River Trail on which it was located. There is an historic grave on the site.

Site 41. Ben Randolph Place (Lower Bramlet Place)

In 1912 Ben and Peyton Randolph, brothers, arrived on the South Fork from the San Francisco Bay area and camped on Scott Flat while seeking a desirable spot for a homestead. A piece of ground a short distance above Collins Creek was chosen. A water system out of Farley Creek was constructed. In 1915 the property was homesteaded and that winter a cabin was built. This became known as the Ben Randolph Place. Peyton Randolph bought the Bob Watson cabin on Rattlesnake Ridge and made his home there (see Site 45.).

In 1927 Mrs. Randolph's parents, Charlie and Elizabeth Bramlet, moved here (see Site 50.). A shop building that still stands was built by Charlie soon after he arrived. The original cabin burned about 1945 and Charlie built a small cabin to replace it; it still stands. The barn collapsed from heavy snow during the winter of 1961-62. Because the Bramlets had lived at two locations along the South Fork their first home upstream at the mouth of Bierce Creek has come to be known as the Upper Bramlet Place and their later home at the Ben Randolph Place now goes by the name of the Lower Bramlet Place.

Site 42. Double Cabin (Tin Cabin) (Petty Place)

At the junction of Farley Creek and the South Fork of the Trinity River, along the Hayfork-Mad River Trail, is the old Double Cabin claim. Originally there were two cabins located here with one fireplace in the middle serving both cabins. These cabins burned and a mound of clay and rocks marks the site. Sometime after 1927 one of the cabins was replaced by Charlie Petty, using sheet metal from the Klondike Mine. Petty was one of the very few miners or prospectors working in this part of the county. Likewise, the Klondike Mine was one of the very few mines that attempted to operate in this area. The Klondike was an unsuccessful venture and after it was abandoned Petty acquired some of the metal for his cabin. It was not a weatherproof cabin and Petty had to put up a tent inside to keep himself dry!

Site 43. Matthews Cabin (Cooksey Place)

Above the mouth of Marie Creek is a river-crossing known as the Upper Ford. Two friends, Charles A. Matthews and Lowell Reese filed twenty-acre mining claims at this place in 1909 and built homes for their families on opposite sides of the river. To facilitate communication between them, various methods of crossing the South Fork were used: first a fallen log, next a pulley rope with a small draft boat, then a suspension mule bridge, and finally the present steel bridge which was built to replace the 1941 suspension bridge that had been lost in the 1964 flood.

The Matthews place is on the west side of the river and was built by Charlie Matthews about 1915; records show that the property was patented that year. The one-story log cabin still stands. The logs are dove-tailed, notched, and chinked and are a good example of a mountain cabin constructed by a Trinity homesteader. It is the oldest cabin still standing along the South Fork.

Matthews was instrumental in establishing a mail route to Forest Glen. In 1920 he had a sawmill here, power for which was generated by a pelton wheel using water ditched in from Marie Creek. The mill provided lumber for the Matthews and Reese places as well as for neighbors and even for the construction of the Hayfork Hotel. Since the Matthews place is accessible only by trail the lumber was hauled down the trail by a narrow gauge wagon.

Following the death of Charlie Matthews, his widow continued to spend summers here but she eventually turned the property over to Mr. and Mrs. Donald Cooksey, Jr., longtime friends. Matthews had known the Cookseys for many years for he had once been personal secretary to Cooksey's grandfather. Donald Cooksey, Jr. had first visited the area about 1909 when he accompanied Matthews on a vacation trip to the South Fork. (Cooksey's father was a professor of physics at the University of California and it may have been his association with Dr. E. O. Lawrence in the physics department there which resulted in the Lawrence family acquiring the Hell's Gate property on the South Fork (see Site 39.).

Site 44. Reese Place (Flint Place)

On the east side of the South Fork near the mouth of Marie Creek is the Flint place, originally known as the Lowell Otis Reese place. The Reese place and the Matthews place across the river from it were homesteaded by two close friends, Charles A. Matthews and Lowell Otis Reese. The first house on this site was probably built about 1910-11 and was a log cabin which soon disintegrated. It was replaced in 1922 with a one and one-half story, shingle-sided gable house which still stands. The lumber for this house came from the saw-

Site 43. This is a 1917 photo of the Matthews homestead which is still only accessible by trail. All materials were made on the premises or packed in.

Site 43. Lumber from the Matthews sawmill which was in operation about 1920 is packed down the trail by a mule-drawn narrow gauge lumber carrier.

Site 44. Ingenuity and resourcefulness were necessary to build and maintain a mountain home far from a road. The Flint cabin is no exception.

mill on the Matthews place. The house was built by a man named Ackerman who had come from Idaho following some marital problems and lived out the rest of his life on the South Fork at the Peyton Randolph place (see Site 45.).

About 1926 R. E. "Tex" Ewell, originally from Virginia and later from Texas, arrived here with his partner Dave Hunt. Ewell became the next owner of the Reese property. In the meantime Chet and Paula Flint had also come to the South Fork from Alameda County. They lived for a while in a cabin at the mouth of Collins Creek and about 1929 bought the Reese cabin from Ewell. It is now owned by their son, Bob Flint. A beautiful fruit orchard and lush meadow make this an appealing homestead.

Site 45. Watson Place (Peyton Randolph Place)

On the south slope of Rattlesnake Ridge is the old Bob Watson place which Peyton Randolph purchased from Watson about 1912-13. Watson had a two-room cabin on the property which still stands but is in poor condition. Peyton Randolph built another cabin about 1915-16; it was a two-room cabin with a loft. He replaced this with yet another building about 1922-24. Mr. Ackerman, who built the nearby Reese cabin in 1922, helped with its construction. Peyton Randolph left the place soon afterwards; Ackerman stayed on, living out his life here. For a time Peyton Randolph worked for the Forest Service, including a short period as assistant ranger on the Mad River District.

Watson, the first owner of this property, had a string of pack mules. It was he who packed the Chinese into their camp near the St. Jacques place. Another of his packing activities was transporting fish, trapped in a fish dam he built on the South Fork, to the miners in Weaverville.

Site 45. This is a 1915 photo of the Peyton Randolph place on the slopes of Rattlesnake Ridge.

Site 47. An older log cabin is enclosed within this newer structure at the Ostrat place. A fine garden and orchard have provided food for this homestead for nearly a century.

Site 46. Stockton Flat (Hoffman Place)

Stockton Flat, located a mile or two up-river from the Matthews and Reese cabins, does not have much historic significance. We simply note that the name given this flat is derived from the fact that a group of hunters from Stockton used it as their main camp when coming here yearly to hunt.

Not far from Stockton Flat on Cable Creek is an old cabin site known as the Hoffman Place. Hoffman was a retired painter who came into the South Fork in the 1920's. Although it was a mining claim, a patent to the land was never obtained. The Hoffman split-shake cabin has burned down. The graves of Hoffman, his wife, and his aunt are on this site.

Site 47. Lewis Place (Ostrat Place)

The first use of this place was probably by James K. Polk Lewis who came into Trinity County in 1887 searching for a place to homestead. He had been a sheepman in Mendocino County where life had become difficult because of conflicts over range lands that existed there between cattlemen and sheepmen. Lewis homesteaded this site in 1888, built a cabin, and dug a ditch to Silver Creek. Confident that the South Fork would provide year-long range he invested everything he had, buying 20 brood mares and 150-200 cattle. But a severe storm the next winter resulted in the death of his horses and most of his cattle. Discouraged, he gave up the homestead and moved to Cottonwood.

George Perl and Bill Hansen were the next people to occupy the homestead. Since Perl was not a citizen, the paperwork involving this place is in Hansen's name. They had a sturdy cabin, large barn, and a fine garden and orchard.

In 1932 the Ostrats bought this property from George Perl. They enclosed the old cabin within a new and larger structure. The thick walls of the kitchen are evidence that an earlier cabin is enclosed within this two-story house. Other outbuildings have also been constructed. The Ostrats did not settle here permanently but used the property as a summer home.

Wild game has always been plentiful here. Lewis' grandson recalls hearing stories from his father about the plentiful deer and bear. A mineral spring on Smoky Creek served as a lick and attracted animals to the area. Bob Watson, an old-timer on the South Fork, built a fish dam here (marks of the dam still show). Watson trapped fish in large numbers, then packed them out over what is still known as the Old Fish Trail that runs along Rattlesnake Ridge. After two days of travel he would reach Weaverville where he sold his fish to the LaGrange Mine and to others.

Site 48. Norris Place (Murphy Place) (Steffensen Place)

A narrow piece of land above Smoky Creek was the location of an old log cabin which was originally known as the Norris place. It was one of the very first sites along the South Fork to be settled. Recollections of the descendants of the Lewis family, who settled on the Lewis (Ostrat) place downstream, indicate that a man named Sims may have been living here as early as 1888.

It is known that in 1917-18 a man named Murphy was living in another cabin on the property. The next name associated with these two cabins is Gosnell. In the 1930's a man by that name was living here. Steffensen is the most recent owner. An old gravesite is on the site.

Site 49. St. Jacques Place — Red Mountain Meadows — Chinese Camp

At a point along the South Fork where Red Mountain Creek comes in from the north and Wilcox Ridge comes in from the south is the site of the Charlie St. Jacques place. In the days before homesteaders came into the South Fork

Site 50. The Upper Bramlet Place was homesteaded in 1915 by Charlie Bramlet. This homestead, shown here in a 1917 photo, had the capability of filling nearly every need of the family.

Site 50. Because of its sound construction the old Bramlet cabin still stands. A portion of the original porch overhang has been enclosed with clapboard siding.

this was the site of an Indian Rancheria. Charles Bramlet who lived a mile and a half upstream for several years tells of having seen impressions on the ground here of eighteen to twenty tepees.

Charlie St. Jacques settled here in the early 1930's. He lived alone but was a friend to everyone along the river—always ready with a helping hand when needed. The place was never patented, so when St. Jacques left, it reverted to the Forest Service which has recently burned the cabin and converted the spot to an administrative site.

Northeast of St. Jaques place along Red Mountain Creek is Red Mountain Pasture which has been used for many years as a pasture for stock. An irrigation ditch provides some water for the area. The site of an early Forest Service Guard Station that was located here is just outside the fence at the lower end of the pasture near a main trail junction. Nothing remains of this cabin today.

One-quarter mile above St. Jacques on the South Fork trail is the site of an old Chinese camp. About six Chinese spent a year here. Rocks from their small 8'x10' cabin are still discernible.

Site 50. Upper Bramlet Place (Bierce Cabin) (Cleveland Meadows)

One of the most beautiful pieces of patented ground on the South Fork is at the mouth of Bierce Creek. It is known as the Upper Bramlet Place and was the home of Charles D. Bramlet and his wife, Elizabeth Hill Bramlet. The Bramlets homesteaded this place in 1913-14. It became a self-sufficient homestead and had the capability of filling every need of the family. Bramlet received the patent to the land in 1920. Charlie had been a teamster by trade before coming here; he continued as a packer, packing supplies of every description for others along the river. In 1923 they left their nice home on the South Fork and moved to Hetten Valley. When they returned in 1927 they settled at the Ben Randolph place, about 12 miles down-river. (Mrs. Randolph was the Bramlet's daughter.) Their new home then became known as the Lower Bramlet place and their former home at the mouth of Bierce Creek was named the Upper Bramlet place. At the present time the Upper Bramlet place is the home of Jim and Julie Lacitignola who are leasing the property from Ray Randolph, the grandson of the original owner. The Lacitignolas are maintaining this 70 acre homestead in beautiful condition and have built some exceptionally fine log cabins on the site. The original log cabin still stands although its condition is somewhat dilapidated. A number of very old fruit trees are also to be seen and are an indication of the age of this old homestead.

Bierce Creek on which the Upper Bramlet place is located was named for a man known to have been an outlaw. Well up on Bierce Creek is a pasture and old cabin site now called Cleveland Meadows. It is speculated that this was the site of the Bierce cabin. The cabin is no longer there, but Charlie St. Jacques who lived on the South Fork nearby remembers that it was standing in 1934.

In the early days of the Forest Service the cabin site in Cleveland Meadows was taken over as a Forest Service Guard Station. The Forest Service, at that time, often took over small pasture spots for administrative sites. These were usually places that had already been fenced and upon which there was an old cabin. As roads were built and travel was facilitated these outlying stations were abandoned.

Site 51. Dutchman's Palace (Penney Place)

A mile above the falls on Prospect Creek and one-quarter mile up its east fork is the site of the old Dutchman's Palace, named for four Dutchmen who lived there in the early 1900's. Traces of their mining activity along the creek are still visible. These men were here for only a short time for it is known that by 1912 Jack Penney was living here. The Bramlets, his closest neighbors, recall that he sought their help at the time his cabin burned. Penney built a second cabin at this place following the loss of the first one; this second cabin was constructed of cedar.

At a later time Penney had a place on the Humboldt Trail, midway between South Kelsey Peak and Hermit Rock. This served as a stopping place for stockmen and packers. Jack Penney was an excellent carpenter. In earlier days he had been a shipwright and was proficient with the broad ax. His craftsmanship was so fine that it is reported that a wooden beam which had floated down the river past the Bramlet Place was identified by Charlie Bramlet as Penney's by the fine workmanship.

Site 52. Payne Ranch

About two miles up the East Fork of South Fork is a piece of patented land that is essentially a very steep open meadow which runs from the Wildwood-Mad River Road down to the river. Three names are often associated with this place: Boney, Eveland and Payne. The Evelands were an Indian family which probably obtained this place under an Indian allotment. Three Eveland graves are on the property: Charley H. Eveland (April 9, 1877-November 27, 1899), Lucy Eveland (June 10, 1843-March 31, 1904), and Elias Eveland (Sept. 25, 1855-September 4, 1904). Believed to be related to this family was an Indian woman known as Liza Jane who ran cattle in this country by herself. A seasonal employee at the White Rock Ranger Station at the time was a man named Lou Payne. Payne married Liza Jane but after only one year of marriage sold her cattle and ran off with Liza Jane's daughter by a previous marriage. (Liza Jane had been first married to a Mr. Ward.) The third name associated with this place is Boney. Ben Boney was a brother of Liza Jane who, it is said, was given his name because he was consistently picking up bones.

Site 53. Jensen Cabin (Blossom Cabin)

High on the slope at the headwaters of the South Fork are two cabin sites which were important during the days when cattlemen used this range extensively. The Jensen cabin, located in the NE¼, Sec. 19, T29N, R10W was first occupied by Tom and Gene Burrill, cattlemen who also built a cabin at Chicago Camp located on the ridge top at the beginning of the South Fork. Jensen was also a cattleman who occupied this cabin at a later time.

In Sec. 13, T27N, R11W, about a mile to the northwest, is the site of the Blossom cabin. It is located just below the West Low Gap road near Hermit Rock. Blossom ran cattle here; he also operated the Wildwood Inn for a while.

According to Clyde Lewis, retired District Ranger for the Yolla Bolly District, the Blossom cabin was built by an Englishman named Bill Brooks who was in the area from about 1905 to 1910. He built several cabins in the Yolla Bolly section of the county, all of which were of unusually sound construction. Nearby Brooks Ridge was named for him.

Site 54. White Rock—Grasshopper

White Rock is located near the Tehama County line in the upper drainage of the East Fork of the South Fork. There is an old cabin here which originally was used by stockmen when they brought their stock from the Sacramento Valley into the mountains for summer grazing. In 1913 it became the summer headquarters of the Harrison Gulch Ranger District for the Forest Service. A row of cedar seedlings was planted in front of the log cabin and barn that were there at the time. Three of these trees have survived. The log barn was replaced in the late 1930's; the log cabin was removed about 1955.

About a mile to the east of White Rock is a pasture area that went by the name of Grasshopper. Before 1905 use of this range was extensive and competitive. Soon after the Forest Service began to administer these lands in 1905, the drift fences in the White Rock and Grasshopper areas were erected.

Site 55. Miscellaneous Place Names and Sites

The use of the upper South Fork drainage as summer range land for both cattle and sheep was extensive in the first part of the century. Before the Forest Service was created as many as 30,000 sheep were driven to and from the Shell Mountain-Mad River area over the Humboldt Trail. The average size band was 2000 to 2200 head. With the creation of the Forest Service in 1905 grazing came under a permit system and use of the range was controlled. Gradually, cattle largely replaced the sheep.

The cattlemen frequently built small cabins for use while on the summer range. Some of these became homesteads. But many of these small cabins have disappeared and little more than their name or their location remains in the memories of a few old-timers. There is no longer sufficient information available to permit detailed reporting. Their mention here, though sketchy, is for the benefit of future historians who might glean some small piece of information from it.

DOUBLE CABINS. This site was about 100 yards up the East Fork from its junction with the South Fork. Double cabins were on this site which was used by Bob Ellis as his cattle headquarters.

FOSS CAMP. The old Fred Foss cabin site, known as Foss Camp, is in Sec. 6, T28N, R12W.

PINE ROOT SADDLE. A seasonal Forest Service Guard Station was at the Pine Root spring near the saddle where the Red Mountain Motorway and the Wildwood-Mad River road now intersect.

HOY CAMP. Just east of Seven-up Cedars in upper Smoky Creek was the summer camp of Hoy who was running cattle in the area during the 1920's. A statement by Charlie St. Jacques indicates that Hoy may have had a corral on Wilcox Ridge, possibly near the trail junction to Cedar Low Gap Ranger Station.

GLEASON CABIN. This is a relatively unknown site located north of Devil Camp above Texas Chow Creek in the NW1/4, Sec. 23, T28N, R11W.

SEVEN-UP CEDARS. A cabin at this place was once under special use permit from the Forest Service. The permit was relinquished by the Jim Duncan family about 1960 when the Forest Service promised to take care of the site for its historic interest. The cabin, however, is now collapsing. Ray Patton recalls that the place received its name as the result of an early episode in which three or four men, while catching wild horses, stopped here and sought shelter in a hollow, fire-scarred cedar tree. While waiting out a rainstorm they played the game of Seven-up, giving the name of Seven-up Cedars to the place. It is in Sec. 15, T29N, R12W.

SWIM MEADOW. This site, located near the eastern end of Rattlesnake Ridge, was patented by a Mr. Swim. It is one of the earliest places in the South Fork drainage to have been used. Clyde Lewis relates that when his grandfather settled at the Lewis Place in 1888 a man named Swim, who had come from the Salmon River area was living here.

MARTIN CABIN. This cabin is located on Buck Ridge below West Low Gap. The cabin here is in good condition. Richard and Isabelle Martin became the owners of the property about 1906.

DONALDSON CABIN. The site of this old cabin is on the South Fork near the Mathews cabin.

CHICAGO CAMP. The reason for the name of Chicago Camp is not known. Chicago Camp, located at the east end of Brooks Ridge, was used as a cattleman's camp. There was a cabin here at one time which was believed to have been built by Tom and Gene Burrill who also had built the Jensen cabin two or three miles away.

Site 56. Humboldt Trail and Tedoc Trail

In the early days of this century there was competition among sheepmen of the Sacramento Valley to see who could first get their sheep onto the summer grazing lands in the Yolla Bolly and Mad River areas. Two routes were used: the Humboldt Trail and the Tedoc Trail. The Humboldt Driveway left Red Bluff and roughly followed the present road to Saddle Camp and Tomhead Saddle. From this point the trail followed the ridgetop to a point about one mile west of Low Gap where it then contoured around the south side of North Yolla Bolly Mountain, then trough Cedar Basin and west around Black Rock Mountain to a location near Hermit Rock. From here the driveway turned south down a spur ridge to the South Fork of the Trinity River and then followed down the north side of the river for a distance of about one and one-half miles to the Penney Place at the mouth of Shell Mountain Creek. From here it climbed west through a glade area on what is now named Trough Ridge to the Mad River Divide just south of South Kelsey Peak.

The Tedoc Trail or Driveway was probably an old Indian trail. From Red Bluff it generally followed the location of Highway 36 through Budden Canyon to a point near the Griswold Place. From there it turned southwest past the Ball Place, around the head of Old Man Spring Creek, over Tedoc Mountain, through Tedoc Gap, and crossed the South Fork of Beegum Creek at the same crossing as on the present trail. There was an old bridge at this crossing; remains of the cribs can still be seen. Sheep were often lost at this crossing, either in fording the creek or being crowded off the bridge. At Stuart Gap the trail forked. One branch went south through Pettyjohn Basin and joined the Humboldt Trail near Cedar Basin; the other branch continued west to a point near the Payne Place, went around the west end of Buck Ridge, crossed the South Fork and up onto Bierce Ridge which it followed to the Mad River Divide, joining the Humboldt Trail near South Kelsey Peak.

There were several short alternate sections of the Tedoc Trail. One followed up Buck Ridge from its west end and joined the Humboldt Trail at the Penney Place. Another left the Payne Place and went through Fern Glade, also meeting the Humboldt Trail at Penney. An Indian family maintained a stopping place in Fern Glade for stockmen and other travelers. Nothing remains to show where this place was but it is presumed that it was near the spring.

Mulligan Glades are located near the top of Bierce Ridge and were an overnight stopping place for travelers on the Tedoc Trail. The main glade, now mostly a ponderosa pine thicket, is where stockmen used to cut hay. As late as 1946 the glades were still fairly open, mostly due to heavy grazing by cattle. For 35 years the Ellis brothers had a permit to graze 250 head in this area. When grazing ceased the trees took over.

Site 57. Red Mountain Motorway

During the 1930's the Civilian Conservation Corps, together with the Forest Service developed a master plan for the construction of a road and trail system

378

that would open much of the Trinity National Forest for greater accessibility. One of the best examples of this work done by the C.C.C. is the Red Mountain Motorway. This road took off from Highway 36 in Sec. 35, T30N, R12W and went southwesterly toward Seven Up Cedars and thence southeasterly, following the ridge past Mud Spring, and on towards Red Mountain. From just below Red Mountain it continued southeast past Pine Root, crossing the Wildwood-Mad River Road and on to Brushy Mountain near the Tehama County line. Here the project was abruptly stopped. Although this road was never completed it did accomplish the purpose of opening up a portion of the county which until then had been inaccessible to cars.

Site 58. Hayfork-Mad River Trail (Hayfork-Hettenshaw Trail)

There were a number of trails in the late 1800's that joined Weaverville and Hayfork with the coast. One of the more important ones was the Hayfork-Mad River Trail. Leaving the Mad River near Ruth this trail went north over South Fork Mountain, dropped down to the South Fork of the Trinity River along the south side of the Farley Creek drainage. Near the Tin Cabin it picked up the trail to the Lower Ford where it crossed to Scott Flat. At the lower end of Scott Flat it left the river and climbed abruptly up over Rattlesnake Ridge, crossed Little Rattlesnake Creek, and contoured along the slope above what is known as the P.G. and E. Flat, paralleling Rattlesnake Creek to a point just west of the Red Mountain Motorway. Here it turned north to the old Post Mountain Road and then followed the divide between Salt Creek and Philpot Creek on down into the Patton Place at Peanut.

AREA I SOURCES

Collaborators for this chapter are Alice Goen Jones and Florence Scott Morris.

BOOKS

Site No.

1, 13, 43	Helen Bacon Boggs, *My Playhouse was a Concord Coach*, 1942
1, 3, 5, 36 37, 39, 53, 56	Issac Cox, *Annals of Trinity County*, 1858
5, 7	Hotz, Thurber, Marks, Evans, *Mineral Resources of the Salmon Trinity Alps Primitive Area, California*, Washington, 1972
2, 5, 14	J. C. O'Brien, *Mines and Mineral Resources of Trinity County, California*, County Report #4, San Francisco, 1965
1	Edwin W. Scott, *California to Oregon*, April 1976, 143 pp.
1, 10, 12, 19-24, 26, 30, 31, 46	Edwin W. Scott, *Memories of Days Gone By*, May 1978, 194 pp.

PERIODICALS, BULLETINS, NEWSPAPERS

7, 14	Donald Francis MacDonald, "Notes on the Gold Lodes of the Carrville District, Trinity County, California", *Contributions to Economic Geology*, U. S. Bureau of Mines Bulletin 530, 1911
2	C. Melvin Swinney, "The Altoona Quicksilver Mine, Trinity County, California", *California Journal of Mines and Geology*, Vol. 46, No. 3, 1950
2, 5, 14	"Trinity County, Its Mines and General Features — Its Hydraulic Mines", *State Resources*, May 1891
5	"The Upper Coffee Creek Mining District", *Mining and Scientific Press*, Vol. 79, Dec. 16, 1899, p. 689
5, 14	"Northeastern Trinity", Redding *Record Searchlight*, Illustrated Mining Edition, Feb. 22, 1898.
2	"The Cinnabar Region", *Trinity Journal*, Oct. 16, 1875, pp. 3
31	*Trinity Journal*, July 10, 1880
29	"Last Toll Road Quits Business", *Trinity Journal*, Dec. 11, 1926, pp. 1
30	"Covington Mill Raised by Fire", *Trinity Journal*, Aug. 3, 1950, pp. 1
30	"Covington Mill Fades into History", *Trinity Journal*, Mar. 25, 1976, pp. 7
3	"Early Day Happenings — Aug. 1878", *Trinity Journal*, Aug. 13, 1953, pp. 1
13, 29	*Trinity Journal*, March 29, 1973.
40	David E. Gordon, "Recollections of a California Mountain County in '49 and the Outlook Today, 1856-59", *Sunset Magazine*, December, 1907

HISTORICAL YEARBOOKS

Site No.

2	Ethel Porter and Chet Flint, "Recollections of a Childhood Spent in the Trinity Mines", *Trinity,* Yearbook of the Trinity County Historical Society, 1958, pp. 40-43

57, 61   "The Van Matres—History and Life on the Van Matre Ranch", *Trinity,* Yearbook of the Trinity County Historical Society, 1961, pp. 4-20

50-53, 58   Philip A. Lydon, "History and Mining in the Southeast Quarter of the Minersville Quadrangle", *Trinity,* Yearbook of the Trinity County Historical Society, 1962, pp. 4-13

4, 9   Viva Tapie, "Early Days on Coffee Creek", *Trinity,* Yearbook of the Trinity County Historical Society, 1973, pp. 6-30

14   "Bucket Line Dredges of Trinity County", *Trinity,* Yearbook of the Trinity County Historical Society, 1974, pp. 8-27

31   JoAnn Baxter, "Bowerman", *Trinity,* Yearbook of the Trinity County Historical Society, 1976, pp. 22-25

2, 4, 5, 7, 12   Henry Carter, "Mines and Miners of Trinity and Siskiyou Counties", *The Covered Wagon,* Annual of the Shasta Historical Society, 1966

MISCELLANEOUS

29   "Statements by Oldtimers", Collection of the Bancroft Library, University of California. Item #71/2496

1, 3   Interview with Warren Messner by JoAnn Baxter, Taped by U. S. Forest Service, Weaverville, California, 1976

31   National Register Nomination for Bowerman Barn by U. S. Forest Service. Nomination written by JoAnn Baxter

14, 17, 18, 27   *Trinity Center Now and Then,* Trinity Center Elementary School Project, 1950

14   U. S. Forest Service Archaeological Site Survey Record, July 27, 1978

52, 53   H. H. Noonan personal papers, Files of the Trinity County Historical Society

18   Historic Resources Inventory Form, "Foster Ranchhouse", Trinity County Historical Society Records, April 1, 1979

28, 55   Trinity County Court House Records

36-61   Edwin W. Scott, "Before the Coming of the Trinity Lake", Essay, Trinity County Historical Society files

INTERVIEWS

The following individuals supplied helpful information for the preparation of this section either directly to the authors or for the Historical Resources Survey:

Mary Foster Abrott, Robert Abrott, JoAnn Baxter, Mr. and Mrs. Joe Belden, Doris Clement Callahan, Ken Collins, Virgil Covington, Melvin Foster, William Foster, Jr., Clara Goetze, Mark Groves, Evelyn Heath Grant, Margaret Yancey Hall, Mary Scott Hamilton, Rita Hanover, Donna Kerrigan, Gussie Lee, Mr. and Mrs. Elmer McDonald, Florence Scott Morris, Leonard Morris, Stewart W. Ralston, Thelma Riordan, Vernon Ryan, Edwin W. Scott, Wally Trapnell, Karl Van Matre, W. P. Van Matre.

PHOTOGRAPHS

Photographs in this chapter are by the following individuals or from their family collections:

Robert Abrott, Mary Scott Hamilton, Janet Lux Johnson, Alice Goen Jones, Nelly Murphy Montague, Florence Scott Morris, Fred Paulsen collection, Anita Van Matre Shuford, U. S. Forest Service, Trinity County Historical Society files.

AREA II SOURCES

Collaborators for this chapter are Florence Scott Morris, Herbert Woods, and Alice Goen Jones.

BOOKS

Site No.

Overview Issac Cox, *Annals of Trinity County*, 1858. pp. 115-146
11, 12, 23

72 J. J. Jackson, *Tales from the Mountaineer*, pp. 123

Overview Franklin A. Buck, *A Yankee Trader in the Gold Rush*

Overview, 68 John Carr, *Pioneer Days in California*

Overview James Bartlett, *Trinity County, California. Its Geography and a Summary of its History*

PERIODICALS, BULLETINS, NEWSPAPERS

63, 75-79, *Trinity Journal*, June 2, 1856; July 9, 1859; April 19, 1873; Sept. 12,
83-92, 94, 95 1874; June 1, 1878; October 23, 1880; September 6, 1890; April 4, 1896

1 *Trinity Journal*, June 28, 1856

9, 11 *Trinity Journal*, November 18, 1876

9 *Trinity Journal*, September 30, 1876

49 *Trinity Journal*, July 18, 1878

30 *Trinity Journal*, August 24, 1878

2 *Trinity Journal*, August 16, 1879

120 *Trinity Journal*, June 21, 1901; July 6, 1901; July 13, 1901; July 20, 1901; August 24, 1901; September 7, 1901; October 5, 1901; November 16, 1901

65 *Trinity Journal*, November 23, 1901

116 *Trinity Journal*, December 12, 1903

101 *Trinity Journal*, September 30, 1905

17 *Trinity Journal*, November 10, 1906

74 *Trinity Journal*, June 21, 1930

68 *Trinity Journal*, September 4, 1952

80 Patricia Hicks, "The Drug Store", *Trinity Journal*, Dec. 15, 1966

74 Patricia Hicks, "The Town Disgrace", *Trinity Journal*, March 30, 1978

74 "The Band Stand", *Trinity Journal* Recreation Guide, March 25, 1976

30 "The Grammar School", *Trinity Journal* Welcome Edition, 1978

"Weaverville Fire", *Shasta Courier*, October 17, 1863

68 "Tong War", *Oakland Tribune*, December 24, 1978

Overview *San Francisco Chronicle*, August 5, 1956

44 "Clara Goetze House", Redding *Record Searchlight*, March 18, 1978

29 Garth Sanders, "The Cemetery That Was Filled Twice", Redding *Record Searchlight*, May 5, 1973

HISTORICAL YEARBOOKS

J. J. Jackson, "Chinese War in America", *Trinity,* 1967, Yearbook of the Trinity County Historical Society, pp. 5-10

Rita Hanover, "The First Brick Buildings", *Trinity,* 1957, pp. 13-15

Donald R. Kennedy, "Early Trespassers of Weaverville", *Trinity,* 1957, pp. 25-27

J. J. Jackson, "Early History of the Weaverville Fire Department", *Trinity,* 1958, pp. 24-29

Rita Hanover, "The Incorporation of Weaverville", *Trinity,* 1959, p. 12-15

85 Pat Hamilton, "He Kept a Diary", *Trinity,* 1967, pp. 32-36

Taylor D. Robertson, "The Chinese in Trinity County", *Trinity,* 1970, pp. 13-17

71-116 "Weaverville Historical District Listed in National Register", *Trinity,* 1971, pp. 6-15

"Old Weaverville Residences", *Trinity,* 1975, pp. 5-19

MISCELLANEOUS

120 Maps: 1894 Trinity County Map; 1950 U.S.F.S. Map; 1930 Townsite Map

106, 108 Abstract of Title

8, 9, 20, 60 Chain of Title, Dero Forslund, Trinity Title Company

34, 35 Chain of Title, Vernon Ryan

54, 55, 56, 69 Official Trinity County Courthouse records

Indices to Records in Trinity County Courthouse

76 Nancy Kelley, "The Confectionery", 1971 report in Trinity County Historical Society files

75 Mrs. Condon Bush, "The Weaverville Hotel", 1977 report in Trinity County Historical Society files

94 Mr. and Mrs. Roy Horner, "Fiftieth Anniversary of Trinity Congregational Church", 1943

71-116 Rita Hanover, "Weaverville Business District from 1856", personal research notes

112 John Thomas, "History of the Timmerman Building", research paper

81, 82 Patricia Hicks, "History of the Edgecombe-Magnolia-Masonic Buildings", research paper

109 Patricia Hicks, "A History of Ryan's Store", *Trinity Journal,* Nov., 1980

116 Patricia Hicks, "Early History of Morris Hardware, 1852-1945", research paper

48-55, 120 Patricia Hicks, personal research file

60 Rita Hanover, "Issac Abrahm", research files

43 Senta Moore, "Todd House", research paper in Trinity County Historical Society files

97, 99, 100 William Hart, "The Chinese in Shasta and Weaverville", 1970 report in Trinity County Historical Society files

97, 99, 100 Bondell Zeugin, "The Chinese Forty-niner", 1970 report in Trinity County Historical Society files

38, 98 Taresa Cathryn McNeil, "The Early Practice of Medicine, 1850-1900", 1970 report in Trinity County Historical Society files

44 William A. Goetze, biographical material in Trinity County Historical Society files

71 Hal Goodyear, "History of the Courthouse", address given July 17, 1976

74 Hal Goodyear, "History of the Band Stand", address given July 4, 1976

120 "History of the LaGrange", files of the California Division of Highways and Public Works, 1939

10, 43 Emily Robb, architectural report for Trinity County Historic Resources Survey

50 Correspondence from A. L. Brearcliff, Puyallup, Washington, Trinity County Historical Society files

17, 19, 21, 22, Walter G. Miller, architectural fieldwork notes, 1978-1979
23, 25, 32, 34,
39, 40, 48, 49,
51, 52, 54, 56,
58

Personal interviews by Florence Morris, with Carl Bremer, Edna Bremer, Harry H. Noonan, Willis Woodbury, Ernest Chapman, and William Richards

INTERVIEWS

The following individuals supplied helpful information for the preparation of this section either directly to the authors or for the Historical Resources Survey:

Dan Adrian, Chauncey and Margaret Arbuckle, Pearl Clement Bigelow, Lucille Caton Borden, Katie Burgess Brabrook, Mary Brady, Gilda Brown, Frank Costa, Maida Hafley Costa, Jim Everest, Shirley Fields, George Files, Lucille Snyder Finn, Hal Goodyear, Rita Hanover, Nora Fields Jepsen, Alice Goen Jones, Moon Lee, Helen Loomis, Thomas L. Ludden, Agnes Rourke Marshall, Henry C. Meckel, Fred Meyers, Judith Davis Moore, Millie Miller, Ruth Blaney Mitchell, James McKnight, Cleone McKnight, Sam Moran, Leonard Morris, Florence Scott Morris, Robert Morris, Vincent Ryan, Vernon Ryan, Ruth Ryan, Edith Smallen, W. P. Van Matre, Karlyn Junkans Van Matre, Herbert Woods, Helen Woods, Allen Young, Robert A. Young, Robert R. Young

PHOTOGRAPHS

Photographs in this section are by the following individuals or are from their family collections:

Jean Breeden, Bill Hall, Walter Miller, Judith Davis Moore, Sam Moran, Florence Scott Morris, Edith Smallen, Trinity County Historical Society files.

AREA III SOURCES

Collaborator for this chapter is Henry C. Meckel.

BOOKS

Site No.

Helena Overview 29, 64 — James W. Bartlett, Annotations to Cox's *Annals of Trinity County.* Eugene, Oregon, 1940

Helena Overview 65 — Frank A. Buck, *A Yankee Trader in the Gold Rush,* Boston and New York, Houghton Mifflin Company, 1930

Helena Overview — Carr, John, *Pioneer Days in California,* pp. 141-142, Eureka, California, Times Publishing Company, 1891

Junction City and Helena Overviews 9, 19, 22 — Cox, Issac, *The Annals of Trinity County,* John Henry Nash, Printing, Eugene, Oregon, 1940

PERIODICALS, BULLETINS, NEWSPAPERS

21 James Bartlett, *Trinity County, California, Its Geography by the Trinity County Board of Education and a Summary of Its History from May 1845-September 1926,* Weaverville, California, News Publishing Company, 1926, pp. 13

21 *Northern California Illustrated,* Sept., 1976, pp. 275

79-80 Thirty-seventh Report of State Mineralogist, *California Journal of Mining,* pp. 33-34, Jan., 1941

10 Vivian Tye, "Where Have All the Indians Gone?", *Trinity,* 1970

23 F. W. Haselwood, "Hydraulicking Highway Cut 210 Feet Deep," *California Highway,* Aug., 1939, pp. 2

19 *Trinity Journal,* Oct. 13, 1978

Trinity Journal, Feb. 2, 1895

21 *Trinity Journal,* May 1, 1858; Feb. 27, 1874

24 *Trinity Journal,* June 29, July 1, 13, 20, Aug. 3, Sept. 7, Nov. 16, 1901; Jan. 4, 11, Mar. 29, Apr. 5, 12, 19, 1902; Apr. 11, 1903

29 *Trinity Journal,* June 13, 1874

82 *Trinity Journal,* Dec. 15, 1888; Nov. 22, 1890; June 13, 1891; Dec. 16, 1893; Jan. 13, 26, July 10, Oct. 16, 30, Dec. 25, 1897; Feb. 12, 1898; Nov. 15, Dec. 26, 1902; Jan. 31, Feb. 6, 1903

83 *Trinity Journal,* Oct. 3, 10, 17, 31, Nov. 14, 1908; Mar. 6, 20, May 1, 8, June 5, July 31, 1909; Mar. 5, Apr. 9, 16, June 4, 1910

MISCELLANEOUS

1, 2, 3 Chain of title sheet for district buildings provided by the Trinity County Title Company.

82 Great Registers of Trinity County

8 Map Collection, Trinity County Clerk's Office, Courthouse, Weaverville

Helena Overview	Map T34N, R11W, Mount Diablo Meridian, Surveyor General's Office, San Francisco, March 12, 1883
29	Official Records of Trinity County, Book I, Patents, pp. 273
Helena Overview	Plat of the Schlomer and Meckel Placer Mine, Book 1 Maps and Surveys, pp. 52. Official records, Trinity County Courthouse
1	Probate papers, Edgar L. Reed Estate, Trinity County Recorder's Office
3	Trinity County Recorder Book of Deeds: Book 24, pp. 354; Book 26, pp. 717; Book 28, pp. 476
19	Report of Trinity Survey Flora Committee, Alice Jones, chairman, 1978
82	United States Post Office records
Junction City Overview	Name file. Trinity County Historical Society Museum Collection

INTERVIEWS

The following individuals supplied helpful information for the preparation of this section either directly to the authors or to the Historical Resources Survey:

Alice Given Bollock, George Burger, Stephen W. Bradford, William S. Bradford, Malcomb Douglas Craig, John Dalldorf, Treva Fullerton, Rita Hanover, Iris W. Kunkler, Creston H. McCartney, Elinor Chapman McCartney, Lois Enos Mikkola, Leonard M. Morris, Nellie Scott Pattison, Richard D. Remick, Vincent W. Ryan, John Shuford, John Souza.

PHOTOGRAPHS

Photographs in this chapter are by the following individuals or from their family collections:

Iris Wilson Kunkler, Henry C. Meckel, Elinor Chapman McCartney, Florence Scott Morris, the Napoli Estate, Odette Saladin Rabout, Walter Robb, Vernon Ryan, Helen Reed Warnock, Eric Woods, Trinity County Historical Society files.

AREA IV SOURCES

Collaborators for this chapter are Elizabeth Bigelow Langworthy, Alice Goen Jones, and Florence Scott Morris.

BOOKS

Site No.

4, 7   James W. Bartlett, *Annotations to Cox's Annals*, 1926

7   Helen Bacon Boggs, *My Playhouse was a Concord Coach*, 1942

1, 3, 4, 5,   Issac Cox, *Annals of Trinity County, 1858*
7, 8, 11,
12, 13, 15,
19, 22, 27,
30, 39

50   G. G. Erwin, *California Gold Camps*, University of California Press, 1975

Stephen Powers, "Tribes of California", *Contributions to North American Ethnology*, Vol. 3, Smithsonian Institution, Washington D. C., 1877

30   Henry Schoolcraft, *Archives of Aboriginal Knowledge*, Vol. III

PERIODICALS, BULLETINS, NEWSPAPERS

50   *Mining Press*, January 24, 1885

Roland B. Dixon, "The New River Indians", *American Anthropologist, Vol. 7, No. 2, 1905*

48   "Register of Mines — Trinity", *State Mining Bureau*, October, 1898

48   "Mines and Mineral Resources of Trinity County", County Report #4, California Division of Mines and Geology, San Francisco, 1965

48   *California Division of Mines Report XXXVII*, pp. 49

"File on Gray Creek Curve Projection", State of California, Department of Transportation, October, 1977, and January, 1978

"The Archaeological Resources of the Proposed Beartooth, Dyer Creek and Mills' Hill Reservoirs in Trinity County, California", report, UCLA Department of Anthropology/Archaeological Survey, June 1, 1968

48, 49   "Mineral Resources of the Salmon-Trinity Alps Primitive Area, California" *U.S. Geological Survey Bulletin* 1371-B, 1972

5   David E. Gordon, "Recollections of a California Mountain County in '49 and the Outlook Today, 1856-59", *Sunset Magazine*, December, 1907

22   *Humboldt Times*, March 3, 1855

26   *Trinity Journal*, March 14, 1857

30   *Trinity Journal*, June 25, 1857; February 12, 1858; February 6, 1864; September 17, 1892; April 14, 1923; December 15, 1928

48   *Trinity Journal*, July 14, 1866; January 10, 1885; January 17, 1885; January 27, 1885; February 7, 1885; February 21, 1885; January 1, 1892; January 16, 1892

26   *Trinity Journal*, May 5, 1877; August 7, 1907; June 6, 1908

39   *Trinity Journal*, August 21, 1880; October 30, 1880; October 22, 1881; October 2, 1882; December 2, 1882

36   *Trinity Journal*, October 19, 1880; March 18, 1893

40 *Trinity Journal*, January 3, 1885

50 *Trinity Journal*, January 10, 1885; February 17, 1885

49 *Trinity Journal*, January 10, 1885; January 17, 1885; February 7, 1885; February 21, 1885; January 16, 1892

51 *Trinity Journal*, January 10, 1885; February 7, 1885

28 *Trinity Journal*, February 15, 1890

25 *Trinity Journal*, September 21, 1895; March 13, 1969

37 *Trinity Journal*, March 23, 1950

38 *Trinity Journal*, September 5, 1974

 Trinity Journal, October 3, 1875

47 *Trinity Journal*, September 12, 1863

HISTORICAL YEARBOOKS

28 Jake Jackson, "The Famous China Slide", *Trinity*, 1957, Yearbook of the Trinity County Historical Society

46-52 Florence Morris, "A Tale of Two Cities", *Trinity*, 1970, Yearbook of the Trinity County Historical Society

19, 20, 30 Robert J. Morris, "A History of Big Bar-Part I", *Trinity*, 1967, Yearbook of the Trinity County Historical Society

19, 20, 30 Robert J. Morris, "A History of Big Bar-Part II", *Trinity*, 1968, Yearbook of the Trinity County Historical Society

45, 47 Earl Raney, "Election Camp", *Trinity*, 1957, Yearbook of the Trinity County Historical Society

48 "The Abraham H. Bar Family", *Siskiyou Pioneer*, Vol. 3, No. 5, 1962, Siskiyou County Historical Society

48-49 "The A. H. Denny Family", *Siskiyou Pioneer*, Vol. 3, No. 5, 1962, Siskiyou County Historical Society

42, 48, 51 "Alexander Brizard", *History of Humboldt County*, 1881

34 *Klam-ity Kourier*, December 27, 1972

34 *This is Hayfork*, Vol. 1, June 1, 1972

34 *This is Hayfork*, Vol. 2, 1973

30 Ernest De Massey, "A Frenchman in the Gold Rush", *California Historical Society, 1927*

MISCELLANEOUS

35 "The Churches of Trinity County", Jean Breeden collection, Weaverville

40 Nellie Fraters, "Notes of Dailey Ranch", Trinity County Historical Society files

46, 47, 48 Wes Hotelling, "A Tribute to Grover Ladd", Trinity County Historical Society files

37 J. W. McCarthy, "Irving Family", Trinity County Historical Society files

44 J. W. McCarthy, "Jake's Hunting Ground", as told to Wes Hotelling, Trinity County Historical Society files

41, 42, 43 J. B. Murdock, "Some New River History", as told to Grover Ladd in 1969, Trinity County Historical Society files

32 Ruth Pippin, "Death of Arabella Beerbower", Trinity County Historical Society files

49 Marjorie Parker Underhill, "Denny Family History", November, 1963, Trinity County Historical Society files

33 Gray Family Records, Trinity County Historical Society files

46-51 Recorded interview with Grover Ladd (prior to 1972) Trinity County Historical Society files

2 Gay Berrien, "Eagle Creek Ranch", U.S. Forest Service, Big Bar, California, 1980.

42, 51 Records of the Post Office Department, National Archives, Washington, D.C., May, 1974 and August, 1978

30 Deeds, Book E, pp. 290; Book P, pp. 398 and pp. 516

31 Deeds, Book G, pp. 139

46 Deeds, Book P, pp. 170-171 and 300-301; Book 12, pp. 44-48; Book 13, pp. 338-339.

26 Deeds, Book P, pp. 398

43 Patents, Book 3, pp. 223-227

46 Patents, Book 2, pp. 496.

48 Records of the New River Mining District, Vols. 1, 2, 3.

39 Great Registers of Trinity County, Trinity County Historical Society files

INTERVIEWS

The following individuals supplied helpful information for the preparation of this section either directly to the authors or for the Historical Resources Survey:

Linda Allan, Gay Holland Berrien, Ruby Bunch, Nita Bussell, Mary Carpenter, DuBay family, Charles Everest, Everett Fountain, Delphine Fountain, Nellie Dailey Fraters, Jay Hailstone, Evelyn Harrigan, Jeffrey Harrigan, Patricia Hicks, Wes Hotelling, Horace D. Jones, Katherine R. McGowan, Mildred Vaughn McMorrow, Florence Scott Morris, Robert J. Morris, Larry Mortimeyer, Jack Murdock, Leonard Nunn, Lloyd Pattison, Idell Rantz, John G. Strand, Elsie (Waldorff) Tye, Annie Irving Wallace

PHOTOGRAPHS

Photographs for this chapter are by the following individuals or from their family collections:

Linda Allan, Nellie Bunner Fraters, Alice Goen Jones, Florence Scott Morris, Katherine R. McGowan, Walter Robb, Lurline Webster, Trinity County Historical Society files.

AREA V SOURCES

Collaborators for this chapter are Richard Krieg and Alice Goen Jones.

BOOKS

Site No.

4, 6, 18, 19   Isaac Cox, *Annals of Trinity County, 1858*
22, 25, 26, 32,
34, 35

35   Edwin W. Scott, *Memories of Days Gone By,* 1978

PERIODICALS, BULLETINS, NEWSPAPERS

1   *Trinity Journal,* April 12, 1873; July 4, 1872; February 5, 1876; May 2, 1903; November 2, 1905.

5   *Trinity Journal,* November 3, 1900.

8   *Trinity Journal,* June 6, 1885

16   *Trinity Journal,* August and November, 1896

33   *Trinity Journal,* March 18, 1937

HISTORICAL YEARBOOKS

9, 14   Frank Ross and Commodore Kise, "A Little About Lewiston", *Trinity,* 1955, Yearbook of the Trinity County Historical Society

24   Florence Morris, "Deadwood", *Trinity,* 1972, Yearbook of the Trinity County Historical Society

27   Marion Karch, "Buckhorn Station", *Trinity,* 1966, Yearbook of the Trinity County Historical Society

MISCELLANEOUS

37   Pat Hicks, "The Clement Ranch", research paper

4   Trinity County Title Company records

22   Lowden Family History, Trinity County Historical Society files

26   Original Incorporation and Settlement Notices, Jan. 15, 1868, January 25, 1872. Trinity County Historical files

27   *Deeds* Book I, pp. 666, 670, 694. Trinity County Official Records

37   *Land Claims* C, pp. 393. Trinity County Official Records

42   Clark W. Brott, "Indian Creek Townsite", Bureau of Land Management Report CA TRI 341, February 9, 1979

INTERVIEWS

The following individuals supplied helpful information for the preparation of this section either directly to the authors or for the Historical Resources Survey:

George Albiez, James Bartlett, David Beans, C. M. Bennett, Pearl Bigelow, Rollin Coumbs, Gilbert Edgerton, LeRoy Eisele, E. E. Erich, Dero Forslund, Dorothy Rourke Goodyear, Hal Goodyear, Rita Hanover, Anne Hennessey, Marion Karch, Agnes Rourke Marshall, Bob McBroom, Florence Scott Morris, Leonard Morris, Mable Rix, L. Stanford Scott, Ruth Conner Snyder, Sam Williams, Johnny Wilson, Bill Wright.

PHOTOGRAPHS

The photographs in this chapter are by the following individuals or are from their family collections:

Jean Breeden, Ruth Lowden Doyle, Marion Karch, Florence Scott Morris, Walter Robb, Trinity County Historical Society files.

AREA VI SOURCES

Collaborator for this chapter is Herbert Woods.

BOOKS

Site No

3, 51   Isaac Cox, *Annals of Trinity County*, San Francisco, 1858

26   Bert Webber, *Retaliation (Japanese Balloons)*, Medford, Oregon, Pacific Northwest Book Co.

PERIODICALS, BULLETINS, NEWSPAPERS

51   Jessee Ranch House, Redding *Record Searchlight*, February 8, 1975

31   *Trinity Journal*, July 26, 1858

51   *Trinity Journal*, March 30, 1895

33   *Trinity Journal*, March 13, 1968

51   Bridge Gulch Massacre, *Sacramento Bee*, Trinity County Historical Society files

HISTORICAL YEARBOOKS

7   Paula Flint, "To Rise Again", *Trinity*, Yearbook of the Trinity County Historical Society, 1967, pp. 15

36   The Klondike Mine, *Trinity*, 1963-65, p. 19

51   Old Settlers' Society Papers, *Trinity*, 1958, pp. 7-14

36   Random Notes on the Upper South Fork of the Trinity River, Part II, *Trinity*, 1966, pp. 43-47, Part III, *Trinity*, 1967, pp. 44-50

MISCELLANEOUS

23   Pearl Bigelow, "Early Blanchard Flat School", Report for History 94A, Roberts, 1970

30   Edna Bland, "History of the Vaughn Family", Trinity County Historical Society files

39   Howard Crews, "Hayfork Ranches of 76 Years Ago", report for History 94A, Roberts, 1970

32-33   Dorothy Rourke Goodyear, "The Dennis Rourke Family", report for History 94A, Roberts, 1970

23   Wilbert Heinz, "The Little Log Schoolhouse in Hayfork Park", *This Is Hayfork*, Vol. 3, 1978

27, 28, 29   "Hyampom, It's History and Development", Hyampom Elementary School project, 1965

26   "Japanese Bombing Balloon", Monument Dedication Program, August 26, 1978, Trinity County Historical Society files

34   James Larsen, "Cuff Barn Notes", San Jose, August 21, 1978

38   *Official Records of Trinity County*, Book 4, pp. 62, pp. 472

34   A. L. Paulsen, *How Peanut Got Its Name*, Trinity County Historical Society files

2, 4, 9, 13   *This Is Hayfork*, Hayfork History Buffs, Vol. 1, 1972
14, 22, 35

32, 33, 37, 39   *This Is Hayfork*, Hayfork History Buffs, Vol. 2, 1973

21   *This Is Hayfork*, Hayfork History Buffs, Vol. 3, 1976

INTERVIEWS

The following individuals supplied helpful information for the preparation of this section either directly to the authors or for the Historical Resources Survey:

Frieda Albiez, George Albiez, Helen Ross Bartlett, Ray Beals, Tom Brezinski, Rollin Coumbs, Charles Crews, Howard Crews, Irene Dockery, Morris Duncan, Harvey Farmer, Paula Flint, Louise Garrett, Ernie Glass, Lena Glass, Walter Glass, Dorothy Rourke Goodyear, Eugene Greenleaf, Jean Hixon, Ivan Jeans, Ray Jessee. Marion Karch, Clarence Laffranchini, Erna Laffranchini, Laverne Laffranchini, Grace McKibbin, Edna Montgomery, Reginald Morris, Geneva Murrison, Wilma Olsen, Ray Patton, Ralph Patton, Idell Hailstone Rantz, Marjorie Schmidt.

PHOTOGRAPHS

Photographs in this chapter are by the following individuals or are from their family collections:

Jean Breeden, Florence Scott Morris, Walter Robb, U. S. Forest Service, Trinity County Historical Society files.

AREA VII SOURCES

Collaborators for this chapter are Alice Goen Jones and Walter Robb.

Site No.

BOOKS

1 Issac Cox, *Annals of Trinity County*, 1858, pp. 252

1 Stindt and Dunscomb, *The Northwestern Pacific Railroad*, 1964

16 Erwin G. Gudde, *California Place Names*, University of California Press, Berkeley, CA, 1969, pp. 173

PERIODICALS, BULLETINS, NEWSPAPERS

1 *Eureka Times Standard*, January 12, 1979

1 "Mines and Mineral Resources of Trinity County", County Report #4, California Division of Mines and Geology, San Francisco, 1965

1 Melvin C. Stinson, "Geology of the Island Mountain Copper Mine", Report, Division of Mines and Geology, Vol. 53, Nos. 1-2

1 *San Francisco Examiner*, October 29, 1948

1 *San Francisco Chronicle*, October 29, 1948

1 *Trinity Journal*, March 28, 1914

1 *Trinity Journal*, April 4, 1914

1 *Trinity Journal*, April 11, 1914

1 *Trinity Journal*, June 6, 1914

1 *Trinity Journal*, November 27, 1915

1 *Trinity Journal*, December 25, 1915

1 *Trinity Journal*, October 19, 1929

1 *Trinity Journal*, November 4, 1937

17 *Trinity Journal*, October 25, 1956

HISTORICAL YEARBOOKS

14 "Zenia", *Trinity*, 1955, pp. 28

36 "Ruth", *Trinity*, 1955, pp. 29

Jake Jackson, "The Longridge Case", *Trinity*, 1957, pp. 21-24

36 "Ruth and Hetten Valley", *Trinity*, 1959, pp. 16-19

41, 50 "Charles D. Bramlet, Biography of a Trinity Pioneer", *Trinity*, 1963, pp. 4-7

36 "Post Office at Ruth", *Trinity*, 1963, pp. 41

38, 40, 42 Chet and Paula Flint, "Random Notes on Upper South Fork, Part II", *Trinity*, 1966, pp. 43-47

40, 42, 43 Chet and Paula Flint, "Random Notes on Upper South Fork, Part III",
44, 45, 49 *Trinity*, 1967, pp. 44-50

3 John Thomas, "Ben Arthur Trials in Erickson Case Recalled", *Trinity*, 1968, pp. 36-42

52 "Who are the Evelands?" *Trinity*, 1968, pp. 45-46

Overview Walter Robb, "South of the South Fork", *Trinity*, 1978, pp. 4-24
3, 4, 6, 8,
10, 13, 14, 17,
21, 22, 23

34   John E. Keller, "The Mendocino Outlaws", Monograph #9, Mendocino County Historical Society, Fort Bragg, CA

MISCELLANEOUS

23   "Records of the War of Rebellion", War Department, Vol. 50, part 1, pp. 50-87, 188-307

8   Leona Miller, "Collection of letters on Southern Trinity History", Trinity County Historical Society files

38   "Old Forest Glen Station," *Forest Sounds,* Newsletter of the Shasta-Trinity National Forest, 1978

9   "Lampley Patent Records", Trinity County Historical Society files

21   California State Archives Reports, 1020 O Street, Sacramento, CA

47   Clyde Lewis, "Early History of the Ostrat Place on South Fork of Trinity River", February 20, 1967, Trinity County Historical Society files

40, 43, 44   Paula Flint, "Upper South Fork River Crossings", 1971, Trinity County Historical Society files

38   Charles E. Brewer, "Forest Glen in Early Days", Trinity County Historical Society files

1   Interview with Fred and Louis Chappell, September 13, 1980, by Walter Robb, Trinity County Historical Society files

Interview with Frank Brown by Walter Robb, Trinity County Historical Society files

10, 22   Interview with Estle Beard by Walter Robb, on tape, October 4, 1978, Trinity County Historical Society files

17   Interview with Andy Scheubeck by Walter Robb, on tape, October 4, 1978, Trinity County Historical Society files

10   Interview with Alan Jamison by Walter Robb, Trinity County Historical Society files

8, 17   Interview with Leona Miller by Walter Robb, on tape, April 14, 1978, Trinity County Historical Society files

Interview with Hazel Willburn by Walter Robb, on tape, April 12, 1978, Trinity County Historical Society files

41   Interview with Ray Randolph and Lena Randolph by Walter Robb, on tape, June 17, 1979, Trinity County Historical Society files

10   Interview with Floyd White by John Thomas, on tape, John Thomas' personal collection

43   Correspondence with Charles St. Jacques, September 26, 1978, November 14, 1978, Trinity County Historical Society files

1   Correspondence, W. W. Duncan to Leona Miller, Trinity County Historical Society files

2   Correspondence from Southern Pacific Transportation Company, San Francisco, July 17, 1978, Trinity County Historical Society files

2   Correspondence from Association of American Railroads, Washington, D. C., June 29, 1978, July 12, 1978, Trinity County Historical Society files

1 Correspondence from Jim Larsen, San Jose, CA, Trinity County Historical Society files

21 Correspondence from John Slonaker, Director U. S. Army Military History Institute, Carlisle, PA, Trinity County Historical Society files

INTERVIEWS

The following individuals supplied helpful information for the preparation of this chapter, either directly for this chapter or for the Historical Resources Survey:

Estle Beard, Zelma Benninghoven, Katie Burgess Brabrook, May Burgess, Betty Elgin, Paula Flint, Mr. and Mrs. Merle Goodwin, Alan Jamison, Ivan Jeans, Leona Miller, Ralph Miller, Florence Scott Morris, Leonard Morris, Ray Patton, Ray Randolph, Lena Randolph, Maxine Burgess Robinson, Blanche Rumley, Andy Scheubeck, Dolly Shannon, Ted Shannon, Irene Stapp, Lee Stapp, Charlie St. Jacques, John Thomas, George Willburn, Hazel Willburn, Ray Willburn, and numerous other southern Trinity residents.

PHOTOGRAPHS

Photographs in this chapter are by the following individuals or are from their personal collections:

Fred Chappell, Florence Scott Morris, Lena Randolph, Walter Robb, Wendy Watkins-Stewart, Trinity County Historical Society files.

INDEX

398

400

405

407

410

412

413

Ozark Mine, 205, 213-4

P. G. and E. Flat, 379
Pacific Brewery, 96, 121, 205
Pacific Gold Dredging Company, 16, 34
Packwood, 358-9
Packwood place, 358
Packwood trail, 359
Palmer, 277
Palmer, Robert, 254
Panther Creek, 255, 266
Panwauket Gulch, 302
Papoose Creek, 49
Papoose Post Office, 49
Papoose Ranch, 49
Parish House, 124
Parker Creek, 10
Parker Meadows, 10, 20
Parks Bar, 184
Pastime Movie Theatre, 133
Patterson, Moses, 254-5
Pattison, Josephine, 239
Pattison, Nellie Scott, 191, 235
Pattison, Lloyd, 237
Pattison, Thomas C., 235
Pattison, William A., Jr., 235, 286
Pattison, William A., Sr., 229, 235, 247
Pattison Cemetery, 234, 235
Pattison place, 233-5
Patton, Arthur, 324
Patton, Ralph, 324
Patton, Ray, 377
Patton, Rayce, 324
Patton, Sam, 324
Patton, Sarah, 324
Patton, William, 324
Patton barn, 324
Patton place, 379
Paulsen, 117
Paulsen, Albert L., 90, 106
Paulsen, Anna, 90
Paulsen, Charles Arthur, 87, 90, 105
Paulsen, Charles, 277, 279
Paulsen, Deda Joseph, 277
Paulsen, Fred, 276-7, 300
Paulsen, Henry, 276, 279
Paulsen, Jacob, 115, 277, 279, 300
Paulsen, Jennie Skinner, 87, 90
Paulsen, Lloyd, 277
Paulsen, Louisa S., 279
Paulsen, Mildred, 277
Paulsen, Peter M., 176, 282, 295-6, 300
Paulsen Brothers Store, 279
Paulsen Company, L. S., 279
Paulsen house, 87, 90
Paulsen Ranch, 277-8
Paulsen's Store, 279-280
Payette, Francois, 223
Payne, Lou, 376
Payne Ranch, 376, 378
Peabody, Commodore, 354
Peak road, 353
Peanut, 312, 324, 379
Pearce, 354
Pelletreau, Alexander "Alex", 210, 213, 214, 235
Penney, Jack, 375

Penney place, 375, 378
Pennsylvania Bar, 189
Perl, George, 373
Petaluma, 337, 366
Peterson, Ola Sward, 189
Peterson Ranch, 38
Pettijohn Mountain, 272
Petty, Charles, 369
Petty place, 369
Pettyjohn Basin, 378
Phelps, D. J., 246
Phelps, Katherine, 246
Phillips, James "Cap", 277
Phillips, Lucy, 277
Phillips, Olney, 277
Phillips and Day's Market, 203
Phillips-Talbott house, 277
Philpot Creek, 379
Pick 'n Shovel, 118
Picket Placer Mine, 184
Picotte, Joe, 239
Pierce, Church and Co., 118, 119
Pilot Peak, 346
Pincus, Isaac, 135
Pine Root Saddle, 377, 379
Pinkham, Ben, 12, 13
Pinkham's Hotel (boarding house), 12, 13
Pioneer Garage, 119
Pioneer Shop, 108
Pit River Hill men, 1
Pittsburg Mining Claim, 193
Pitzer, Jesse H., 215
Platina, 324
Plummer Creek, 253, 261
Poage, Levi P., 179
Point Bar, 297
Poison Camp, 354
Poison Gulch, 176
Poison Spring, 342
Poker (Polka) Bar, 297
Poker Bar Dredge, 284
Pony Bar Extension Mine, 250
Pony Bar Mine, 250
Pony Bar Placer Mine, 250
Pony Buttes, 257
Pony Creek 256, 257, 266
Pony Mountain, 256
Pony Ranch, 317
Porch and Pantry, 123
Porter, 62
Portland-Sacramento Stage, 2
Portugese Meadows, 10
Posey Gulch, 49, 272
Post Mountain Road, 324
Potter, Sheldon, 345, 347
Poverty Bar, 299
Powder house, 146
Powers, Austin, 330
Powers, O. H., 241
Powers Mill, 330
Prairie Creek, 234, 237, 239
Prairie, Little, 237
Pratti, Bill, 366, 368
Preacher's Peak, 9
Price, Sam H., 342
Price, Thomas Boles, 233

418